TRADITION(S)

Studies in Continental Thought

John Sallis, *general editor*

Tradition(s)

Refiguring Community and Virtue in Classical German Thought

STEPHEN H. WATSON

Indiana University Press

BLOOMINGTON AND INDIANAPOLIS

The paper used in this publication meets
the minimum requirements of American
National Standard for Information
Sciences—Permanence of Paper for Printed
Library Materials, ANSI Z39.48–1984.

Manufactured in the United States of America

Library of Congress Cataloging-in-Publication Data

Watson, Stephen H., date
   Tradition(s) : refiguring community and
virtue in classical German thought /
Stephen H. Watson
      p.   cm. — (Studies in Continental thought)
   Includes bibliographical references and index.
   ISBN 0-253-33328-8 (cloth : alk. paper). —
   ISBN 0-253-21152-2 (pbk. : alk. paper)
   1. Tradition (Philosophy). 2. Philosophy,
German—18th century. 3. Philosophy,
German—19th century. I. Title. II. Series.
B2748.T73W38   1997
148—dc21   97-1225

1 2 3 4 5 02 01 00 99 98 97

CONTENTS

ACKNOWLEDGMENTS

With the exception of sections of chapter 2, the materials united here are original to this work and have not been published elsewhere. Previously published sections of chapter 2 appeared originally in *Kantstudien* 77, no. 2, in an article entitled "Kant, Autonomy, and the Possiblity of Morality." On the other hand, a work written on materials from a period during which education became so paradigmatic a theoretical problem—both in content and institution—would be negligent were one to rest without mentioning one's own students. As Levinas would see, still fully in line with classical German thought's elevation of education, beyond all "maieutics," the fact becomes plain that one cannot teach without being taught. Those that ought to be mentioned not only in this regard but in the more tedious sense of participating in the drafting and production of this book are David Vessey, Marya Bower, and John Davenport, all of whose contributions, sense of humor, and persistence are gratefully acknowledged. Finally I would like to thank my typist Cheryl Reed, whose patience throughout drafts too numerous to count is gratefully acknowledged.

ABBREVIATIONS

The following abbreviations refer to works frequently cited throughout this book and will be noted with page numbers in parentheses. The works and their abbreviations are listed alphabetically first by author name and then by title within each author. I have tried to use standard and widely available English translations where possible. The references include the date of the original language first publication, or the date of composition where this differs from the date of original publication.

Theodore Adorno
ND   *Negative Dialectics* [1966], trans. E. S. Ashton (New York: Continuum, 1973).

Walter Benjamin
Trau   *The Origin of German Tragic Drama* [1924–25], trans. John Osborne (New York: New Left Books, 1977).

J. G. Fichte
SE   *The Science of Ethics* [1798], trans. A. E. Kroeger (New York: D. Appleton and Company, 1897).

SK   ———, *The Science of Knowledge* [1794–95], trans. Peter Heath and John Lachs (Cambridge: Cambridge University Press, 1982).

SR   ———, *The Science of Right* [1796], trans. A. E. Kroger (New York: Harper & Row, 1969).

VS   ———, *Some Lectures Concerning the Scholar's Vocation* [1794], in *Early Philosophy Writings,* trans. Daniel Breazeale (Ithaca: Cornell University Press, 1988).

Michel Foucault
OT   *The Order of Things: An Archaeology of the Human Sciences* [1966] (New York: Random House/Vintage Books, 1973).

Hans-Georg Gadamer
TM   *Truth and Method* [1960], revised and trans. Joel Weinsheimer and Donald G. Marshall (New York: Crossroad, 1989).

G. W. F. Hegel
Dif   *The Difference between Fichte's and Schelling's System of Philosophy* [1801] (Albany: SUNY Press, 1977).

FK ———, *Faith and Knowledge* [1802], trans. Walter Cerf and H. S. Harris (Albany: SUNY Press, 1967).

FPS ———, *System of Ethical Life and First Philosophy of Spirit* [1802–04], trans. H. S. Harris, T. M. Knox (Albany: SUNY Press, 1919).

Aesth ———, *Lectures on Aesthetics* [1835], vol. I, trans. T. M. Knox (Oxford: Clarendon Press, 1988).

HP ———, *Lectures on the History of Philosophy* [1833] (three volumes), trans. E. S. Haldane and Frances H. Simson (New York: Humanities, 1953).

L ———, *Logic,* part 1 of the *Encyclopedia of Philosophical Sciences* [1830], trans. William Wallace (London: Oxford University Press, 1968).

NL ———, *Natural Law* [1802–03], trans. T. M. Knox (Philadelphia: University of Pennsylvania Press, 1975).

Phen ———, *Phenomenology of Spirit* [1807], trans. A. V. Miller (Oxford: Oxford University Press, 1977).

PH ———, *Philosophy of History* [1830], trans. J. Sibree (New York: Dover, 1956).

PS ———, *Philosophy of Mind,* part 3 of the *Encyclopedia of Philosophical Sciences,* trans. A. V. Miller (Oxford: Clarendon Press, 1971).

PR ———, *Philosophy of Right* [1821], trans. T. M. Knox (Oxford: Clarendon Press, 1967).

WdL ———, *The Science of Logic* [1812], trans. A. V. Miller (New York: Humanities Press, 1969).

I-XX ———, *Werke in Zwanzig Bänden* [1832–1845] (Frankfurt am Main: Suhrkamp, 1971).

Martin Heidegger

BP *The Basic Problems of Phenomenology* [1927], trans. Albert Hofstadter (Bloomington: Indiana University Press, 1982).

BT ———, *Being and Time* [1927], trans. John Macquarrie and Edward Robinson (New York: Harper & Row, 1962).

LH ———, "Letter on Humanism" [1947], in *Basic Writings,* trans. Frank A. Capuzzi and J. Glenn Gray (New York: Harper & Row, 1977).

Thomas Hobbes

Lev *Leviathan* [1651], ed. C. B. Macpherson (New York: Penguin Classics, 1985).

Edmund Husserl

K *The Crisis of the European Sciences and Transcendental Phenomenology*

[1934–37], trans. David Carr (Evanston: Northwestern University Press, 1970).

Immanuel Kant

Anth   *Anthropology From a Pragmatic Point of View* [1798], trans. Mary J. Gregor (The Hague: Martinue Nijhoff, 1974).

CJ   ———, *Critique of Judgment* [1790], trans. Werner S. Pluhar (Indianapolis: Hackett Publishing Company, 1987).

CprR   ———, *Critique of Practical Reason* [1788], trans. Lewis White Beck (New York: The Bobbs-Merrill Co., Inc., 1956).

(A.../   ———, *Critique of Pure Reason*, trans. Norman Kemp Smith (New
B...)   York: Macmillan, 1973). Following the standard practices, references to this work will list pages of the first [1781] and second [1787] editions, or "A" and "B" paginations.

Ed   ———, *Education* [1803], trans. Annette Churton (Ann Arbor: University of Michigan Press, 1960).

Found   ———, *Foundations of the Metaphysics of Morals* [1785], trans. Lewis White Beck (Indianapolis: Bobbs-Merrill, 1959).

Ethics   ———, *Lectures on Ethics* [1924], trans. Louis Infield (Indianapolis: Hackett, 1979).

Logic   ———, *Logic* [1800], trans. Robert S. Harman and Wolfgang Schwartz (Indianapolis: Bobbs-Merrill, 1974).

OH   ———, *On History,* ed. Lewis White Beck (Indianapolis: Bobbs-Merrill, 1963).

T-P   ———, *On the Old Saw "That May Be Right in Theory But It Won't Work in Practice"* [1793], trans. E. B. Ashton (Philadelphia: University of Pennsylvania Press, 1974).

Tugend   ———, *The Metaphysical Principles of Virtue* [1797, part II of the *Metaphysik der Sitten*], trans. James Ellington (Indianapolis: Bobbs-Merrill, 1964).

Rel   ———, *Religion within the Limits of Reason Alone* [1793], trans. Theodore M. Greene and Hoyt H. Hudson (New York: Harper & Row, 1960).

F. W. J. Schelling

Natur   *Ideas for a Philosophy of Nature* [1797], trans. Errol E. Harris and Peter Heath (Cambridge: Cambridge University Press, 1988).

Leo Strauss

NR   *Natural Right and History* (Chicago: University of Chicago Press, 1953).

PREFACE

What follows is the first of two books that comprise a series of studies organized around the theme of the origin and significance of the concept of tradition in recent continental philosophy. These investigations follow an itinerary of problems usually associated with the domain of the ethical. Their results will show that the concept of tradition both is contested within and itself overdetermines the interpretations of the history (conceptual and real) in which we still participate, involving the problem of its competing rationalities, and the recurrent question of the passage "between the ancients and the moderns." Accordingly, these studies also address current debates in Continental thought concerning the exclusions and retrievals of the past, belief and enlightenment, theory and practice—in short, systematic knowledge and its lived experience. The overall thesis is that we have still not emerged from the complication wrought by tradition—which enframes current debates concerning the intelligibility of the present as much as the past. The problem of tradition surely does not provide the solution to the contemporary theoretical debates with which it is so intimately involved, but its investigation may well assist in their assessment and evaluation.

It follows that such an investigation can depend neither upon the work of a single author—the unity of the *oeuvre*, as Foucault says—nor on a single research program or 'traditional' canon. Indeed, as will become evident, the question of tradition forces us to reacknowledge the problematic relations of any single author to the past which result from the dependence on 'traditionality', even in articulating the specific difference, critical 'deformation', and refiguration of tradition that a single author might undertake. Thus we can see how closely the problem of interpretation accompanies the question of traditionality "as such." We stand then not only, to use Arendt's terms, between past and future but equally, again to use Foucault's terms, "between tradition and oblivion," divided between remembrance and anticipation, coherence and critique, the canons of tradition and the demands for creative invention and current relevance. As a result, no author writes in a vacuum; nor, on the other hand, can there be something like a tradition in itself determining history. Hence we will see the problematic status of the concepts of individuality and 'subjectivity' with respect to both authorship and traditionality.

Such considerations doubtless complicate the assessment of intertraditional debates as much as the interpretation and evaluation of individual thinkers themselves. But they likewise limit the attempt to define categorically the internal margins of any given (or ontic) tradition itself. Analysis here will be as schema-specific as it is elsewhere, always requiring interpretation and reinterpretation. Everything hinges instead perhaps on grasping the complex relation between analysis and interpretation, 'principle' and 'transcendence'. Here as elsewhere relations between the ontic and the ontological, experience and judgment, remain unwieldy—but, as later analyses will disclose, neither unprincipled nor unreliable. The fact remains however that the relations (and limits) between tradition and its analysis, hermeneutic and critique, will be neither fixed nor, doubtless for the same reasons, themselves devoid of the need for reinterpretation.

Even standard accounts of the tradition of Continental philosophy inevitably confront such margins, as becomes evident for example in attempting to grasp this tradition's complicated emergence in "the collapse of [traditional] idealism," to use Heidegger's terms. A similar 'collapse' spurs the origins of much of contemporary philosophy; doubtless for example, this collapse accompanies the emergence of "analytic" philosophy as well. This relation to idealism is, after all, maintained not only in Husserl or Heidegger's relation, say, to Hegel before them, but equally in Russell and Moore's emergence in critiques of idealists such as Bradley. Even this, however, plays down the complicated relations at stake in what has recently been aptly called "the middle European origins of analytic philosophy" in figures like Meinong and Wittgenstein. Here it becomes incumbent that we view Husserl's or Heidegger's "origins" (both historical and conceptual) in relation not only to Fichte or Hegel but equally in regard to figures like William James or Bergson—as much as all these thinkers have a problematic relation to Kant, Brentano, Nietzsche, or Frege. The problems of theoretical (or political) 'constitution', the question of the 'the given', and the opposition of critique and tradition thus became ubiquitous in twentieth-century philosophy. But, uncannily, their analysis led thinkers almost everywhere to worry about the failure of traditional concepts and the end of metaphysics or philosophy itself—as is evident in the line from Carnap to Rorty as much as it is evident in the line from Heidegger to Derrida. The conclusions here, as will become apparent, will be more reserved: it will be necessary to deny the "all or nothing" thesis that accompanied such opposing claims. In the place of these extremes we will exhibit the rationality that accompanies the endless (and unavoidable) refigurations of the reinventions of the traditional. Inevitably, perhaps, this rationality involves a venture divided between those who would preserve tradition and the "tradition" of revolt.

Provisionally, I will begin by focusing upon the status of Heidegger's 'reciprocal rejoinder' between past and future, and the questions of coherence and critique such a venture itself entails. What this initial interpretation of Heidegger provides however is a preliminary view of the historicity of 'factical' or ordinary life that resists the reduction of transcendence to formal decision procedure. Nor does it rely on ancient appeals to authority, to teleology or unbroken tradition. In this respect, the space of Heideggerean reflection occurs out of the already fractured experience of modernity and the event of 'detraditionalization' which lies at its origin. Precisely in acknowledging the problematic relation to tradition in which we live, Heidegger articulates a history in which interpretation unfolds (and the historical experience itself includes) both the 'genealogical' relation to the past and our pluralizing distance from its inheritances. In short, 'experience' itself is a venture or attempt (*experiri*) always already divided between experience as systematic knowledge (*Erfahrung*) and lived experience (*Erlebnis*) and involves a reciprocal rejoinder that upholds both the questions of critique and the bonds between history and innovation. In this respect, as will become apparent, Heidegger rejoins a problematic which begins in classical German thought.

Following this initial encounter with Heidegger, I turn then to analysis of the concept of tradition itself. Here I will further detail both the problematic conceptual character of tradition as well as the ambiguity of its history. What is revealed again is an experience in which, like the ancient problem of analogy that always accompanies it (hence the Heideggerean problem of the *Seinsfrage* itself), reason's own history becomes ambiguous: divided between the demands of coherence and critique, event and allegory, repetition and renewal, continuity and difference.

Nonetheless, 'tradition' itself as the hinge between history and reason (or in its modern guise as 'ordinary' or 'factical' life), reveals itself to be problematic in the same moment as it reveals in its own genealogy both the possibilities of retrieval and the constant need for reinterpretation. Indeed, the status of the notion of "the ordinary" and factical life itself will become particularly pointed as we consider the reciprocal relation between tradition and interpretation and its links with the vernacular and the *renovatione* of classical virtù—hence the elevated status of problems of translation, difference, and recognition that already accompany encounters with classical wisdom (or the *humaniora* as Kant still calls it). The rationality that accompanied the modern experience at stake in fact already arose as 'hermeneutic', divided between 'self' and 'Other', one language and another, one 'culture' and another. Provoked by a transcendence with respect to the Good that had become as problematic as had the relation between sovereignty and Justice itself in modern life, the question of tradition in this experience could not help but be counterpoised between a mourning before the withdrawal of tradition and demands for liberation from its constraints.

Finally, the initial protocols outlined in the Introduction and first chapter will be articulated and filled out through three chapters focusing on central figures and topics of classical German thought. It is here that the problem of tradition decisively emerges in post-Enlightenment thought, where classical notions in the itinerary of ethics, e.g., virtue, community, nature, and justice themselves have already begun to be refigured, both in light of the theoretical advances of modernity and in light of the freedom that the distance from tradition that modernity acknowledges—and disperses. The result, as will become apparent, in large part lays the basis for the emergence of recent debates in continental philosophy. A later work, *On the Dispensation of the Good*, will offer these more contemporary debates their own reciprocal rejoinder and evaluate the debates themselves.

TRADITION(S)

Introduction

Our 'Reciprocal Rejoinder' with the Past:
On Heidegger's Erwiderung

At a particularly crucial point in his exposition of truth as disclosure or *aletheia* in *Being and Time,* after having just decried all word mysticism, Heidegger declared that we will avoid the problem of dogmatic Interpretation "all the more if we succeed in demonstrating . . . how [the ordinary conception of truth] came about" (BT:262). In thus complicating his account, the rationality of truth as expressed in the "elementary word" *alethiea* became linked both to a reappropriation (*Aneignung*) of tradition and to the possibility of its critical disavowal or 'destruction': i.e., to the twofold gesture of an essential reciprocal rejoinder (*Erwiderung*) with the past. Although *Being and Time* would thereby furnish an "Interpretation (*Interpretation*) of understanding, meaning and interpretation [*Auslegung*]" in general, it would do so in a complex way (BT:245). Heidegger linked reason both to the need to interpret and to a confrontation with its own emergence—even when that interpretation concerns, as Heidegger thought it did, the extent to which tradition may have obscured the evidence. What is crucial to grasping Heidegger's account is the relation formed by these gestures—and perhaps the admission that appears in their 'juncture': namely, that interpretations by themselves do not suffice and "cannot be built in midair."[1] Instead the narrative of their emergence both buttresses and defuses the link between their venture with respect to truth and simple ideology—a problem that doubtless threatens all of *Being and Time,* as it would all such interpretation (and all 'hermeneutics') in its wake.

Hence emerges the complexity of Heidegger's "genealogy of the different possible ways of Being" (BT:31). This syntagm itself would unite Nietzsche and Aristotle at once: thereby acknowledging, as Hobbes said, both the "dangers" of tradition and the truths that might be wagered in its wake— perhaps even in hope of attaining another virtue and a "new justice," to use Nietzsche's already "postmodern" term.[2] At stake in both regards was almost a conflict between the heritage of philosophy and its account of the good, i.e., the *pros hen* or 'that for the sake of which' (*hou heneka*) of tradition and the shattering of its limits (or exclusions): *incipit tragoedia.* But Heidegger distinguishes his account both from Aristotle, insofar as the categories must remain hermeneutic for Heidegger, and from Nietzsche, insofar as, granted Being's transcendence, it would not be interpretation "all the way down." Yet what was once called Being's *transcendens* would inevitably be complicated in Heidegger's account. Genealogy always presupposes interpretation; analysis always presupposes genealogy. Hence arises the complexity of the events of repetition (*Erwiderung*) in which all three participate—and the diversity in reception, even among Heidegger's students at the time (who included figures as different as Hannah Arendt, Leo Strauss, Hans-Georg Gadamer, and Jacob Klein).

Although the word "*Erwiderung*" itself occurs but once in *Being and Time*, perhaps more than anything else this treatise attests to the complexity of the "*Erwiderung*" essential to interpretation. As Heidegger's comment on the ordinary conception of truth indicates, at stake is an event combining the remnants of tradition, the remainder of the ordinary and the everyday, and our critical resources for dealing with both. Moreover, the result becomes again complicated in the problem (and the *poiesis*) of interpretation, that venture through which, by a certain *Voraussprineng*, reason might still preserve another "primordial" truth within the appearances. Hence originates the venture of *aletheia* itself—in hopes, as he would later put it, of "another history."[3] If Heidegger almost inevitably privileged *poiesis* (and interpretation) over against the plurality of *praxis* or the demonstrations of *theoria*, he did so in light of both their dangers and impoverishment—if never perhaps sufficiently. In fact all of Division One of *Being and Time* would testify to this impoverishment, not only in articulating the failure of modern functional instrumentalism in the critique of *Das Man*, but also through resorting to a certain confirmation (*Bewährung*) of its own interpretation of the '*Daseinanalytik*' in the myth of care and its Stoic past—a compounding of narrative upon narrative. This Stoicism is one to which modernity (and Heidegger himself) would return again and again—not only in the *ethos* of care, but in the account of the experience of detraditionalization and the onslaught of the new science of nature, in which not only 'tradition' but symbol, law, and reason would be similarly fragmented and refigured. And writers today who would deny the relevance (and the ironies) of such fragmentation miss its explanatory import, which both underlies the venture of interpretive significance and motivates the genealogical project in general, granted the underdeterminacy of interpretation itself.

Notwithstanding this productive 'impoverishment' in hermeneutics (the term is Foucault's), what follows in the analyses of the subsequent chapters is precisely a series of such *Erwiderungen* with respect to post-Kantian Continental philosophy.[4] These investigations explicate an interpretation of both tradition and its genealogy. Moreover, each of the expositions involves—to invoke an equally complicated term that has similarly reappeared in such contexts—the 'experience' of traditionality itself, traced specifically with the markers of ethics in mind. Texts in classical German thought become initially privileged, since both the problem of ethics and the issue of traditionality emerge in close proximity in these texts, complicating their reception of the avid antitraditionality of theoretical modernity. In this regard, classical German thought forms the last vestige of (and perhaps the last attempt harmoniously and systematically to resolve) the "quarrel be-

tween the ancients and the moderns." As Heidegger put it, "both Kant and
Hegel still stand fundamentally on the soil of antiquity" (BP:112). But
classical German thought thereby becomes the origin of a wide spectrum
of debates in contemporary thought, including not only debates about the
ethics of tradition, but also debates about the status of enlightenment itself.
The many links between ethics and tradition (and especially its modern
conceptual origins in classical German thought) are too often omitted in
recent quarrels concerning the status of 'traditionality' and the 'question' of
ethics—not to mention the remnants that inform the specificity of the
experience (and the narratives) in their 'phenomenologies'.

Such an experience at one time articulated the unicity of past and present,
of anticipation and recollection (or retention and protention as Husserl
codified it), and the analogical unity of *synthesis* and *diaresis*—so much so
that a tradition flowing from Cicero to Aquinas and Vico, long before Hegel
or Gadamer, viewed *prudentia* itself as uniting memory of the past, understanding of the present, and foresight of the future. Perhaps no one would
express more strongly than Hobbes the fracture of this continuity, declaring
prudentia to be essentially about the past and at most a presumptive sign of
the future. Such signs are consigned to the providential and infinite knowledge of the creator, to use Boethius's terms—as Hobbes does (Lev:I.3).[5]
Hence history is less about the ideal than about the avoidance of its failure.
As the word 'experience' itself attests in being connected with the disavowal
of the past and the experiments (and empiricisms) of the modern age,
'experience' after Hobbes steadily became the explication of detraditionalization, a rupture (and perhaps violent *destruktion*) that transformed not only
authority, but theory itself, as the science of nature testified. Both science
and nature would be refigured in the "revolutions" that followed, including
even political revolution itself, as Arendt has indicated.[6]

Such transformations seemed almost inevitably to participate in that modern outrage against "vain" and "fabulous tradition," (Lev:IV.46) as Hobbes
called it. But this outrage itself involved the experience of a kind of Babel
of language and theory in which both the danger of theory and the problem
of recognition [*Anerkennung*] came to the foreground. Thus arose the attempt to remove the ethical from any link to power—even to the extent of
removing it from theory itself—an attempt that extends beyond Hegel to
Sartre, Levinas, and beyond. Like the metaphysical *agon* to which Kant
would attest in opening his own critique of reason, such theoretical Babel
(as Hobbes regarded 'metaphysics') answered the "extreme need" that had
accompanied the failure of traditions. At this point the dangers haunting
tradition, reason, and the decay of the past intersect: ethics and danger

thereafter inevitably need to be thought together, as the result of an agonistic that is both historical and theoretical in scope.

As Hobbes also attested, "All laws, written and unwritten, have need of interpretation." This is especially true of the agonistic that accompanies the natural law, in light of the polemics of modernity, concerning not only 'law' but 'nature' itself. Consequently, Hobbes insists, natural law has "the greatest need of able Interpretors" (Lev:II.26). Here again, Hobbes declared, we must rely "not on the reading of other mens Writings but a mans own natural Reason"—and by no means rely on the benevolent harmonies (or transcendence) of nature to which the ancients appealed. Instead, above all, we rely upon principles of equity in these matters (Lev:II.26). But, like Reason, equity had become calculative in Hobbes (Lev:I.5) not only as a means of analyzing law, but also in order to provide a certainty that answers the extreme need and profound doubt resulting from the dangers of fantasy and the "decay" of imagination and memory: "whatsoever we imagine, is Finite. Therefore there is no Idea, or conception of anything we call Infinite" (Lev:I.2).

Jürgen Habermas (among others) has recently recharacterized modernity in these terms, by declaring "the bond between the right and the good is broken."[7] The foibles that accompanied the interpretation of the latter would now be foregone, replaced by the algorithmics of decision procedure, traceable most directly to Kant's own codification of the natural law in terms of a determinate formula (*Bestimmt formul*). And yet, as will become evident in subsequent chapters, Kant's own transformation did not dissolve the problem of the dialectics and interpretation of law. Instead, Kant's dialectic gave rise to a refiguration whose symbolics became increasingly more complicated, ultimately resting neither with tradition nor principle, neither with the substance nor the form of law, neither its syntax nor its semantics. Even at its most exact, Kant's venture thus escapes neither uncertainty nor even its own indeterminacy and its own *Erwiderung* with "the ruins of the ancient systems."[8] But in one sense this very excess or underdeterminacy confirmed Leo Strauss's view that "transcendence is not a preserve of revealed religion. In a very important sense it was implied in the original meaning of political philosophy as the quest for the natural or best political order" (NR:15).

But, again to use Strauss's terms, what Hobbes's "extreme need" underlines (and doubtless Strauss continually avoided it) is the problem of this quest's default.[9] The problem is precisely the status of such transcendence when we are without the traditional markers of certainty or a way of distinguishing the 'inside' and the 'outside'. Instead we confront the dispersion, the history, and perhaps even the event in which rather than founding community "nature should thus dissociate" (Lev:I.13). What results is a dispersion of the classical orders both theoretical and social. Hence arises the problem of interpretating or their reinterpretation—not to speak of the complex link between experiment and interpretation that accompanies modernity from the outset. When Bacon similarly stressed the need for "passing beyond the ancient arts" by means of interpretation, which is "the true and natural work of the mind when freed from impediments,"[10] it was precisely at this point that experience would require not simply repetition but *innovatione,* in Machiavelli's term, or experiment, in Bacon's. Both, as we will see, are part of a humanist *renovatione* that was more general in scope.

It was not accidental that Bacon, in articulating the meaning of morals or virtue, elevated the issue of "application" and argued that it requires the study of history (and its phenomenology), since one must find the material for such deliberations in "history, poesy, and daily life."[11] Rather than indicating a weakening of reason (as Strauss thought), such considerations indicate at least as much the weakening grip of the past.[12] Bacon's emphasis on application reflects an experience of detraditionalization that adds to the "peremptory" codes of past conduct the recognition of an event in which "nature admitteth a latitude" and an experience "not reduced to written enquiry."[13] Moreover, rather than simply denying either reason or virtue, Bacon has understood their 'transcendence' otherwise, and seen that its interpretation required another way of philosophizing (*alia ratio philosophiae*)—and both reason's and virtue's links to *fortuna* were thereby refigured. Interpretation (as opposed to anticipations arising in midair) must involve an articulation distinct both from 'intuition' and 'induction', yet inextricably linked to both in responding to the "obscurity" in which the ideal and real are now encountered.[14] As Montaigne similarly said in his essay, "Of Experience," likewise interrelating experience and interpretation beyond the classical harmonies: "Multiplication of our imaginary cases will never equal the variety of the real examples."[15]

Accordingly, experience in all its dimensions will remain fragmentary; it will form less a continuous linear history than a history ironical (and dialectical) in structure. As involved in traditionality, experience will have the complexity of the *Erwiderung* itself, whose method is less a diachronic gesture than (in the ancient sense of 'interpretation' itself) a 'ciphering' and 'reinterpretation' (the term is Lefort's) of the fragments that articulate its permutations.[16] It is just in this sense that recent theorists who dismiss the theoretical significance of irony—like the *Seinsfrage* itself, from whose history irony again emerges—miss both the complexity of historical time and the explanatory purport of the genealogies that accompany it. Similarly, those who dismiss experience entirely from the structure of moral enquiry, exchanging such experience for formal rules of validity, miss the irreducibility of experience: as Kant himself would come to see, we will need both principle and transcendence. Theorists on all sides of the debates on these matters have lost sight of precisely this complex indispensibility of both principle and transcendence, syntax and semantics, experience and judgment. In this regard, the problem may still be as Aristotle found it: "All the partisans of different forms of government speak of a part of justice only."[17]

Recent theorists in a number of quarters, but especially in Continental philosophy (e.g., Gadamer and Derrida, and, perhaps nascently, their apparent theoretical adversaries) have stressed, like Aristotle himself, the history and the *remainder* of friendship. This book also will trace the event of friendship through its ontic as well as ontological, ethical as well as epistemic, implications. Again, like the term 'law' itself, the symbolics of friendship became complicated by the figures that underlie its apparent objectivity. The effect transformed interpretation into demonstration under the hope, to use Fichte's claim, that "the more extended this intercommunication is, the more does truth (objectively considered) gain and I likewise" (SE:260).

The doctrine of morality, thus conceived, conjoined the Good not simply to law and principle, but equally to what can be publicly communicable and institutionalized. Yet this revision, uncannily enough, occurred at the same time that modernity had rendered the possibility of community and the bonds of tradition questionable and come to regard them as matters of "tutelage," to use Kant's term. The ancient reserve of virtue—which like friendship itself was always as much a mode of Being as an act—now seemed to lay everywhere in ruins. Where once reciprocity, reliability, recognition, communication, and benevolence all seemed to coalesce, now neither nature, community, recognition, nor benevolence, neither the public nor the private, seemed to be harmoniously conceivable. The continuity of the dialogue that constitutes the humanist tradition lay—like nature itself—in tatters. Indeed it is precisely the rational dialogue that for Aristotle distinguished human beings in the very sharing of thoughts among friends (and distinguished them *as rational* from grazing animals [NE:170b]) that now seemed either futile or exclusive. As a result, the ancient analogies of the Good "beyond the true" were eclipsed in the elevation of justice (as equity), and the latter methodologically (and fatefully) refigured in terms of decision procedure.

Few exceptions indeed can be found for this leveling of ancient virtue and character or the hopes of their refigurations: views such as Schlegel's, for example, that understood manners as "characteristic edges"[18]—linked like the novel itself to the refiguration of both virtue and character—could seemingly only be countered by Hobbesian denials. For granted the difference of manners and "the diversity of passions in diverse men . . . there is no *Finis ultimus* (utmost ayme), nor *Summum Bonum* (greatest Good) as is spoken of to the Books of the old Moral Philosophers" (Lev:I.11). Consequently, "felicity consists not in the repose of a mind satisfied," but in the "continual progresse of the desire . . . a perpetuall and restless desire of Power after power that ceaseth only in Death" (Lev:I.11). Devoid of original co-mmunity, the most we could hope for (or presume) was not "decency" in manners, but hope for peace among such differences. Or as Hobbes proclaimed, fully in accord with the competitive *commercium* of modernity, such peace could be hoped for neither through love, friendship, nor generosity: "The affection wherewith men many times bestow their benefits on strangers is not to be called charity, but either contract, whereby they seek to purchase friendship, or fear, which maketh them purchase peace."[19] Even post-Hegelian attempts like Mead's to claim that manners implied a sense of community as the "generalized Other" seemed timid responses to the breach that Hobbes and modernity in general had experienced, a breach that would color all moral theory in its wake—not to speak of what has been properly called the "surrealist manners" that accompanied its *avant-garde* challenges.[20] Hobbes's "fight to the death" seemed to be mirrored in Sartre's own inversion of Aristotle. Notwithstanding his emphasis on reciprocity, Aristotle was adamant that the love which accompanies friendship consists more in loving than in being loved.[21] Sartre however was equally adamant: "to love is to want to be loved."[22] Levinas's ethics—mobilized in the problem of the recognition of the Other and attempting to save ethics from the dangers of theory—seemed itself only to remain hostage to Hobbesian premises in insisting, by a certain reversal, upon our need to submit to the needs of the Other. Hence the overdetermined repetition of *Totality and Infinity*'s opening sentence: "Everyone will readily admit that it is of the highest importance to know whether we are not duped by morality."[23]

Still, as Strauss put it, "people often speak of virtue without using the term."[24] But they do so not simply out of ignorance, but experience. Indeed we should insist that this silence (or its limit—and here, as Montesquieu put it, even virtue itself must be limited[25]), occurs perhaps less out of ignorance than out of the very experience of virtue's lapse—and the risk accompanying the possibility of its refiguration. It is just this "risk" in refiguring virtue that is usually omitted from contemporary analyses, doubtless under the mistaken concern that to let virtue become at all accidental would deny its rationality, when in fact it is just this venture that underlies rationality itself—that is, the very interpretive complexity uniting law, form, and logical syntax that remains at stake in the joint problems of rememorization and nostalgia in post-Enlightenment accounts. Similarly in their varying ventures to articulate such an event beyond the constraints of modernism, this complexity remained at stake in phenomenological attempts to articulate lived experience, a task whose theoretical naïveté concerning fact and narrative doubtless still privileges the narratives of phenomenology at the same time that it demonstrates the failure of all post-Copernican attempts to "save the appearance."

This problem would in any case complicate all 'phenomenologies' in their attempts to extricate the originary phenomenon from history—Hegel's and Fichte's after Kant as much Scheler's and Heidegger's after Husserl. Scheler, for example, had openly worried not only about the remainder of the ancient virtues, but equally about their leveling in modern society, lamenting "the rubbish left by the inner decomposition of communities."[26] The question was whether the repetition involved would be a simple restoration or whether the "automatism of the good" and tradition, to use Sartre's terms, in merely *equating* Being and the Good with what "already is," would simply amount to bad faith before the inevitable transformations that awaited them.[27]

Still, apart from the limited scope of the "phenomenological movement" we will see that these complications were part of a "phenomenon" (theoretical and practical) much broader in scope than attempts at a strict science of phenomenology—just as phenomenology's theoretical descriptions betrayed in their very articulemes a history broader than the domain of 'pure consciousness' itself. This is true even of the Husserlian *epoché* that would provide access to the 'things themselves', thereby complicating the lifeworld. Indeed, while it has been often said that Husserl's own work involved a retrieval of a manifestly Aristotelian tradition, its method was, on the other hand, not only Cartesian but even Hobbesian in its attempted refiguration of the Stoics' '*epoché*'. At the outset of modern philosophy, Montaigne had emphasized the importance of the Stoics' *epoché*, in spite of all that had threatened in the defoundation of the Copernican turn. Hobbes, on the other hand, as Herman Weyl noted, began *De Corpore* with a "destruction" of the world in order to construct it anew with certainty—an *epoché*, it should be added, that led him ultimately to deny that such mind-dependent terms as "Entity, Intentionality, Quiddity" could be significant at all (Lev:I.4).[28] Heidegger, however, at the end of the techniques of modernity, made the connection between the Stoics and Husserl's *epoché* by reinterpreting it (explicitly responding to Hobbes) and denying that objectification or methodical exclusion sufficiently accounts for the event of this *epoché*. Returning to the "early sign" of Being's truth, or *aletheia*, Heidegger insisted that actually the *epoché* belongs to Being itself and is the opening or lighting of Being. Thus he again articulates our relation to it as a care that allows something to be itself "in withdrawal."[29]

Recognizing (and insisting upon) the overdetermined (and inextricable) status of such articulemes will play a prominent role in the following analysis. Such reciprocal rejoinders would, after all, hold true as much for those who speak of the remainder of virtue and the experience of tradition without mentioning them, just as it holds for those who insist upon its dispersions. Indeed, as Lefort (following Merleau-Ponty)[30] saw, this was the reason for privileging the 'Machiavellian moment' (against Hobbes) in reinterpreting the remainder of the political (*politeia*). Hobbes hastened the collapse of tradition with scientific progress in hopes of a successor theory in which, now finally "purged from ambiguity," calculative reason would form "the pace, the increase of science, the way and the Benefit of man-kind the end" (Lev:I.5). Machiavelli, on the other hand, sought to articulate the remnants of the ambiguous event still uniting *virtú* and *fortuna*, perhaps still holding fast to Boethius's *via media*.[31] This ambiguity is also found in other ambiguous "Boethian" distinctions that articulate historical intelligibility: reason and understanding, interpretation and explanation, 'speculation' and sense, even perhaps meaning and reference. Moreover, the ambiguity at stake and the problem of reinterpretation that accompanies it is just the experience of tradition (and detraditionalization) itself, divided between Hobbes and Machiavelli, both of whom, after all, had affirmed the problem of interpretation with respect to it. The question was whether the keys for such interpretation would be imported from the models of mathematics and the new science of nature or from the 'experience' of detraditionalization itself.

When in contemporary debates accounts of the subject are said to be hopelessly antiquated, it is important, consequently, to grasp both the complexity that attaches to the experience of subjectivity and its rationality. This is in no way just to privilege or reinstate the subject. This is true even of Heidegger's own ideal of inquiring "into the possibility of a suitable interpretation of the subject, one that is free from the entire tradition" (BP:146), which must initially seem if not naive, then at least precritical. It became increasingly clear to Heidegger that the phenomenological tradition's claim to pretheoretical meaning often instead articulated conflicts much more antecedent to it, preventing the very purity such phenomenological explications sought. Such conflicts were also involved in the very idea of saving the appearance by relying upon our reciprocal rejoinder with a past from which reason "must nurture itself" (BT:194)—as Heidegger explained the reliability of Being and the hermeneutic circle. Because of this hermeneutic interdependence, history, reason, and event cannot be readily distinguishable. Moreover the historicity (and the hermeneutics) of this event is no less obvious in Heidegger's fundamental claim concerning the question of the *pros hen* of Being and experience: "the transcendence of Dasein's Being is distinctive in that it implies the possibility and the necessity of the most radical individuation" (BT:62). In this individuation—in addition to explicitly refiguring the medieval notion of *actus* [BP:101f] (as Arendt would refigure Boethius's *nunc stans* as human 'natality', or Husserl, as the "streaming presently")—Heidegger articulates a passage between the ancients and the moderns in a text that betrays the difficulty Hobbes's account has before such transcendence perhaps as much as it does Aristotle's reliance upon them.[32]

To cite Hobbes in conjunction with Heidegger may still seem errant, or at the very least, anachronistic. But it is Heidegger himself who taught us to be leery of standard views; we would rather read Heidegger, as Sloterdijk did, as the representative of Weimar schism; or as Adorno did, as the last breadth of a failed bourgeois defense of traditional individualism (a reading to which Habermas too readily accedes in attempting to find a successor theory for the *Daseinanalytic*); or even as Derrida did, as opening a questioning which only the likes of Nietzsche could comprehend. But we do not often (or often enough) think of Heidegger in connection with Hobbes (nor with Machiavelli). Yet—without denying outright any of these standard views—it should be recalled that it was Hobbes who emphasized the threat of the Other and the leveling of community in the *commercium* of Dasein, in the war of each against all, the disruption of the ancient harmonies. At least as significantly, it was also Hobbes who thought of the copula as mere equation and calculability. And precisely in this regard, as Heidegger saw, "Hobbes's view . . . is of particular significance for the understanding of contemporary logic because the latter also adhere to this thesis" (BP:190).

Heidegger railed against reason in this reduced sense, against *ratio* (and the calculative) as the limited translation of *logos*: "Hobbes necessarily has to be blind to the fundamental significance of the transcendentals" (BP:190). Heidegger himself nevertheless was forever reinventing this encounter, refiguring it, even in understanding its "uncanniness" otherwise and with a different direction (BP:101)—and perhaps especially in appealing to the ancients for its mythemes as "basic words" (*Grundwörter*). The best of thinkers were similarly refiguring reason—including, as will be seen, those who were refiguring 'humanism' from the outset—as Vico's own "interpretive" etymologies already attest. In fact, 'humanism', rightly understood, essentially involved this refiguring, and it is this that makes its relation to tradition both uncanny and unavoidable. The connection with Hobbes surely emphasizes both the uncanny experience at stake in "the rupture of detraditionalization" in the same moment that it raises the question of legitimation or justification—again in the pairing of *Destruktion* and interpretation itself.

Still, it will be objected, what is really uncanny is the extent to which the meditation on tradition and even Heidegger's refiguration of truth as *aletheia* risked their own demise in affirming the possibility of the end of philosophy or the simple overcoming of tradition. On this view, what is uncanny is how ontology in Heidegger's analysis became quickly entwined in a conceptual elaboration of the end of metaphysics, how both truth and Being became increasingly questionable, and how finally, even Aristotle (under the guise of Nietzsche) seemed ever to lead back to Sophocles, who, as Heidegger would claim, understood the word '*ethos*' better than Aristotle (LH:232–33).

On this view, we should refuse such hermeneutics (and religions) of first negation in which a philosophy that had begun with Scotus ended, by passing through Suárez into nominalism, or in which a philosophy that began in challenging the limitations of realism ended not in idealism, but in scepticism—or at least, aligned with the scepticisms of the twentieth century. Most of all, we should refuse the uncanniness in which a hermeneutics that began by tracing the failure of modern civil society and the thoughtlessly random leveling of the *Alltäglichkeit* led neither to its refiguration nor even to a return to its past, but instead to a concentration of its *katastrophe*—exaggerated (if only for a moment) in the politics of the grand style, still recoiling from *fortuna* and the "tragedy of beings as such."[33] In the 'shattering' that results, it was almost as if (to paraphrase Merleau-Ponty) Heidegger's thought had taken seriously the claim that the phenomenological could not find ultimate explanations without destroying the very fecundity upon which it relied.[34] And indeed, the logic of *aletheia* itself time and again revealed this very fragility—and its own proximity to Sophoclean fatalism:

> A sceptic can no more be refuted than the Being of truth can be 'proved'. And if any sceptic of the kind who denies the truth factically is, he does not even need to be refuted. In so far as he is, and understood himself in his Being, he has obliterated Dasein in the desperation of suicide; and so doing he has obliterated truth. (BT:271)

Roughly a decade later, appropriately in confronting Nietzsche, Heidegger returned to this matter, claiming that such words as "truth, beauty, Being, art, knowledge, history, and freedom" are fundamental, Grundworte—or, roughly it might be said, his 'transcendentals'.[35] Not without heeding Hobbes's admonition that we must remember what the original names stood for, Heidegger also sought—despite their "essential ambiguity" and "plurality"—to grasp the univocal meanings of their terms.[36]

> The life of actual language consists in multiplicity of meaning. To relegate the animated, vigorous word to the immobility of a univocal, mechanically programmed sequence of signs would mean the death of language and the petrification and devastation of Dasein.[37]

In the background of this claim one may still hear Heidegger's confrontation with Carnap; both were still trying in their own way to rid usage (as Hobbes called it) of its "jargon." Heidegger did so by calling for a semantics of the basic words—still appealing to a unicity (of Being, and of Being and time) within the irreducible multiplicity of meaning—i.e., a semantics that would overcome metaphysics as a systematically failed art as strongly[38] as Carnap's logical syntax had denied it. And both had seen Nietzschean emotivism as the only remaining alternative.

But this much, in any case, is true: to use Husserl's terms, now "everywhere the problems will be historical," and, in this regard, now "our human existence moves within innumerable traditions" (K:369, 354). Husserl himself would be led to articulate the 'passive synthesis' underlying all transcendental presence through the problem of tradition—an Urtraditionalität he too would ultimately explicate through associative deconstruction (Abbau) and reconstruction (Rekonstrucktion).[39] By contrast, however, Heidegger, in accord with a genealogy that informs his work from the outset, held that such a historical approach could no longer presume either inner coherence nor the continuity that Hobbes called the sure "increase of science." This history would not record the simple repetition of the same, the legacy of philosophia perennis, but rather the breach in continuity, the agonistics and Ruinanz out of which such views emerged. It is in just this sense, again, that interpretation requires genealogy, or as Heidegger's 1927 Grundprobleme lectures had already put it, all phenomenological reduction and construction (or projection) must be augmented by destruction or deconstruction (Abbau) with respect to tradition. Accordingly, all "construction in philosophy is necessarily destruction, that is to say, a de-constructing of traditional concepts carried out in a historical recursion [Rückgang] to the tradition"

(BP:23). The *Grundprobleme* itself provides Heidegger's most explicit example of such a historical recursion and genealogy with respect to logic and ontology. Within its account even the indifference of the copula is not simply negated: "the indifference of the copula is not a defect [*Mangel*]; it is merely characteristic of the secondary nature of all assertion" (BP:211). Propositional 'meaning' is secondary, that is, with respect to the pre-thetic "contextual interconnection" of the historical traditions and hermeneutic practices from which declarative judgments emerge (BP:207).

All this is to say that the link with the past (or with the Good that Heidegger describes as always being a "heritage" that is transmitted or "handed down" [*überliefern*] [BT:435]) will not simply be abandoned. Indeed it is precisely by acknowledging the breach in question that such a heritage (*Erb*) might again become viable, or again that there might be "a positive appropriation of tradition" (BP:23). Nor is it to ignore the radical demand of justification that this breach requires. And Heidegger acknowledges it—even in his strongest investments in the poetic. Even art, as he glosses Nietzsche, "is not only subject to rules, must not only obey laws, but is in itself legislation"—even if such legislation is "inexhaustible."[40] Nonetheless, despite his critique of modernity and his attempt to retrieve conceptual resources that escaped its requisites, 'justification' would always be the sign of a certain *lacunae* in the Heideggerean text.[41] Like the resources he continually sought with respect to the question of Being, such 'justifications' will doubtless always be 'endangered' and 'underway'. Without attempting to resolve this issue we can mark its conceptual *aporiae*, but we should be forewarned that to affirm their presence is not to claim that the *aporiae* are irresolvable—nor to exonerate the difficulties in Heidegger's own texts surrounding them.

Divided between its ancient and modern inheritance, divided between justice as *transcendens* and justice as determinate formula, justice became as complicated, in Derridean terms, as trying "to calculate the incalculable"—a syntagm that again attests both to our need to calculate and to the latter's limitations.[42] Hence Derrida (again explicitly returning to Montaigne) also reemphasizes the ever-present need for reinterpretation: "each advance in politicization obliges one to reconsider, and so to reinterpret the very foundation of law such as they had previously been calculated or delimited."[43] In appealing to a "justice [that] exceeds law and calculation," Derrida thus still acknowledges its modern necessities: even "incalculable justice requires us to calculate." As a result of this paradox, we will need to confront the fragmented inheritance of justice itself.[44] But the peril for Aristotle was already clear, for whom inequity was seen as a source of revolution.[45]

Although the account of the moderns conceived objectivity in terms of the iterability of universal relations and substitutability, the account of the ancients remained inherently a multiplicity whose elements could not be substitutable *salva veritate,* a multiplicity whose differences could not be reduced to the indeterminate or neutrally 'equitable' without remainder: justice therefore could not be simply a matter of external difference.[46] Here too, as Heidegger had asserted in the *Grundprobleme,* "ancient ontology . . . is fundamentally not unimportant and can never [simply] be overcome because it is the first step that philosophy in essence has to take" (BP:111).

Equality or "decency" for the ancients remained recalcitrantly—like Being itself—a matter of (qualitative) proportion [*analogia*]. In other words, equality remained proportionate with respect to an 'equity', a *pros hen* in the Good that escaped strict calculability or demonstration. The paradoxes attending meaning and reference here (the paradoxes of the calculable-in-calculable), which are both theoretical and practical (as Hobbes attests), only became fully intelligible as a result of modern demands for proof, critical enquiry, and the dissolution of ancient analogies of proportion. As Jacob Klein pointed out, however, this process occurred only through a sequence of interpretations that involves systematic *innovatione* and *reno-vatione.*[47] With respect to theoretical *analogia* itself, this history lead steadily to both the dissolution of the 'hermeneutic' multivalency of the copula and, correspondingly, to the reduction of analogy to quantitative proportion and the latter to a general theory of equations, finally construing the *doctrina quantitatis* as *universal Mathesis.*[48] And the influence of these transformations became all-pervasive. Even Nietzsche was not immune: while he railed against the view that "the only justifiable interpretation of the world . . . [is] an interpretation that permits counting, calculating, weighing, seeing and nothing more," it did not prevent him from saying that "mathematics is merely the means for general and ultimate knowledge of man."[49] And when this view becomes absolute, the result will be that justice must be calculable or it cannot exist at all.

Heidegger (and those after him) similarly railed against the elevation of calculability as the measure and advocated in its place what remained irreducible, still appealing to "the root of transcendence" in the idea of the Good (*idea tou agathou*) that lies still beyond the essences (*epekeina tes ousias*).[50] As Heidegger's oeuvre from beginning to end attests[51]—but without simply affirming either Plato or Aristotle (whose 'that for the sake of which' [*hou heneka*] lies in close proximity)—it is just this experience of transcendence that escaped the leveling of modernity and (as Nietzsche had claimed before Heidegger), the leveling of utilitarianism in particular. Even

Heidegger's attempt to articulate an *ethos* of care as fundamental ontology could not attempt simply to recapture such transcendence without interpretation, however; nor, as has been seen, could it deny the indispensibility of justification or even the need for "calculation." Interpretation is, in this regard, just the problem of adjudication, the remainder of Aristotelian *synesis:* the just and sympathetic perception of the equities common to all good humans.[52]

Both interpretation and adjudication are conjoined, as Hobbes realized, in the problem of sovereignty and authority (Lev:II.26)—the very issues that had come to the fore in the experience of detraditionalization, where the origins of legitimacy, power, and right itself came into question (Lev: II.26). And even if one were to dissociate the question of power from the problem of its *transcendens,* even if one were to speak of power only as institutionalized, or as 'micropowers' in Foucault's sense, the *pros hen* does not dissolve. As Derrida has put it, "the question remains of knowing what the unity of signification is that still permits us to call these decentralized and heterogeneous microphenomena 'powers'."[53]

The point is that neither version of justice can claim sufficiency—neither *synesis,* sympathy, care, and friendship, on the one hand, nor universal calculability on the other. There can be no simple choice between the ancients and the moderns; no narrative finally exhausts justice (and neither of these versions can be done without the other remaining necessary, despite its own insufficiency by itself.) It is just the task of interpretation itself to hold these incompatibilities together, to understand the multiplicity of thought that does not preclude unity—even while it remains a multiplicity which, rather than being articulated through the genre of tragedy, is more amenable to the multiplicities (and justifications) of democracy itself. Thus we can see the sense in which, notwithstanding the requisites of calculability and decision, as Levinas put it, "justice would not be possible without the singularity, the unicity of subjectivity."[54] Such a conception will neither dissolve the subject, nor ultimately ground it, nor even (as Heidegger often enough hoped) formulate an account beyond all traditionality.[55] Despite the Hobbesean limitations (or admonitions) that may continue to accompany even his thought, Levinas may have understood such pluralism better. Returning in fact to the very archive Heidegger had traced in the *Grundprobleme,* he stated:

> Across the theology of the analogous attributes of the Middle Ages this [equivocal relation between Being and beings] goes back to the conception of the only analogical unity of being in Aristotle. In Plato it is found in the transcen-

dence of the Good with respect to being. It should have served as a foundation
for a pluralist philosophy in which the plurality of being would not disappear
into the unity of number nor be integrated into a totality.[56]

What this implies still remains oblique, not fully removed from the *Abbau*
Heidegger required. The 'plurality' Levinas calls for here is not simply other
than that Heidegger had glimpsed in the ontological difference—nor certainly distinct from the possibility of appropriation and *renovatio*. Like the
latter, however, this plurality surely requires both interpretation and judgment, being an event devoid of neither theory (even the relations at stake,
analogical or not, remain conceptual) nor judgment (both evidential and
rational, as Levinas acknowledges). The problem is how to understand it
otherwise and how this plurality differs with respect to the tradition from
which it departs.

These writings are intended to provide an investigation of this inheritance, forming thereby both an interpretation and a genealogy, history and
critique—precisely in accord with Heidegger's twofold gesture. This twofold
gesture is not one without its own past, theoretical and historical. Granted
the multidimensionality of the issues and the plurality of interpretation
itself, such exposition can by no means be definitive. Nor, on the other
hand, however, can these studies be undertaken uncritically—without, to
use Heidegger's terms, neglecting the need for disavowal (*Widerruf*). We
articulate in this regard both our belonging to tradition and tradition's
inherent instability: this book articulates, as Heidegger himself did, both the
lasting effect of tradition and its fragmentation. Such an investigation will
remain then equally fragmentary; its analyses in no way are intended to
provide a "history" in the standard sense. Indeed it purports to show just
what underlies and exceeds such history, but without dissolving it. Accordingly, rather than attempting to offer a theory of traditionality, it will become
evident in what way the problem of traditionality always underlies (and
limits) the emergence of theories themselves.

The logic of traditionality lends itself neither to the monologic narrative
of a book nor the continuous diachrony of a history: no single book either
constitutes or comprises a tradition, nor is any tradition exhausted by a
canonical set or oeuvre of such texts. To speak Foucauldian, the concept
belies such classical attempts at classification. Correlatively, no interpretation either simply originates or completes a tradition. In this regard, nothing
is more antitraditional—and surely more dangerous—than to pronounce
that a tradition has acquired the status of completeness. Indeed, as Umberto

Eco has recently claimed regarding the cult of tradition, it is precisely such claims to completeness that provide the first principle of twentieth-century facism.[57]

Inevitably, it will be claimed, granted such paradoxes, the concept of tradition (transcendentally) disrupts the metaphysical continuities of *historia*, divided between the order of being and the order of knowledge. Still, if so, as has become provisionally evident, such is the paradox which constitutes what phenomenologists articulated in the temporal passage of recollection itself—the passage of interpretation between retention and protention, which transforms its fragments into allegories without simply dissolving them. Hence, as has already become evident, complicated relations arise between the history of the concept of tradition and that of allegory itself. Allegory, Gadamer points out, always depended upon a firm tradition (TM:79). Still, to force such claims would be to render both allegory and tradition itself impossible. The allegorical, as Benjamin knew, likewise depended upon, if not a certain disenchantment with the obvious or the immediately evident, then at least a certain distance from such immanence: hence emerges the affinity between allegory and irony. In this regard "allegories are, in the realm of thoughts, what ruins are in the realm of things" (Trau:178). We encounter both only through our difference and distance from them. Gadamer himself had linked this distance both to the problem of hermeneutics and its experience of the classical (TM:288).

It is perhaps not surprising that the problem of hermeneutics emerged as a phenomenon of general significance (like the problems of fragmentation and irony) in such authors as Schleiermacher and Schlegel. All three "topics" require a certain distance from and rupture before neoclassicism. Thus if the problem of tradition is an ever-present accomplice of such hermeneutics, it is because hermeneutics emerges as a general problem from the experience of detraditionalization itself—an experience fully divided between its dependencies and its disenchantments. Irony here, as Kierkegaard saw, would need to be distinguished from Theophrastan "dissimulation," marking an experience of freedom cut loose from the continuity of our past, and an individuality irreducible to the practices and concepts it inherits. In other words, irony involves an experience of individuality (or subjectivity) irreducible to an *individuum* (or *subjectum*).[58] As Schlegel had already seen with respect to irony (and Schliermacher with regard to hermeneutics), this experience would need to be distinguished from a particular genre in the same way that interpretation would need to extend beyond strict conceptual subsumption. And, not without retracing Aristotle's own *pros hen*, Schlegel declared that irony (like allegory) must be understood problematically, "in the first place [as] something that happens in more ways than one."[59] However, the 'irony' out of which interpretation emerges here neither requires religious resolution, as Kierkegaard thought, nor succumbs to scepticism before monological demands for a final demonstrative vocabulary.[60] Only in this respect does this 'irony' authorize a certain self-trust—namely, that the present out of which we speak need not blind our judgment to history nor lead us simply to substitute private conscience for rational certainty.[61] Rather, it is in just this sense that judgment is both normative and transcendent at the same time, as Kant realized in setting a precedent for the post-Kantian 'ironists' in his wake.

It has recently been charged by thinkers as diverse as Rorty and Habermas that "ironist thinking" is irrelevant to politics, indeed that it is destructive of social hope. In one sense this is true: if we start from an empirical concept of politics whose accounts of meaning and truth are imported from the natural sciences such thinking often gives the impression of a "negative dialectic" or a "weak thought" that seems only to instantiate the very nihilism it decries—and in this regard, that it is still, to use Nietzsche's terms, "nihilism that stands at the door." But by stepping beyond such a limited concept of politics, the irony out of which interpretation arises, by the ancient inheritance denoted by the *Seinsfrage* itself, is equally the encounter with the remnants—and the problem—of "the political" as such.[62]

The passage of interpretation, thus understood, cannot be reduced to its (traditional) origins, nor gain intelligibility apart from the origins from which it departs. Hence, however, the relevance of the lingering appeal (*hermeneuein*) of tradition—an appeal thereby already enigmatic and allegorical. Tradition thus becomes a process bound both by its own limits and never devoid of the need for interpretation and critique (and thereby transformation and refiguration). But it is precisely this disequilibrium that underlies the very event of traditionality—and one that doubtless accompanies the event of *Erwiderung* itself in the venture of its own difference with respect to origins.[63]

1. Traditionis Traditio[1]

> I can tell you the tradition that has come down from our
> ancestors, but they alone know the truth of it.
>
> —Phaedrus (274c)

1. On the Figures of Tradition

To privilege the concept of tradition in philosophical analysis is to embark
upon an investigation of the ambiguities of contemporary thought, an undertaking that is conceptually polyvalent: theoretical and metatheoretical,
practical and historical at once. Moreover, it is to encounter the limits of
analysis itself, confronted with an event that, although clearly not devoid
of legitimation, remains internally disrupted in incommensurability, difference, and agonistic. The concept of tradition, then, remains anomalous, one
of those ancient but paradoxical 'transcendentals' that, as Heidegger or
Foucault recognized, underwrites philosophical analysis—although only
perhaps by betraying the nonsystematicity and historicity of philosophical
'systems'.[2] That neither Foucault nor Heidegger sufficiently emphasized the
complexity of the paradox at stake, it might likewise be argued, simply
attests to the extent to which each of their own thoughts continued to
depend upon its reserve. Adorno had equally confronted the remainder of
this event, one he too could call at most "quasi-transcendental" in character.
"Although reflecting the transcendental moment," tradition, Adorno declared, is "not a point like subjectivity but itself the properly constitutive
factor," albeit one still articulated by him in terms of what Kant called "the
mechanism hidden in the depths of the soul" (ND:54). And yet like this art
itself, the idea of such a traditional 'reserve' involved both an event and a
concept, which like the ancient semantics of analogy that continually intruded on the critical system, involved a play between the determinate and
indeterminate, the univocal and the equivocal, identity and difference, between past and future.

This reserve—the remainder of tradition itself—announces a concept that
is not a concept; that is, it announces a concept that is the *pros hen* of
conceptuality—or, to invoke an uneasy term that has always accompanied
its descent, the "life" (and schematism)—of conceptuality. Hans-Georg
Gadamer's account, doubtless the most direct in its retrieval of the conceptual archive of traditions, pays testimony to this past by emphasizing the
speculative concept of life (and its *Erlebnis*) as its foundation.[3] The 'concept'
of tradition would provide, to speak precisely, a concept of the (historical)

life of conceptuality. In so doing, it would paradoxically and continually draw upon an ancient—indeed if not mythological, then surely an analogical—past of conceptuality; an event that involves, as Husserl put it, "tradition producing tradition out of itself"[4] (K:374). And, while the significance of the concept of tradition thus became almost universally acknowledged in the wake of what Heidegger called "the collapse of idealistic systems," this concept likewise imparted a complex legacy, not only with respect to being and time, but as the hinge between memory and imagination, meaning and value, truth and reference.[5]

As early as 1874, F. H. Bradley argued, in what Collingwood recognized as a still unsuccessful "revolt against positivism," that the intelligibility of human tradition involved a complex interchange between analogy and disanalogy.[6] Heidegger similarly recognized the importance of analogy in his early encounter with Brentano's *The Manifold Sense of Being in Aristotle,* an issue which thereafter would accompany the itinerary of his *Seinsfrage.*[7] Indeed Heidegger himself recognized in both Brentano and Dilthey the emergence of "an Aristotelian tradition."[8] Retrospectively, it can be seen perhaps just how complex such appeals to analogy are. Granted the ancient archive of analogy itself, the paradox of such appeals for the hinge between history and Being is determinate. Like those paradoxes that haunted Russell's foundational concerns in his reliance upon set theory to overcome Bradley's indeterminacy, 'Being' both is and is not a being: both does and does not contain itself (and its 'appeals' are as much explication as complication). Indeed the result of such 'hermeneutic' appeals to the analogies of tradition was a circle of interdefined 'concepts' whose reference was as much invention as discovery. If, as Foucault put it, on this construal "to know must therefore mean to interpret," the legitimation of such appeals must ultimately come face to face with "the plethoric yet absolutely poverty-stricken character of this knowledge" (OT:30f.).[9] The question is perhaps what to make of its arguments and its evidence.

Doubtless such an economics will always remain complex then—and yet still this complexity sustains a gathering of ancient elements, ones that already form as much as are informed by Aristotle's ancient discussions of analogy itself in the *Metaphysics.* For one already finds there the rudiments: that nature creates similarities, that memory is the mental faculty for the articulation of such iterability, that learning arises within such repetitions as a matrix of determinate repeatables—and perhaps too, that time is then paradoxical with respect to such continuities, both a bridge as well as a "cause of decay."[10] It is true, of course, as Bradley's (Nietzschean) casting of analogy against analogy attests in its account of the historical, that the nineteenth century too becomes perhaps as much the invention as the rediscovery of this event of tradition.[11] Still the very intensity of its retrieval equally demonstrated a rupture. As Benjamin recognized, "the observable world of modern man contains only minimal residues of the magical correspondences and analogies that were familiar to ancient peoples."[12]

If nothing is more traditional in this regard than the concept of tradition itself, then perhaps what is most crucial for its analysis is that the complexity of such "Hegelian" commitments to the historicity of the rational are equally the retrieval of premodern resources: not only those of Aristotle, but equally Platonic *anamnesis,* later Augustinian (or Ciceronian) *memoria* and onwards. To speak as Heidegger did, all these aspects would invoke still the perdurance of "the quiet force of the possible" (BT:446). Heidegger's claim nonetheless occurred only by invoking, as will be seen, the most ancient predicates of *traditio* as the handing down (*Überliefern*) of a treasure (*Erb*), and its heritage (*Erbschaft*). Only on this basis could *Being and Time* continue to declare that, "everything good is a heritage" and "the character of 'goodness' lies in making authentic existence possible" (BT:435).

Yet here too the figure of analogy interrupts. Is this "possible" the mere repetition of the once actual, an event in which "ontic" and "ontological," *mythos* and *logos* coincide? Is it thereby simply too often forgotten in our search for the modern, ultimately then to be parsed by destiny and the fate of the True? Or, is it the invocation of a promise, perhaps to speak Benjaminian, an "exclusion," never yet fulfilled? What then might limit the concept of tradition, and what continuity integrate its coherence?

The concept of tradition in this regard also wears its modern itinerary on its sleeve. Not only is the articulation of tradition a matter of belonging-together, of 'co-mmunity'; not only is the concept always already "Aristotelian" in the defense of the recurrence of the ordinary and the everyday; equally, to be traditional is to be tradition-*bound*, to demarcate a norm, a criterion—and to be bound to coherence. Indeed the claim in this regard becomes that all assertion would be incoherent beyond such boundaries (or in any case before a limit always in need of translation), but always, as Hegel put it with respect to limits, a determinate relation to Otherness (*Anderssein*) (WdL:131f.). While Heidegger sought the treasure of tradition, it was equally an inheritance, he claimed, that would need to be wrestled away from its remainder. This commitment, moreover, continually grounded his suspicions of the everyday as a system of prejudice, as a "tradition" that "blocks our access to those primordial sources" that are at stake within it (BT:43). If in this regard his account betrays its modernist, foundational overtones, it also reveals his close proximity to Nietzsche. The *Genealogie* of the modes of being that *Being and Time* encountered required the herme-neutic *destrucktion* of a tradition that had been hardened up (*härteten Tra-dition*), a destruction critically—and axiomatically—to be aimed wholly at the 'today' (*'Heute'*) [BT:44]. As Nietzsche's own genealogy had similarly declared, this critique required that "we philosophers need to be spared one thing above all; everything to do with 'today'."[13]

Even those apparently at odds with such claims regarding tradition and origin remained strangely in concurrence. Despite his own antihistoricism, and at odds with both Heidegger and Nietzsche, Leo Strauss's defense of the origin of tradition precisely concurred: "philosophy appeals from the ances-tral to something older than the ancestral. Nature is the ancestor of all ancestors or the mother of all mothers. Nature is older than any tradition, hence it is more venerable than any tradition" (NR:91-92). Philosophy appeals from the ancestral to what is intrinsically good. Indeed, as Strauss claimed, philosophy appeals to what is good by nature, precisely thereby uprooting "the claim of the ancestral in such a manner as to preserve an essential element of it" (NR:91). But that, of course, was just Nietzsche's suspicion as he pondered whether its noble lie were not a "lie indeed": "Impossible to rebel against this past! Impossible to oppose the work of gods: It's to count as an unbreakable law of nature."[14]

From the beginning, the problems of law, nature, and tradition were linked as permutations in the "repetition" of an inexhaustible origin, the perduring of a certain living history. It remains significant to recognize that, their differences notwithstanding, all three could in the end concur with Strauss's claim that the "whole history of philosophy is nothing but the record of the ever repeated attempts to grasp fully what was implied in that crucial discovery which was made by some Greek twenty-six hundred years ago or before" (NR:82). The intelligibility of tradition has always depended upon the significance of such origins. From the beginning of his work, accordingly, Heidegger had argued that all of history required the distinction between quantitative and qualitative events: "even the beginning of time computation indicates that it commences with an historically significant event (Founding of Rome, the Birth of Christ, Hedschra)."[15]

2. After Strange Gods

The 'life' of traditions always verges—here and elsewhere—upon becoming less that of a universal truth than that of a finite (and fallible) consensus. Its coherence, that is, remains always ultimately specific, always verging upon a certain reduction to the conventional. Hence its complex relation both with conventionalism and with questions of the (vicious) circularity of historicism. It is no accident that the issue of traditionality emerges in recent theoretical debates from the question of historicism—nor that its reappearance with figures as diverse as Heidegger, Gadamer, Popper, or MacIntyre (every bit as much as Burke and Herder) provided a similar response to the formalism of the Enlightenment. Nor is it accidental then that tradition is claimed to provide the hinge between structural and genetic forms of explanation, the link between atemporal origins and temporal genesis, reason and cause, explanation and narrative: the extensions of formal iterability and the transcendence of ancient inheritance. Such reliance on the symbolics and iterability, the perdurance of 'tautology' has in fact always depended upon an excess or potential never exhausted, the inheritance of a past whose founding or natality always seemed miraculous—although never being more than provisionally vindicated. The wonders of tautology, praised not only by the intuitions of logicians but the intuitions of "Romantics," would always indicate a symbolics at least as well captured by the grids of Freud or Nietzsche as by those of Russell or Schelling. And it would attest to the incursion of the traditional (and the symbolic) in even the most antitraditional works—as Kant had already betrayed.

If Schelling (or Coleridge) was perhaps most direct in parsing the logic of mythological thought precisely as "tautogorical," Russell's 'intuition' about the tautological propositional extent of the formal was logically (if not historically) never far from it.[16] All three gambled on the fecundity of syntax against the threat of drift into the margins of semantic indeterminacy (and historical relativity).[17] And little could escape this excess: neither the judgment of predication nor the judgment of relations, neither the explication of internal relation nor the analysis of external relation, not the identities of intentional fulfillment nor that of logical typology.[18] The permutations of symbolic iterability always, in their dependence on what escapes them, turn allegorical: their analysis is already synthesis, or their "observations" are always theory-laden, or their assertions are always already interpretation.

The point, as the history of polemics here attests, is that such elevations of the syntactic once more collapse before their own determinate impoverishment, before the very conceptual indeterminacy which had furnished the foil for Russell's and Moore's arguments against idealism. Here, as T. S. Eliot, for example, said in his own thesis on Bradley, "beyond the objective worlds of a number of finite centres, each having its own object, there is

no objective world."[19] Each thinker would be similarly plagued by the
indeterminacy of interpretation, lacking sufficient foundations. Against all
reduction to logical or metaphysical facts, "any assertion about the *world*,
or any *ultimate* statement about any *object* in the world, will inevitably be
an interpretation."[20] Although this *blick ins chaos* here as elsewhere in philosophical modernity led him by a certain inexorability to a retrieval of the
past and to the conceptual problem of tradition that it entailed, even at his
most conservative, Eliot realized that precisely what it ruled out was the
idea of a changeless, inalterable 'tradition' sufficiently permanent to ground
a formalism. Moreover, the paradox of its event, for reasons now evident,
remained as irreducible to pragmatics as it was to demonstration.[21] If Hannah Arendt, for example, had seen the perdurance of tradition in England
and America as a matter of good fortune, the author of the 1922 *The Sacred
Wood*, having rightly noted that in English "we seldom speak of tradition,"
likewise declared that

> if the only form of tradition, of handing down, consisted in following the ways
> of the immediate generation before us in a blind or timid adherence to its
> successes, 'tradition' should be positively discouraged. [Instead] the past should
> be altered by the present as much as the present is directed to the past.[22]

Although the relations for him would remain intentional and the interpretations at stake even bound by 'objective correlates' (hence related still to
Meinong, Husserl, and Brentano), it would take a J. N. Findlay to see what
had been accomplished thereby: Eliot's *Waste Land* would furnish the exposition of Meinong's *Aussersein*, a world where the timeless identities, still-
born from Leibniz's *ars analytica* are encountered as a labyrinth lacking
sufficient determination.[23] Hence Eliot's ultimate objections "to the drawing
and quartering of reality into real and ideal objects."[24]

The underdeterminacy that results would continually foil Russellian
hopes to found a more "robust sense of reality." The shortcomings of logical
analyses would become obvious on their own terms. Indeed, they would
become as apparent from without as they would from within. As writers
even more directly in the wake of Bergson and Hegel than Eliot would
continually attest, a certain fissure opened up with respect to both "experience and judgment." And, this fissure, as will be seen, was especially portentous in the ruins of idealism for those attempting to bridge the gap
between time and meaning. As Husserl put it himself while attempting to
found the iterability of *Sinn* in internal time consciousness, the problem is
precisely that "the life of consciousness does not merely piece itself together
link by link into a chain." Rather, "everything new reacts on the old," in a

relation of reciprocal involvement (and dependence) between retention and protention, condition and conditioned.[25] The problem of this "interaction" would continually foil Husserl's attempts to link the static analysis of absolute idealism to its genetic temporal emergence. Those in Husserl's wake would continually discover it: the problem of the interrelation between temporal facticity and projection beyond it, to use Heidegger's terms; the problem of tradition as extension, to use Arendt's. As Gadamer similarly realized, the very idea of tradition as a sequence of determinate repeatables thus becomes incoherent: "It is by no means settled (and can never be settled) that any particular perspective in which traditionary thoughts present themselves is the right one" (TM:535). Indeed to justify such a claim it would be necessary to confront the complicated intertwining between transcendent meaning and concrete event, repeatable narrative and actual practice, history and idea, and theory and observation. It is perhaps this as much as anything that explains what Royce aptly referred to, in discussing Husserl's *Logical Investigations,* as the latter's "long farewell" to psychologism.[26]

The same abyss awaited the science of phenomenology in general, appearing under the auspices of meaning analysis and the intentional correlate, specifically in the problem of the *noema*. While Moore (like Husserl's Göttingen students) had praised phenomenology in 1922 for its realism, its realism was precisely what seemed to be most precarious.[27] The idealizations that underwrote the constitution of the *noema* of phenomenological iterability equally required defense against claims that would render it indistinguishable from fictional pretense.[28] Indeed the authentic (*Eigentlich*) fulfillment of intentional (rational) adequation that the sixth of Husserl's *Logical Investigations* had sought would equally be turned problematic in the forgetful and unauthentic ambiguity (*Zweideutigkeit*) of Heidegger's *Das Man* analysis.[29] Here, unlike the (positive) ambiguities of the classical analogy of Being, Heidegger articulated an event in which reason and history, institution and judgment had been cast adrift (cf. BT:§37)—a world surely recognizable on Prufrockian virtues.

Even Husserl's account of the origin of geometry as a tradition of "the logical chains of the centuries" had likewise emerged as an interplay of determinacy and indeterminacy; always what is "handed down" has "only relatively self-sufficient being in traditionality, only the being of nonself-sufficient components" (K:372). But that is just the problem of traditionality: like the science of phenomenology itself, it invokes a necessity always lacking in sufficiency, its evidence always lacking in ultimate adequacy, its 'science' one of "infinite tasks." It is just in this sense that the epistemic relation to tradition will be inevitably complex, one involving, to use Merleau-Ponty's term, the break-up (*éclatement*) and disillusion of the origin to which all transcendentalism appealed.[30] Jacques Derrida, not simply opposed to such claims—and a propos the text of Plato's *Phaedrus* from which we departed—would point to the paradox of writing such a tradition. Both required and yet eschewed as inadequate, such writing would remain paradoxical, a "repeating without knowing."[31] Depending upon the perdurance and preservation of past truth, the fact remains that "memory is finite by nature," underdetermined and overdetermined.[32] Walter Benjamin would similarly claim the fragmentary form of the ruin to be always of the essence of such writing itself (Trau:174f.). But the insight again remained the same. As Benjamin rightly saw, having similarly, like the phenomenologists, distinguished origin from genesis:

> That which is original is never revealed in the naked and manifest existence of the factual; its rhythm is apparent only to a dual insight. On the one hand it needs to be recognized as a process of restoration and reestablishment, but on the other hand, and precisely because of this, as something imperfect and incomplete. (Trau:45)

Even the "conservative" Eliot would directly confront the internal limitations of the concept of tradition in pronouncing—by a figure struck against the very logic of tradition as received inheritance (*traditio*)—that tradition "cannot be inherited." Rather, it is the result of a complex interplay of presence and absence, encounter and distance—indeed of fact and fiction.[33] The reception of tradition will always in this regard be an interpretative event.

In his 1916 piece on Leibniz, Eliot openly declared that "the genesis of the common world can only be described by admitted fictions" in which, on the one hand, "my experience is in principle essentially public" and, on the other, "everything, the whole world is private to myself." In this experience the very idea of preestablished harmony or the one Absolute is, if not simply fractured, at least "the most unnecessary of [Leibniz's] mysteries."[34] And yet that such Leibnizian mysteries had accompanied the modern concept of tradition had been evident at least since Herder. Kant, as will be seen, will have similar objections to both, as is evident in his own demurrals regarding the concept of tradition, a demurral regarding both its metaphysical naturalism (which avoids the distinction between the sensible and the intelligible, theory and observation) and its lack of independent criteria for theoretical adequation.[35] It would be surprising, of course, if a sufficient account could be provided for that which seems always to escape adequation. And, the point was as clear to Eliot (and his teacher, Royce) as it would be to Heidegger: "The role played by interpretation has often been neglected in the theory of knowledge."[36] As Royce had realized before him, the very notion of interpretation required a time, a past, a memory, a community, and an infinity: the infinite sequence of interpretation itself.[37] And it did so, as Royce also realized, because interpretation always intervenes within the fragmented event of human rationality.[38]

But again Eliot claimed Royce was wrong to consider interpretation to be an inherently self-correcting process; no judgment is "more than more or less true."[39] To acknowledge all this is by no means to deny classic refutations of idealism (for example, Moore's of Bradley, or Brentano's, Ingaarden's, or Sartre's of Husserl) any more than it is to deny the evidential bases of interpretation. To be aware of an appearance (or an interpretation) is indeed "already to *be* outside the circle of our own ideas," — or, to use Ingaarden's phrase, other than I (*Ichfremd*).[40] On the other hand, it is not to claim that interpretations simply determine meaning. *Esse est interpretari* will need in this regard to be distinguished from *Esse est percipi* in acknowledging that, beyond strict syntactic entailment, no *evidence* simply guarantees the truth of its conclusion — that is, that truth always remains underdetermined with respect to certainty. The *Ichfremd* divides certainty from within, if not also justification or obligation. Interpretations *simpliciter* again are devoid of neither argument nor evidence — any more than, granted the complications between evidence and entailment, they lack ideology or myth.

We can see that the result of such complications bars ultimate resolutions. Granted the underdeterminacy of this opening, nothing would be more meaningless than to point to an account of *the* tradition. This monomyth presupposes of course that someone (e.g., the Romans, or Christians, or Renaissance humanists, bourgeois liberals, nostalgic Romantics, critical rationalists, causal theorists, hermeneuts, or postmodern pagans) got their appeals to tradition definitively, determinately, and ultimately right.[41] But it is precisely this view about which we should be leery. If the canons of tradition are not simply given but articulated, and if the question of interpretation is never finished, if then traditions are in fact never homogeneous, never 'metaphysical' — in themselves, never determinate — it is precisely their truth, ever relied upon and ever appealed to, which escapes ultimate demonstration or reduction in such wagers. And, curiously, despite everything else that divided the work of Martin Heidegger and Rudolf Carnap in the 1930s — the one thing both shared was the view that metaphysics had become a systematically failed art.[42]

At the very least, however, such reductionist views presupposed a view

of metaphysics, a metaphysical 'tradition' as a governing One and a meaningful system where concepts were in fact systematically defined. Such a
system presupposed that concepts were intertranslatable, determinate, and
complete—and in this regard that their 'transcendental signified' could be
ultimately vindicated. In general however, it presupposed that concepts like
'Welt', 'Sein', 'ousia', or 'physis'—or 'subjectum', 'certitudo', or 'repraesentatio'—
or 'person', 'virtue', 'power', or 'value'—were all concepts with unified and
determinate extension, strictly definable "as such."[43] Finally, such views
presupposed that a metalanguage for their adjudication might be noncon-
troversial and that such 'concepts' could be viewed under the aegis of
'completeness'—a completeness the analogical past of conceptuality itself
always belied. The result of these assumptions moreover would invest these
concepts with a status nothing less than mythic. Such views, however,
presupposed that traditions—conceptual, rational, moral, or cultural—were
in this respect finished, without specific (conceptual and real) history and
thus simply opposable to the 'post-traditional', the universal, the real, the
factual, and the true.

3. On the Sayable and the Said

If the fertility in the "concept" of tradition lies precisely in an excess that
provides a narratological and interpretive bridge between observation and
theory, between theory and practice, between 'internal' and 'external' time,
or between genetic and static explanation, then there is a sense also in which
it never fully completes the bridge, insofar as the events it is invoked to
explain always remain yet to be vindicated. Despite the historical affinities
between 'tradition' and 'orthodoxy', or tradition and conservatism (even
Eliot's high church defense of orthodoxy admitted at the same time that
"most of us are heretical in one way or another") 'traditionalism' (in the
monolithic sense) seems to be precisely what is ruled out thereby.[44] The
world of tradition is indeed like the world Malebranche invoked, a world,
that is, never finished. Its historical concepts never become fully explanatory, its genesis and structure never become fully demonstrative. Accounts
of traditionality emerge in a certain chiasm, in a leap from the underdeterminacy of description to explanation and demonstration, always a venture of interpretation that would save—albeit only at the same time by
'constituting'—the appearances. It is the virtue of recent philosophy to have
recognized the divided status of such symbolic investiture, the complicity
between tautology and myth (or 'metaphysics' and 'apophantics') and to

have traced its 'phenomenological' remainder, the difference that divides all appearance from within.

As Wittgenstein began to realize in the early thirties, theory in the end, pace Russellian (or Fregean and Husserlian) hopes to purge the ordinary from its equivocity, would always remain 'phenomenological'; the ambiguity that accompanied the 'appearances' or the 'object language' in theory construction would remain underdetermined and irreducible. But if that eventuality must be legitimately acknowledged to be part of the logic of justification, it nonetheless cannot be mistaken for justification understood classically. The latter became complicated by the idea of appearances in which "reason comes to an end"—strictly speaking an event neither rational nor irrational which is there "like our life."[45] We should not be surprised that such 'phenomenological' turns to current practice, to the everyday and the grammar of the ordinary became linked to talk of traditions. Nor should we be surprised that the science of phenomenology itself became similarly complicated by traditionality, insofar as it was divided between 'Cartesian' demonstration and the inexhaustibility of Aristotelean 'lived experience'—which remained in uneasy synthesis (ontological, epistemological, and moral).

The reasons for this rapprochement between Wittgenstein and phenomenology remain still to be clarified—and we will confront the issue more specifically elsewhere. Yet even if this rapprochement is undeniable, the intricacies of the relationship in its specificity are both manifold and complex, as is perhaps most obvious in the insufficiency of our standard accounts. Pace these standard accounts, such a rapprochement cannot be accounted for simply because phenomenology analyzed grammar rather than logic; nor because such an analysis could not be carried out successfully without regard for 'internal' relations; nor simply because the objects (*Gegenstande*) discovered in such analyses were dependent upon both, on 'use'; nor because such use was a matter of *Lebensform;* nor that all of this implied that meaning was as much a matter of implicit as explicit definition; nor that the criteria for evaluations, as public as they might be, likewise remained internally generated; nor that the relations between syntax and semantics would be similarly complicated in the complexity of *Sprachspielen* or *Spielbedeutungen.* The accounts of Husserl and Wittgenstein would be further complicated not only by the complexity of the histories from which they emerge, but also, as will be seen, by both the archives and the languages of theory that divide them. We can see retrospectively as a result that Husserl would never understand the extent to which grammar (traditionally, the judgment of relation) would not simply form meaning, but must also

limit and determine meaning. Similarly, Wittgenstein would never understand objections that the judgment of predication could not simply be
reduced to its criteria or role. And neither would grasp the extent to which
the event of judgment as thus differentiated—as an event of interpretation[46]—itself proceeded because of a specific excess (classically understood,
that of intentional anticipation, the *intendit significare,* as the medievals put
it) and because of the underdetermination at stake, dependent upon a play
of analogies which would both underlie and underdetermine phenomenology itself: the problem of the silence that accompanies the expressible and
the demonstrability of the said. Hence Adorno's claim arises that "the fact
[is] that all approved traditional philosophy from Plato down to the seman-
ticists has been allergic to expression" (ND:55).

Surely the contested status of 'phenomenological' commitments to the
ordinary or modern attempts at saving the appearances must be discovered
here. It is unsurprising that such commitments would lead inexorably to
questions of practice, institution, history, and finally tradition—albeit not
without the concomitant demonstrative shortfalls. As Aristotle realized from
the outset, *epagoge,* the articulation of the apparent or the received, remains
always equivocal, always less demonstrative than dialectical. The problem
of the ambiguous status of the phenomenological converges again in this
regard with the equivocity which has classically haunted the problem of
analogy and its *pros hen.* The latter marks precisely what Levinas, from a
post-Heideggerean standpoint, appropriately called, "The ambiguousness of
the Logos."[47] While he traces the ambiguity at stake in the analogical unity
of Being to Aristotle (and Plato), as we have seen, the very indeterminacy,
he claimed, "should have served as a foundation for a pluralist philosophy
in which the plurality of being would not disappear into the unity of
number nor be integrated into a totality."[48] Moreover the fact that it did not
led him to assert with certain proto-Foucauldian admonition that "ontology
as first philosophy is a philosophy of power."[49]

As those like Foucault have insisted—and surely not at odds with the
latter claim—we should be suspicious, granted the demonstrable shortfall
which always haunts conceptual analysis with regard to traditions, of attempts that would transform interpretation into a logic of discovery with
unambiguous links to the given. We should be suspicious, it is again insisted, of the accompanying progressivism, appeals to enlightenment, or
alternately, appeals to origins, the hope to return to 'home ground,' to
'natality' and the natural, to the 'classical,' or its decline. Indeed, as Gadamer
rightly saw, this account of removal or distance from origins was now
constitutive of all "classicism" (TM:288). Moreover the problem of such

distance was always accompanied by the problem of the mythic status of foundations—indeed in this regard the mytheme 'Rome' itself and the question of 'decline' and decadence—one which extends from Gibbon to Montesquieu, Winckelmann to Nietzsche, Heidegger, Arendt, Eliot, or Strauss. We should, in short, be suspicious of such claims when the complex logic of traditionality would dictate quite otherwise.

Hans Blumenberg claimed, in researching the rationality and descent of myth, "Every economy of ideas for which no rational foundation is given becomes suspect when it presents itself as the demand for submission to something for which no rational foundation can be given."[50] Yet, again, without simply vindicating traditional 'truths', the fertility of the 'concept' of tradition rested precisely in imparting this complex remainder in mediating the invented and the received. It would be equally remiss to claim rational uniqueness for this concept as its privilege. The privilege that can be claimed for this concept in this regard is its exemplary status, that is, a fertility capable of generalization based upon the breadth of its impact—albeit always by a complication. It is true that the concept of tradition itself articulates how, for example, demonstration depends upon background; why interpretation as a logic of iterability, repetition, and reproduction, demands a *Vor-Strucktur,* a domain of the 'said': the 'life of the concept' is inevitably a historical event and reason always depends upon a language, the ordinary, and the public realm. As Wittgenstein put it:

> Any interpretation still hangs in the air along with what it interprets. Interpretations by themselves do not determine meanings.

Interpretation must ultimately—to invoke the transcendental perfect—'always already' depend on some prior understanding,

> some way of grasping . . . which is *not* an *interpretation,* but which is exhibited in what we call "obeying the rule" and "going against it" in actual cases. Hence there is an inclination to say: every action according to the rule is an interpretation. But we ought to restrict the term "interpretation" to the substitution of one expression of the rule for another.[51]

"Hermeneuts," following Heidegger, similarly distinguished an "active" sense of interpretation from the meanings of its inherited *Vor-structur* (indeed *Being and Time* is an example of the former and we will insist upon stressing the latter with respect to it). But it is important to recall that Heidegger himself introduces the problem of interpretation and tradition in this regard precisely to avoid the naive antinomies of traditionalism, on the one hand, and the "opinion that a philosophy can be built in mid air," on the other. Hence emerges, as we have seen, the twofold synthesis of genealogy *and* interpretation in Heidegger's thought. Nor will simple description of our background practices suffice: this same twofold synthesis remains underway here as well. It is just in this regard that *Being and Time* becomes itself an *explicatio* of such an "active" Interpretation of Dasein, providing *inter alia* "an Interpretation (*Interpretation*) of understanding, meaning, and interpretation [*Auslegung*]" (BT:245).[52] The complications in recognizing this twofold character of interpretation and its 'semantic' backdrop cannot be dissolved: analysis and synthesis will be inevitably linked (BT:201–202).

The "linguistic turn" limiting rational underdeterminacy through semantic analysis in twentieth-century philosophy surely accomplished much. It could not, however, simply replace epistemology with the semantics of natural language; nor did it replace issues of justification with simple appeals to ordinary language; nor did it simply facilitate the substitution of pragmatics for the question of truth. The analysis of language could not, then, replace foundational questions regarding the legitimacy of the public domain (and its analysis). Neither could it circumscribe the semantic potential of the ordinary by leveling off its variants to current practices under incommensurability arguments that ended with the rhetoric of resignation—that is, a rhetoric that argued, in default of strict criteria, we might as well call most of what we unproblematically think "just" true. Such attempts simply to "overcome the tradition" or the problem of translation and truth tend to dissolve the question rather than resolve it.[53] The origins of such attempts, as will become evident, are doubtless as complicated as the origins of the concept of 'objectivity' itself. In reducing the complexity of the issue, as Royce recognized about such pragmatisms during the debates at their origins (but already confined to the 'aesthetic' categories of these debates), they commit us to still "a poorer sort of life from which the artists can and do escape."[54] Indeed, as the aesthetic (but not simply the aesthetic) attests, 'ordinary' usage is already invested with the potentials of such 'escape', refiguration, and transformation. Against this, such attempts at reductivist theoretical construction involve a dissolution which in the end mystifies (and doubtless analogizes) such Wittgensteinian markers as 'language', 'use', 'custom', 'institution'—not to speak of the 'ordinary'. Similarly, it should be added that justified "deconstructionist" insights regarding underdeterminability could no more end by claiming we might as well call most of what we think false. Although the *Tractatus* restricted meaning to what could be said, that did not prevent the book, after all, from talking about what indeterminately—and inexpressibly—extended beyond it in silence.[55] And, thinkers as far afield as Lyotard and Derrida would not miss this Wittgensteinian limit. Still, this is not simply to relegate such silence to the ineffable, nor to assign what cannot be 'said', articulated, or perspicuously 'shown' in notation to the meaningless *simpliciter*. Rather it is to open the horizon of the indeterminately sayable always (and only) in relation to a certain determination—which itself in turn becomes hermeneutic at least in this respect, that it remains always schema-specific and potentially underdetermined. Moreover, when this indeterminacy began to be recognized to be anything but incidental or exceptional to language games as forms of life, both became recognized to be similarly of a piece: "The concept of a living being has the same indeterminacy as that of a language"—to speak Kantian, both are strictly taken, 'purposive', that is, without *definite* purpose.[56]

The standard account of "the linguistic turn," as much as it provided justifiable advances in either epistemology or the science of linguistics, too often succeeded in instituting the protocols of the Vienna Circle which ran together questions of meaning, testability, and 'objective knowledge'. The history of the emptying of metaphor within modern philosophy provides proof in itself of the paradigms that dominate such investigations, pivoted around strict demonstrability and fixed reference. Yet "expressivist" counterexamples, emerging from the medievals or the idealist tradition, and culminating in a modern hermeneutics that privileges the literary and extends beyond such theoretical protocols, are again rampant. Far from reducing the literary, Von Humboldt, who can be credited with founding both linguistics and history as disciplines in the wake of German Idealism, claimed that, rather than being theorized on the model of scientific literality, language should be seen through the foundations of literature. Indeed he argued that only during the flourishing of literary periods does language fulfill itself and take on its specific character. Hence "poems and songs, prayers, proverbs, and stories . . . become the foundation of language" and "react upon it from its earliest beginnings."[57] The point would not be lost in twentieth-century thought and its retrieval of a grammar, an account of the *modi significandi* with "the task of liberating grammar from logic"—the latter involving as Heidegger (like Royce) put it, "a domain not more rigorous but narrower" (BT:209, 195). This task moreover was evident not only in Heidegger's return to the ancient resources of the *Seinsfrage* and its ultimate emphasis on poetics, but equally in avant-garde accounts privileging the poetic and the literary, extending from Mallarmé to Benjamin, Sartre, Foucault and beyond. As Adorno put it, (like tradition) rhetoric has been tabooed in recent philosophical history (ND:55). But perhaps more to the point is the way the 'taboo' undercuts the ancient 'quarrels' or antinomies between philosophy and poetry, the literal and the literary.

At stake in these accounts, as Heidegger's recognition concerning 'rigor' implied, was less a simple choice between antinomies than a discovery of a means for reckoning with the difference that divided them. The point, without needing to endorse either view, is that the antinomies between the literal and the literary, which threaten linguistic analysis, remain both significant and intractable. It is equally necessary to note that those following Saussure rather than Frege would meet the same objections, forgetting the expressivist excess that belies perspicuous analysis in general as well as the historical origins of Saussure's *Cours* itself. Besides revealing Saussure's use of formalism or *combinasion* to account for what he significantly called the *mecanisme* of language, these origins, after all, likewise reveal (without, as has been argued, subsuming the latter beneath it) an emphasis upon the syntagm, an individual and inventive element that is the choice of each: "this is parole, because it is the execution."[58] And the latter shows its effect even in the published version of Saussure's theory—again notwithstanding its algebraic model. If "at each moment solidarity with the past checks freedom of choice," it remains the case that "speaking is characterized by freedom of transformation," and that "the synchronic law is general but *not* imperative . . . and the arrangement that the law defines is precisely precarious because it is not imperative."[59]

Knowing that the making-sense of an utterance will restrict its intelligibility to coherence within the public domain neither reduces coherence (or transformation) to simple reiterability, nor restricts novelty to the repetition of the past, nor entails that usage in accord with a rule precludes variance, nor dictates that the rules of syntax (or semiotics) strictly determine either 'use' or semantics. 'Following a rule' must nascently instead equally involve knowing when to transform it, knowing when to give it up. While doubtless reflecting Fregean (and Kantian) insights about the normative character of prediction, too often the paucity of Wittgenstein's talk about the introduction and transformation of rules likewise seemed to mirror his scant (and romantic) talk about traditions—that if you don't have one you can't get one.[60] Notwithstanding his admonitions regarding interpretation, Wittgenstein admitted the possibility that "successful and influential innovative practitioners may also modify the rules," which is crucial to any account of meaning and rationality.[61] In addition, neither iterability nor repetition is limited by the constraints of fixed objective knowledge, to what we can "get away with" within fixed constraints. Although every Platonist must return to the "middle realm" of linguistic image, this does not either preclude 'knowing' more than what is said, nor restrict the sayable to the mere ciphering of past statements, the 'treasure' of tradition. Rather it includes equally knowing both *more* than and *other* than the finite limits of the already said. As was becoming clear even as the *Tractatus* was being written—or becoming clear to Pound, Joyce, or Eliot at any rate—the limits of the 'natural' language could not be bound by the rigors of such synchronics. Instead these synchronics equally involved a certain piling of fragment upon fragment which expressivists tended to grasp and logicists tended to reduce. For the former the natural languages of modernity would be as much complicated by their past as by their interfaces, and hence as much discontinuous as continuous, giving rise to the task of analyzing not only their permutations but their differences and translations. Beginning again with Herder and von Humboldt, the problem of translation itself became—as it had been with the Renaissance humanists—essential to accounts of the rational. Only now, unlike as was not the case with earlier humanist retrievals, translation was likewise connected with the problem of recognition of the other or *Anerkennung*.[62] The ever-feared Babel of language, that is, would now be seen to be essential to grasping its internal coherence. The later Wittgenstein's revolt against logicism simply attested to this from within.

The very idea of a conceptual scheme, as those like Davidson or Rorty insist, surely is "well lost," but not because 'truth' could be localized or reduced, but rather because, without simply dissolving its evidential origins, judgment likewise never exhausts the differences in which it is constituted.[63] The recognition that there is no final vocabulary need not simply result in out-and-out relativism, nominalism, and historicism—nor even consequently sceptical irony.[64] Rather, as the interpretations of ironists like Schlegel and Schleiermacher and their multiple descendents realized, there is likewise an irony of self-trust and invention that neither confuses claims regarding the plasticity of language (or character) with simple subjectivism ('intentionalism' or 'speaker's meaning'), nor views discourse as a system of final monological constraints either to be enforced or escaped (and truth a placeholder for what we can get away with). Rightly understood, the 'ironist' neither simply attempts to escape the present nor succumbs to it, but rather is aware of the extent to which judgment (as again Kant realized) is both 'normative' and 'transcendent', assertive and expressivist at once—and so likewise is the language upon which it relies and in which it "dwells."[65] The point to all this cannot be that such expressivist accounts (or deconstructivist suspicions in light of them) might form a replacement for more 'calculative' or demonstrative accounts. Rather, any account that simply dissolves the heterogeneity underlying language will remain as dangerously insufficient as are the accounts of rationality, history, and the ethical that would spring solely from protests regarding the exclusions of such accounts. To lose the expressivist margins of discourse is also to lose the pluridimensionality of language and reason—and thereby their inventive potential.

In one sense the recognition of the polymorphous and expressivist character of the ordinary has been too "well lost" for a long time. Since the Renaissance, at least, literature has been explicitly multilingual in character—a recognition that gained an essential glimpse of the rational and fueled Hobbes's demand that in order to prove them not meaningless, the accounts of the Scholastics should be translated into modern tongues (Lev:I.9). Thus, in this regard, the valorization of "ordinary language" and the vernacular over against the excesses of speculation that would again be emphasized by Wittgenstein, had already been accomplished by Hobbes; both, moments of detraditionalization. The elevation of the ordinary, the vernacular, or the 'vulgar', surely was not mistaken in this regard; what was mistaken was to think that the ordinary itself simply lacked the 'jargon' and the madness of the speculative—to use Hobbes's terms—or, finally, to think that such translations might resolve the underdeterminacy of speculation. If reason would now rely upon the 'ordinary' for the 'silence' and the inexpressibility that surpassed logical perspicuity, it would not replace it, nor solve its paradoxes, nor even, strictly taken, shore up its foundation. Indeed it is just in this sense that the problem of translation is inherent to the problem of the rational, to "knowing how to go further"—or so it seemed to expressivists everywhere. To use Novalis's terms, everywhere the rational similarly involves the question of extension and fidelity (*Erweiterung und Treue*), and thus, the problem of interpretation itself.[66]

The hinge of iterability between the sayable and the said would be more complex, attesting instead to what Merleau-Ponty aptly called an "exceeding of the signified by the signifier essential to 'reason'."[67] Just as the epistemic paradigms governing objectivity have forced the issues of legitimacy to be ever-present, they have likewise often needlessly constricted the limits of our accounts of intelligibility and rationality. If expressivists have often been too quick to adopt the poetic, realists have been too fast to abandon it for the sake of certainty, embracing in its stead a privilege for the literal which amounts to a certain linguistic conservativism. Heidegger's analysis of *Das Man*, mechanistically leveled to material anonymity, is surely on the one hand historically or 'factically' (as Slojteridik realized) a Weimar matter; on the other hand, logically, it is the precise depiction of Popperian (platonist) Third-World indifference [*Gleichgultigkeit*]—and the sociologist of knowledge ought surely to see them to be of a piece.[68] And notwithstanding his own 'Averroism' concerning intersubjective iterability, even Husserl had seen the effects of its constraints concerning meaning and truth in the Vienna Lecture: "A one-sided rationality can certainly become an evil."[69] Still, he too seemed clear that reason could not receive its norms from "the naive experience and tradition of everyday life"[70]—even if it was his own commitment to the importance of the time-analysis that ultimately had led his students to center upon the issue of tradition, and even if, as has been seen, they hoped by so doing precisely to escape it. Even if Strauss's retrieval of the natural law remained similarly committed in this regard, as critical as Husserl of all historicism, he too wedded his project to a mining of the natural world underlying the "theoretical attitude" and purported to solve the latter's modern "crises" by a *Rücksfrage* and an *Ursprungsklärung*, the latter being precisely an "essential" history of "historical origins" (NR:79, 96). Husserl ultimately realized, however, that the very intelligibility of such a project demanded a rapprochement with the rationality of traditions, the problem of the *traditionis traditio*. It is precisely in this sense that Husserl ultimately came to acknowledge, against all his logicist instincts, that even the most "pure" of rational exemplars are linked to the problem of traditions: even "'geometry' is a tradition" and "everywhere the problems—are historical" (K:369-70). It is not accidental that all three—Popper, Husserl, and Strauss—sought respite from the onslaught of historicism by means of a *critical* tradition. Although the first two thought that tradition would involve completing the rise of modern science, Strauss thought it meant more emphatically a retreat to classical origins, but he knew as well that both attempts were obfuscated in the threat of Nietzsche.

4. On the Translation of the Ancients

Traditions both depend upon (and simultaneously generate) robust forms of coherence, providing not only syntactic (or semiotic) reiterability, but reliability, predictability, and thereby a certain minimal 'intertranslatability' or 'communicability' from present to present—and, consequently, between past and future. The logicist principle of expressibility—that everything that is expressible can be said—involves a certain transcendental illusion: at most the expressible and the sayable, to use Kant's terms for such illusion, approach one another 'asymptotically'. It is not possible to say everything, nor will just any innovation be susceptible to rational warrant. We should admit that the recognition of such boundaries alone is not enough to deny modern (and already) Cartesian claims for the freedom of imagination, nor

even need it deny 'reflective equilibrium', both of which are perhaps problematic enough on other grounds. It still remains the case that although
Husserl could ultimately admit that reason exists only through tradition, he
also never would deny that "we have the capacity of complete freedom to
transform . . . in this activity of free variation."[71] It must also be admitted,
however—and Husserl ultimately saw it as well—that transformations are
always parasitic upon prior practice for rational coherence.

Granted the bonds between coherence and invention, traditions are themselves the demarcation (if not the limit) of the real and the imaginary.
Consequently, the dialectical, trial and error at stake in their transformation
always forces us to admit that traditions tacitly carry with them, as Blumenberg put it, "a distribution of burdens of proof" and that "the burden
of proof lies on the person who demands that the proceeding be reopened."[72]
This point by itself perhaps remains conservative, an argument against the
irrationality of revolution (of all sorts), one which tellingly occurs already
in Burke, and even more forcefully in Hegel:

> Experience has revealed that it is not so easy to know the nature of the law, of
> the constitution, of the good. The isolated individual all too easily believes
> himself to be qualified for this. . . . Far more must one know that positive laws
> carry enormous authority, the authority of millennia, of the entire human race.
> The whole of mankind has laboured upon them, and it is not so easy to judge
> this work of spirit, or to be more clever than this world-spirit.[73]

Knowing that critique as well as coherence limits transformation, however,
neither authorizes the blind need to submit, nor the refusal to transform.
Indeed, as Blumenberg quickly stated, "It can be rational not to be rational
to the utmost extent."[74]

It is this interrelation between tradition and transformation, this "reciprocal rejoinder [Erwiderung]," to speak Heideggerean, which ambiguously
opens the weight of tradition, adding to its dissymmetry over time (BT:438).
If reliability can be found in repetition, it can also be invented in the form
of repeatability.[75] Both then are bound by the trace of the past. Indeed,
notwithstanding the strange psychologism that burdened such claims (we
are one step from the psychologism of associationism, after all), we can still
make sense of Blumenberg's claim that imagination could not be credited
with simply inventing the past: "No imagination could have invented what
ethnology and cultural anthropology have collected in the way of regulations
of existence, world interpretations, forms of life, classifications, ornaments
and insignia."[76] Indeed, "the fact that the choice of world interpretations, the
decision between forms of life, has already been accomplished is what con-

stitutes the circumstance of having a history."[77] As Emerson similarly put it, in a statement axiomatic for his defense of the ordinary, "tradition supplies a better fable than any invention can."[78] This however is not to say that anything goes or that our narratives simply turn into myths. "Myth" as Blumenberg put it, "can derive anything from anything but it cannot tell just any story about anything."[79] But this is because "myth" is less about the origins than about the intelligibility of the world—to speak in accord with an itinerary that goes back to Dilthey (and beyond), its "significance." It is precisely the pressure for mythic intelligibility that breaks up appeals to the origin. And science itself will not be exempt, being, as Popper realized, less about the accumulation of knowledge than about its refiguration, the products of myth-making and tests: science is a "second-order tradition," that is, a "tradition of adopting critical attitudes towards the myths."[80] Still, Popper realized the naïveté in the hope "that we could ever free ourselves entirely from the bonds of tradition"; rather for Popper, perhaps as much as for Eliot or Heidegger, it becomes a matter of making conscious what had been unconscious and perhaps "only after they have begun to fall into desuetude."[81] The problem of traditions would in this regard be inseparable from the problem of the unconscious.[82] Consequently we cannot preclude the tendency to turn the past mythic *tout court*. Lefort warns us in this regard against "the mythical function that we make [the past] play in order to assure ourselves of a truth which is already given and which will not betray us, in order to conjure away, in sum the indeterminacy which constantly re-emerges in the history that we live."[83] As debates in this area reveal, it is precisely this substitution of the work of art for the state, the remythologizing of the state that proved so dangerous in twentieth-century facism.[84]

5. Ransacking the Ancient Ruins of Prudence: On the *Renovatio* of the Vernacular

Neither the unconscious power of the past nor the mythic appeal of traditions simply limits transformation, metamorphosis, or invention—and this is surely true of the metamorphoses of architectonics in general. Architecture itself discloses this complexity in its richness. As has already become evident, we should do anything but preclude the relevance of the work of art in these matters even in acknowledging the dangers in aesthetic rationality itself. What should be precluded instead are abstract accounts regarding both its inventions and rationality. It is indeed tragic, to recount the events by which science and *theoreia* became replaced by art or *poiesis* in twentieth-century political theory, and tragic to think that either simply could be replaced by—or substitutable for—*techne*. It is important, moreover, to recognize the danger of techn-ology—to recognize the leveling off of 'nature' when treated as the objective correlate of *mathesis*. But perhaps it would be equally dangerous to simplify its complicated emergence within the inventions of the modern, beginning with the translations of the 'Renaissance'—for this would be to risk losing both the rationality at stake in such translations and the transformation of technology itself.

It should be noted, however, that even here the question of radical translation is overstressed—a matter that afflicts the will to *renovatio* in all 'architectonics'. In architecture itself, for example, even the Renaissance never quite did forget its received medieval, traditional, and regional or vernacular forms—nor their origins. Here too, the issues that govern such interpretations, those of translation, repetition, and invention, acquire a certain poignancy, disrupting the ideologies of standard accounts. In this regard, "a 'modern' ideology which measures the Renaissance purely by the classical elements it contains would end in absurdity."[85] Indeed, the "classical" texts of Vitruvius himself were never simply absent only then to be rediscovered—they were for example already quoted by Bocaccio. Grasping the difference that intervenes in such "citations" instead is crucial to grasping the aesthetic and the 'fittingness' of aesthetic rationality. However, Brunelleschi's models were as much late gothic of the trecento as they were Romanesque or even simply Roman—and in fact they were both at once.

The transformations remain unmistakable. Jan van Eyck's use of the Romanesque arch, for example, was not simply to ornament the backdrop of his paintings, but to mark an iconographic differentiation between old and new, specifically emphasizing the antithesis between Judaism and Christianity and depicting the Old Testament by one order and the New Testament by another. Equally unlike previous use of the Roman arch in the medieval *renovatio* that integrated the classical into the gothic phantasmagoria, Brunelleschi clearly attaches to the Romanesque arch a universal and systematic significance that orders anew the structure of architecture. This 'repetition' constitutes an invention that is itself the invocation of a certain *novus ordo saeclorum*—and yet one that in fact remained quite tentative since there is some evidence that he never clearly conquered the syntactic difference between the classical orders (Doric, Ionic, Corinthian, Tuscan, Attic). Without the later works we would not be able to identify the "purity" of Brunelleschi's classicism. And yet those works cannot provide the clue to his transformations: neither as a whole, nor separately can they stand on their own. Moreover, even if Brunelleschi himself thought he had broken the bonds of tradition, seeking new forms because the old ones reportedly no longer pleased him, this intention to 'break' with the old order should not confuse us. Clearly, without his knowledge of Roman construction the solution to the problems afflicting the construction of the cathedral in Florence could not have been carried out—first and foremost the problem that the Duomo's very size precluded the possibility that available timber would be either long enough or strong enough to use as centering on which to build a dome. Roman vaulting, absorbing side thrusts into immense walls, was however equally precluded by Arnolfo's plans: the solution would require a translation between the architectural languages of the ancients and the "moderns" of his time (the medievals)—and yet one which could neither structurally nor stylistically simply amount to a mythic return to either. Not only does the Duomo depend upon its Tuscan predecessors at Pisa, Sienna, Massima Marittima, and Arezzo, for a 'tradition' of domes emerging from the "Romanesque" central tower or the Baptistry in Florence (which likewise owes its origins to the Pantheon); its structure also arches skyward wholly and necessarily gothically, thus providing the strength that had been lacking in Arnolfo's walls.

Thus there is much more than simple repetition or *imitatio* at stake in Brunelleschi's (or Donatello's) return to measure the ruins of Rome. The Abbot Suger of St. Denis had differentiated the Romanesque and the "Gothic" in his own invention of the latter—a distinction between the *opus modernum* and the *opus antiquum,* to use his terms, an event which in all continuity and progress constitutes its "modern" fulfillment. Brunelleschi would equally undertake his task anew in crowning the cathedral of Florence not so much by means of a structure reducible to the Gothic or the Romanesque, but as a translation or transformation that differentiates both—precisely in this 'between' that utterly transforms architectural (and cultural) space. Yet it does so only by truncating and inventing in its difference a 'space' in which the very ideal of intertranslatability reaches its limits. Taken by themselves, the syntactics of this space mimic the geometrics of classicism, which, in the eighteenth century, would become detached from the art and the virtue of its invention to become a technological system wholly devoid of its artful institution. Still, what is revealed by the Duomo is precisely the art of this order's invention and the 'virtú', the fittingness of its solution—without claiming that it was the only possible one (let alone ideologically 'pure').[86] Beyond him in any case, all Gothic would seem for better or worse, 'neo-Gothic'—and beyond all modern 'ideology', the classical would seem to be 'neoclassical'. Michelangelo's St. Peter's may be the Duomo's most famous successor, but it is evident equally in American state capitols and county court houses.[87] The point is the rational solution Brunelleschi had furnished to a specific problem: one that involves not simply imitation, but invention, translation, and refiguration. And the example of architecture, the most public of the arts, may be crucial in this regard in its combining of *poiesis, techne,* and the political. As prone to 'ideology' and political incursion as any of the arts, architecture is perhaps no less amenable to theoretical simplification or reduction, poetical, metaphysical, or otherwise.

The complexity of both the potential and dangers involved in such "retrievals" is clear. As Brunelleschi and Donatello had masterfully found in the ruins of Rome a solution, it would not be long before Piranesi's *Achita romane* would find—in advance of both Gibbon and Goethe—and alongside of Winckelmann—a sublimity which defied all solutions, precisely a *mise en scène* whose ruin ominously loomed over the world-play of history in withdrawal and abjection, a past that is as dangerous as its repetition is attractive.[88] It would take Schelling's concern with the unconscious to link the complications attending the analysis of this event, "bringing into mutual contact" the issues of natural law, art, culture, and history—a link which historically "seems to start with the expansion of the mighty Republic of Rome."[89] The point, however, is that "solutions" appealing either to the fertility of such an "absolute synthesis" or their simple rejection defy simple rational alternatives in the same moment that they defy simple repetition or *mimesis.*

As Claude Lefort has seen with regard to Machiavelli and the "renewal of civil spirit," the humanist work of art (and consequently the repetition and refounding it inaugurates) cannot be understood apart from a consciously new relationship to the work of art. Specifically, Lefort argues—and explicitly against the trace of essentialism or a certain *philosophia perennis* he still finds lingering in Arendt—the work of art remains unintelligible apart from the "time-difference" in which it is constituted.[90] The ancient world was less simply "recollected" than transformed in its being "rediscovered." The commission for the Duomo itself demanded that "it surpass anything of its kind produced in the times of their greatest power by the Greeks and the Romans." From the first it was to be anything but an imitation. It is not, after all, that the ancients or the ancient world had been simply been lost, but more that it was instituted as a past that was *different* from the present now to be recovered—even in those works most systematically classical.[91] The Renaissance, in other words, explicitly relies upon the experience of distance and estrangement, and it explicitly affirms the 'between' which its *innovationi* invoke in the *renovatio* of the past.[92] Consequently, as Lefort says, the experience of *temporal separation* is a precondition for communication, or in its extreme form, identification with the ancients; it is also the precondition for an opening on the future, an opening created by deeds, knowledge, art and pedagogy, by a work of creation which is legitimized by the creation of the past.[93]

In one sense, even Gadamer claimed, "the humanistic ideal implies no content, but is based on the formal idea of the greatest variety" (TM:202). In quite another sense, however, the humanistic ideal is through and through a commitment to content. Indeed in the very refusal to privilege any particular content as substantial form, its ideal acknowledges that rationality is ventured only in our ability to interpret the differences of particularity itself—precisely insofar as only in such differences is Being itself articulated. Translation, interpretation, and the encounter with the Other, far from lying at the limits of rational coherence, are instead what underlie the virtues of the rational—and the opening of modernity itself insofar as this recognition (indeed the problem of recognition itself) emerges as an effect of detraditionalization itself.

The prominence of translation in the works of the Renaissance thus only underscores the complexity of the effects of this history, poised between the ancient "sciences" of poetics and dialectics and the emerging "sciences" of invention and experiment. Hence emerges the privilege given to its texts among recent writers stressing the problem of interpretation. Phillipe Sollers has similarly stressed the specificity of this historical distance already in Dante's *Divine Comedy*. For Sollers, the originality of Dante's 'upheaval' articulates a certain "total expansion" of the letter in the 'universality' of the vernacular. With Dante there is already the emergence of the "multiplicity of the signifier"; Dante's text erupts as an event between heaven and Babel, a "symbol" in the midst of time "of antiquity's resumption and herald of modern times"—a symbol in fact "of the temporal line on which we are located."[94] A rupture portentous indeed; while, as Eco has shown, Dante had transferred the poetics of Aquinas's sacred theological tropes to the poetic domain, Bruni and his followers would find the tropic to be a general feature of language itself and the Babel of language, again, essential to its origins.[95] While a medieval work like Hugh of St. Victor's *Didascalion,* a treatise on reading, could distinguish between deeper levels of intelligibility which required both "interpretation and commentary" beyond the literal, now, to use Soller's term, the problem would be one of *lisabilité* writ large.[96]

Doubtless this transference from symbol to sign (and heaven to earth) marks the beginning of modern expressivist accounts, as Foucault also has noted. But it begins too, in the same transference, that other instrumentalist and voluntarist itinerary that accompanied and equally overdetermined its descent—as critics of humanism have often noted. If we should insist that the two are not of a piece—neither translation nor expression can be confused with or reduced to a sheer act of will—it is true nonetheless that the illusion had accompanied its tropic generalization from the outset. Beginning with Dante's *De Monarchia*, this expressivist extension had brought charges of an elevation of the *universalis civilitas humani generis* before the sacred—and a corresponding Averroism.[97] Humanists have often been read as having elevated, indeed inflated genius in the work of art. At stake too, however, was always an elevation before the withdrawal and separation that underwrites the tropics of language itself—its revelation always emerging from "behind its veil," to use Boccaccio's term. Gadamer had of course argued just this about hermeneutics in general (cf. TM:291ff.). What should be added, though, is that the 'between', which the experiment of the difference acknowledges, less facilitates an event of will than opens the issue of legitimation and invention. The latter 'opens', in short, beyond the canons of tradition, precisely as the venture of difference, reason, and freedom.

The same must be said of course for philosophy, e.g., Pico's platonism. As Kristeller noted, even the "neoclassicist" invention of the tradition of philosophy as *philosophia perennis* emerges only in this difference and its inventions—an "invention" classicists like Strauss would continually deny.[98] Lefort's reading of Machiavelli similarly demonstrates that the latter's venture to recover and to articulate the *virtú* of the ancients is equally figured, undertaken under conditions in which it could be regarded at best as a hope in uncertain times. In all this too, the relationship is not just one of simple reproduction. The difference that intervenes is decisive throughout, as it was in the case of Brunelleschi. Lefort is perhaps right to capture it as a matter of dialogue, thereby reemphasizing an itinerary which haunted modern philosophy, as will be seen. To figure this critical retrieval as *dialogue*, of course, is to invoke an overdetermined relation that truncates the difference itself. Indeed, it is precisely the shared practices that sustain such univocity and co-mmunity that are now discontinuously problematic in the ruins of ancient virtue—and the problem of its remainder, "the virtues of the vernacular." And, as Lefort likewise realized, the difference can be cast in terms of the most complicated of ancient 'virtues', that of the amiability and venture of *friendship,* a matter as complicated as—and perhaps, with respect to the concept of tradition, inseparable from—the question of Being itself.[99] As will become increasingly evident in what follows the question of the status of friendship (both theoretical and otherwise) will be a matter to which it will be necessary to return. The

transformation of both friendship and Being in the conversations (or agonistics) of modernity would be no more evident than in the venture of the
vernacular itself—and as Lefort likewise saw, both were at stake in the
humanist's gloss on dialogue.

The point of grasping such transformations, however, must be detached
from any reading that could be underwritten by an *arche* or *telos*—by either
the mythemes of decline or those of progress. What should likewise be
acknowledged, however, is that the simple contrast between the traditional
and the posttraditional will now be inevitably abstract. The same of course
must be claimed of the concept of the 'antitraditional'; and as has been seen,
the conservative "restorations" of 'traditionalism' are something else again.
It is doubtless just because of the disequilibrium at stake that sociologists
have had such problems in articulating the difference between traditional
and posttraditional cultural practices.[100]

6. *Ordo Traditionis*

The best accounts of tradition have always acknowledged this complexity.
To begin with, however, it must be equally acknowledged that the history
of the concept of tradition itself is complex. Indeed its derivations in fact
are complex enough that when theoreticians have faced the task of its
analysis they have almost always been driven into nostalgic appeals to
origins, and as is often the case with analysis, by a need to overcome the
interpretive indeterminacy that inevitably accompanies (and often under-
mines) conceptual development in general—not to speak of the reliability
and stability of traditions themselves. At stake on both counts are the need
to refound, to preserve, to legitimate—in this case, to legitimate the concept
of tradition itself. The importance of the problem of foundation—and the
figure of 'Rome' as connected to that problem—now becomes clear.

As Arendt acknowledged in this regard, throughout its history the problem of tradition unites event and legitimation. This history in fact has
determinate beginnings. "The very coincidence of authority, tradition, and
religion, all three simultaneously springing from the act of foundation, was
the backbone of Roman history from beginning to end."[101] In *auctoritas*,
permanence and change were inexorably tied together, as its etymology
indicates: *augere* means to augment or increase. By religion, in *pietas*, in
being bound back (*re-ligare*) to one's own beginning, Rome could be linked
to—and handed down (*traditio*) from—its ancient past, to its first founding.
As Cicero put it himself in articulating this *memoria*:

> So let our citizens be convinced of this at the outset: that the gods are the lords
> and rulers of things, that all that is done is done by their might, dominion, and
> authority, and that they have treated mankind well; that they also observe what
> sort of man each individual is, what he does, of what wrong he is guilty, with
> what intention, with what piety he keeps ritual observances; and that they take
> cognizance of the pious and the impious, for minds imbued with these beliefs
> will surely not reject useful or true doctrine.[102]

It may well be that the concept of tradition would be continually—and dangerously—refigured thereby. This passage is cited by Burke even in modern political theory. Foundation is always re-foundation: as Arendt openly quoted Harrington, always "a ransacking of the archive of ancient prudence."[103] Strauss would credit Burke with being the last great representative of the natural law tradition formalized in Aquinas: Burke remains closest in spirit to Cicero—yet not without transforming him (NR:294f.). As Arendt realized, beginning with Machiavelli's refiguration of 'Rome', such refigurations would parallel the histrionics of political modernism.[104] Indeed the reinvocation of Rome itself would overdetermine both the extensions and the transcendental illusions of modern political theory—as well as decisively influencing the *humaniora* and, (as Hegel put it) "the honor done to the Human and to the development of Humanity" as the result of the study of antiquity.[105] Gadamer's explication of the *Geisteswissenschaften* would still appeal in this respect to the perdurance of "something immediately evident"—his characterization of the classical itself—in the *vita memorae* at stake in the Roman classics, and, in particular, the extended account of *sensus communis* in its *historia* and prudence (cf. TM:19ff.).

However, the first to ransack this archive—and indeed arguably, to invent the *theoretics* of tradition—were not Romans but those for whom the revelation of the divine and "tradition" itself were identical, i.e., the Christians of late antiquity. While, as has become evident, the problem of the justification of tradition always involves the problem (and the invention) of difference, the conceptual innovation by Christian theologians developed precisely in raising the question of their own origins. As Blumenberg rightly saw in this regard, the emergence of dogma is a dialectical matter; it occurs precisely under "pressure of the demand that they be associated with something to which response, corroboration, approval, or advice is being addressed."[106] Insofar as both the word and the practice of "tradition" contains a complicated and varied past, it was perhaps paradigmatic to Christian theology to undertake explicitly its theoretical construction. In other words, it was perhaps characteristic to Christian theology that such a response to the dialectics of enquiry took the form of the articulation of the *ordo traditionis*.

It was of course not simply "prudence" that was at stake even for their Roman predecessors. Roman law had initially distinguished *tradere* and *traditio* as legal terms literally related to appropriation: to hand over an object with the intention, in the one person, of surrendering possession, and, in the other, of acquiring possession. The thing that was transferred or transmitted, consequently, became a *traditum*. For example, the transfer of ownership of a house in delivering over the keys was called a *traditio clavium*. A specific authorized performative thus emerged here: a question of a handing over, *traditio*. It is just this performative transmission that struck the medieval church fathers as significant; subsequently they viewed ordination as a *traditio instrumentorum*, the marriage rite as a *traditio puellae*, an installation of a bishop as a *traditio episcopatus*, and so on. What is clear about these transformations from the Roman to the Christian rite, as theologians have noted, is that, although the vocabulary might be the same, the difference between a juridical and a living ecclesiastical *traditio* is clear. As Yves Congar's classical treatise explained, "in the former, the first owner relinquishes his possession, but in the latter, he brings another into communion in a good which he does not relinquish."[107] This difference with respect to the co-herence and belonging-together (*communio*) of *traditio* marks the explicit development of tradition not simply as a performative but also as a substantive event: it is as much a matter of being and identity (and individuation) as institution (and identification).

Initially, St. Irenaeus is often credited with characterizing tradition as part of explicit doctrine, and with affirming it so emphatically that it became translated into images derived from biological ordering, which would moreover accompany its 'lineage' even in more recent accounts: its iteration is always 'figuration', a propagation, by sowing or generation from the first seed. Christian doctrine was construed in this regard to be primordially a matter of transmission, *tradere*, a "handing on." In this way its ministers received authority to teach the faithful in continuity with the mission of the apostles. Not only did the rule of faith find justification through appeal to its origins by this conception; the latter likewise provided the limitations on interpretation. Thus St. Irenaeus paradigmatically wrote against gnosticism in *Against the Heretics*:

> True gnosis is the doctrine of the Church throughout the whole world, the distinctive (recognizable) mark of the Body of Christ, which consists in the chain of succession by which the bishops, through tradition, have established the Church in every place: the most comprehensive explanation of Scripture which has come down to us without alteration, addition, or subtraction.[108]

It can be seen that from the outset the concept of tradition binds the divide between genetic and structural forms of explanation, interrelating narrative and event, law and emergence, explication and origin, coherence and identity. Later, Tertullian would articulate this interdependence more explicitly by extending the term *traditio* to encompass not simply those practices accompanying scripture but also what had been customary in the church for long generations. It is this interrelation of genealogy with form that binds authority (*auctoritas*), transmission (*tradere*), and event together as "a rule of truth," that is, as an epistemic event that both founds and guarantees truth through appeal to origins precisely insofar as "truth precedes its copy."[109] Tertullian explicitly claims this appeal to be sufficient for questions of demonstration and proof. Beyond the disruptions of finite certainty, what Iraneaus already called the "rich storehouse" of the tradition becomes accessible in its abundance, constituting thereby "the tradition of truth."[110] It is precisely this epistemic 'surplus', however, that demarcates tradition from mere custom, from irrational repetition. Indeed, "it is not the assumption that an act was previously performed that makes it tradition; rather it becomes traditional when it is replicated precisely *because* it was performed before. In every bona fide tradition there is always an element of the prescriptive."[111]

Even these cursory considerations show that although the sacred penumbra accompanying the descent of traditions (like that of the *Nomos* or *Logos* itself) may never simply disappear, those who would appeal to the simple idea of a univocal tradition with no need for epistemic vindication equally forget its divided origins. For better or for worse, in other words, we will need to see the concept of tradition, to use Foucault's term, as always already a *"counter-memory."* However, unlike the Gnostic's account against which the concept of tradition had been polemically extended, tradition for Irenaeus requires no additional secret insights, nor augmentation; it remains, Irenaeus declared, "publicly" available and recognizable even to those "barbarian" believers who had believed "without letters."

The theoretical origins of the concept of tradition itself already then included a reliance upon its twofold fecundity, first to legitimate the reliability of its own resources and second to delineate certain limits *"adversus haerses"*—and perhaps especially in matters of (dialectical) interpretation lacking extrinsic demonstration. Yet from the beginning 'tradition' emerged as an epistemic and ratiocinative event. Still, those who would attempt to exchange its dialectics for deductions and its play of analogy for ultimate determinacy would forget the plurality that underlies the concept of tradition itself—to invoke again Eliot's words, the extent to which we are all, strictly construed, 'heretical'. Tradition exists, as Gadamer put it "only in the multifariousness of its voices" (TM:284). We should not in this regard confuse the diversity of a religious tradition with the strictness of an axiomatic system nor neglect the matter of its complicated interaction with (and assimilation of) other cultures or religions, as the torturous history of Christianity itself attests. The concept of the 'sacred' is not only as theory-dependent as any other, it is equally underdetermined. Indeed this underdeterminacy, in one sense, has always been taken to be just the sign of its transcendence, a sign that the infinite "overflows" the finite.

If, however, the history and the (sacred) narrative that accompanies the concept of tradition is thereby intransigent — in its underdeterminacy, problematically linked now to the penumbra of the modern — then it is necessary to insist that the problem of its account, its experience, and 'phenomenologies', are neither substitutes nor apologies for dogmatics. Beyond (or perhaps despite) such apologetics, we are forced to confront within them the inextricabilities (the transcendental analogies) which haunt their conceptual analysis, overdetermine their history — and undermine any attempt simply to detach them from the *problem* of 'transcendence'. Indeed 'experience' in the modern sense opens precisely in the rupture of 'detraditionalization' and the uncertainty that haunts the 'unicity' of retention and protention. This explains not only the complexity of turns to the *phronesis* of tradition for 'precedent' (or "analogical precedent" as Burke rightly termed it in his defense of tradition) but equally the complicated remainder of the 'sacred' or the transcendence it subtends, which would surely be contested within theoretical modernism.[112] We should not forget Hobbes's invectives against "vain tradition" and its "kingdom of darkness" or Nietzsche's suspicions, not to say outrage, at the passion of Tertullian's exclusions.[113] Neither the question of significance nor its sacred 'penumbra' is a simple matter. It remains intimately connected with the problem of symbolic institution, as Lefort discerned, the theological-political underpinnings of modernist theory and what exceeded its demonstrative pretensions, dividing the symbolic and the real.

7. *Ars Analytica* (and) *Trauerspiel*

The reciprocal interdependence of tradition and interpretation here too, therefore, remains irreducible. Any grasp of the 'rule of faith' — epistemic or otherwise — would require (as not only the tradition demanded, but its contemporary authorities acknowledged) that theoretics be augmented by practice. Theoretical analysis would always be augmented by the silence of this 'lived' excess, even as the rule of prayer was claimed to augment the proofs of dogma itself (or practice, scientific theory). Such appeals (evident, as we have seen, even in the early Wittgenstein) however must again be disconnected from the simple appeal to the ineffable. The demand that such augmentation must be acknowledged has less to do with claims that such a 'silence' is recuperable than that it occurs precisely as an excess which is indeterminately problematic. The encounter with tradition is indeed, as those such as Dilthey, or Collingwood, or Gadamer insisted in attempting to generate a critical history, always already and inexhaustibly "a lived experience." Yet they perhaps still remained confident that all that exceeds demonstration could still be determinably retrieved, a retrieval moreover always based upon the *factum* of our being-in-it. As has become evident, however, narrated between past and future, such claims could be articulated only by a step beyond *the* tradition determinately construed.

Arendt aptly questioned whether Boethius's medieval term for eternity, the *nunc stans,* might be properly understood to be metaphorical. Like all such figures, it was dependent upon a narrative and a narrating, symbolizing "the small inconspicuous track of non-time beaten by the activity of thought." It is not surprising that Husserl would attempt directly to 'demythologize' it, invoking the *nunc stans* as the theoretical articuleme of the transcendental ego. Indeed, as Arendt herself put it, the *nunc stans* invoked a certain "non-time," the time of a 'between' that (again) "cannot be inherited and handed down by tradition" precisely because it is the 'eternity' of a between in which tradition erupts: between *mythos* and *logos,* narrative and event.[114] The question is always how to evaluate such transfers. So construed, this *nunc stans* remains equally the possibility for differentiation and invention, that is, "the time and space given to natal and mortal men," the possibility "to overcome the perplexities inherent in every beginning."[115] Yet, while the theoretical concept of tradition can be claimed to underlie the invention of Christian philosophy—and perhaps even its lived experience is the result of the great Augustinian synthesis—like this synthesis it inherited the Roman paradigm of foundations. Here religion, politics, and authority could be assured in an already accomplished, sacred, indeed 'mythological' past.

To recognize this, however, is equally to recognize the problem with such foundations, that is, the *mythoi* of origins and foundation themselves. In the third *Critique's* culminating considerations on the double function (*doppel Geschaft*) of the symbolic, Kant had already borne witness to the analogical prefiguring of such foundations (*Grunden*) by recognizing that such a

Geschaft "has not been analyzed much so far" (CJ:227). In the analysis of the metaphorics of 'foundation' itself, Kant claimed, the word *grund* is figured both as to *depend* (to be held from above) and to *flow*. The event of foundation remains similarly divided: complicated between its vertical and horizontal 'transcendence', between the appeal to authority and narrative and the requisites of judgment. The difference at stake imparted a double function to judgment itself—and as Kant saw, one with immediate (and symbolic) political implication: "Thus a monarchy ruled according to its own constitutional laws would be presented as an animate body, but a monarchy ruled by an individual will be presented as a mere machine (such as a handmill); but in either case the presentation is only *symbolic*."[116]

Accounts devoid of the intervention and the difference which occurs in the event of *Fundierung* fail to capture both the invention and the fragility at stake in these mythemes. They miss the venture by which, as Michel Serres put it in recognizing 'Rome' itself as the 'book' of such foundations, "the origin repeats itself."[117] In other words, we cannot overlook both the accomplishment and the danger inherent to such foundings. The issue, obviously, is not merely a theoretical one, but equally one of *Realpolitik*. And it is perhaps just in this respect that Arendt, having equally detailed the mytheme of Rome in modern revolutionary theory, came to the conclusion that Christianity's real contribution to the political was the acknowledged desire to be free from it.[118] As St. Jerome put it in founding the monastic life:

> When winter comes with its frost and snow, I shall not have to buy fuel, and whether I sleep or keep vigil, I shall be warmer than in town. . . . Let Rome keep to itself its noise and bustle, let the cruel shows in the arena go on, let the playgoers revel in its theaters.[119]

Arendt was neither the first nor the last in the *traditio* of the elevations of Rome as *Roma aeterna*. Indeed she shares in Eliot's affirmation of Rome as a "highly civilized world of dignity, reason and order," an affirmation that led him to privilege Virgil, since "he is the symbol of Rome; and as Aeneas is to Rome, so is ancient Rome to Europe."[120] Still we should be careful in approaching such claims. Such appeals are not simply ideological *tout court*. They do not simply imply, as Eliot put it, that at issue is "the extension and justification of the *imperium romanum*"—a conflation of fact and symbol. Indeed Virgil's account is clearly credited with formulating "an ideal for Rome, and for empire in general, that was never realized in history." In turn, Eliot argues, this ideal provides an "analogue and foreshadow" of

Christian humility before its inheritance of religion and tradition—again out
of respect and love "due the object."[121] If the lesson of Roman foundation,
as Arendt put it, was "quite reassuring and consoling," it likewise required
justification.[122] The same doubtless holds, as will become evident, of the
virtue of Roman character (*humanitas*) itself and its accompanying theoretical operators, not only with respect to virtue, but those regarding even the
notions of law, community, and universality themselves. Such appeals and
their warrants, of course, are not merely narratological and theory-laden.
They are equally laden in myth. Indeed, 'Rome' was invoked and transferred
again and again, not only in Montesquieu and Gibbon, but equally in
Milton, Nietzsche, Spengler, or Heidegger after them. The paradigm for such
political transfers had been theoretically accomplished already in medieval
thought. As Kantorowicz realized, from the outset, "'Rome' migrated from
incarnation to incarnation, wandering first to Constantinople and later to
Moscow, the third Rome, but also to Aachen where Charlemagne built a
'Lateran' and apparently planned to establish the *Roma futura*."[123]

The problem is of course the legitimacy in the series that constitutes
'Rome's' metamorphoses, that is, the relation between ontic institutions and
their 'transcendental' requirements. As Kantorowicz demonstrated—not far
from Kant—the problem that underwrites such "translations" is identical
with the problem of the monarch's two bodies itself, the problem of this-
worldly political reason and its next-world vindication. But there is little
reason to think that either the question of embodiment upon which such
sovereignty pivots (or incorporation, as it came to be called) or the problem
of transcendence that haunts it has been eliminated in modern political
theory—or perhaps even that it is eliminable at all.[124] It is this link that
(politically) intensifies, after all, both the problem of the 'body' and the
problem of transcendence in recent analyses in the 'Humanities' and 'Social
Sciences'. Both the problem of the body and the problem of transcendence
would instead divide the 'phenomenologies' of such a *traditio*—between its
productions or institution and the symbolic realm; between the inescapable
attempt to grasp the significance of the lived and the indeterminacy (and
the risks) in which its excess would be ventured. Such insights may not
then be simply historical but also conceptual and logical in character.[125]

Seen in this regard there is always a disequilibrium that haunts the
'grammar' of such foundings. This disequilibrium is figured historically in
the iterations of the concept of 'Rome' itself: a certain underdeterminacy
that destabilizes all iterability and even the ensuing complication of the
formal concept of *multiplicity* itself. Trading upon such formal analyses,
Michel Serres's discussion reflects the fact that the issue is not simply sym-

bolical but logical in impact, one that in turn reflects the itinerary of the concept of multiplicity itself extending from Riemann to Husserl and onward.[126] Moreover the need to disavow this disequilibrium overdetermines, he claims, the concept of tradition itself as it emerges within the critical and demonstrative requisites of philosophical modernism, giving rise to attempts to openly deflate the demands of Reason through speculative appeals to what exceeded its grasp. Without simply affirming or denying Serres's interesting suggestion,[127] we should first recall the "disequilibrium" that we have noted regarding the concept of tradition itself.

First, granted the requisites of coherence—this disequilibrium within multiplicity could not simply entail an escape from tradition. Again, although Popper argued—as strongly as Husserl for example—for the idea of a critical attitude toward myth, a "new tradition the Greek philosophers invented" (doubtless as 'mythic' in its conception of invention as it is ethnocentric), he also acknowledges that uncritical acceptance is in some respects unavoidable, as 'unconscious' as Eliot or Gadamer had insisted it is.[128] Despite the critical ideal, Popper states, we cannot avoid accepting tradition uncritically, "often without being aware of it. In many cases we cannot escape this; for we often just do not realize that we are faced with a tradition."[129]

Secondly, however, and against such claims, the demonstrative requisites of theoretical modernity become equally intransigent. Tradition is, once again, not only inexhaustible, a sublime principle of rich inheritance, as Burke put it—its plethora the infinite reservoir of truth—but it is likewise a sublimity overwhelmingly dangerous.[130] "The streams of tradition" as Walter Benjamin put it, "surge down violently, often from opposite directions" (Trau:106). The act of founding in itself is neither rational nor intrinsically necessary, just insofar as it is never simply bereft of the arbitrary. In other words, it is subject to errancy and a certain excess which withdraws before the grips of the rational. Hence after all the motivation for the genealogy of suspicion. As Foucault realized, such a genealogy "is not the erecting of foundations: on the contrary it disturbs what was previously considered immobile; it fragments what was thought unified; it shows the heterogeneity of what was imagined consistent with itself."[131] But even more to the point is the danger perhaps in our dependence upon its presumption, i.e., that rationality, the conditions of assertion, presuppose coherent background assumptions. There is a certain naïveté then in thinking—and even Arendt was occasionally guilty of it—that we are somehow beyond tradition, that recognizing its indeterminacies and inadequacies provides us with "the great chance to look upon the past with eyes undistracted by any tradition."[132] At most we proceed differentially, by juxtaposition and internal critique. As Blumenberg put it, the fact remains that "any rational action assumes a certain system of reference which responds in a predictable or partly predictable way."[133]

In the extreme even this argument remains both overly conservative and potentially irrational. If it is true, as Burke put it, that "criticism is almost baffled in discovering the defects of what has not existed," any descriptive inventory of its inheritance too remains conditional, that is not only underdetermined and interpretive, but complicated and overdetermined.[134] The interpretation of tradition remains constituted in historical difference, a difference that precludes in principle a timeless account of *the* tradition. Here Arendt is doubtless aware of the danger: "it sometimes seems that this power of well-worn notions and categories becomes more tyrannical as the tradition loses its living force."[135] Traditions emerge not only in a tissue of differences but of power relations—and both perhaps exclude simple resolution. Hence then the intransigence of Serres's (formal) insistence that the event of (phenomenological) *Fundierung*, which occurs when a multiplicity emerges that is not a unity, but always an origin that would constitute (that is, found itself) within the multiple, always explicating—and perhaps always thereby excluding—the multiple itself. The result is a 'unity' always symbolic in character: an event, that is, again divided between the symbolic and the real. As such this event remains both foundational and indefinite, precisely to the extent that it remains always schema-specific.[136] If Arendt was naive in thinking we might be beyond all traditionality, this recognition alone is sufficient for us to concur with her that "the break in our tradition is now an accomplished fact. It is neither the result of anyone's deliberate choice nor subject to further decision."[137] "From here on," to borrow a phrase from Paul Ricoeur, "we will have to speak of traditions"—but equally we will have to speak of traditionality—as indeterminately plural, 'tradition(s)', a unity within multiplicity, a schematic differentiation within the indifference of the possible.

As Blumenberg recognized, however, this 'indifference' is precisely what remains at stake in what Heidegger called "the endless multiplicity of the possible" (BT:435). Again, this 'indifference'—to speak Kantian the *difference* itself between the sensible and the intelligible: to speak Heideggerean, the ontological difference between Being and beings—irreducibly disrupts the Leibnizian synthesis that might inform, as Herder for example continued to hope, a modern metaphysics of tradition. Again, to speak Kantian, in its reduction of the 'indifference' at stake, such a metaphysics remained "onto-theo-logy" (A632/B600). It was this very indifference of the multiple that provokes, beyond all formalization, the need for significance: precisely the 'indeterminacy' (*Unbestimmtheit*) that provoked the interpretive *Seinsfrage* from the beginning.[138] The ancients could recognize in it a certain wonder at the origin of learning.[139] The demonstrative requisites of the moderns, on the other hand, yielded in the rational both an unwieldy intensity and plasticity, divided between institution and symbol, coherence and interpretation, the "need" for intelligibility and the heterogeneity of the rational. Moreover, the *Seinsfrage* attests to this transition explicitly: 'Being' is not a result of generalization (producing an abstracted universal) nor a formalization applicable to the something in general, das *Etwas überhaubt*: Being is not a bound variable. Instead the *Etwas* to which Dasein is related here (as *Gegenstand*) is not an *Objekt* nor, granted its indeterminacy, can it simply be the correlate of formal *Objektivität*. The univocity of the *intendit significare* became disrupted in the reductive extensions of the moderns' *combineatoire*. If the former had always been accompanied by a semantic (and expressive) excess indicative of transcendence, the latter could parse it only under the auspices of the inadequate and the underdetermined (and in the extreme, the fictional and the false). Heidegger himself however never simply gave up on the 'reliability' in the ancients' account of *transcendens*. Indeed even the later Heidegger would retrieve it in claiming that this heeding at stake in the question of significance confronts the "quiet force" of the possible as "the favoring enabling . . . of the possible" (LH:196). But such talk always in the end sounded more allegorical than assertoric. The allegorical, as Hans Robert Jauss has put it, always attested to a certain "collapse of the outerworld" that owed as much to the latter's inadequacies as it did to the possibilities of the internal in extending beyond it.[140] Indeed, as Benjamin himself claimed, this is precisely why the inventions of the allegorical—like that of the conceptualization of the tradition itself, as has been seen—could not originate in the immanence of Greek naturalism. On the contrary, both concepts intrinsically required a certain lapse from origins—a lapse which not only does not simply disappear in the demonstrative immanences of modernity but becomes—in tension with it—perhaps most evident (Trau:224). Despite the success of the *ars analytica*, beyond the logicist distinction between *Sinn und Bedeutung*, a third semantic category, the problem of 'significance' continually demarcated the ruins of allegory: the interpretive excess that has always accompanied the itinerary of theoretical modernism, both irreducible and irreconcilable with the analysis of formal recursion. As Blumenberg said:

> The entire need for significance is based on the indifference [or "nondifferen-
> tiation": *Indifferenz*] of space and of time—on the inapplicability of Leibniz's

principle of sufficient reason to space-time positions, an inapplicability that had
driven Leibniz to the step, as desperate as it was daring, of denying reality to
space and time and making them into mere modes of ordering employed by
reason.[141]

'Significance' rightly understood undercuts both bad accounts of objectivity, 'the view from nowhere' and its skeptical or simply fallibilist perspecti-
val replacements, insofar as the latter invoked an iterability only schema-
specific. It is true: all *determinatio* emerges only in fragments.[142] It is just
this that provoked Heidegger's denial of Leibniz's principle—a denial that
'Being' could just 'mean' ground/reason. Still, the disjunction between the
'ontic' and the 'ontological' is precisely what provokes our reliance upon an
excess that adjoins 'intensity' and iterability—and what withdraws from
strict demonstration and 'ground'. The Enlightenment's demonstrative commitments to certainty could not but level off the excess: its indeterminacy
could only accompany Leibniz's gamble as a shadow.[143] What Heidegger *et
al.* added in this regard in venturing the continued relevance of tradition
was "the repeatable possibilities of existence" at stake within it (BT:443).
This venture, in the wake of the dissolution of transcendence, and precisely
in the hinge of the reciprocal rejoinder between the past and the present,
made possible "the perdurance of the possible," the reciprocal play between
the received (repeatable) historicity of significance and the 'upon which' of
(invented) projection as interpretation in which Being might still appear:
hence its culmination in a general hermeneutics. Just as we have seen such
a *Wechsel* in Eliot's and Royce's responses to idealism, this was too, as
Blumenberg acknowledged, the effect of Gadamer's construal of Heidegger's
account as *Wirkungsgeschichte*.[144]

Surely this same *Wechsel* and its *Spiel* provoked Gadamer's own hermeneutic archaeology of *Erlebnis,* which, by both figural condensation and
intensification, provides the hinge that unites autobiography and event,
teleology and existence, symbolics and allegorics (TM:66). The 'unities' and
the expressions that result arise in the lived event—indeed, as he rightly
recognized, "the experiment" (TM:251)—that unites speculation and life
(TM:66). But it does so—like the concept of tradition which it figures,
precisely because 'life' and 'self-consciousness' are, again, something analogous (*etwas Analoges* [TM:252]). Like all transcendental analogies, then, the
relation ventured remains, too, 'figured' in a regulative extension that exceeds determination. Interpretations are always as much anticipation as
demonstration, as much 'hope' as 'proof', arising then as much out of need
(or rational insufficiency, or "impoverishment," to use Foucault's term) as
argument or return to origin—emerging again by a fragmentation and loss

that are undeniable. The *'nunc stans'* that opens in this difference between past and present is itself 'ciphered' in the indeterminacy which erupts between—and that exceeds the adequation of—sense and signification, fragment and narrative, metaphor and metonymy, the intelligible and the unintelligible. This is a point potentially not without Freudian implication, as Lacan's own explication of *signifiance* realized, similarly construing the *Deutung* of Freud's *Traumdeutung* through Saussure's algorithmic calculus as a surplus always excluded from signification.[145] There was, indeed then, to use Benjamin's term, always a certain *Trauerspiel* that allegorically accompanied the desubstantialized, modernist symbolics of Leibniz's *ars analytica* (Trau:47f.). As Gadamer concurred, allegory is always already the invocation of a traditional remainder, albeit now fragmented—and reason inevitably evokes the ruins of history and myth in its wake (TM:79).

Eliot had similarly articulated the effects of this insight in a 1923 review of Joyce's *Ulysses* and its *scienza nuova*. The result of this interplay between sense and significance, he claimed, would be less a matter of simple continuous narrative and more the opening of "a continuous parallel between contemporaneity and antiquity." It would be, in other words, granted the *Aussersein* he had encountered before Bradley's version of Leibniz's failure, a matter "of ordering, of giving a shape and a significance to the immense panorama of futility and anarchy which is contemporary history."[146] And, as he had realized earlier in "Tradition and Individual Talent," the difference which intervenes is insuperable. At stake is neither mere repetition nor conformity: "It is a judgment, a comparison, in which two things are measured by each other. To conform merely would be for the new work not really to conform at all."[147] Thus use, again, is never simply iterative, never completely 'rule-governed'. There is the sense instead in which all language, as Joyce realized, is tacitly *Finnegans Wake*. Moreover, as Beckett would realize, it is precisely in the disequilibrium that Joyce became the model for contemporary letters and the heir of Dante, Bruno and Vico.[148] It should be recalled that Gadamer equally recognized in Vico a retrieval of Roman oratory, Cicero's account of *historia,* claiming we "must laboriously make our way back into this tradition (TM:20ff.)." Still, to gauge such retrievals it is critical to recognize the perilousness of their venture, one whose implications Beckett understood perhaps at least as well as Gadamer. The traditional origins which bound together the link between the verisimilar and the true are now lacking in the requisite fixity which might facilitate their simple reinstitution or retrieval. To interpret cannot mean simple reiteration. While all intelligibility is bound by its coherence with tradition such intelligibility is not simple repetition: "It is enough to say that we understand in a *different* way, *if we understand at all*" (TM:297). The relations between origin and repetition, foundation and institution, assertion and interpretation are both underdetermined and various—and yet ones whose evidence is thereby never simply dissolved.

Devoid of such fixities, however, beyond the "well-formed" origin, the disequilibrium of foundations, the peril demarcated through such monolithic semantic markers as 'Rome' and their imperatives, continuously incurs, continuously denying the distinction between the symbolic and the real out of which both the fertility and the rationality of interpretation emerge. As Serres saw, the result could no longer be articulated by the semantic guarantees of such determinate indices, not, that is, by "the *sensorium dei* of human narratives" 'divinely' guaranteed within the well-founded logic of substance. Instead it is subjected to the play of the multiplicity of events that can go astray and whose dangers are nondefeasible—a matter where *Fortuna* itself, as Machiavelli's venture was perhaps the first to gauge, even to 'calculate,' had become both ambiguous and in peril.[149] And, as Lefort saw in Machiavelli's risk or venture, this recognition at the threshold of modernity became the first to gauge truly the opening of "universal suffrage," in a realm from which the natural foundation of things had withdrawn and which would now require the art of invention in its lapse.[150] In other words, Machiavelli had glimpsed an originary realm in which, as Merleau-Ponty put it before Lefort, "values are necessary but not sufficient"[151]—almost in the same way that Gadamer would claim in returning to Cicero's *vita memoriae* for a source of (historical) truth totally different from theoretical reason, that 'method', that "reasoned proof is not sufficient" to account for it (TM:23). In fact both—both interpretation and memory—are needed, but neither naively; thus arise both the task and the problems accompanying our narratives and their "phenomenologies"—and the mixed virtue they summon. Political founding is less miraculous than inherently human and unstable, its risk inherently irrecuperable, ventured in a contingency that arises precisely as this 'between' that adjoins the past and the present, 'retention' and 'protention'.

8. The *Wel Ordynat* and the *Every Dayes*

No more overdetermined notion arises in relation to the disequilibrium of tradition and the remainder of its recurrence than that of the everyday, its *restance* the heir of the Renaissance affirmation of things vernacular. In the first place, however, undergirding this affirmation was doubtless still a pair-

ing of Aristotlean *empereia* and *dialectic,* of the particular and received view.
At stake still are remnants of Aristotle's account of "induction" as *epagoge*—
an epistemic event that, from the outset, had troubled philosophical modernity's struggles concerning certainty and method that accompanied the experience of detraditionalization. As Heidegger realized, the customary
translation of this complicated event as 'induction' remains "totally errone-
ous" and, limited to the logic of scientific thought, the term *epagoge* itself
becomes "immediately suspect."[152] Such 'translations' had already succumbed to the moderns' usurption of the ancients. Beyond all methodolog-
ical reduction *epagoge* indicated a complex exchange between the received
and the discovered, the apparent and real. Parsed on the one hand as the
inexhaustible resource which tradition preserves and yet on the other hand
as all that it endangers in its 'leveling', the exchange now bequeathed the
destabilized 'inheritance' of the past itself. The result coupled the appeal of
Aristotle to the *phainomena,* all their puzzles (*aporiai*) not withstanding—
with all the dangers of 'common sense' that Plato recognized. Without
simply denying their veracity (and we should not), Gadamerian appeals to
the *sensus communis* of Cicero or Marcus Aurelius could not help but be
complicated by this event—the recognition, that is, of the dangers lurking
in the remnants of tradition, the experience of detraditionalization that has
accompanied platonism from the outset—and complicates in turn any 'hermeneutic' of the lingering resources of the everyday itself.

The recognition of such dangers would be sublimely present once more
in Hegel's critique of modern civil society and its own articulation of the
commonplace or everyday. If Hegel's account furnishes the remainder of the
conjunction between life and the good life (*zen kai euzen*) which is an-
nounced in Aristotle's *Politics,* it equally explicitly traces its disruption, its
Entzweiung, to use Hegel's term. It is no accident, to use Findlay's terms,
that, here as elsewhere, Hegel becomes "the Aristotle of our post-renaissance
world."[153] The origins of the 'concept' of the everyday risked within this
account are also complex; as with that of 'tradition' itself, the attempt to
articulate these origins is always ventured within the relation between the
remnants of the aura of the sacred and the profane. Indeed, as is evidenced
by standard etymologies, the 'everyday' originally just meant those days
other than the sabbath; accordingly, the ordinary just meant the "well ordered." As Chaucer put it in his own 1374 translation of Boethius's *Consolation,* speaking through the guise of Fortune:

> "O thow man, wherfore makestow me gyltyf by thyne every dayes pleynyngs?
> What wrong have I don the? What godes have I byreft the that weren thyne?

[*Quid tu homo, ream me cotidianis agis querelis, quam tibi fecimus iniuriam, quae tua tibi detraximus bona*][154]

Thus it becomes possible for him to speak of the effect of the consolation upon a person:

Whoso it be that is cleer of vertue, sad and wel ordynat of lyvynge [*Quisquis composio serenus aevo* . . .].[155]

The interconnection of fortune, *vertú*, and the everyday did not portend their simple dissolution. This medieval past should *inter alia* already provide a warning for simple readings of modern (secularized) 'levelings' of the everyday: as has been seen, whatever else was at stake, the *nunc stans* was the invocation of the possibility that *fortuna* might not be irrational, that the time given to mortals might not be lacking in significance. Precisely in emphasizing the difference in which time opens to mortals, that is, in contrasting the time of the *nunc stans* and its finite apprehension, however, Boethius's *Consolation* demarcated the problem of human finitude and its originations.[156] In fact, it is just here that we must trace the backdrop of its modern eruption (and perhaps even its first vindication) to Machiavelli and the problem of *fortuna*—both in the dangers of the everyday, and equally in the interrogation of a risk of its originary resources. Moreover, even in continuing the legacy of mythic origin, as Lefort and others have pointed out, what Machiavelli finds anew in 'Rome' was precisely a certain disorder that produced a new order and that was represented politically by the disunion and interaction (and perhaps nascently the check and balance) of the senate and the plebians. This is a history to be understood not simply as the degradation of a primitive good form, but also as the opening of the remainder of 'Roman' invention.[157] Its mythic repetition, however, now like-wise attests to the problem of ideology and legitimation—and once again to the question of its significance. Hence, as Lefort puts it, Machiavelli's "critique of tradition oscillates between two poles"—divided between the simple affirmation of ancient narrative and a politics without principles.[158]

Strauss, of course, had found the same double gesture in Hobbes, whose continual trust in the possibility of political philosophy requires that we "pay proportionate attention to his emphatic rejection of the tradition, on the one hand, and to his silent agreement with it on the other" (NR:167). While Hobbes sought recourse in his critique of "Fabulous Tradition" from science (Lev:IV.46), however, Machiavelli utilizes the political practice of classical antiquity and especially republican Rome against itself.[159] At the same time, that is, Machiavelli employs this critique both to undermine the ancient conceptions of the state in which monarchy and the absolute could be simply identified, and to denounce the politics "without principles" of the "pseudo-sages" of Florence.[160] By denying the simple uncontested status of philosophy and religion, by acknowledging the complicated relations between power and knowledge, by substituting for them a 'non-knowledge' (*non-savoir*), Machiavelli traces in their place the opening of an originary realm which, again invoking the 'ideology' of 'Rome', invokes it against itself. In this regard Machiavelli explicates "an oscillation," Lefort declares, "which is neither a sign of confusion nor scepticism" but a realm which was itself *suigeneris* political. Unlike Hobbes's modernist reduction, however, this realm remains inseparable from the ancient question of *virtú*. The question of ideology thus remains inseparably intertwined with the political citation of *virtú* that closes *The Prince* by reference to Petrarch—just as a similar reference to Petrarch closes Machiavelli's "Exhortation to Penance," recalling "that worldly pleasure is a short-lived dream."[161] The question is grasping Machiavelli's gesture in its complexity. And it is no accident in this regard that it provokes the conclusion of Lefort's work into a lengthy discussion of the interrelation between oeuvre, ideology, and interpretation and what Lefort called elsewhere "Machiavell's dialogue with the ancients."

Without simply endorsing this account of Machiavelli's theoretical innovation, Arendt concurred that in the opening of the Italian city-states, the secular had achieved "a dignity and splendour of its own."[162] This recognition at the same time attested that the virtues of the ancient narratives could find renewed application in the latter's collapse, in the *combineatoire* of *virtú* and *fortuna*. Yet everything depends, as becomes evident again, upon grasping the event of this emergence and withdrawal, that is, the oscillation between immanence and transcendence, tradition and innovation, which is at stake.

Like many other thinkers, Arendt and Lefort do not simply agree on Machiavelli here—and we have already witnessed their differences over humanism. If Arendt had credited Machiavelli with confronting for the first time "the perplexity in the task of foundations designed in such a way that it would fit and step into the shoes of the old absolute," she was perhaps more inclined (as was Strauss) to simply view Machiavelli with suspicion.[163] The American revolution—though not unequivocally—better captured for her the fertility of this turn to Roman 'tradition' in instituting a revolution which acknowledged the disequilibrium of foundations.[164] The question is whether the latter had not already presupposed Machiavelli's twofold gesture toward the tradition and the rupture concerning *politeia* that had

occurred. Still, their ultimate concurrence in acknowledging the complexity
(or double gesture) in the return to the ancients can be evidenced in that
both would similarly claim of Montesquieu that he had opened, in the wake
of the ancients' *politeia*, the sphere of (originary and nonguaranteeable)
representation in modern democracy, fulfilling the humanist's invention by
elaborating the conditions of internal constraint upon power. Here again, it
was a matter of the necessity of analyzing politics as an 'empirical' or middle
realm from which transcendence had withdrawn. For reasons already evident, even though what would unhappily be identified in this oscillation as
the merely 'secular' had emerged with "a dignity and splendour of its
own"—words that doubtless should be taken in their most ancient of
senses—the event of foundation (or refoundation) remained one in which
the Absolute remained continually problematic. Hence, granted the indeterminacy and withdrawal at stake, explicit demands now emerged for the
necessity of checks and balances, for a multiplicity of powers and limits.
Indeed it required even the limit of *virtú* itself: *"la vertu même a besoin de
limites"*—an eventuality that Montesquieu admitted to be "strange but
true."[165] The question of this 'errancy' was inevitably linked with the disequilibrium of power. As even Burke himself realized, if virtue is generally
a private matter, when it becomes a public matter it becomes a matter of
power. Whether this theoretical discovery is credited to Machiavelli or to
Montesquieu, however, it might be said that the move was already related
to, indeed culminates in, the contested phenomenologies Hegel sought to
articulate, divided between the epistemic demands of theoretical modernity
and the affirmation of its 'experience', the vernacular, and its histories. And,
failing to resolve this tension—in many respects still a tension between the
ancients and the moderns—it proved to be the site of Hegel's greatest failures. Although the *Philosophy of History* had originally credited Machiavelli
with having recognized the problem of founding the state in uncertain
times, this work ultimately exchanged such ambiguities for the certainties
of the development of history as the cunning of reason itself and the ultimate elevation of the speculative subject (PH:403).

Hegel recognized that neither the laws of nature nor the laws of tradition
could find ultimate vindication in themselves—justice, again, is analogical
through and through. If the doctrine of right (*Rechtslehre*) is based upon
justice, the problem is "where do we turn in order to know what justice
is?"[166] Clearly for such a question, no simple theoretical deductive response
can be provided. Granted this indeterminacy, law and freedom will be intimately connected. The term 'natural law' would now need to be a "flexible
one" charged again with a certain *plasticität*. Indeed the concept itself, Hegel

claimed, was to be retained only if it could be allowed that now too "freedom is the nature of the thing." Moreover, it would be necessary to grasp both the institution of justice and its 'concept'—an event at once institutional and historical. Still, although the doctrine of the separation of powers had been acknowledged to contain "the essential moment of difference," even this did not prevent Hegel from attempting to transform this indeterminacy into its other through the mediation of the monarch (PR:175f.). Moreover, attempts to deal with the indeterminacy of positive law, i.e., the problem of the *application* of justice, was excluded as a nonspeculative matter at the outset of the *Rechtslehre*.[167] The Hegelian monarch's arrival on the scene would once again always threaten to dissolve all forms of indeterminacy—including obviously the indeterminacy which underlies democracy itself.[168] The *virtú* and the venture of this indeterminacy, always relied upon in the figurative excess of the speculative over the propositional, then encountered the limits of its own transcendental subreption. From now on, the issue of the law of nature or natural right would be inextricable and problematically linked to history. And it is here that the explications and institutions of primary and secondary principles, the implicit and the explicit, would find their context of discovery.

The originary domain that opens in Machiavelli's venture would remain inextricably linked to and complicated by its connection with the ambiguity of appearance, inextricably a 'phenomenological' matter. Yet, pace Hegel, it also excluded a grand narrative of its totality, or its totalization. From the beginning Machiavelli's venture—and its dialogue—had begun in the collapse of such univocal absolutes, always the effect of the experience of detraditionalization and the dispersion of totality. Machiavelli doubtless should be credited with a new term in political theory, the state (*"lo stato"*) —but only by placing it within the disequilibrium in which his thought itself opens. As Jean-Luc Nancy has rightly put it, "there would be no phenomenology of the state."[169] Instead the state would ultimately be the site (and the history) on which all 'phenomenology' would be pluralized, decentered, and abandoned within the very disequilibrium of 'retention' and 'protention' itself—which is not to say *dissolved,* but rather ventured to the extent that the metaphysical and traditional foundations of community had become problematic. To say simply that Hegel had dissolved the tensions at stake in modernity however would be too quick: the requisites that formed the theoretical lineaments of Hegel's absolute science would only be matched by the indeterminacy his own narratives had opened up, openly marking an indeterminacy and withdrawal that had haunted theoretical modernity from the outset.

9. The Prose of the World

Indeed it remains crucial in this regard to grasp the philosophical 'destiny' of this indeterminate figure, the 'order' and 'history' that manifest themselves in the *quotidien* and that ambiguously culminate in Hegel. While Findlay saw Hegel's role as "the Aristotle of our post-Renaissance world," it occurred by certain elevation of memory that Findlay thought to be "eccentric."[170] Yet Hegel's lingering (neoclassical) emphasis on the *vita memoriae* was again distinct from mere reiteration or reproduction; it involved, again, a 'hieroglyphics' of transformation that remained irreducible to formal reconstruction or analytic designation (hence, Hegel's charge that Leibniz was misled by the model of the hieroglyph [PS:215, §459]). Instead, the rational would again depend upon a 'productive memory' in the articulation of intelligibility (PS:212f., §458). Reason would be divided between narratives just as it would be divided between past and future—and in precisely the same way that Hegel had divided "speculation" and *Witz,* that is between memory and imagination.[171] Indeed, Hegel continually grappled with this event, attempting to articulate the "thick" abundance of the ancient order by means of modern categories. To trace the full effect of this in Hegel, however, it will be necessary to look beyond the constraints of the *Rechtslehre* and its reception of Aristotle. For even Aristotle's doctrine of the mean itself was reduced in this book to a formal operator, a move whereby Aristotle's account of prudence became charged with being too formal, too Kantian, and thus too abstract. Yet Hegel accomplished this, it should be insisted, only by tracing the disequilibrium of virtue within the *diaspora* of modernity:

> The individual as he appears in this world of prose and everyday (*Welt des Alltäglichen und der Proza*) is not active out of the entirety of his own self and his resources, and he is intelligible not from himself, but from something else. For the individual man stands in dependence on external influence, laws, political institutions, civil relationships, which he just finds confronting him, and he must bow to them whether he has them as his own inner being or not. . . . Even the great actions and events in which a community cooperates are in this field of relative phenomena confessedly only a manifold of individual efforts. This or that man makes his own contribution with this or that aim in view; that aim miscarries, or it is achieved, and at the end, in fortunate circumstances, something is accomplished which, compared with the whole, is of a very subordinate kind. (Aesth:149)

This relativity of aims, interests, needs, and institutions traceable through Machiavelli's transformation of the tradition is nonetheless too relative for the (demonstrative) demands of Reason, lacking the bridge between idea and substance Hegel had sought since the 1803 *Natural Right*. And yet Hegel realized equally, as Pöggeler has also seen, that Machiavelli would again be irreducible to a simple theoretician of power, linked openly by Hegel to the problem of natural right and the modern experience of indeterminacy in which Machiavelli's insight originates.[172] It is suggested moreover that Machiavelli's experience is already linked by Hegel not only to Petrarch's *virtú* and the retrieval of Cicero and its account of *virtú* as *fortitudo*, but also to Montaigne's and Shakespeare's renewed "discovery of life"—all matters to which it will be necessary to return. Suffice it to say, however, that at stake is precisely the experience of transcendence in modernity itself.

Here again it is critical to demarcate the gesture in our complex relation to the ancients. No one, of course, is more critical of Hegel in this regard than Leo Strauss.[173] Nascent to Hegel's affirmation of this *proza* is a modern trajectory whose origins Strauss found in Bacon. Bacon's account of "history, poesy, and daily experience" again abandoned the ancient's question of *politeia* in order to trace its deficiency: the hope that is to discover, against the "frauds, cautels, impostures, and vices of every profession . . . the best fortifications for honesty and virtue that can be planted"—a 'dialectic' between suspicion and discovery that Strauss (among others) links to Bacon's stress on invention.[174] Indeed here 'prudence' would be connected to history as laying forth the wealth of the possible, thus rendering further assistance to the question of application. Moreover, it is under the guise of such 'invention' that the overdetermination explicitly linking knowledge and power—and the accompanying suspicions of tradition—erupts in theoretical modernity, an overdetermination not without its own tragedies. Indeed it is precisely here that Adorno would have us choose Shakespeare over Bacon: "Shakespeare was a dialectical dramatist who, unlike Bacon, looked at the theatrum mundi from the perspective of the victims of progress."[175] Benjamin had similarly declared in this regard that "invention is incompatible with tragedy" (Trau:106). As will become evident, the legacy of tragedy, however, would loom ominously in German Idealism's discovery of Shakespeare, and we will return to it. Yet, at the same time what distinguishes Hegel's "speculative correction" upon the legacy of Hobbes consists precisely in grasping recognition (*Anerkennung*) as an *ethical* possibility *beyond* the struggle to the death that might make of history "a slaughter bench," to use the unfortunate term before which even Hegel himself 'gives way'.[176] As will be seen, perhaps nothing would prove more unwieldy for ethical thought in his wake to grasp—let alone the complicated link between such recognition and the theoretical inventions of modernity—a link usually

simply eschewed. Nor perhaps would anything prove to be more decisive
for grasping the experience of traditionality (and detraditionalization) itself.
It would not be accidental, for example, that Gadamer's classicism would
likewise be refigured in the problem of recognition, nor for that matter that
Lefort insists on characterizing humanism as a dialogue across differences—
nor finally that both would stress the ancient problem of "friendship" as a
result. All would be at stake in the originary 'prose' discovered in the world
of the everyday.

Without denying the tragedies which attend modern instrumental rationality, we should not forget, either, the complexity of such invention, the
essential detraditionalization (or delegitimation of "vain tradition") under
which the argument on behalf of invention arose, nor indeed the "argument
of hope," to use Bacon's terms, it ventured. We should not forget then the
complexity of its history (Bacon in the above-cited passage, hoping to sustain virtue, again cites Machiavelli) nor, even under this gloss, its Aristotelean moment—even with respect to *arete,* and the event of detraditionalization (and refiguration) implied thereby. The whole of the *Ethics,* after
all, can be read as Aristotle's attempt to venture the possible, and the highest
possibility (*Eudaimonia*) against fate—and, with respect to the genre of
tragedy itself, a certain *Erwiderung* with tradition. Not simply dissimilarly
did Bacon's "argument of hope" arise in its explication of the poesy of daily
life, nor its exploration of the relations between knowledge and power. If
the scientific practices that emerged would too often reduce the underdeterminacy and transcendence at stake, they could not eliminate the invention
and reinvention that the *Erwiderung* with tradition as such would require.
This complexity, in any case, is surely what unites hermeneutics, the *interpretatio naturae,* and the rise of modern science, a complicated conjunction
that amounts both to the fragmentation of *transcendens* and the possibility
of understanding it otherwise both further and beyond the constraints of
tradition.

If the contingency of this *prosa* would be generally identified with the
developments of civil society itself, throughout its intelligibility involves,
Hegel claims accordingly, "the recognition of the Secular [*Weltlichkeit*] as
capable of being an embodiment of Truth; whereas it had been formerly
regarded as evil only, as incapable of Good" (PH:422). Moreover, doubtless,
not only with such an account of the Good in mind, but also both the
problem of freedom and equality political modernity had bequeathed its
theorists, Hegel claimed it would require also "a different order of virtue":
eine andere Tugend. The fact remains nonetheless that if Hegel had briefly
glimpsed the fecundity of these developments, he could articulate its in-

determinacy only while demanding its resolution and ultimate subsumption and dissolution. He had, in other words, interrogated this prose of the world as an event not as "sundered and split into many parts," but as an event that could be articulated only as acquiring its intelligibility from something else (*aus anderem verständlich*) (Aesth:149). And, he could interpret it only through its reabsorption into totality, to the "higher" sublimity. For Hegel 'Reason' required a higher sublimity, an elevation beyond the relative existence of prosaic particularity, finitude, circumstance, and historical detail. And it required a pure thought beyond understanding and a pure narrative beyond historiography—in short a pure poetics beyond all prosaics.[177]

Often enough, however, for theoretical modernism—and Hegel still belongs here—such indeterminacy ultimately signals the failure of foundations and the absence of the divine, as Hölderlin would put it. It would be intelligible first and foremost as failure or dispersion, articulating the *Zerstreutsein* character of the everyday, to use Heidegger's term. And it would also force the need to recur to tradition not only for what has been passed down (*traduit*), but for what had been leveled and even buried within the everyday. Freud's *Psychopathology of Everyday Life* identified it as not only "preferred forgetfulness" but "false recollection." Indeed, Freud too was as worried as any modernist about what Hobbes called our tendency to disregard the references of the original names.[178] The problem, as Hobbes attested, is the collapse of the univocal *ordo traditionis* and its dependable links to the laws of nature—a matter of both traditional and epistemic conflict. That such is the fate of civil society is apparent from Locke's own defense of natural law *against* tradition. As Locke's manuscript on natural law states, in a passage deserving quotation for the break it demarcates between the natural light of reason and the ruptured inheritance of past tradition:

> In such a great variety of traditions, warring among themselves, it would be impossible to establish what the law of nature is, difficult even to judge what is true, what false; what is law, what opinion; what nature commands, what interest, what reason persuades us of, what civil society teaches. Indeed, traditions everywhere are so varied, men's opinions so manifestly contradictory and in conflict with one another, not only in different nations, but within the same state; [and since] every opinion we learn from others is 'tradition' [and] finally, since each contends so fiercely for his own opinion and demands that he be believed, it would be impossible to know what that 'tradition' is or to choose the truth in such a great variety, were tradition alone to dictate the principle of our duty, since no reason can be discovered why the preponderant authority

of tradition should be granted or a more submissive belief given to [the claims of] one man rather than to another who claims the dead contrary, unless reason can discover some way of distinguishing between traditions themselves.[179]

What is at stake in such analyses (as is clear from Locke's own attempts to refigure the medievals by way of Hooker and Grotius) is perhaps less the dissolution of transcendence and more a matter of grasping the specificity of the difference that had intervened—the transformations that constitute modernity. It would be inappropriate to simply characterize modernity, as does Strauss, as demanding that "one must lower one's sights."[180] Even less can it be claimed that modern 'secularization' was simply an emptying of transcendence (NR:317). Recall that Strauss himself realized that the question of transcendence remained unwieldy: "Transcendence is not a preserve of revealed religion. In a very important sense it was implied in the original meaning of political philosophy as the quest for the natural or best political order" (NR:15). With the modern, it provoked the need for discerning transcendence 'otherwise', for discerning a transcendence which might be identified, as Merleau-Ponty put it in his own treatise on the *Prose of the World*, neither by "vertical transcendence" nor "horizontal transcendence." It would be a milieu nonetheless identified by him once more as that of the everyday (*de chaque jour*), an interpretive domain in which "even the purest of truths presuppose marginal views" and—confronted with the rigors of purity themselves, the requisites of strict science—"there is a risk of destroying what one is trying to understand."[181] Granted the indeterminacy and ambiguity out of which the "figure of everyday meaning" emerges, the account of transcendence would require, (precisely as Machiavelli had already begun to realize) a new ontology beyond the classical hierarchies—and yet not one simply incommensurate with the old ontology.[182]

The narratives of phenomenology, as Husserl realized, depend both upon "the single subject's and the community's whole daily life."[183] Yet they likewise occur, as even he came to see, within a history and a modern tradition of *Technisierung* essentially disconnected from such origins, which in its extreme "can certainty become an evil" (K:291). To condemn Machiavelli and Hobbes, for concern with "the extreme case," as Strauss put it, or to condemn them for the preoccupation with certainty is to forget that history is not simply the perduring of the Good, but the history of violence and the narration of events under which "the social fabric has completely broken down" (NR:196). It is to forget that modernity is not simply the history of nihilism but—ambiguously—both repression and liberation. Even Husserl's defense of the evidence of lived experience and the 'daily life' or *Lebenswelt* that was its 'presupposition' demanded "a *criticism of the naive concepts of evidence and truth,* or true being, that govern the whole logical tradition"—again, once more to make the evidence in question certain.[184]

Contested in these very antinomies, disfigured in the chiasm between the visible and the invisible, the problem of the ordinary and the everyday would force itself to prominence time and again in twentieth-century thought. Again and again, however, the disequilibrium of the everyday lifeworld would be theoretically appropriated by subsumption or reduction—cast between claims that see in it as (1) only a 'leveling' secularization, the dissolution of the Good, and the elevation of *techne* in its place, or (2) as the presentation (*Darstellung*) of the Absolute itself within the ordinary. In both respects it would indeed involve "the logos as ontic," to use Charles Taylor's gloss on Heidegger's considerations on its 'aesthetic' remainder—or perhaps even more pointedly, Lyotard's on Barnett Newman's, "the sublime as now."[185] As Kierkegaard had already put it in Hegel's wake (and as Cavell has stated more recently), the point is to find "the sublime in the pedestrian"; a way of asking if "the extraordinary (*Ausserordentlich*) is happening."[186] It must be emphasized however, as Kierkegaard also put it in his most antitraditional work, that what was at issue was less the extraordinary of mere nature, the transcendental genius, than (as Hegel's *Naturrecht* had already blinkingly glimpsed) "the ordinary of freedom."[187]

The lineaments of such a "logic" in one sense are doubtless already present in Hegel's prosaic of the ordinary. From the standpoint of the ancients, the play of modern ordinary life, Hegel realized, would seem only "vulgar and worthless." From this standpoint, his *Aesthetics* continues, the role of art would be to "lift us above the whole sphere of needs, distress, and dependence" (Aesth:245). The division between the transcendent and the ordinary, and its "disdain for everything on earth," Hegel himself warns, is however a false one, indeed, a viewpoint still bound to the abstractions of modernity itself. Still, if Hegel had then been poised to exhibit the conceptual significance of the everyday, he doubtless remained, again, bound by the technical paradigms of modernity itself—and in particular its account of truth as the equation of subject and object, one which becomes particularly ominous in the tragic histrionics at stake in the *realization* of the *Zeitgeist*.[188] The result, in effect, refounds Herder's metaphysical tradition (not to speak of its *Weltgeist*) on the basis of Fichte's act. What, Hegel claims, limited modernity in this regard was its lack of courage to control or to realize itself in the everyday—hence its incompleteness: that it did not transform the transcendence of the everyday into self-immanence. For

Hegel, that is, the demeaning of the ordinary derived still from "a superior abstraction made by that modern subjective outlook which lacks courage to submit itself to externality" (Aesth:245). But, as has become evident, even though Hegel once more protests against such dichotomies, his own account of destruction as lack of fortitude surely itself attests to his own idealizations about tragedy, viewing both suffering and need as simply failures of will, attesting to a certain inadequate voluntarism. As the *Phenomenology* puts it, "I err insofar as I suffer" (PS:284).

To think the transcendence at stake in the ordinary—to use Benjamin's terms, the "surprise in the everyday"—we will likewise need to recognize its refusal of such self-immanence, both in the refusal of the commonplace and the acknowledgment of both its 'transcendences' and its 'catastrophes'. Equally contested in the domain of the ordinary is the question of the Other and the bitter truths that accompany the failures of the commonplace—the anonymous historical fate of the everyman, the Nobody, *Chacun, Personne* and the *Jedermann, Niemand*.[189] But before we simply consign such aspects of the everyday to outsider status, or condemn them to the "inauthentic" history of *Das Man,* or a chapter in the history of madness, we should not forget (at pain of losing its rationality) the fertility of appeals to the *idiota* or folly, or the layman in Cusa, Erasmas, Rabelais, or Vico, or their narratives in Bocaccio—a point at which Bakhtin and Gadamer rightly converge.[190] These narratives provide not only a critical hermeneutic in the articulation of the experience of detraditionalization but are also critical—as Vico's case exemplifies—of the experience of modernity (and the method of the "new" science) itself. They are, moreover, a continuing legacy of aesthetic modernity's ambiguous explorations of the everyday.

In his classical text on the problem of artistic modernism, *The Tradition of the New,* Harold Rosenberg claimed:

> Under the slogan for a new art, for a new reality, the most ancient superstitions have been exhumed, the most primitive rites re-enacted: the rummage of generative forces has set African demon-masks in the temple of the muses and introduced the fables of Zen and Hasidism into the dialogue of philosophy. Through such dislocations of time and geography the first truly universal tradition has come to light, with world history as its past and requiring a world stage to flourish.[191]

Even the aesthetics of high modernism could not simply deny its "traditionality," however; it could not escape the problem of extension by transformation, dislocation, and dialogue. If what modernity adds to this dialogue is the possibility of a "truly universal tradition," as we have seen, the latter escapes neither the limits of time nor place: it adds instead the twofold gesture which Heidegger calls reciprocal rejoinder (*Erwiderung*) itself—destruction and retrieval: a logic not simply of continuity and identity, but, like the modernist collage itself, superposition, montage and difference. The horizon of the universal, that is, remains a horizon, a question that no work of art (and no work of theory) finally answers. Hence emerges the importance of *dialogue* itself, which, like its Socratic antecedent, as Bakhtin saw, combines fragment, irony, and narrative in surpassing the epic 'absolute past' of tradition in order "for the first time [to initiate] truly free investigation of the world, of man, and of human thought."[192]

The impact of aesthetic theory in this regard still remains telling, since it trespasses and transforms domains from which it is usually excluded, and its implications become both epistemic and moral, metaphysical and political. Such, as has already become evident, was true of the role of Hegel's *Aesthetics* in his system, and so its resources contested from within their subsumption beneath the concept of 'aesthetics'. It is this rupture that became preeminently evident in Hegel's ambiguous exposition of the prose of the world itself—acknowledging the transcendence of the ordinary in the very moment that he attempts to reduce it to self-immanence. And it is even more true of the work of art afterward: for example, the twentieth-century avant-garde's proclivity for the "found," the ready-made, and thereby, the everyday—which, as Gadamer has justifiably claimed, does not simply break with tradition but instead remains both enlightening and traditional, simultaneously symbolical and allegorical.[193] But the work of art here emerges equally in disruption, always proceeding, to use Proust's term, by a certain logic of 'juxtaposition'. Having discovered in the transcendental past a moment upon which all reflection relies, all transcendental phenomenology encountered in such cases a problem that could not be reduced to the techniques of the *ars memoriae*. The past upon which all reflection relies is more an event than an act, and has in fact become juxtaposed (or juxtaposes itself) with simple (intentional in the purposive sense) reflective acts. It is precisely in this regard that Proust's juxtapositions became crucial. The counterorientation of Proust's *memoire involuntaire* would radically contest Husserl's emphasis upon the past as simple repository and guarantee of the iterative act, complicating the rationality of transcendental phenomenology at its (unifying temporal) core—precisely in contesting the self-transparency of the predicative judgment from within. As Heidegger's *The Origin of the Work of Art* equally grasped in this regard, the ordinary in all this had become complicated through and through: "At bottom, the ordinary is not ordinary; it is extra-ordinary, uncanny."[194] Appeals everywhere to "the familiar, the reliable, the ordinary," in the phenomena remain always perilous in missing the discontinuity, not to speak of the dangers, denounced therein: the truth at stake remains uncanny, a matter of unconcealment and often enough is "dominated throughout by a denial."[195] Even Husserl himself perhaps recognized the problem that haunted any scientific phenomenology in this regard, in acknowledging that "we cannot discover the psychical in any experience, except by a 'reflection,' or perversion of the ordinary attitude."[196]

10. *Ars Memoriae* and *La recherche du temps perdu*

What remains true concerning such 'phenomenologies' of the ordinary, as is often claimed, is that the pre-positing (*Voraus-setzung*) that such appearances presuppose cannot be simply equated with mere prejudice. They involve, rather, a question of the historical origins of 'positing' in general, as Gadamer realized (TM:270–71). Husserl claimed before him that such positing indicated a certain absolute, "beginning with the pre-positing [*Voraus-setzung*] which gives rise to all presuppositions" (*Voraussetzung*)—a certain *Ur-traditionalität*.[197] It provided the origin of an evidence and an experience, that as unwieldy as it remains, had all the characteristics of an absolute, except absolute demonstrability. As Sartre had seen already in 1936 however, never would such evidence *imply* truth, but only our 'relation' to it.[198] Insofar as such 'transcendental' 'absolutes' were inextricable, they could never be simply vindicated. Nor could the suspicions that accompanied appeals to their 'phenomena' be accepted without suspicion, accepted, that is, as 'ready-made'. In this regard, even the phenomenology of perception with its emphasis upon 'lived body' becomes less a return to origins than the discovery of a dimension and a complication beyond traditional hierarchies, an emphasis, as Bakhtin again realized, also emerging with the experience of detraditionalization itself.[199] With the problem of embodiment there emerges a materiality whose *transcendens* would, again, be of a different order than its idea, explicating a rationality '*au dehors*' or '*autrement que*' its reflective origins, and an original time that has never been in this regard reflectively present. Hence emerges perhaps the problem of the distance between the "epics" of reflection and the "prose" of the everyday—and the exclusion of the latter from our accounts.

It is this, moreover, that confounds naive commitments to the ordinary. If Emerson is all that Cavell made him to be concerning the Romantic's transgression of scepticism, such claims must equally be posed against Emerson's own internal disillusionment—and externally, posed against Poe's horrors. If Emerson is right in claiming that "Man is an analogist, and studies relations in all objects," it is because 'man' is, after all, an allegorist, and in both cases, the human is fragmented through and through, his time as much *distentio* as *extensio,* his inheritance, his *traditio,* always *une recherche du temps perdu.*[200] Henry James would be perfectly on the mark in these matters in reminding us about Emerson that "there were certain complications in life which he never suspected."[201]

What naive quests for the ordinary have too often missed, in short, is the *dissonance* of the ordinary: the event in which, to cite the brilliance of Adorno, the radiance has turned black.[202] As Marx put it in *The Eighteenth Brumaire,* and against Burke's definition of society as a partnership built up over generations between the living and the dead, here "The tradition of all the dead generations weighs like a nightmare on the brains of the living."[203] Tradition equally here takes on that other sense—*tradere*—"to betray." In all this, Marx shares in the defiance of modernity, a defiance proclaimed in Baudelaire's 1846 proclamation that "the great tradition has got lost and that the new one is not yet established."[204] For Baudelaire, the great tradition, "a habitual, everyday idealization of ancient life," is now the subject of a certain funeral cortege, once more an object of Piranesian abjection.[205] Marx's own revulsion doubtless pivots around the transcendental subreptions which haunt "philosophic analogy" and those to which Burke had appealed in the "sublime inheritance" of tradition. Burke had, after all, turned the contract (and the community) into a system of intransitive and nonreciprocal relations based upon the inheritance of property, one "whose characteristic essence is to be unequal."[206] Recently Julia Kristeva has aptly said in this regard "to those who are concerned with renewing the tradition, I would say that it appears to me indispensible to maintain the tradition of revolt."[207] The problem is doubtless sorting out the experience which reveals both.

Before Marx, Hegel claimed that modernity would need recourse to the ancients for their positive account of life, nature, and human well-being— and from the beginning, even a certain retrieval of the ancients' materialism.[208] The nineteenth century's discovery of time likewise forced it to grapple with tradition as a critical resource in such matters. Indeed, as Benjamin ironically noted regarding Baudelaire's account of modernity, "among all relationships into which modernity entered, its relationship to classical antiquity stands out. . . . Modernity designates an epoch, and it also denotes the energies which are at work in this epoch to bring it close to antiquity."[209]

Despite again the convulsions that separate it from those who defended tradition, Baudelaire's account of "a constant, unchangable element . . . and a relative limited element"[210] as the interchange between the modern and antiquity would be repeated again and again in defenses of the classical. But if it would thus be naive to think that the 'negations' of tradition simply surpass traditionality, it would be equally remiss to overlook the fact that they too have their reciprocal rejoinder (*Erwiderung*) with—and critical disavowal (*widerruf*) of—the past. In fact, the negations of tradition are themselves 'traditional', participating in a complex history of critique and "counter-tradition."[211] Indeed, as has been seen, science itself depends upon such a second-order tradition.

As even Adorno realized, the tendency of modernism to "negate tradition itself" was equally ideological. It caused one to forget the ambiguity and historicity, the *Vor-struktur* out of which all interpretation proceeds—and which, as both Benjamin and Gadamer rightly recognized, makes its analogical appeals always inseparably allegorical, conditional (and traditional).[212] Surely Adorno was equally right about this much, however: the continuous ideal of tradition, "conceptualizing it in terms of perpetual relay race with one generation, one style, one master, etc., [a] handing over the baton" from one to another, is surely mistaken.[213] The invocations of analogy are both historicist and metaphysical, ideological and empirical. The result then is a complex gesture, again a double movement of appropriation that gains legitimacy only as disappropriation and disavowal:

> Whoever seeks to avoid betraying the bliss which tradition still promises in some of its images and the possibilities buried beneath its ruins must abandon the tradition which turns possibilities and meanings into lies. Only that which inexorably denies tradition may once again retrieve it.[214]

The characteristic of analogy, as halfway between the univocal and the equivocal, remains equivocally dangerous, however: the everyday is itself not immune from the "levelings" of tradition. Indeed it is precisely in this guise that it becomes the object of modern criticism. Throughout its modern challenges, all revolutionary consciousness—from de Beauvoir to Du Bois to Gramsci—would concur in this regard with Sartre's claim that *la moralité quotidienne* excludes *l'angoisse éthique* from its midst.[215] Moreover its own internal "levelings" would similarly lead to bad faith, a certain obedience to tradition and an "automatism of the Good."[216] Consequently, Benjamin claimed, "In every era the attempt must be made anew to wrest tradition away from a conformism that is about to overpower it."[217] It is in just this sense that the everyday cannot, consequently, simply furnish the ideal of a quest that might provide the solution to modern scepticism. Rather it is the place in which transcendence has become problematic. No more, then, could it be reduced by recourse to the *semes* of ordinary usage, to the analysis of the lexicon of ordinary language and its assumed security in the world of "ordinary middle-size dry goods." Here in fact Aristotle's Good has indeed been, to use Taylor's Hegelian term, "inverted": its 'transcendence' transposed into the economies of production.

Simple affirmations of the ordinary in this regard remain too abstract. If the Absolute (real or ideal) has withdrawn, the external reference in relation to which the relativity of the *quotidien* might be grounded, measured, and articulated cannot simply be exchanged for something else, even for a return to what was once present. It is "measurable" only in terms of an intelligibility whose placeholder remains, as Lefort said, "empty." This is, as Arendt realized, the predicament of all modern political bodies, of their profound instability. It is now a question of reckoning with the remainder—to use Gadamer's term, now a question of reckoning with the *problem* of the Good. And this problem, after all, has figured the question of analogy since the outset.

11. On the "Aftereffects" of Tradition

Everything depends upon grasping the prose in question as the opening of what, within the epics of classical reason, remains always a certain "blind spot," to use Foucault's term. This opening involves the wager of a reason that, in its reliance on the ambiguity of the everyday, answers to a "lesser" reason. It relies, that is, on the possibility that there remains a reason which answers to 'unreason', an order in 'disorder', even a certain *virtù* which answers to the alternatives between *fortuna* and *chaos*—and perhaps even more anciently, thereby provides a bond between *chaos* and democracy. Here again, as Lefort would concur, fully prompted by the *Entzweiung* discovered in the opening which figures Florence in its own disarticulation of 'Rome':

> Modern democratic society seems to me, in fact, like a society in which power, law, and knowledge are exposed to a radical indetermination, a society that has become the theatre of an uncontrollable adventure, so that what is instituted never becomes established, the known remains undermined by the unknown, the present proves to be undefinable, covering many different social times which are staggered in relation to one another within simultaneity—or definable only in terms of some fictitious future; an adventure such that the quest for identity cannot be separated from the experience of division. This society is *historical* society *par excellence*.[218]

The question is how to interpret this result and its community of heterogeneous time, especially when many have claimed it is only time itself that
we now possess in common (*co-mmunio*). But it is in any case the question
of interpretation that it unlocks, its indetermination a matter which precludes simple reinstitution of the *ancien régime*.

Indeed it is precisely this rupture which has accompanied the task of
interpretation since the beginning of modernity and Hobbes's (and, as has
been seen, Machiavelli's) demurrals before tradition. Confronted with the
Babel of languages, theories, and traditions, Hobbes declared, "All laws,
written and unwritten, have need of interpretation"—and this is especially
true of the natural law, that has "the greatest need of able Interpreters"
(Lev:II.46).

The interpretation of the remainder of such a 'natural law' is doubtless
problematic, the problem of the *dispensation* of the Good: the complex
remainder that ensues in calling the Good into question. And, beset by the
fragmentation that ensues, the interpretation—or explication—of this remainder, of what might still perdure in its withdrawal, is the *problem* that
accompanies the dispensation of the Good. In both senses, both as rupture
and as possibility, the result impacts litigants on all sides—not least of which
are hermeneuts themselves. Hence even if Gadamer, for example, could
claim that he remained Aristotelian, he realized full well that the idea of the
Good as "neither capable nor in need of justification" was mythic.[219] It
remained an old story (*alte Geschichten*) whose historical remove and indeterminacy, (the indeterminacy Serres had discovered through the multiplicities of Rome and Gadamer himself had discovered in historical consciousness) now required anew legitimation and application. And, of course, all
that remains true of the *regime ancien* likewise holds true of its traditions,
now multiple, instable, and at risk.[220] As Lefort again has put it: "Thought
may be able to free itself from certain images; but what resists this attempt
is the relation that we maintain with the representation of the past, the
mythical function that we make it play in order to assure ourselves of a
truth which is already given and which will not betray us, in order to
conjure away, in sum, the indeterminacy which constantly re-emerges in the
history that we live."[221] Hence again emerge the dangers accompanying "the
tenacious fidelity to a tradition."[222]

All of this—both as resource and danger—doubtless circulated in the
great analyses of the everyday in the twentieth century, and particularly
those who had felt the penumbra of Hegel's effect. Most directly, this became
evident in those authors we associate with continental philosophy—
Husserl, Heidegger, Buber, Merleau-Ponty, Benjamin, Adorno, Foucault,

Levinas, et al. Implicitly, however, as has been seen, it became realized in those authors that struggled with its effect, for example, in Moore's and Russell's or Eliot's struggle with Bradley—or more recently in those like Taylor or Cavell, who would seek, to use Nietzsche's loaded term, "redemption" of the everyday. But, as all realized, the genealogy of the modes of Being as everyday, to speak Heideggerean (BT:11), or as Lefort called it, the "genealogy of democratic representations"²²³ would be irreducible to power, although inevitably complicated by it. The moderns realized that—and realized quite early as has been seen—the question of the political is inseparable from the question of power. As Nietzsche rightly saw in this regard, in all difference of form there lies always a question of difference in power. The question of the difference at stake is not, however (as Nietzscheans always suspected), simply a matter of external difference, but equally of a difference that might intervene between forces.

Hence "Marcusean" (post-Heideggerean) claims, about the one-dimensionality of the everyday (like "Lacanian" claims about the inevitable exclusivity of its laws) are less false than overblown, that is, false in the extreme, missing inevitably not only the problem of 'errancy' and judgment but the question of transcendence which continually interrupts—to speak neutrally, its plurality. The questioning of tolerance it provoked was again strictly taken no less false, forcing us again and again to requestion in fact modernism's commitments to tolerance. Like all the transcendentals, such "tolerance" involved less the simple dissolution than the withdrawal of truth. The *telos* of tolerance, in short, is less truth or Being—both of which after all escape in this withdrawal—than rationality.²²⁴

Indeed, both truth and rationality become "regulated" in an economics that, as Hegel saw, haunts the conceptual limits, and the *Anderssein* of tradition itself. At stake, consequently, is an economics infinitely complicating the "thick" descriptions of the everyday—an economics that extends, as has become evident, through Marx, Heidegger, Husserl and beyond. Witness, for example, the complications of Levinas's attempts to grasp the problem of significance, acknowledging both the complexity of the *quotidien* and the problem of attempting to derive a pure meaning (*sens*) from within it:

> The world, as soon as one moves on from the humble daily tasks [*humble taches quotidiennes*], and language, as soon as one moves on from commonplace talk [*conversation banale*], have lost the univocity which had authorized us to ask of them the criteria of the meaningful [*sense*]. Absurdity consists not in nonsense, but in the isolation of innumerable meanings [*significations*] in the absence of a sense [*sens*] that orients them. What is lacking is the sense of the

meanings [*sens des sens*], the Rome to which all the roads lead, the symphony
in which all the meanings can sing, the canticle of canticles. The absurdity lies
in multiplicity in pure indifference.[225]

While noting that this absurdity is classically or metaphysically linked to
the death of God, Levinas himself still searches for the restoration of the
sens des sens beyond all identity, a *sens* that would still unite univocity and
freedom in proceeding freely from the Same to the Other.[226] In this respect,
while reconfronting the question of univocity itself (and the issue of certainty), he again retrieves (while extending) the question of analogy and its
pros hen. The question, however, now becomes one of the ethical relationship, and its complicated status—not only conceptually but historically. In
the complexity of his own reinvocation of the *sens des sens* Levinas would
have us reconfront the alterities and antinomies between Same and Other,
violence and metaphysics, right and respect—in quest, as he still somewhat
naively hoped (and, as has been seen, beyond Machiavelli's and Montesquieu's insight), for a moment that was determined "neither by knowledge nor power."[227] What remains at stake for Levinas, in any case, is the
"extraordinary and everyday event of the responsibility for the faults or the
misfortunes of others."[228] But, the question is whether *virtú* and the investment of power and knowledge can be so readily separated—both were, after
all, even classically, thought to be "powers" of the soul.

The order of things, dispersed between the fortunes of necessity and the
contingencies of forces and external effect, as Machiavelli knew, surely did
not exclude the wager of *virtú*. The whole question is how to calculate
legitimacy while acknowledging its limits. This is, *inter alia,* doubtless a
question of empowering the "people" in the same moment (of errancy) in
which, as Arendt realized again, even *virtú* itself could not be simply un-
leashed.[229] The revolutionary tradition itself, she reminds as, is a Copernican
matter, linked both to a science and a politics (of freedom) unknown to the
ancients.[230] The question of interpretation in general might be claimed,
similarly, to be one of what it means in this regard to be beyond the
traditions of the ancients—which is not at all to say beyond the everyday.
But the remainder of the appearances at stake would indeed be complex.
And, as Levinas's task attests again, nowhere is it more complex than in
connection with the problem of recognition (*Anerkennung*) itself, both as
originating with and as departing from tradition, in an interplay of forces,
theoretical and otherwise.

It is here that Heidegger—often enough, almost despite himself—sums
up the event we have traced and reveals the dispersion in which its interpretation takes place, precisely in confronting, if not solving, the question

of the "double aftereffect of tradition" (*doppel Nachwirkung der Tradition*) (BT:45). These ruins, the reciprocal rejoinder of the ontic and the ontological, the visible and the invisible, were precisely, after all, the remainder that Heidegger's attempts had sought, despite the failures of his "ambiguous" hopes either to return to their primitive sources on the one hand, or to violently wrestle and gainsay their future potential on the other. The point is that neither of these responses were adequate to "the between" that had erupted in the question of tradition, nor could they provide resolution to the nostalgia (or tragedy) he hoped to overcome precisely by overcoming first and foremost the problem of the everyday—and especially the potential it had raised for the indeterminacy and reciprocal rejoinder its interpretation necessitated. At stake in one sense would be a step beyond theory, confronted with an encounter that opened only in the reciprocal rejoinder with the possible that the logic of its inheritance had made necessary.

> Laying the foundations, as we have described it, is rather a productive logic—in the sense that it leaps ahead [*vorspringt*] as it were, into some era of Being, discloses it for the first time in the constitution of its Being, and, after thus arriving at the structures within it, makes these available to the positive sciences as transparent assignments for their enquiry. (BT:30–31)

It was, nonetheless, the most baroque of Heideggerian monuments, a fragment allegorical beyond respite, *inter alia* in its appeal to what within the limits of theoretical modernity, to speak Wittgensteinian, cannot, strictly speaking, be said. The *pros hen* of analogy and application, that is, the *pros hen* of interpretation is always 'deconstructive' with respect to such origins; subject, to speak Kantian, to a "double-function"; its analysis always symbolic: analogy is always indeterminately 'analogous'; interpretation always interpretative, tradition always already extension by default. There will be in this sense no ultimate foundations, only 'ruins' and 'refoundations'; there will be no positive sciences to receive assignment from such inspections: only fragments, and their archaeologists, and their interpreters—and their possibilities. The interplay between theory and observation, *Vor-struktur* and articulation, will complicate any attempt to privilege such productive logics. There can be in short no logic of discovery. But this *Vorspringen* remains nonetheless disarticulated between sense and sensibility, the aftereffect of a potential, one in which "interpretation" receives in this passage its first (and arguably its last) theoretical gloss in *Being and Time*. As Werner Marx realized early on in focusing on Heidegger's transformation of Aristotle's *ousia*, it was a question of grasping the new within tradition, namely "the other meaning of Being and essence in Heidegger, as departing from the

tradition."[231] In this doubtless Heidegger's transformation still maintained
its complex link with a certain humanism—even a certain Machiavellian-
ism, if as Heidegger rightly saw, there is still room for us "to restore"
meaning to the word "humanism" (LH:224). It was, after all, Machiavelli
who, confronting the fragility of foundations, saw all *innovationi* as a complicated undoing of the violence of the past, and in this sense always an
overcoming of tradition. But it was not simply a matter of accident that he
chose the most ancient of ethical terms, *virtú,* to confront this risk.

Similarly it was not at all accidental that the question at stake in this
reciprocal rejoinder itself was also the most traditional, the problem of Being
itself. Moreover, it was the remainder in Heidegger's own work of an initial
investigation that had begun with Scotus's sense of existence (*haecceitas*)
that had sought out a "breakthrough into reality and real truth" which
"cannot be deduced" but "can only be pointed out" in response to "our duty
to see."[232] It remained an attempt still to grasp both transcendence and
historical individuality.[233] As *Being and Time* would bear witness, the latter
would also reveal too the remainder of the effects of civil society, its cultural
and theoretical practices now dirempted, dispersed, and ungrounded. If the
investigation of the ancient problem of analogy had provided the
grundmarkmal of metaphysics, it had also provided the limit concept between unity and diversity—itself indicative ultimately of a certain shattering.[234] But thereby its status became critical to thought. So much so that
Adorno too would claim that "there is one variant that should not be
missing from the excessively narrow questions in the *Critique of Pure Reason*
and that is how a thinking obliged to relinquish tradition might preserve
and transform tradition" (ND:54–55). Doubtless it is just this complexity
in the relations between preservation and transformation that we have
traced in the lineaments of the concept of traditionality. The question perhaps is whether it had not from the beginning lain at the heart of critique
and the critical system itself.[235]

2. Kant, the Architectonics of Reason, and the Ruins of the Ancient Systems

On the Symbolics of Law

1. Tradition, the Prudence of Precedent, and the Requisites of Theory

The preface to Kant's 1793 *Theorie-Praxis* essay contains a reference to a "certain worthy gentleman" who had argued that political rationalism was too deductive to meet rational criteria for reasonable political change, who had argued for his own brand of empiricism based upon the inheritance of tradition. Against it Kant specifically denied that "a practice calculated for an outcome probable in line with *past* experience" should be "made master of self-existing theory" in the belief that a person "can get further than theory might take him by fumbling with experiments and experiences without specific principles" (T-P:42–43). The reference here may well be to Burke's *Considerations*, a work translated into German shortly before Kant's essay appeared, and to which Kant may have felt impelled to react because it denied the rationalist foundations of the very sort that he had demanded.[1] That Kant left the reference oblique, it has been suggested, itself pays testimony to the dangers of the public realm and his need to avoid the Prussian censors. The matter will then be complex—from the outset matters in which principled autonomy and historical necessity are inextricably intertwined.

The problem of tradition had already been prepared by Herder's 1784 *Outline of a Philosophy of the History of Man,* whose principles were founded on tradition:

> Hence the principles of this philosophy become as evident, simple, and indubitable, as the natural history of man itself: they are called tradition and organic powers. All education must spring from imitation and exercise by means of which the model passes into the copy; and how can this be more aptly expressed than by the term tradition? But the imitation must have powers to receive what is communicated or communicable, and convert it into his own nature, as the food by means of which he lives. Accordingly, what and how much he receives, whence he derives it, and how he uses, applies it, and makes it his own, must depend on his own, the receptive powers. So that the education of our species is in a double sense genetic and organic: genetic, inasmuch as it is communicated; organic, as what is communicated is received and applied. Whether we name this second genesis of man, cultivation from culture of the ground, or enlightening, from the action of light, is of little import; the chain of light and cultivation reaches to the end of the Earth.[2]

The issues which burdened the concept of the *ordo traditionis* are thus fully active in Herder: the limits and fecundity of *mimesis* as origin, the limits of a 'copy' and its 'communicability', nascently thereby the encounter with the foreign and the limits of translation, and finally the problem of its 'enlightenment' and 'reappropriation'. Kant reviewed this work in January 1785, a time when his own concerns with the "teleologics" of history and the political were only just emerging. Indeed he openly disclaims scholarly expertise in the matter, saying he is "inexperienced in scholarly philology and the knowledge or critical examination of ancient documents."[3] And yet it is clear too that the claim that "all progress in culture would be a projected communication and fortuitous proliferation of an original tradition" doubtless conflicted with Kant's own critical contributions to the German Enlightenment.

Such a tradition is not without danger, even for Herder who would not sanction Burke's own account of tradition as divine inheritance. As Herder later states:

> Tradition in itself is an excellent institution of Nature, indispensable to the human race: but when it fetters the thinking faculty both in politics and education, and prevents all progress of the intellect, and all the improvement, that new times and circumstances demand, it is the true narcotic of the minds, as well to nations and sects, as to individuals.[4]

Kant's reply to all this is indeed 'Crusoesque': in an unchartered desert a traveler must be free to choose her route at discretion.[5] Moreover, the idea of succeeding generations extending like a species into infinity—an idea that accompanied the descent of the concept of tradition for Kant—could be at most asymptotic, an idea and not a nature. What Kant denied most stringently is the latent naturalism in the appeal to a natural kind or species that might underlie these concepts. Such an idea lies outside the realm of "empirical natural science"[6] as well as outside of the prescriptive requisites for moral imperatives. It seems then that Kant's account of tradition, bound by his Enlightenment commitments, would remain entirely negative.

This much Kant never denied. If the idea of tradition was to Kant a kind of "tutelage" to which he remained quite opposed, it was true too that he neither simply rejected the idea of history *as idea*, nor denied the essential link with the past it implied. As his precritical work on *Education* remarks, "The maxim *Tantum scimus, quantum, memoria tenemus* [We know just so much as we remember] is quite true—hence it is very necessary to cultivate the memory" (Ed:72). Indeed, as he remarks in the *Anthropology*, it is because we can voluntarily remember "that the mind is not a plaything of the imagination" (Anth:57). And although he admits that "the proper mechanism for the study of history has yet to be found," history itself, as the *Education* imparts, not without a certain Baconian resonance, "is an excellent means of exercising the understanding in judging rightly" (Ed:72). But that is precisely the point for Kant—what is at stake is not simple recollection *but judgment*.

> The inferior faculties have no value in themselves; for instance, a man who has a good memory, but no judgment. Such a man is merely a walking dictionary. These beasts of Parnassus are of some use, however, for if they cannot do anything useful themselves they at least furnish material out of which others may produce something good. (Ed:71)

The production of something good, that is, requires judgment, "the application of the general to the particular" as he puts it in anticipating the first *Critique*'s definition (A133/B172). If Kant's work seems in this regard the extreme counterpoint to the "inheritance" which would bind one to tradition, it is also true that the problem of proper application of concepts is inseparably bound up with the question of legitimation and enlightenment itself. From beginning to end critique is itself linked to application. Precedent, however, is at best a guide, not a rule. The prejudicial and the provisioned, as Kant put it in the *Logic*, must still be distinguished (Logic:83). Here the production of something good will require again *fortitudo*, virtue being definable as a moral strength of will, but also (in a human being at least) as a will in accord with duty (*fortitudo moralis*) (Tugend:37). Such a will doubtless must have a history, even a cultivation, and finally an education, a catechism—and in this respect it will be bound to a 'tradition' in the sense that Burke or Herder imparted. Kant admits "the experimental (technical) means for the cultivation of virtue [*Mittel der Bildung zur Tugend*] is the good example of the teacher himself (his own conduct being exemplary)," implying that the experimental and the moral do not exclude one another—in fact far from it, as will be seen. Yet such examples are not in themselves justified:

> The good example (exemplary behavior) should not serve as a model but only as proof of the feasibility of what is in accord with duty. Thus, it is not comparison with any other man (as he is) but with the idea of humanity (as he ought to be), and so with the law, which must supply the teacher with an infallible standard for education. (Tugend:148)[7]

These vagaries of example and exemplification are recognized by Kant to be intrinsic to judgment, which the first *Critique* describes as "a peculiar talent which can be practiced only and cannot be taught, the specific quality of so-called mother wit [*Mutterwitz*]." Moreover, even if physicians, judges, or rulers have rules available to them, they may "stumble in their application" because of insufficient training and examples as well as be "wanting in natural power of judgment" (A133-4/B172-3). Any transcendental and critical doctrine, on the other hand, must "have as its peculiar task the correcting and securing of judgment, by means of determinate rules," providing thereby "by means of universal but sufficient marks the conditions under which objects can be in harmony with these concepts" (A135-6/B174-5). In a claim those already identified as post-Kantian would not miss, he states that the object of practical reason will nonetheless have to "show its reality and that of its concepts in actions" (*durch die Tat*) (CprR:3), in accordance with self-prescribed rational laws.

While Kant is doubtless clearly attending to classical accounts of virtue and to Stoic conceptions of law—perhaps both at the same time—they will undergo transformation and refiguration in the process of articulating anew the transcendental aesthetics of practical reason. Habituation (*Angewohnung*), he acknowledges, is a precondition of virtue (and a matter of "aesthetic" preconceptions, as the *Religion* will explain), a first establishment (*Begrundung*) of firm inclination for those who are still without the rational means of deliberation, i.e., "without the use of maxims." As such, however, it remains a mechanism of sensibility without, as he put it, ultimate *Bildung*. Examples cannot simply be reiterated without the subjective autonomy required for practical reason. Only rational recognition in accord with the law itself can serve as incentive for virtue here, not merely received maxims. Kant is clear about such an inheritance, therefore; "whatever others give us can be the foundation of no maxims of virtue" (Tugend:148). From this standpoint, the problem then is breaking loose of the prejudice. The problem of morality is one of how the "single individual [is] to work himself out of life under tutelage."[8] The Kantian focus would never be more firmly fixed. He insists equally however that the problem is a broader one, insofar as it is not simply a matter of overcoming bad desires, but also overcoming "statutes and formulas, those mechanical tools of the rational employment or rather misemployment of his natural gifts."[9] Both are cases of heteronomy, a matter to be overcome in pure rational respect for the law. If then Kant had reiterated habituation, retrieving thereby practical reason in the classical sense, he had still radically altered it. Faced with the onslaught of the proof-theoretical paradigms of modern physics, he had been forced to divorce the mechanistic laws of nature from (teleological) accounts of the Good. The law which guides practical action as its *Summum Bonum* must instead be universally rational and not rational by determinate event: any ontic inventory of the Good remains contingent. Granted Kant's deferral to classical accounts of virtue, however, the problem becomes how the *Nomos* itself can be an incentive, a problem for which Kant attempted time and again to provide an account. Indeed the critical project itself in this regard pivots around the question of how such consciousness of the moral law is possible. The question is how virtue is to be made rationally intelligible granted both the rational requisites of modernity and the substantive accounts of the tradition—both, if you will, principled and significant—and how the legacy of the ancients might thereby find legitimation within the rational demands of the modern. It is pivotal to note then that, unlike many modern thinkers in this regard, Kant does not simply deny the existence of a *Summum Bonum* but instead seeks to render it rationally intelligible, to refigure it within the demonstrative constraints of theoretical modernity. Moreover, he aims to lose nothing in the translation. Kant opens his investigations into the foundations (or perhaps refoundation) of the metaphysics of morals precisely by claiming that he wishes to improve on "ancient Greek philosophy" only by "supplying its principle" (Found:3).[10] Kant's original preoccupation with Garve (and Burke) in *The Old Saw on "That May Be Right in Theory But It Won't Work in Practice"* *inter alia* revolves around this issue—with, evidently a double effect, retrieving and transforming tradition. But it is the complexity of his transformation that is too often missed, and missed precisely with regard to the complex generation of the intelligibility of those principles themselves: an agency that might, if you will, both be 'principled' and 'teleological' at once. Here it is evident that Kant's transformation of the tradition becomes portentous: both conceptual and symbolic, analytic and hermeneutic.

The implications of this transformation resonate throughout contemporary debates on the interpretation of the ethical, the status of morality, the 'transcendence' of the sacred, and the incursion of the political. Moreover while most such debates have centered upon the symbolic extensions of the third *Critique,* what will become evident is that such symbolics are already pivotally at stake in the second *Critique's* account of the rational and its complicated 'conjunction' concerning the requisites and narratives of law, the experience of freedom, and the hermeneutics of transcendence at stake in its possibility. Indeed it is just the complications that accompany such an experience, the experience of freedom, that render it portentous. And pace standard "formalist" readings, no one, prior to contemporary thinkers such as Sartre or Arendt, had confronted what the latter termed "the abyss of freedom" more than Kant himself.[11] Doubtless, moreover, nothing was more problematic for theoretical modernity, as Arendt realized, than combining the inheritance of Augustinian free will, the ancient narratives of human origin and foundations, and the determinate certainties of the new sciences. Moreover while she too privileges Kant's account in this regard, again focusing on the account of judgment in the third *Critique,* the specificity of Kant's transformation here and his passage between (and not simply beyond) the ancients and the moderns becomes perhaps most fully apparent only in the theoretical constructions in Kant's itinerary leading to the double function of judgment itself in the third *Critique*.

Far from it being the case that "the bond between the right and the good is broken"[12] in Kant's 'postmetaphysical' ethics, what becomes decisive instead is precisely the manner in which he refigures the narratives attached to both—and not least decisive of all is the extent to which these narratives must now operate in conjunction in confronting the remainder of the metaphysics of morals. Indeed it is just the problem of the status of such narratives that emerges in articulating the possibility of *how* human freedom might be both 'principled' and 'teleological' at once, and how consequently principled enquiry and 'transcendence' might coalesce. In this regard, the issue becomes as important to understanding Kant's reciprocal rejoinder with the ancients as it would be to understanding the legitimacy of Kant's principled "formalism" and its attempt to make freedom both significant and efficacious in their wake.

2. The *Experimentus Crucis*: The Possibility of Freedom

Initially however the question opens preeminently upon the Kantian ethical problem, the rational status of the will itself—or how, that is, rational agency could be possible without in fact being determined by (made conditional upon) an end. Instead, Kant held, such an unconditioned will would be motivated purely out of respect for the law, that is, a will that remained wholly rational and autonomous, one whose maxims are wholly disinterested and universalizable. While this presents certain theoretical difficulties to classical accounts of human agency that require, as will be seen, specific humanistic exposition vis à vis the concept of *homo criticus,* its impact in fact extends beyond the ethical to epistemic and even ontological implications that emerged only within the antinomies of theoretical modernism. Kant's extension beyond both classical or traditional accounts of virtue and the modern transformation of natural law must consequently be sought in the conflict between theoretical and practical reason in a way which divides the ancients and the moderns.

At the outset it can be said, in accord with standard interpretations, that Kant solves the problem of the relation between theoretical and practical reason by affirming the possibility in which the latter establishes its own actuality beyond the limited gaze of theoretical knowledge. The dilemma of morality—of pure practical reason—would thereby seemingly be dissolved.

That Kant saw it as a dilemma, however, itself pays tribute both to his modernist, Enlightenment-based commitments and to his recognition of the "unfinishable" nature of the project of modernity. Notwithstanding all his attempts at formal analysis of principles and his retrievals of the ancients for their intelligibility, there is indeed something already 'post-modern'. At the heart of our rational practices, Kant saw, there lurks a heterogeneity whose irreconcilable character may be insurmountable. It might be said that what was irreconcilable were two 'incommensurables': the discourse of determinism and that of freedom. The limitation on metaphysics which Kant underwrites in the first *Critique,* tying knowledge to a specific experience, recognized that no discursive practice can be absolutized, totalized. Kant's account recognized that the conditional character of what he called experience could not provide a final idiom for unifying science (*Wissenschaft*). And yet the account of experience was ultimately to remain modern. Despite all the limits he was to place upon that project, Kant continued to labor under the influence of the Enlightenment, the rise of modern science, and specifically, Hume's understanding that it required rejecting traditional metaphysical enquiries on the basis of a foundation that had seemingly become unquestionable: the domain of the mathematical and the experiential, the "empirical."

As the development in the first *Critique*'s categories, schemata, and principles demonstrates, what Kant had in mind here was in fact a specific 'experience'; the experience of Newton and Galileo. He claimed this experience to be both objective and determinate; as he points out in the first edition of the *Critique*'s Preface, this experience is to be used as a paradigm for the sure, progressive advance of knowledge. Yet Kant also saw that despite the victories thereby achieved, this experience could not be called absolute, or absolutely determined.

This was, of course, his solution to Hume's skeptical difficulties. Certain of our synthetic a priori propositions remain transcendental as the conditions for the possibility of experience insofar as it arises for a finite rational being. Consequently, if we could claim such knowledge to be universal—universal to our experience—we could not apply it as a 'predicate' of things in themselves. Metaphysics was impossible insofar as one meant by it what had been done under that banner prior to Kant: the attempt to arrive at being *qua* being, objective knowledge of things in themselves. The Transcendental Deduction states categorically that the analysis of our experience presupposes and is conditioned by a prior synthesis: the 'interpretative' process that subtends all finite (nonoriginative, i.e., *discursive*) rationality (A68/B93).

Specifically what escapes this limiting of experience could not then in the strict sense involve an 'experience' (i.e., structured through the principles of the understanding), although it remains, Kant claims, inevitably a "fact of pure reason" (*Faktum der reinen Vernunft*) of which we are conscious (CprR:48). Grasping this facticity (and its interpretation) would be decisive for the critical system since it is an event that all but defied Kant's constraints on both experience and its conceptual framework for *Sinn und Bedeutung*. The implications of such a *factum*, after all, escaped the simplicity of determinate experience, disarticulating its referential connection to the sensible. Instead, drawing upon the internal speculative excess accompanying this *factum*, Kant was led to undertake a hermeneutic of what exceeds such 'determinacy', a hermeneutic that discloses possible domains of being other than those depicted through our categories and schemata underlying 'experience' normally constituted. Indeed, such domains could be brought to light only by a series of transfers—in fact, tropes upon our categories as normally used. The requisite transformations can be shown through Kant's use of the categories of modality. For example, while sure that there is no experience of the moral law and the event it would denote, and he will claim consistently with this that such an event could not be called 'actual', (since actuality requires a perception in the empirical sense) he points out that it is in fact *actualized*:

> The moral law, itself needing no justifying grounds, shows [itself] to be not only possible, but actual in beings which acknowledge the law as binding upon them. (CprR:49)

Likewise, the category of necessity will similarly need to be transferred from its application to a grid of external events to characterize an internal necessity (autonomy) that reason prescribes to itself—even though there is no sensible intuition for it to apply to in the latter case.

Nonetheless, this series of tropes would not be completed within the categories of modality—and for essential reasons. The first category, that of possibility, remains intransigent. The notion of an entity's possibility relates an object merely to its 'thinkability' and not its 'knowability'. It precedes, that is, the differentiation between the theoretical and the practical, between one schematization (and its justification) and another. Indeed it is for this reason that possibility, as enframing the question of justification, takes on such importance in the series of questions which enframe the critical tribunal, e.g., "How is metaphysics possible?" The question here takes the form, "How is the categorical imperative possible?", or more pointedly "How is consciousness of the moral law possible?"—which means, as shall be seen, how does such a law acquire 'significance'?

Since the answers lie beyond the demonstrative means of a strict analytic of understanding, however, they cannot be as simple as other critical enquiries on possibility. Indeed the difficulty involved—and not accidently, granted the underdetermination at stake—will elicit several sets of answers from Kant. What is in question is not only the origins of human reason (of practical reason in this case) but also the (premoral) origin of human susceptibility to reason, since to have reason here is not simply to apply it by subsumption as one does the categories to the manifold of intuition. The enquiry will, therefore, impact not only upon the examination of the character of pure practical laws, but also the beings who undertake them and the status of *their* possibility—an enquiry that now reciprocally articulates both sensibility and intelligibility, the received and the required, and ultimately requires a much more demanding account of receptivity and spontaneity. On the other hand, the other transformations in the categories of modality are quite classical, following a tradition of 'actualization' that doubtless can be traced back to the 'gap' that Aristotle's practical syllogism places between premises and conclusion. All the while, that human beings, for Aristotle, were *capable* of such actions was not in question; they were so as "rational animals."

3. A Hermeneutics of Freedom's Nature: the Typic's Gordian Knot

Kant's "solution," finding its certainty in the Galilean-Newtonian "schemata," could not have Aristotle's luxury. The gap between premises and conclusion here, the gap between theory and practice, the gap between the moral law and its instantiation, is neither merely ethical, nor merely logical. The instantiation must be *ontologically* "hermeneutic" as well, so that the link is forged through the 'actualization' of the agent's own being as autonomous; one which inevitably will, *qua* free, escape empirical determination, thus opening a realm—and a 'nature'—otherwise than the known. The results will consequently be especially oblique for a system in which ontology had itself become oblique and was ultimately reduced, as a result, to the ontic science of physiology (A845/B874). But the *pros hen* at stake is not simply reducible in this sense, as will become especially apparent in the economy of practical reason itself.

The moral law is projected away from determinate nature and the conditional as it had become experimentally ascertained and yet remains inexorably (and critically) tied to it. The tenuous and fragile nature of such a connection is immediately evident. There is, seemingly, nothing inherent to this heterogeneity which could make possible a proper coalescence. Indeed, everything certain goes the other way, since the *seme* of the concept of nature had been bound by Newtonian constraints. Kant quite rightly in his correspondence with Beck during the summer of 1792 affirms in principle the possibility of the impossibility of their homogeneity: "if you mean, a definite order of nature, for example, that of the present world."[13] He affirms in fact that no easy solution can be found, since we have no schemata for the "nature" of intelligible world.

This dilemma overdetermines the problem of the Typic (*typus*), of practical reason, the derivation of a law of (noumenal) 'nature' (CprR:72). The dilemma forces us to consider just how it is that these two orders intertwine, not only at the logical level, but also at the ontological level—in the *being* who combines both incentives and obligations. Moreover this ambiguity stands at the center of debates that continually plague both Kant interpretation and the general problem of interpretation in ethical thought. If grasping the ethical requires, as Cassirer, for example, claimed, that one "gives up the schematism" through which the phenomenon becomes intelligible, how does the world of autonomy become intelligible?[14] And if a finite intellect in the former finds semantic intelligibility through the schematism that had provided the link (and the warrant) for the relation between the intelligible and the sensible, how does a finite intellect, having "abandoned" such receptivity, find its own autonomy intelligible? As Heidegger responded, "We cannot discuss the problem of the finitude of the ethical creature if we do not pose the question: what does law mean?"[15] What is the nature of the possibility of law and what is the relation between its syntax and its semantics, its pure form and its intelligibility? While Kant classically divides the will into two parts and assigns one to the intelligible world and one to the sensible, this assignment presupposes what Kant's modernism had denied: that the laws of sensibility and the laws of intelligibility might simply coincide—but freedom and nature go different ways.

Kant had in effect proposed a double-edged sword for himself, perhaps even a certain *Wechsel*, as those after him thought. The experiment of the Copernican turn had linked categories and intuition, sense and *sensibilia*, assuring cognitive content to knowledge—if only understood from the standpoint of a finite intellect. Pure practical reason based upon non-Newtonian causal premises had been robbed of these links. While it could derive principles and categories, the status of their link to the (noumenal) world—to the "nature" of pure practical reason—remained oblique and, as will become apparent, figural, leaving the link between syntax and semantics ultimately indeterminate. As a result, in a complex gesture, Kant's theoretical construction would be led to transform—even deconstruct—the conceptual resources of the tradition, albeit precisely by refiguring and articulating at one and the same time the intelligibility of practical reason within the figures of principled 'objectivity'. It would be doubly complicated thereby: in the same gesture in which he explicated the possibility of practical reason (i.e., the rationality of moral action) he would likewise articulate the rational status of the traditions in which it became intelligible. And finally perhaps he revealed thereby, by what he fittingly identified as "the schematism of analogy," the complicated status of transcendental constitution for reason in general (Rel:58).[16] To think then that pure practical reason is devoid of interpretation is as spurious as it would be to think that nature itself could supply a law to reason. Reason will instead be both principled and hermeneutic. Both claims, consequently, would be subject to similar illusions—both the claim that the pure syntax of law might provide the basis for deducing its object, or alternatively, that pure principles might be deduced for the 'experience' of such objects, a pure 'semantics'. Kant himself perhaps had no such delusions—and doubtless in this respect provides a model for all such "hermeneutics" in his wake.

The third antinomy in the *Critique of Pure Reason* had discovered the paradigm which would form the structure and limits of the development of the ethical domain. The solution to the third antinomy discovers the possibility of a causality through freedom, one in harmony with the Universal Law of natural necessity. Humankind, in this exposition, must be viewed "on the one hand (as) phenomenon, and on the other hand, in respect of certain faculties the action of which cannot be ascribed to the receptivity of sensibility, a purely [*bloß*] intelligible object" (A547/B575). The noumenal would be outside the series of appearances and yet possessed by a causal agent that also is an appearance. Therefore, human beings as agents may have both an intelligible character and an empirical character. A space would be thereby opened for the requirements of morality, which "necessarily presuppose[s] freedom (in the strictest sense) as a property of our will," to be fulfilled (Bxxviii).

Establishing this fact outlines the possibility of Reason's being a law unto itself. In this the manifestation of Reason (however finite) as in a sense creative would become a *fait accompli*, an *ordo naturae* generated from its own *materia*. Indeed Kant here is specific:

> Reason does not here follow the order of things as they present themselves in appearance, but frames for itself with perfect spontaneity an order of its own

according to ideas, to which it adapts the empirical conditions, and according
to which it declares actions to be necessary. (A548/B576)

Kant's analysis allows for a *compatibility* in the conjunction of the two
causes in one being. Nevertheless, what has been discovered is narrowly
limited. Neither the reality nor even the possibility of freedom is *demonstrated*. In the former case an experience would have to be given, while in
the second case we cannot know the possibility of any real ground and its
causality from mere concepts. What has been established is merely the logical
possibility of freedom in accord with the necessity of humans standing under
the laws of natural causality. This perhaps is of little comfort, but of great
import given that what is at stake is the possibility of a spontaneous beginning (A533/B561). Indeed, in one sense it is upon this cornerstone that all
that is put to the test in the *Critique of Practical Reason* was to be grounded.

Despite Kant's constraints upon knowledge and truth, the task that practical reason inherits from the speculative then would be grounded (or in fact
figured) not in knowledge, but in thought. "But though I cannot *know*, I can
yet *think* freedom . . . provided due account be taken of our critical distinction between the two modes of representation, the sensible and the intellectual, and of the resulting limitation of the pure concepts of understanding
and of the principles which flow from them" (Bxxviii). Significantly, however,
such 'thoughts' nonetheless remain devoid of *Sinn und Bedeutung* in the strict
sense, since they extend beyond the validity conditions of the senses by
which a finite intellect acquires knowledge and, thus, strictly speaking, remain trapped in the figments of imagination—in mere narration, as he had
put it elsewhere. Indeed, whatever warrant they might still retain will be
restricted to the pure principles of practical reason; consequently, the classical
narratives of morality will themselves be transformed, invested, and legitimated precisely insofar as they "flow out" of, are limited by, and are prefigured in the ground of "the mere concept" of the law itself.

The moral will in itself is determinable only *formally,* and this determinability (*qua* unconditioned) is possible only through causality by freedom.
Morality is itself a nomothetic of freedom, one delineated in difference to
"all material . . . principles [which] are, as such, of one and the same kind
and belong under the general principle of self-love or one's own happiness"
(CprR:20). In this way, freedom and the unconditioned practical law reciprocally imply one another:

A free will must be independent of all empirical conditions . . . and yet be
determinable, a free will must find its ground of determination in the law, but
independently of the material of the law. But besides the latter there is nothing

in a law except the legislative form. Therefore, the legislative form . . . is the only thing which can constitute a determining ground of the free will. (CprR:28–29)

The achievement of this mutual implication, this homogeneous coalescence of the free will and the moral law, is the basis for the rupture between natural causality and causality through freedom; morality per se constitutes the institution of their separation and difference. Nevertheless, the differentiation as it has been accomplished remains abstract. What is not provided is the exposition of the event through which such a possibility might become intelligible. The only means of accomplishing morality as a real possibility is to articulate the link between the modern (non-ateleological) sense of law as universal regularity and its possibility (and significance) for human rationality. And perhaps Kant's separation of those problems, which are handled in the second *Critique's* Analytic, from others dealt with in the Dialectic adds to this abstraction. Indeed, having established a nomothetics of freedom, Kant is led to consider both the specificity of the 'nature' such a nomothetics articulates as well as the 'nature' of the being who inhabits it—both considerations which bring his *ars analytica* of moral imperatives into dialogue with the traditional narratives of human virtue.

4. The Analogies of Form: The Permutation(s) of Categorical Imperative

It is precisely here that the unwieldy problem of the Typic intervenes in the *Critique of Practical Reason*, drawing in fact upon an analogon which already had been explicated in the *Foundations of the Metaphysics of Morals* (1785), one which moreover further clarifies Kant's inheritance and in particular his proximity to Stoicism. Judgment in general, as has been seen, involves a question of application. Pure practical judgment will require universally necessary rules for such application for the subsumption of specific cases under general rules. As Kant reiterates in the second *Critique*, pure reason in its theoretical use had means of escape (*Mittel*) from the problem, that is, the categories, schemata and principles linked immediately to sensibility by the "middle" of imagination. While this bridge to *sensibilia* is lacking in practical reason, Kant claims that there is "a favorable prospect" in these circumstances—precisely since it liberates pure practical reason from determinate causality. And here again it is worth quoting the text in detail:

But to the law of freedom (which is a causality not sensuously conditioned) and consequently to the concept of the absolute good, no intuition and hence no schema can be applied for the purpose of applying it in concreto. Thus the moral law has no other cognitive faculty to mediate its application to objects of nature than the understanding (not the imagination) and the understanding can supply to an idea of reason not a schema of sensibility but a law. This law, as one which can be exhibited in concreto in objects of the sense is a natural law. But this natural law can for the purposes of judgment be used only in its formal aspect and it may therefore be called the type of the moral law. (CprR:71–72)

Kant's preface to the second *Critique* claimed that it presupposed the *Foundations* "only insofar as that work gives a preliminary acquaintance with the principle of duty and justifies a determinate formula of it" (*ein bestimmt formel*) (CprR:8). Nevertheless, Kant's exposition of the Typic is imported as a transformation of the third of the "formulations" of the categorical imperative Kant provides in the *Grundlegung*.

It may be, however, a questionable abstraction to see these three formulations as mere algorithmic permutations, or simply "analytic" versions of the categorical imperative—even if Kant tells us that by the application of categories of quantity he derives the definite characteristics that all moral maxims are contained therein and hence that they are only "so many formulas of the very same law" (Found:54). The question of the application of the universal to the particular is never far from the problem of wit (*Witz*) in the critical system (cf. Anth.354). The problem that haunts this differentiation, as Kant will say in the *Tugendlehre*, is that such a plurality remains inevitably problematic: mathematical construction "allows a plurality of proofs for one and the same proposition" while a plurality of proofs for moral principles yields only plausibility, a matter of rhetoric and not logic (Tugend:62). If Kant is to strictly distinguish pure practical reason from the rhetorics and dialectics of the ancients, here too the demarcation must be unequivocal. Immediately, the *Foundations* in fact imparts that the difference between the formulations here is more a "subjective difference" and its qualification as subjective is critical to the theory of practical reason and perhaps even to the Copernican turn of the critical system in general: "There is nevertheless a difference in them, but the difference is more subjectively than objectively practical, for it is intended to bring an idea of reason closer to intuition by means of a certain analogy" (Found:54). As such, these permutations of the categorical imperative are ampliative, not simply analytic: they are, that is, three different synthetic a priori formulations derivable *not by mere analysis* but by analogue—an analogical extension which becomes particularly prominent in the Typic. At stake in the *Foundations* are differences which are subjective conditions of maxims embodying the univocally determinate categorical imperative. Accordingly, Kant states in this text that despite these differences, all maxims have:

1. A form which consists in universality: and in this respect the formula of the moral imperative requires that the maxims be chosen as though they should hold as universal laws of nature.
2. A material, i.e., an end: in this respect the formula says that the rational being, as by its nature an end and thus as an end in itself, must serve in every maxim as the condition restricting all merely relative and arbitrary ends.
3. A complete determination of all maxims by the formula that all maxims which stem from autonomous legislation ought to harmonize with a possible realm of ends as with a realm of nature. (Found:54–55)

It is most directly the third which Kant transfers into the Typic—notwithstanding the fact, as has been seen, that he had categorically precluded the possibility of moral maxims being grounded in nature as we *know* it. The first formulation, after all, could still be construed to be merely drawing the parallel distinction of universality which pertains to the logical syntax of laws in general (a refiguration of the ancient's form [*morphe*] in accord with modern mathematical 'construction').[17] That the third must do more, indeed that it does so paradoxically, in fact is already evident, and for reasons which were twofold: such maxims as based upon nature would be generalizations and would fail not only the criterion of categorical necessity but also the thesis of autonomy in the agent, granted the first *Critique's* commitment to 'natural' determinism. Hence emerges the ambiguity of the Typic: a 'nonnatural nature' which is not without applicability in the realm of the senses. Instead, in accord with the antinomy (or again, the *Wechsel*) he had brought to light, at stake is a certain counternature which is to be conceptualized by principles wholly other than the nature of the first *Critique*; it is 'denaturalized' if you will, in accordance with the negative principle which itself derives from the conditions of moral autonomy—and yet one for which we have no intuition, no knowledge, and no determining ground other than the pure spontaneity of the will itself. How then are the events which are to be ordered by this *lex naturae* intelligible?

Kant suggests that the subjective condition which articulates the application of the categorical imperative originates in a certain transference. By the transference in question we are "allowed to use the nature of the sensuous world as the type of an intelligible nature" precisely insofar as it "takes from sensuous nature no more than that which pure reason can also think for itself, i.e., lawfulness, and conversely transfers (*hineinträgt*) into the supersensuous nothing more than can be actually exhibited by action in the world of sense according to a formal rule of natural law in general" (CprR:72-73). This "transference," the traditional (rhetorical) language of figure and metaphor, is however less demonstratively justified than discerned. Indeed, as befits expositions by analogy, by invoking the language of rhetorics he claims that this transference is a "suitable" one. And in fact, Kant's argument restricts itself to the requisites of the categorical imperative's form (again its logical syntax), while at the same time limiting the (analogical) extension or Kathexis[18] its intelligibility presupposes: any explication itself will not be simply categorical in the 'literal' sense but symbolical, as he immediately imparts—and in this sense its conceptual exhibition not simply distinguishable from its subjective significance.

In a telling example Kant states that happiness and the infinitely useful consequences of a will determined only by itself certainly "could serve as a very adequate type for the morally good but still not be identical with it" (CprR:73). Our ultimate happiness might provide a perfectly adequate (and coherent) "symbol" of the good but yet not be determinate with respect to it. To take it as determinate remains nonetheless dogmatic, a matter of mysticism, as Kant puts it. At the root of the Typic there remains a certain cathexis, one which, as figured in the concept of nature itself, remains analogically and symbolically inscribed. If, that is, "life is the faculty of a being by which it acts according to the laws of the faculty of desire" (CprR:9n), then 'life', subjectively considered, understood from the 'standpoint' of a finite rational intellect, will be inevitably symbolic. In delineating the facultas signatrix in the Anthropology Kant refers to the symbol precisely in terms of its poverty of determinate concepts, a thought which remains figurate (Anth:38). The third Critique is perhaps even more direct in claiming that all intuitions that are a priori are either schemata or symbols, of which the former contain direct, the latter indirect presentations of the concept—"the former do this demonstratively; the latter by means of an analogy," such as the beautiful indirectly a presenting of the good (CJ:§59).

Kant's construals in the Typic also authorized only an indirect reference to a law of nature 'otherwise' than nature as we know it. Indeed, if we turn to the third Critique where the symbolization of the Good is treated in further detail, we can find the process itself quite rightly referred to as a matter of analogization. "For the imagination [in its role] as a productive cognitive power is very mighty when it creates, as it were, another nature out of the very material that actual nature gives it" (CJ:182).

In fact such is the general interpretative function of analogy. As the Logic imparts: Analogy, a form of reflective judgment, concludes from "partial similarity of two things to total similarity according to the principle of specification." Unlike induction, which involves the principle of "one in many, hence in all," analogy is a matter of "much in one (that is also in other) thus also the remainder in one" as in the other, and only the identity of the ground is required. Kant allows that analogy and induction are both "useful and indispensable to the expansion of our experiential cognition" (Logic:137)—as the first *Critique* too had demonstrated, where, it could be argued, a similar indeterminate symbolization of the cognitive field (of metaphysics) occurs in the Transcendental Dialectic's account of regulative employment of rational ideas. Indeed the conclusion of the Analytic itself has acknowledged as much: lacking (sensible) intuition, or even pretension to such, "we have an understanding which *problematically* extends further" (A255/B310). And such extensions were perhaps not simply without theoretical impact. As Kant himself recalls in the third *Critique* the critical project's search for foundations depends itself upon the metaphor of *grounds,* (CJ:227–28) in its grounding, the spontaneous joining together of sensibility and understanding, a chemical analogue, that of 'affinity' (*affinitas*) (Anth:52–53). But in this regard theory and trope again would not be simply distinguished.

In practical reason, however, the 'analogization' is doubly complex. Kant draws not only upon certain causal similarities between autonomous and heteronomous determination of the will, but likewise refigures the concept of natural law with the figure of the absolute good. This figure is itself complex: 'natural' necessity is refigured by Newtonian, i.e., mathematical nomology, while this in turn becomes *cathectic* as the *Summum Bonum.* Indeed in this regard we can reiterate about this transformation what Jacob Klein stated of the general passage of ancient mathematics into modern conceptualization in general: "the relation of our concepts to those of the ancients is oddly ruptured. . . . the edifice of this 'new' science is now erected, but erected in *deliberate opposition to the concepts and methods of the former.*"[19]

Now the transfer of this "ground" is a complicated one, certainly, but its antecedents and precedents are both conceptual and historical. Kant has refigured the concept of the natural law in accord with the formal requisites of practical reason, emptying the concept of cognitive reference—as Kant openly admitted, it remains a formal typic and not a concrete instance: syntactic and not (strictly taken) semantic. That the transfer itself is not a refiguration without concrete historical antecedents is perhaps equally evident. As is often noted, Kant's Stoicism may well be traceable to Garve's translation of Cicero's *De Officiis,* a work Garve annotated, as Kant's *Theorie-Praxis* essay notes (T-P:52n). Indeed, in this respect all that we have been tracing is not only a refiguration of the ancient's account of natural law but the virtues of wisdom, justice, courage, and self-control. And the point is not simply historical: the Typic's gloss on natural law, for reasons now clear, cannot be simply conceptual, but must be symbolical as well: nothing in the concept of autonomy, after all, determinately *demonstrates* its links with this figural law of supersensuous nature. Hence the precision of Kant's syntax: act "as if . . ." Nor can this acting "as if" be simply spelled out, as will be seen, without more fully tracing the symbolic investments with the Good it entailed, a transfer once more laden with conceptual and historical antecedents.

Finally, given this complicated "transfer" which underwrites the third formulation of the categorical imperative (as the Kingdom of ends), it is perhaps easy to see the same process at work in the second formulation (Humanity as an end in itself). Here the ancient and again Stoic conception of the love of humanity becomes transformed into Kant's pure *respect* for humanity. This transformation occurs by an invocation and an invention whose grammar itself—one repeated time and again under similar circumstances in Kant's work—indicates the transfer of this (analogical) investiture: "Now I say [*Nun sage Ich*] man and in general every rational being exists as an end in himself" (Found:46). If we should see Kant's natures as split, divided, and ana-logical in use, equally it will be necessary to see this formulation of humanity as analogizing anew the most ancient nature of "individual rational substance," that is, a 'person', to cite Boethius's original definition. Both substance and person will in fact be overdetermined in Kant's wake, divided between freedom and nature, experience and category, individual and universal, *factum* and schematism. If later writers like Trendelenburg took Kant in all this to be finally "scientifically" codifying the various senses which attach themselves to the word 'Person', parsing it between the permutations of theoretical and practical reason, we can see the refiguration such codification also employed, and, as will be come apparent, the omissions in Kant's codification.[20] While Kant's Paralogisms had, in accord with his critique of all ontology, removed the attributes traditionally associated with rational substance (in fact of the transcendental and epistemic attributes Leibniz had already prefigured: self-consciousness and temporal iterability), the account of practical reason offered in Kant's *Nun sage Ich* reintroduced rational 'nature' as an end in itself having dignity and the soul's immortality as a postulate of practical faith. The same grammar's complex symbolics is also apparent in the third *Critique's* declaration:

> Now I maintain that the beautiful is the symbol of the morally good; and only because we refer the beautiful to the morally good (we all do so naturally and

require all others also to do so, as a duty) does our liking for it include a claim to everyone's assent. (CJ:228)

In both cases, beyond the rational syntactics which undergird Kant's mathematization of theory, we are left with a question of how concepts with such a symbolic investiture arise—in particular with respect to practical reason, how such pure love, that is, respect, becomes possible,[21] and perhaps even more to the point, granted modernist constructs of the sort for which Newton (and Hobbes) had argued, even plausible. Here the complex argument in the second *Critique*'s Dialectic becomes an *experimentum crucis* for the exposition of the conceptual grids delivered in the Typic.

5. The *Symbiosis* of Law and the Dialectics of Reason: The Refiguration of Transcendence

The problematic of the Dialectic of the second *Critique,* including its "retrieval" of the *Summum Bonum,* can be read as an explication of the symbolic investiture of concepts; in fact it provides a conceptual exposition of the subjective conditions of the determinability of a finite rational will as ethical. The Dialectic does so again by further articulating the character of the link that exists between the purely formal and the *materia,* the abstract and the concrete, the significative and the symbolical, within the faculty of desire in its relation to such determinability. Moreover in the Dialectic we can more specifically measure Kant's debt to ancient accounts of desire, the good, and 'natural law.' Indeed in articulating the symbiosis of the sensible and the intelligible that accompanies the will, the Dialectic amounts in this regard to a double hermeneutic of the problem we saw beginning to emerge with the Typic. It provides both a hermeneutic of the will and a hermeneutic of the domain of traditional practical reason. Pace standard accounts, this is not a problem which occurs exclusively in the later ethical writings, however. Rather, it is found and expressed in all of the major ethical works. It can be found as early as the first *Critique.*

> It is necessary that the whole course of our life be subjected to moral maxims; but it is impossible that this should happen unless reason connects with the moral law . . . an operative cause which determines for such conduct as is in accordance with the moral law an outcome. (A813/B840)

However great the importance of the discovery of the perfect spontaneity of reason's self-legislation, it must be aligned with a discovery which is

equally important in the end and once more articulates Kant's connection
with classical accounts.

> To be happy is necessarily the desire of every rational but finite being, and thus
> it is an unavoidable determinant of its faculty of desire. (CprR:24)

This "fact" is not something that disappears when the analysis moves
from the empirical will to the pure will. Willing per se is necessarily involved with happiness as happiness is the "one end . . . which we may
presuppose as actual in all rational beings so far as imperatives apply to
them" (Found:33). The exposition of happiness dislocates the purity of the
former analysis—to use Klein's term again, it too is "oddly ruptured"—for
it forms a certain reciprocal rejoinder upon those matters which are "conditional":

> Happiness is the satisfaction of all our desires, *extensively,* in respect of their
> manifoldness, *intensively,* in respect of their degree, and *protensively,* in respect
> of their duration. (A806/B834)

To be able to speak of morality only in conjunction with happiness, only
in conjunction with *ends,* forces all that was implicated in reason's perfect
spontaneity back upon its limits, upon its finitude; in short, upon the
paradoxical nature of its *im*perfection. Kant is perhaps most explicit on this
in *Religion Within the Limits of Reason Alone:*

> It is one of the inescapable limitations of man and of his faculty of practical
> reason (a limitation, perhaps, of all other worldly beings as well) to have regard,
> in every action, to the consequence thereof, in order to discover therein what
> could serve him as an end and also prove the purity of his intention—which
> consequence, though last in practice (*nexu effectivo*) is yet first in representation
> and intention (*nexu finali*). (Rel:6n.)

There is in this a hint ("a limitation, perhaps, of all other worldly beings
as well") that, notwithstanding the unconditional iterability that underlies
rational autonomy, forces human rationality back upon its animality (upon
human nature), and that it is indeed this intersection that is being analyzed
here. Indeed, it is precisely this recognition which provides the protocols
for Kant's explication of the matter in *Theorie/Praxis.* He states, "Man is not
. . . expected to renounce his natural aim of attaining happiness as soon as
the question of following his duty arises: for like any finite rational being,
he simply cannot do so" (T-P:45–66). If, for a finite rational being, "thought
as a means is directed [to] intuition," practical reason and ethicality in
particular are directed undeniably to happiness. No relation to intuition, no

knowledge. And, likewise, without reference to outcome, to results, to *materia*, to ends, there is no willing:

> In the absence of all reference to an end no determination of the will can take place in man, since such determination cannot be followed by no effect whatever; and the representation of the effect must be capable of being accepted . . . as an end conceived of as the result ensuing from the will's determination. (Rel:4)

There can be no morality apart from the "extension" which occurs in the aspect of happiness. Moreover, at stake in this extension is the link between sign and symbol, reason and imagination—precisely, that is, insofar as it remains true, as the *Foundations* claimed, that "happiness is an ideal not of reason but of imagination" (Found:36). Imagination in both cases, cognitive or conative, both complicates and facilitates, both makes possible and limits the transition from syntax to semantics, principles to reference.

This renewed link with the figures of imagination, however, only truncates the problem once more. The second *Critique's* discussion of the Typic had seemingly divested itself of the imagination in distinguishing the Typic from transcendental schematism. Kant clearly claims that "the moral law has no other cognitive faculty to mediate its application to objects of nature than the understanding (*not* the imagination); and the understanding can supply to an idea of reason not a schema of sensibility but a law" (CprR:73). But, as we have seen, here the argument is that reason has a right to use the concept of nature (devoid of the conflicting elements of the schematism) for the application of its law to the extent that it pertains to the form of lawfulness in general. Moreover, Kant adds, reason "has a right and is compelled to do so" (CprR:73); a right, insofar as the result remains principled, a 'compulsion' insofar as it is through the figures of this analogue that freedom becomes intelligible, that is, that a 'principled virtue' becomes possible. Such a typic not only guards against heteronomy, but also against mysticism, namely that "which makes into a schema that which should serve only as a symbol, i.e., proposes to supply real yet nonsensuous intuitions (of an invisible kingdom of God) for the application of the moral law, and thus plunges into the transcendent" (CprR:73). Such a "plunge into the transcendent" is surely not identical with the formal articulation (the expounding) of the categorical imperative and yet (as the affinity of Kant's example of the third formulation demonstrates) this articulation remains inseparably linked to such "mysticism" in its application—and one supposes, therefore, is not *sensu stricto* separable from the symbolic extension of imagination, precisely again to use Kant's later terms, in the form of "a schematism of analogy" (Rel:58). Hence the complicated remainder of the ancients' *Summum Bonum* within the figures of proof-theoretical rationality: virtue will by 'right and by compulsion' be both principled and hermeneutic.

The final two of the three questions which open the "Canon of Pure Reason" in the *Critique of Pure Reason* are then inexorably (and symbolically) tied together by Kant. What I ought to do is inevitably connected with what I may hope. The purity of the ethical can only be accomplished in conjunction with the 'necessity' that willing implies. The 'thought' that arrives at the former must face at the same time the facticity of the "subjective conditions" of the latter. The account which found their separation meaningful, and in fact necessary must now—if it continues to cling to anything like the logical requisites concerning the principled purity of morality—acquiesce not only before the analogical complexities in the transition between syntax and semantics but also thereby directly articulate the status of the being that is to undertake such a requirement.

The need to account for the event as intelligible, that is, *really* possible (again, if the intention is to be possible), itself forced the transition from moral theory to rational "faith," the transition from the rational principles to the excess and symbolization that would facilitate both its instantiation and fulfillment. The connection between the nomothetics of Kant's refigurations, between morality and nature ('free' causality and natural) is, taken by itself, totally contingent on the achievement of virtuous happiness. Thus, in order for a connection to be made between intention and happiness and the two domains which they implicate, a ground of their mediation must be posited outside them, yet homogeneous to both. This ground and the postulates which arise with regard to it for Kant open the domain of a rational and moral theology.

This ground of highest mediation would complete the system of morality—and yet once again, it too still presents a bare outline. If Kant has articulated thereby both the complex syntax and semantics of practical reason, we have still not grounded the latter's possibility, thus distinguishing, to use his terms, its narration from "mere fiction." For granted that pure practical reason necessarily lacks empirical confirmation, an assurance of its possibility requires an account of the event in which it has its occurrence. It is in this occurrence that the final substantiation, the realization, of the Kantian ethics would need to be constituted.

Thus far Kant's *system* of ethics has been seen to evolve from a 'conjunction' between its analysis of the nature of the faculty of desire (i.e., the problem of the determinability of the will) and Kant's modernist (i.e., mathematical) conception of a lawful nomothetic. This, however, is abstract—even on his terms. It evades and disregards again both the problem and the *significance* of the fact that the foundation of morality is not purely analytic (derivable from the fact of free will), but is constituted through a synthetic a priori principle. Hence the critical question, that is, the question of origins, has been deferred—categorically, granted Kant's Newtonian commitments with respect to transcendental knowledge and all that theoretically ladens the account of its experience. Kant himself first faces this perhaps most explicitly in the *Foundations:*

> If the freedom of the will is presupposed, morality together with its principle follows from it by the mere analysis of its concept. (Found:65)

In this sense, problems of the determinability of the will amount in the end merely to a limitation of the analysis of a nomothetic of freedom, of its passage from syntactics to semantics by means of 'symbolics'. To displace the problem of the synthetic a priori in this respect, however, amounts to a *petitio principii*. It uses the concept of freedom regardless of its problems of substantiation, ones which the developments of the third antinomy only initiate.

Freedom is *not,* however, a concept that can be morally *constructed,* but rather is one which must be derived. As the *Critique of Practical Reason* finally makes clear, if morality is to be possible only under the condition that it proceeds from our *knowledge* of freedom, then it cannot be possible. Our knowledge of the unconditionally practical

> cannot start from freedom, for this we can neither know immediately, since our first concept of it is negative, nor infer [it] from experience, since experience reveals to us only the law of appearances and consequently the mechanism of nature, the direct opposite of freedom. (CprR:29)

It is then necessary to discover that from which freedom is derived. In one sense, this condition is disclosed in what has already been exposed to be the correlate of freedom in the *Foundations:*

> It is therefore the moral law, of which we become immediately conscious as soon as we construct maxims for the will, which first presents itself to us; and, since reason exhibits it as a ground of determination which is completely independent of and not to be outweighed by any sensuous condition, it is the moral which leads directly to the concept of freedom. (CprR:29)

This is the same exposition that the resolution of the third antinomy of *Critique of Pure Reason* brought about (B575-6). The concept of freedom arises necessarily out of, or in reference to the priority of its object viz. the consciousness of the moral law. And, this consciousness, to which freedom is referred, and rises immediately out of, is nothing other than "the sole fact [*Faktum*] of pure reason" (CprR:31).

The first condition of morality, and thereby freedom, is not a construction of reason; it is not derived, nor is it simply an object of intuition. Rather, Kant claims, it is a *Faktum* of reason itself. Through its presentation reason "proclaims itself as originating law" (CprR:31). Since a free will finds its origins in morality, "therefore a free will and a will under moral laws are identical" (Found:65). In this there is the corollary to the statement that a lawless freedom would be absurd; freedom in its origin arises *as* lawful.

If this account were adequate, the foundation of freedom would then have been discovered. Lacking the means by which other forms of knowledge are substantiated, "the moral law assures us of [the] difference between the relation of our actions as appearances to our sensuous being and the relation by which this sensuous being is itself connected to the intelligible substrate in us" (CprR:103). The task, however, now becomes the substantiation of the *Faktum* itself.

6. The Phenomenology of Kantian Conscience: Consciousness of the Moral Law

In this regard the issue of morality appears to reduce to the solution of one question in the Kantian problematic. Granted the solution to this question (the question, that is, of reason's substantiation of itself as ethical; i.e., the substantiation of its ability to be an "originating ethical law"), human beings may be affirmed as ethical beings—that ethicality *is* their possibility:

> How is consciousness of the moral law possible? (CprR:29)

In fact, however, Kant puts forth more than one set of answers to this question. The first one, as has been just seen, bends the problem back upon its previous formulation and upon the mechanics of reason itself:

> We can come to know pure practical laws in the same way we know pure theoretical principles, by attending to the necessity with which reason prescribes them to us and to the elimination from them of all empirical conditions, which reason directs. The concept of a pure will arises from the former, as the consciousness of a pure understanding from the latter. (CprR:29)

This is the provisional answer of the second *Critique* (and it runs parallel to corresponding statements in the first *Critique*). We have seen how peremptory it is, especially granted the absence of a referent and the problem of its intelligibility. It is, perhaps at best, an explanation of its operation (a factor which, as will become evident later, is of great importance for Kant), rather than an exposition which gives an account of *origins*—the task, again, that lies at the ground of critical procedure (cf. Logic:91; A55/B80).

Kant appeals here to the immediacy of the transition and reciprocity that he has analyzed in the notion of a free will and the moral law. In many respects it remains identical to the blunt yet haunting statement which opens the *Foundations:*

> We have, then, to develop the concept of a will which is to be esteemed as good of itself without regard to anything else. It *dwells already* in the *natural sound* understanding [*so wie er schon dem natürlichen gesunden beiwohnet*] and does not so much need to be taught as only to be brought to light. (Found:13)

At stake in the question "how is consciousness of the moral law possible?" devoid of extrinsic criteria for verification, reference, and deduction is a 'pure phenomenology' of moral obligation, and surely attests to the problem of such phenomenologies in Kant's work.

Once the consciousness of the moral law in its uniqueness as a rational fact is achieved, the "deduction" or the transition to the free will as its substantiation follows immediately—and, as has become evident, the transition to its symbolics. We have seen, however, the complexity in which the intelligibility of such a concept of the 'natural understanding' is figured—both logically and historically, the disequilibrium of such phenomenologies.[22] The question at hand then is one regarding the status of the rational fact: the question of its actualization, a question whose implications are less logical (or analogical) than more directly epistemic and ontological. And, it is here perhaps that Kant makes his mark, granting a domain of *validity,* and even priority, to the practical beyond the limits of theoretical enquiry, a move which subverts—without inverting—the epistemic hierarchy between *theoria* and *praxis* which enframed the tradition. The priority of practical reason is established without need of external justification or criteria:

> Thus, the objective reality of the moral law can be proved through no deduction, through no exertion of the theoretical speculative, or empirically supported reason; and even if one were willing to renounce its apodictic certainty,

it could not be confirmed by any experience and thus proved a posteriori. Nevertheless, it is firmly established of itself. (CprR:48)

The practice—or event—in which reason, by a certain exception (or a certain counternature and counterintuition) raises the problem of its own principle thus opens a domain previously closed by the constraints of critique and need for theoretical justification. Moreover, Kant is clear that through this event, albeit in a manner quite other than theoretical enquiry, practical reason sufficiently establishes its own actuality: not in some verifiable deed, but in articulating a domain whose justification, beyond extrinsic constraint, allows for a kind of evidence otherwise than proof-theoretical rationality. No deed, after all, could provide either its demonstration or verification. What is established is not established *by* a deed but *in* a deed: the event in which reason itself raises the possibility of its own principle and thereby the possibility of a domain otherwise than that of causal efficiency and instrumental rationality. We have traced this exception (and perhaps its scandal) to be precisely that moment in which Kant thought both the law and freedom, principle and transcendence, sign and symbol, nomothetics and hermeneutics together.

Still, even if this consciousness and the event it implicates need no extrinsic justification, or better in the consciousness of the categorical imperative and the problem of its significance it would explicate the extent of its own possibility, this cannot simply dismiss the problem of its origins. *Inter alia*, as the above text notes explicitly in renouncing (like all such phenomenologies)[23] deductive certainty, it lacks determinate proof, if not possibility.

If transcendental logic is always a question of origins it would be dogmatic to either simply assert or to defer the problem of origins here, knowing that "empirical proof" is impossible. If from the outset the complicated relations between autonomy and happiness had been apparent, the problem of the 'origin' that might articulate their belonging together doubtless continued to dog this analysis. Again to assume the theoretics of phenomenology, 'static analysis' always requires the augmentation of 'genetic analysis'.[24] And Kant perhaps knew it and attempted in his later writings to provide further clarification of the nature of its event through an exposition of the concept (and doubtless the attendant 'experience') of humanity implicated in the position on practical reason the second *Critique* had delineated. In such "phenomenologies" moreover, he in fact further details the character of the symbolic extension that arises in the *factum* of practical rationality, again returning to a hermeneutics whose scope is then broader in impact.

Kant's second "set" of answers to this question, developed in the later writings, comes at the problem from a different side, openly amplifying the aesthetics of practical reason, its hermeneutic refiguring the symbolics of practical reason through the account of moral feeling—and openly responding in the process to Hutchinson (CprR:41). In *The Metaphysical Principles of Virtue* and *Religion Within the Limits of Reason Alone*, Kant deals with this question of moral feeling under the aspect of the conditions of *human susceptibility* to ethicality. Like both the postulates on happiness that arise with the problem of will's determinability (termed "subjective effects"), and the threefold formulae of the categorical imperative which render the latter intelligible, these conditions of ethicality too are termed "subjective conditions" in the *Tugendlehre*.

The sensitive basic concepts (*Ästhetische Vorbegriffe*) of the mind's susceptibility to the concepts of duty, as related in the *Tugendlehre*, are specifically called the *means* by which humans can be obligated. They are four in number. First, "moral feeling" becomes the susceptibility to pleasure or displeasure merely from the consciousness of the agreement or disagreement of our action with the law of duty. It constitutes a "susceptibility of free choice for being moved by pure practical reason" and without it a person would be "morally dead . . . the moral vital force could no longer produce any effect on this feeling, his humanity would be dissolved into mere animality." Secondly, Kant claims that conscience, which is practical reason holding up before man his duty under a law, is "originally within him." Thirdly, love must be included because it cannot be willed and yet it is "subject to a law of duty. Love is a matter of sensation, and not of willing" (Tugend:58–60). Finally, respect (*reverentia*) is the ground of certain duties, for respect must be original within man "in order [for him] to be able to conceive duty at all" (Tugend:62). These predispositions are something which every person has. They cannot be regarded as a duty, precisely because they are the condition *sine qua non* of duty. They are both natural and antecedent then to duty. In short, they are the ground, the possibility of duty itself.

Religion Within the Limits of Reason Alone again takes up the problem in "Concerning the Original Predisposition to Good in Human Nature." Here the predispositions are divided into three, and are explained less specifically, but the substantial agreement with the *Tugendlehre* is generally evident. The first of these is that of the predisposition to animality in man, taken as a living being. The second of the predispositions is that to humanity. It is the desire for equality and mutual love. Third, there is the predisposition to personality in us, taken as a rational and at the same time, an accountable being. It involves the capacity for respect of the moral law as in itself a sufficient incentive of the will (Rel:21–23).

What was in the *Tugendlehre* merely stated is here specifically spelled out:

> All of these predispositions are not only *good* in negative fashion (in that they
> do not contradict the moral law); they are also predispositions *toward good*
> (they enjoin the observance of the law). They are *original*, for they are bound
> up with the possibility of human nature. Man can indeed use the first two
> contrary to their ends, but he can extirpate none of them. By the predisposi-
> tions of a being we understand not only its constituent elements which are
> necessary to it, but also the forms of their combination, by which the being is
> what it is. They are original if they are *involved necessarily in the possibility* of
> such a being, but *contingent* if it is possible for the being to exist of itself without
> them. (Rel:23)

The possibility of human susceptibility to the moral law (i.e., the possibility of reason's susceptibility to itself, and to be self-constituted through
the will, however finite) will remain contingent upon a definite set of
circumstances, the particular circumstances (and origins) of its 'nature'.
Reason itself must be constituted (anterior to its self-constitution) in order
for the occurrence of the ethical to be possible.

In contradistinction to the predisposition to the good, the *Religion* also
demarcates the propensity for evil in human nature. A propensity is defined
as the subjective ground of the possibility of an inclination, so far as humankind is liable to it. Here again there are three: the weakness of the
human heart in its observance of moral maxims (the frailty of human
nature), the propensity for mixing unmoral with moral motivating causes
(impurity), and the propensity to adopt evil maxims (wickedness).

Kant is quick to differentiate these propensities from the nature of the
predisposition to good. "[We] can call this a natural propensity to evil, and
as we must, after all, ever hold man himself responsible for it we can further
call it a *radical* innate evil in human nature (yet none the less brought upon
us by ourselves)" (Rel:28). Nevertheless, unlike those related to good, these
cannot be taken as a natural predisposition. They are not "bound up with
the possibility of human nature" and therefore are not original but deriva-
tive. "The original predisposition (which no other than man himself could
have corrupted, if he is to be held responsible for this corruption) is a
predisposition to good" (Rel:38). Evil therefore resolves itself into a straying
from human origins. The willing of the moral law amounts to a return,
perhaps a repetition. Morality is already original to humankind; it is a matter
of it being chosen ("reason has a respect for reason's law": humankind
rechoosing itself).

Yet if this reveals the ground of human susceptibility to the moral law (which involves both our capacity to "give ourselves" the law as well as to understand and respond to it), nevertheless it cannot explain the primordiality of good over evil. It is at this point in the *Religion* that Kant again acknowledges the limits and dissolution of such investigation into the origins of morality. The fact that humans *have* such a possibility now confronts the analysis as an "incomprehensibility."

> There is one thing in our soul which we cannot cease from regarding with the highest wonder, when we view it properly, and for which admiration is not only legitimate but even exalting, and that is the original moral predisposition itself. (Rel:44)

However "awesome" and "incomprehensible" this matter is, Kant is emphatic that it is not miraculous, its appearance notwithstanding. Kant states that a miracle is something "in the world the operating laws of whose causes are, and must remain, absolutely unknown to us" (Rel:81). Now, it is just the operational laws of the moral principle which were exposed in the first "set" of answers to the problem of the moral principle's possibility. There is nothing "miraculous" involved in Kant's renewed "plunge into the transcendent"—it remains, he claims, principled and we should not miss its *significance*. Indeed, it is just the latter which justifies the transcendence of virtue: both in its "reciprocal rejoinder" with the past and the future it portends, now fully cognizant of the rational requisites of the modern. In fact, Kant here turns again decisively back to the precedent of the Typic and its confidence in the "sublime analogy" of the Newtonian model: this moral origin is no more incomprehensible, Kant claimed, than the laws of gravity (Rel: 129n–130n). It cannot be said, then, that there is something simply mysterious involved in the grounds of morality:

> We shall not be entitled to number among the holy mysteries the *grounds* of morality, which are inscrutable to us; for we can thus classify only that which we can know but which is incapable of being communicated publicly, whereas, though morality can indeed be communicated publicly, its cause remains unknown to us. Thus freedom, an attribute of which man becomes aware through the determinability of his will by the unconditioned moral law, is no mystery because the knowledge of it can be *shared* with everyone; but the ground, inscrutable to us, of this attribute is a mystery because this ground *is not given* to us as an object of knowledge. (Rel:129)

Now as has been seen, since the second *Critique*, Kant had fought to preserve the distinction between the grounds of morality and their dogmatic investment—what, recall, he referred to as "the mysticism of practical reason"—that would confuse signs and symbols (CprR:73). Nonetheless, at the same time, as the postulates of practical reason had demonstrated, reason inevitably turned symbolic in the practical realm through investment in practical cathexes. If such symbolization was a necessary accompaniment of the will's determination in the transition from syntax to semantics, such symbols could not be regarded as axioms of practical reason—if they did reveal the complex historionics in which consciousness of the moral law became possible. Hence results the complicated status of the sacred it sub-tends, not to speak of the complex field of symbolization—both principled and hermeneutic—that constitutes the objectivities of the public realm for Kant (and modernity). We have indeed traced them throughout; conceptu-ally underdetermined (*qua* symbolic) and potentially overdetermined (*qua* cathectic), the extensions at stake can never be without risk. And doubtless the risks here are both theoretical and real, epistemic and ideological.

To grasp this remainder nonetheless will require grasping that other sym-bolic effect within the Kantian text. If the schematism of analogy had evidently provided the means for articulating the categorical imperative, it is the other form of the aesthetic, the *sublime*—which Kant admitted was both somewhat "farfetched and the result of some subtle reasoning" (CJ:121) that guides his articulation of its motivation. Against the eudamonistic bases of classical morality constructed in one form or another on the basis of pleasure, Kant's account of respect for the law was to be based instead precisely in denying pleasure the highest position, in favor of respect for *another* (sublime) order at the heart of the self, a good beyond the egoistic goods that had threatened the mechanistic reductions of philosophical modernism. This account in ap-pealing to a strangeness at the heart of consciousness, resulted in a semantics and an 'experience' whose 'other' order approximated the allegorical rather than analogical. The experience of respect in this regard "places before our eyes the sublimity of our own nature" (CprR:90). In fact the (transcendental) aesthetics of respect is carried out precisely in the same terms as those of the experience of the sublime, as characterized in the third *Critique*. Notwith-standing morality's inevitable systematic connection with happiness, first and foremost the "effect of this [moral] law on feeling is merely humiliation (*Demütigung*)" (CprR:81).

While this phenomenon has been the subject of a number of critical and especially psychoanalytic analyses,[25] connecting the account of repetition it entails to the superstitions of neurotics, Kant's struggle was precisely against the leveling of the 'sacred' to such fantastic projections (or to a meaningless asceticism). In both cases he declared "we must be attuned to quiet contem-plation and our judgment be completely free" (CJ:122). The Stoic remnants of this event are perhaps equally manifest—not only in Kant's Stoic retreat into the self but equally in the cataleptic moment that overcomes the uncertainty accompanying ethical egoism and the irrationality of the passions.[26] Not without irony perhaps, in these texts Kantian ascetics is closer to Nietzsche's than to Freud's. He strongly distinguishes, consequently, the sublime from "submission, prostration, and a feeling of impotence" (CJ:122). Indeed Kant's "symbolics" were intended to pave the way for a refusal of both fanaticism and deism: like the "more dangerous" of dogmatisms of materialism to which Kant opposes them, all are transcendentally "subreptive"—in short illicit reductions. The heterogeneity which divides the subject from within, on Kantian terms, could not be so readily reduced without delusion. Indeed this heterogeneity marks a sublimity which announces, without succumbing to its own incomprehensibility. Unlike the Hobbesean protocols that Freud still shares, there is ultimately no material 'law' that ultimately governs Kantian desire and it is precisely this which announces its sublimity;[27] announcing the possibility of a *Stimmung* beyond the *chaos* of nature (CJ:99). Still the intelligibility of this event remains always and in this respect still not without its own "plunge into the transcendent."

7. The Dangers of Civil Society and the Remainder of Modern Friendship

This final incomprehensible sublimity completes and, at the same time, limits the attempt to expound the possibility of the ethical domain. It also constitutes an enigmatic placeholder of the sacred in the Kantian system. While insistent upon the differentiation of the moral and the miraculous, in speaking in turn of the *ground* of this possibility, Kant has been unable to fully affirm their total heterogeneity. In the *Religion* text, the moral predisposition itself, in light of the incomprehensible and miraculous nature of its ground, announces a divine origin—albeit only by serving as the inauguration to "the holy mysteries" (Rel:129). Seen in this perspective, the problem becomes one of clarifying why "it is absolutely incomprehensible to our reason how beings can be *created* to a free use of our powers" (Rel:133). The problem then is again one of the origins of the finite, albeit origins that are still to be seen from the site of the finite itself. And, in this regard, we are not far from the ambiguities of the *Opus postumum*.[28]

Still, if Kant is surely correct in saying that the consideration of the possibility of ethicality does not detract from the purity of ethical laws, nor cast any doubt on their a priori origin, it does nonetheless lead into considerations on the tenuous *nature* of its determination. Even if Kant's *Religion* text opens with a proclamation of morality's self-subsistency, this does not mean that this proclamation holds for all possibilities, but only under the circumstances (the contingencies) of *its* own possibility. Thus, the purity of rational analytics is subjected to the disequilibrium of its own origins. In this regard, the possibility of law's subjective significance (the problematic of a rational 'faith', reason's relation with the infinite) opens up a domain in which the practical becomes interspersed through the symbolic, —now, *not* as the *prius* or metaphysical *arche,* but as the *telos* of rational endeavor, the infinite "striving of Reason," before the dispersed remainder of transcendence: a transcendence whose nature remains nonetheless fully transcendent. In one sense, it is just this dispersion of the theological across the domain of the finite —'dispersion' because the sacred remains an ineluctable and yet unencompassable object —that remains Kant's legacy. Writers after Kant will continuously grapple with its instability. Reason and the sacred, *Glauben und Wissen,* while never simply reducible to or interchangeable with one another, will be inevitably linked by a certain underdeterminability, difference, and excess.

Again, this transformation may in one sense be explicitly tracked in Kant's development. Kant's precritical *Lectures on Ethics* rejected the view he identified with Zeno that virtue had no motive that could be identified with the senses and that virtue itself could be self-satisfying. Instead, Kant claimed, the Gospels alone could provide a pure and adequate account, insofar as the ideal of happiness beyond this world provides both "the purist morality as well as the strongest motive —that of happiness as blessedness" (Ethics:10). The second *Critique,* however, in accord with the analytic of moral imperatives, categorically denied such an independent motive for morality, thus bringing Kant in closer proximity to Zeno —and yet without simply succumbing to Zeno's dogmatism. Never in fact did Kant hold that the bond between the right and the good is broken. It is precisely Zeno's dogmatism that Kant rejects from the outset, arguing by counterexample that were virtue sufficient unto itself "all men would be virtuous" (Ethics:10). And yet, if it is to remain rational, i.e., if morality is to accord with the (universal) logical syntax of obligation, virtue cannot simply be (conditionally) motivated or determined by happiness. Hence the complex hermeneutic and refiguration of the ancient narratives that ensues regarding both the nature and possibility of morality.

For Kant himself, however, one thing remains certain in this search; only under the auspices of the specific circumstances which constitute its possibility (logical, epistemological, metaphysical) can it be said that for man, who despite a corrupted heart yet possesses a good will, there remains hope of a return to the good from which he has strayed. (Rel:39)

While affirming this hope of a return to origin(s)—and that the 'transcendence' in question might be rendered intelligible—as possibility, Kant at the same time was forced, even in making room for faith, and in order to avoid dogmatism, to introduce the end of dogmatic metaphysics, indeed the end of theological metaphysics: "Cosmo-theology" or "Onto-theology" as he called it. In all this he reaffirmed his modernist commitments—his piety notwithstanding. And yet, against these commitments, a hermeneutics of humanity is ventured in his work which, while not closed off in advance, also cannot be guaranteed. In this respect Kant opened both the logical space of such a hermeneutics and the problem of its heterogeneity. This conception of humanity, after all, was developed with cognizance of modernist (Humean) skepticism, but likewise with cognizance of the meaning and implications of the theoretics at stake in modern science—as the problematic of the third antinomy ultimately demonstrates in opening up a sphere where freedom might again be ventured.

It is doubtless important to emphasize—perhaps especially granted the *Atheismus-streit* that would haunt Fichte in his wake—that while Kant's answer to that dilemma doubtless does, as he hoped, effectively provide room for his symbolics for 'faith' (and hence Kant's hermeneutics of the *symbolae fidae,* as the creeds used to be called), "providing room" is exactly what it does. Never, even across the landscape of his 'religious' writings, does he allow himself to make this venture safe: both theoretically and practically Kant had acknowledged Reason's propensity to stray. Hence the problem, as we have seen, of not only the evils but also the ideologies of reason. The failure of metaphysics (the search for a total schematization of Being) and the failure of modernism (that totalization as determinately mechanistic) here coincide. And, Kant, consequently, was unable either to ultimately affirm or deny the possibility he worked to secure. To return to the problem of the Typic, he was unable to move fully beyond possibility to actuality; in the end he was able only to truncate both its possibility, its undecidability, and ultimate underdeterminacy. Moreover it was Kant who claimed, writing to Fichte to assist him with the Prussian censors in the publication of the *Attempt at a Critique of all Revelation,* that this extension could be warranted precisely because at stake was (again) a matter of subjective necessity, its propositions always articulated beyond the *literal,*[29] divided already between the spirit and the letter.

The venture in this regard remained "hermeneutic" through and through, yet it was sufficient to open the possibility that Kant had worked to liberate from metaphysics—namely, the possibility that practical reason could not be viewed simply as a regional or adjunct captive of theoretical enquiry, or as a determinate subsumption of the constraints of referential transparency. Nor, finally would the problem of *significance* consequently be excluded from the concept of morality. Like all hermeneutics, here too the presumptions of rational obligation need not be vicious. It is precisely this possibility which is at stake in the claim which radically broke with Western thought that "Pure reason of itself (*für sich*) can be and really is practical," privy to a domain to which it alone has access and which it justifies 'otherwise'—again, not by abandoning either law or nature, but, precisely in this hermeneutic venture that, conjoining principle, interpretation, and narrative, refigures them in the retrieval Kant marks in the "schematism" of analogy itself.

We should be careful, however, to avoid the subreption that would substitute symbol for sign, a priority or interest for a solution, a hermeneutic venture for an axiom: in short, Kant's questioning of the transcendent for an answer, or his "phenomenologies" for a science of metaphysics. While many of the pure speculative expositions and "phenomenologies" that followed in Kant's wake saw it to be such, they remained unmindful of the very critical limits (and the antinomies) by which this phenomenology had been generated. Grasping this antinomial origin of its move from pure syntax to a semantics articulated through symbolics becomes crucial to grasping Kant's accomplishment. No strict deduction of these "possibilities" will be possible and their "analysis" always presupposes synthetic extensions inextricably linked to (if not simply reducible to) subjective conditions (the historicity or facticity) of Reason's obligation. The result articulates the indeterminate 'phantasm' (*Schein*) of freedom's possibility, i.e., the (principle) narrative(s) of morality. We have measured the "reciprocal rejoinder" in this regard with the narratives of Stoicism and his "principled" reply to Burke's skeptical traditionalism.

What is decisive in this again is Kant's internal acknowledgement of the account's hermeneutic status.[30] Kant admitted it from the outset of the critical system, after all; and he admitted it explicitly, as has been seen, in his 1792 letter to Beck. Moreover the practical extension, analogically constructed, as has been seen, relied upon this possibility—the possibility that things could be 'otherwise.' And surely they could have: Christian theology, *inter alia* could, after all, have been substituted with the narratives of a number of "theologies"—precisely in accord with the plurality of the symbol. But nothing would be more unwieldy for those in his wake—as both those hoping to capture Kant's "extension" through a single return to metaphysics as well as those who sought positivistically to dissolve it would attest. For the same reason, however, it would be equally as mistaken to limit the ramifications of Kant's venture simply to the theological as it would be to take him to have rationally substantiated the theological. Instead Kant's venture beyond the requisites of the "literal" would be broader in impact.[31] The theoretical accomplishment at stake is precisely the exposition of how principle and symbol, the analytic and hermeneutic might (and inevitably do) interact—"pluralistically" as the third *Critique* will ultimately allow (CJ:140). While Kant had insisted upon the distinction between principle and narration (*Erzählung*) [A835/B864], in the same way that he had demanded the distinction of reason and tradition, we have witnessed the complex transformation and the venture that results in the exposition of both.

8. Critique, History, and Dialogue: The *Humaniora* and the Nonsubstitutability of Individuality

Having noted this advance and both the complexity and the symbolics which underwrite Kant's venture we would miss its full interpretive effect (and peril) were we not likewise to trace the breadth of its impact vis à vis classical accounts of reason and community, a point where we again encounter Kant's transformation of tradition. Its emphasis on the rational status of the will had certainly depended on a split between the 'inside' and the 'outside', between reason and nature—yet as has become evident, not without invoking what it could no longer rely upon. Based still upon the account of the *lex naturae* Cicero, for example, could appeal directly to what *De Officiis* calls a *communis humani generis societas* as a concept which expresses the supreme moral law: human beings should care for one another just because each is a human being—a common law to which everyone is subject.[32] Kant's exposition of the categorical imperative, as has been seen, similarly expresses such Stoic respect for *humanitas* as an end in itself, undertaken in accord with universal reason. Recent commentators (e.g., Pierre Hadot) have reemphasized the Stoic precedents of Kant's formulations.[33] Moreover, the *Religion's* predispositions had encountered it again in the predisposition to humanity and mutual love. In his treatise on friendship Cicero could accordingly proceed to claim that nature spurs us to friendship through an innate principle which causes us without a regard for our own benefit to love anyone who manifests virtue. We are moved to love their virtue for its own sake, "by the feeling of love which it generates"—and thus it is that "good will and charity come into being when we have seen clear signs of virtue."[34] Such conditional limitations violated Kant's transformation of the *lex naturae,* which requires a 'charity' and respect that are unrestricted. As the second formulation had made clear, categorical "reformulations" of this ideal required respect for humanity as a rational Idea and not as a generic nature (cf. Found:49). And what had been given ideal content in the second formulation became in the third, the kingdom of end, a *communio* of hope.

If Kant's account fundamentally alters the classical order of reasons, transforming habituation into rational deliberation and love into respect, no more significant transformation will occur than in the culmination of classical virtue theory's account of community and friendship. Here respect for humanity (*humanitas*), which Kant too identified with friendship—even categorically transformed—will openly acknowledge the historical uncertainties under which it would now take place. Here Kant attests as well to the dangers, to use Machiavelli's term, of *fortuna* and such dependence on community, the uncertainty of civil society and the problem of private judgment—and *inter alia,* a return of the vagaries which haunted the first *Critique's* account of judgment. Intimacy, what the medievals had called "tenderness," now becomes transformed into a certain confidence regarding private judgment in a world respite with danger (the very dangers, recall, that Herder had likewise acknowledged). With Cicero the connection between *honestum* and the public good remained homogeneous: that is, the idea of *communis humani generis societas* could be viewed as the culmination of the law of nature. Kant denies this position first on the basis of the naturalistic fallacy: one cannot deduce universal principles from (empirical) nature. Utilitarians would skeptically attempt to conventionally reconstitute such universality by the calculation of utility, a procedure Cicero himself denied, on the basis that friendship was too rich for such calculations.[35] In the end "nature" and virtue for Kant remained strictly opposed to one another—indeed antinomial. The move from barbarism to culture would be instituted on insecure foundations. Nonetheless, not only formal insufficiency, but the "natural" danger of society itself dictates such demurrals as well. The common good has withdrawn: civil society was no longer simply a realm of virtue but of power.

As Arendt realized, as a result of this history, "we are wont to see friendship solely as a phenomenon of intimacy." But insofar as we limit it thereby "it is hard for us to understand the political relevance of friendship." Thus it is hard to grasp that when Aristotle claimed that *philia* is one of the fundamental requirements for the well-being of the *polis,* he was speaking of the absence of faction and civil war and friendship's role in the latter. "But for the Greeks the essence of friendship consisted in discourse. They held that the constant interchange of talk united citizens in a *polis*."[36] Roman citizenship added to this a certain cosmopolitanism, a certain recognition of the universality, transforming Greek *philanthropia* into *humanitas,* which is a "political background [that] distinguishes Roman *humanitas* from what the moderns mean by humanity, by which they commonly mean a mere effect of education."[37] Her argument moreover proceeds to claim that Kant had lost all this (while Lessing retrieved it), transforming the plurality and dialogue of friendship constituted in gladness, "entirely permeated by pleasure in the other person and what he says."[38] All this gets sacrificed, for Arendt, to the univocally decidable criteria of the categorical imperative, one she condemns both for its "inhumanity" and its "concept of one single truth."[39] Surely, granted Kant's emphasis upon the search for a "determinate formula" in these matters, something of this is true. And yet, beyond both the "hermeneutics" that accompanies Kant's principle and his own amplifications of the "aesthetics" of practical reason, Arendt's claim perhaps misses the specificity and the ambiguity of Kant's own return to friendship, which is especially evident at the end of the *Tugendlehre*—and perhaps thereby she misses its theoretical fertility.[40]

The 1797 *Metaphysics of Moral's* distinction between part one (the *Rechtslehre*) and part two (the *Tugendlehre*) had already acknowledged the split between the internal and the external, individual and community, in the practical domain. In the *Rechtslehre*, Kant had defined justice in terms of external laws (again affording univocally determinate application and denying *inter alia* the idea of a conflict of obligations) consistent with the coexistence of wills in accordance with laws of freedom. Against this backdrop, however, the *Tugendlehre's* account of friendship takes on an ominous acknowledgement of the predicament of civil society. Nothing in Kant's theoretical considerations, neither formal nor symbolical, prepares us in this regard for the *Tugendlehre's* conclusions. These conclusions, impelled by necessities which remain more steadfastly historical than 'theoretical', once again fill out the transcendental aesthetic of practical reason, delineating now the precariousness of its intersubjective field.

> Moral friendship (as distinguished from sensitive [*ästhetisch*] friendship) is the complete confidence of two persons in the mutual openness of their private judgments and sensations, as far as such openness can subsist with mutual respect for one another.
> Man is a being intended for society (even though he is also unsociable). In the cultivation of the social state he strongly feels the need to open himself up

to others (even without thereby aiming at anything). But on the other hand, he is also constrained and admonished by his fear of the abuse which others might make of this disclosure of his thoughts; and he therefore sees himself compelled to lock up within himself a good part of his judgments (particularly those concerning other people). He might like to talk with someone about what he thinks of the people with whom he associates, what he thinks of the government, religion, and so on; but he must not risk it because others, by cautiously holding back their own judgment, might make use of his remarks to his own detriment. (Tugend:138)

Friendship makes possible the bond of humanity under the real (historical) conditions of civil society, conditions which require as much risk and venture as the venture of freedom itself, a step beyond tutelage. In a full analysis, it would be necessary to investigate all that Kant invests in respect for humanity in one's own person and in the Other—a matter which combines both considerations on tutelage, and on its empowerment, with those of morality and the critical requisites of *objectivität*. Here the experience of freedom (not to speak of the experience of detraditionalization itself) precludes a simple return to the model of the Greek *polis* and its communal *praxis*—which is still not to say that detraditionalization makes community irrelevant.[41] It is decisive that moral friendship—unlike Kant's refiguration of the ancients' love of humanity in the second formulation of the categorical imperative—is judged by Kant to be no mere ideal. If the ideal requisites of the moral law had led him to conclude that "in men all good is defective,"—if, that is, "man is certainly unholy enough," turning morality, to use Adorno's term, utopian in the same moment that it turned it 'social' (ND:258)—the same cannot be said of friendship (CprR:80,90). "This (purely moral) friendship is no mere ideal, but (like the black swan) actually exists now and then for its perfection" (Tugend:139). It will be necessary to see friendship in this regard, as the *Anthropology* says, as a domain of "mixed goods," complicated by their forms, and endangered by evils that threaten both from without and within. It will likewise be important to grasp the history in which Kant writes to investigate more fully the significance of such mixed forms within their own history.

Indeed we can measure Kant's transformation here by considering post-Kantian elevations of universality, iterability, and communicability as the condition of objectivity and truth, all of which (doubtless) continue Kant's own investments in modern accounts of the rational based upon deductive exemplars. Bacon, for example, could say of friendship in his essay on this topic that it supports judgment by virtue of "faithful councel." Kant would not be far behind in claiming that communication between friends is "a human necessity for the correction of our judgments" (Ethics:206). Still, neither of them had simply equated truth with communicability, as Fichte would demand in the practical realm, in accord with modern epistemic constraints on objectivity. Moreover, the "equation" would in fact lead Fichte into a dilemma, committed both to the importance of conscience ("conscience never errs and cannot err") and the demand that the fallibilism of finitude must give way to the constraints of intersubjective communication, insofar as "the more extended this intercommunication is, the more does truth (objectivity considered) gain and I likewise" (SE:183,260).

The Fichtean equation of intercommunication with certainty and security, anticipatory of Popperian iterability, is, if clear in the privileging of conscience, perhaps one step away from the dissolution of private judgment—and not only in those cases for which demonstrable, "public" adjudication is lacking—but equally in those cases which motivate Kant's (proto-Foucaudian) admonitions concerning "man's . . . fear of the abuse which others might make of this disclosure of his thoughts" in the public sphere (Tugend:138).[42] Without openly acceding to the requisites of dialogue, Kant had perhaps realized what was at stake in turning against the classical metaphysics of friendship based upon similarity. As he put it in the *Lectures on Ethics*, not identity but "difference of thought is a stronger bond for friendship, for then the one makes up for the deficiencies of the other" (Ethics:207). The *Tugendlehre* would perhaps grasp this need for 'difference' even more strongly, precisely in its concern for the dangers of the public realm. If truth requires communicability in order to gain 'objectivity', the latter cannot guarantee it. This difference itself is what makes dialogue both necessary and dangerous—and dangerous with respect to the recognition of the Good. As the *Anthropology* states:

> Man must . . . be *educated* to the good. But those who are supposed to educate him are again men who are themselves involved in the crudity of nature and are supposed to bring about what they themselves are in need of. (Anth:186)

Indeed, Kant adds, even scientific progress is similarly limited and "fragmentary (according to time) and has no guarantee against regression, with which it is always threatened by intervals of revolutionary barbarism" (Anth:187).[43]

Still, neither should we miss Kant's transformation on the idea of *humanitas* itself, an idea, which, as Arendt rightly realized, itself enters the Kantian text under the problem of education. First, it is not insignificant to note that the second *Critique* centers its analysis of education as a model for morality on a Renaissance humanist, that is, on Montaigne—a matter doubly complicated, granted both Kant's and Montaigne's shared skepticism regarding the (modern) dangers of the political and the importance of friendship in its lapse. In fact the problem of education is variously analyzed as a question of the status of education and the ancients, a question then of the impact of the ancients upon the moderns, and equally then a question of the status of historical knowledge, a discipline for which the lectures on *Education* itself had denied we had proper knowledge. In fact, as becomes apparent in Kant's *Logic* and in the first *Critique*'s Dialectic, the development of such an epistemics of the history of pure reason is underway in Kant's later work.

The *Logic* assigns the *humaniora*, humanistic studies, to instruction in what serves the cultivation of taste according to the standards of the ancients. As such, *humaniora* retains a link with the *polis, paideia,* and the political insofar as it involves the unification of science and taste and thereby "furnishes the communicability and urbanity in which humaneness consists" (Logic:51). Nonetheless this reliance upon the ancients is not without its dangers, which specifically require reason and philosophy to avoid mere "polyhistory," "a cyclopsean erudition that lacks one eye, the eye of philosophy"—and thus becomes a domain without determinate limits.

Moreover as such, insofar as the *humaniora* takes place under the aegis of education, as the *Logic* itself explicitly likewise imparts, it resumes the method of the *dialogue*. Rational education requires that one question. As simply a matter of memorizing it involves catechizing, a method "valid only for empirical and historical cognition [while] the dialogic method, however, [is alone valid] for rational cognition" (Logic:150; cf. Ethics:81). And it is clear that the conjunction of the criteria of universalizability, communicability, and the kingdom of ends in this regard renders the categorical imperative itself a dialogical principle. This is not to say that rational cognition is then devoid of historical connection. Reemphasizing the model of optics, which generates the first *Critique*'s model of conceptualization, in the *Logic* Kant turns this figure historical and conceptualization into a rational process within the field of historical horizons. In the first *Critique* Kant had claimed that all concepts are standpoints for a finite intellect, and that "the sum of all the possible objects of our knowledge appear to us to be a plane with an apparent horizon—namely that which in its sweep comprehends it all, and which has been entitled by us the idea of unconditioned totality" (A760/B788). In the *Logic,* before introducing the *humaniora* and precisely in order to extend and demarcate our cognition, Kant proposes a number of rules that will "determine in advance the absolute horizon of the entire human race (as to past and future) and in particular also determine the place occupied by our silence in the horizon of all cognition" (Logic:48).

Discussing the latter, he speaks in terms of a "critique of reason of history and historical knowledge, a universal spirit which goes into human cognition comprehensively."

Here too, however, we should not miss Kant's own neoplatonic accounts of the development of the critical system itself, precisely as it impacts upon the status of Kantian critique, the question of tradition, and the status of its humanist remainder. Insofar as Kant had transformed nature into idea, the moral law into an ought, humanity and the kingdom of ends not into a real event in which we participate, but into what we can hope for, the transformation between the ancients and the moderns had been decisive. This conflict is not simply a matter of the rejection of the concept of tradition, however. Not only is its archive still active in Kant, but we even find the remnants of the naturalism of which Kant accused Herder. Kant himself claims that "a power higher than human reason" figures its development—a certain return of neoplatonic ideas. The history of reason is itself understood as an internally developing schema—its own internal original 'germ' posited in the first *Critique*'s account of architectonics:

> Systems seem to be formed in the manner of lowly organisms, through a *generatio aequivoca* from the mere confluence of assembled concepts, at first imperfect, and only gradually attaining to completeness, although they one and all have had their schema, as the original germ, in the sheer self-development of reason. Hence, not only is each system articulated in accordance with an idea, but they are one and all organically united in a system of human knowledge, and so as admitting of an architectonic of all human knowledge, which, at the present time, in view of the great amount of material that has been collected, or which can be obtained from the ruins (*Ruinen*) of ancient systems, is not only possible, but would not indeed be difficult. (A835/B863)

Moreover, there is in this a certain affirmation of rational tradition as a continuous descent of generations of reason, a "march of human affairs . . . worthy of life and well being." As the "Idea for a Universal History" put it:

> It remains strange that the earlier generations appear to carry through their toilsome labor only for the sake of the later, to prepare them a foundation on which the later generations could erect the higher edifice which was Nature's goal, and yet that only the latest of the generations should have the good fortune to inhabit the building on which a long list of their ancestors had (unintentionally) labored without being permitted to partake of the fortune which they had prepared. However puzzling this may be, it is necessary if one assumes that a species of animals should have reason, and, as a class of rational beings each of whom dies while the species is immortal should develop their capacities to perfection.[44]

Still, (consistent with the argument against Herder) these ruins do not provide an ultimate vindication. Since metaphysics itself has proved deceptive, critique of dialectical illusion is required for all such narratives in order to "prevent the devastations of which a lawless speculative reason would otherwise be inevitably guilty" (A849/B877). Kant's retrieval of the logic of analogy, specifically explicated in *reflective* judgment, and in contrast to the logic of (deductive) subsumption of determinate judgment, likewise remained fully attuned to the former's fragility, its danger—and its (transcendental) illusions.

The *humaniora* would involve less a memory, an imitation, than a dialogue of legitimation carried out within the ruins of the ancient systems: it is doubtless just such a dialogue concerning practical reason (and the *humaniora* in general) that we have traced throughout here. The result, however, brings such principled 'deductions' into closer proximity with the narratives Kant hoped to exclude from his account of the rational. Moreover it does so by another "natural predisposition" Kant typically opposes both to determinate judgment and universality, that is wit (*Witz*) (Anth:89). Although wit is always more a matter of play (*Spiel*) than the business of knowledge, it is precisely in the interface of imagination and judgment that wit emerges, emphasizing both the talent and 'abandonment' of rational individuality.

It is doubtless just this complex link between the *humaniora*, the symbolics of laws, and the ineliminability of individuality that would continuously link in turn the problem of interpretation (or characterization) and the republican idea in those immediately following Kant; e.g., von Humboldt, Schleiermacher, and Schlegel.[45] Reason, that is, would increasingly become linked both to the 'speculative' possibilities of authentic *Individualität* and the internal limitations (epistemic, moral, and political) of 'law' itself—and firmly thereby to liberalism. Moreover, without simply denying the 'transcendence' at stake in the 'sacred'—indeed remaining fully aware of its role in the symbolization and interpretation of the law—all three would likewise be quick (in ways Fichte was not, as will be seen) to ground their problematic status *through* the articuleme of individuality, i.e., neither simply by means of tradition nor the canons of 'objectivity' nor the practices of the public sphere—fully aware of the underdeterminacy at stake and the venture indicated therein.

Surely the legacy of Kant's transformation of the concept of individuality also becomes in this regard a central effect of his encounter with the ruins of tradition: an event in which universal and individual can no longer simply be claimed to coalesce. If, that is, "man becomes man by education," if indeed "he is merely what education makes of him" (Ed:6) it is also true that opposition between individual and society is both dangerous and "inevitable" (Ed:27) and that "one generation may have to pull down what another had built up" (Ed:14). This helps explain the complex transformation by which the *Sumum Bonum* becomes now *both* a dialogical transformation of the *lex naturae* and a matter of freedom. And both are at stake in Kant's description of the goal of education: "the education of a personal character, of a free being, who is able to maintain himself, and to take his proper place in society keeping at the same time a proper sense of his own individuality" (Ed:30). Or, as Montaigne put it in his own essay "On Education," similarly disparaging the method of simple memorization and affirming Cicero's claim that the authority of those who teach is often an obstacle to those who want to learn, "Let him be taught not so much the histories as how to judge them."[46]

As has been seen, for all his differences with Herder's account of tradition, in the question of application Kant remained in close proximity. Moreover in retaining history as teleological and "organic," the accounts were not simply uncommensurable—though Kant's institution of reflective judgment had transformed the latter into an idea, thereby taking his distance from it. Reflective judgment, after all, remained insurpassably linked to the individual—and precisely thereby to the problem of application. Herder originally denied neither the importance of application nor the problem of the threat of traditions to individuality, as has been seen. Only after 1806 did the account of origins based upon tradition and nation become identified with the notion of a political struggle. Thereby an account which had originated in the constitution and translation of tradition finally, by a certain transcendental subreption, excludes it. The *humaniora* after all had always required the acknowledgement of the foreign (at least in the sense of the classical) as essential to understanding oneself, all mediated through the linchpin of reflective judgment. Here Kant's account becomes less a legalism or a dualism than an account of the social interaction of "incorporated" agents, a dialogue of legitimation and passion, symbol and symbiosis. The result, as Arendt emphasized, is an account of judgment as a realm of an extended art of thinking (*eine erwerterte Dunkungsart*) that is both the acknowledgment of other conceptual standpoints—and thereby the opening of a universal horizon (CJ:§40). It is precisely here moreover that the third *Critique* had encountered the *humaniora*, articulated between "the universal feeling of sympathy and the ability to engage universally in intimate communication" (CJ:§40). But we would miss the importance of the conjunct if we did not see Kant's account in its richness: this interrelation of sympathy and communicability, is, after all, just the complexity that has emerged in Kant's account of friendship, the remainder of an ancient inheritance that underlies

(and interrelates) both virtue and the rational, the hermeneutics of transcendence and the analytics of principle combining—as even Aristotle's
treatise did—love and respect, affection and communicability, benevolence
and equality, reciprocity and "universality."[47] If the categorical imperative
had formulated the necessary conditions of such a universal, only this
combination could provide its ultimate sufficiency, an opening constituted
dialogically in the *Wechsel* of history and judgment, education and culture.
In the same way that dialogics or acroamatics, i.e., philosophy, augments
mathesis, so judgment augments analysis—and finally politics augments
morality. And in all cases hermeneutics, an *ars inveniendi*, augments critique; the question of law is always a question of the relation to this extension, its plunge into the "beyond," and in both respects its symbolization
and institution.

Kant's reflective judgment would accordingly impact both his political
theory and his account of community, providing laws for the institution of
participation in the public sphere. In the third *Critique* this occurs explicitly in the account of teleological judgment, and by analogy with nature in
the teleological sense, since in legal organizations "each member in such
a whole should be not merely a means, but also a purpose" (CJ:§66) and
yet without thereby *determining* their ultimate social forms. Hence it can
be claimed once more that the kingdom of ends will be symbolic, equivocal, an ambiguous *politeia*. The result similarly shows itself in Kant's republican arguments for representational government (since "every form of
government which is not representative is, properly speaking, without
form") which equally demand a separation of executive and legislative
powers (OH:96), denying both pure democracy and pure despotism. If a
republican form of government is that which preserves both law and the
free play of the symbolic order, the latter will again require a prudence
(OH:125) that will draw on both the equivocal narratives of nature and
history's "contradictory examples."

9. Beyond 'Formalism'

Kant's emphasis upon the single individual as a process of rationalization
anticipates later accounts in German Idealism of tradition and virtue as
matters of individualization and experiment, figuration and judgment—the
plasticität of virtue. It would, however, require acknowledging once more
the question of the determinability and interpretation of lawfulness. This is
the problem of Kant's "formalism," as Hegel already argued (WdL:764ff.).

But rightly seen, this recognition and its complication is already at stake in Kant's dialectic itself. Hence arises, as we have seen, the complex relationships between immanence and transcendence, history as genus and history as idea, organics and heuristics, risk and warrant, judgment and "danger."

Equally, the "Idea of a Universal History From a Cosmopolitan Point of View" had in a sense set up Hegel's problematic in its opening paragraph, trading upon a distinction the Transcendental Dialectic had already made between historical and rational knowledge. The "prose" discovered in the narrations of history is a matter of "the play of freedom" albeit, Kant says, one which gives us hope that out of its chaos we may discern a regular movement in it.[48] The problem is a provocative one, however. For while it is the occasion for hope, this great world stage (*grosse Weltbühne*) makes it impossible to suppress a certain "indignation" granted vanity, malice, folly, and destructiveness. The great world stage is then a certain tragicomedy already for Kant. And "since the philosopher cannot press upon any [conscious] individual purpose among men in their great drama, there is no other expedient for him except to try to see if he can discern a natural purpose in this idiotic course of things human."[49]

We should not miss the (interpretive) play—indeed the *Wechsel*—of teleologies which has been at stake in these developments. A footnote in the *Grundlegung* from Kant's original account of the analogization accompanying the threefold formulation of the categorical imperative brings these together:

> Teleology considers nature as a realm of ends; morals regards a possible realm of ends as a realm of nature. In the former the realm of ends is a theoretical idea for the explanation of what actually exists. In the latter is a practical idea for bringing about that which is not actually real. (Found:55)

As became evident, both were made possible by the extensions of reflective judgment, which is, as the *Logic* once more claimed, and perhaps finally made evident, the effect of analogization itself: "Reflective judgment has only subjective validity, for the general to which it proceeds is empirical generality only—a mere analagon of the logical" (136).

Doubtless this complexity itself explicates the "ruins of ancient systems" which Kant had insisted haunt the history of pure reason and from which his own architectonic emerges (A835/B863). What is clear is the incursion of both: that Kant's edifice depends upon the ancient ruins, critically incorporates its elements, and transfigures its result in a complex hermeneutic of principles.

3. On the Rights of Nature

I do not know any substantive word under which the actual and operative activities, thought in the spiritual world, and motion in the corporeal world, could be comprehended with so little constraint as they are under the concept of force, power, organ. With the word, 'organic force' one signifies at the same time the inner and outer, the spiritual and the corporeal. But it is still only an expression, for we do not understand what force is, nor do we claim to have explained the word 'body' by it.

—Herder[1]

Spinoza is everywhere in the background, like fate in Greek tragedy.

—Schlegel[2]

The self is to encounter in itself something heterogeneous, alien, and to be distinguished from itself.

—Fichte[3]

Nature once rebuffed soon returns to claim her rights.

—Schiller[4]

We have an earlier revelation than any written one—nature. [Apart from this, philosophy] has no other way than to strive to orient itself historically and to take as its source and guiding principle the *tradition* to which it was referred earlier with similar results.

—Schelling[5]

1. Nature's Dissonance

The very term 'Nature'—which we now hear, beyond all 'terminology' in the strict sense, as the *dissonance* of 'Nature'—doubtless still requires explanation in a time that has seemingly determined the logic of explanation and completed its Romantic excursions. As a result, the semantics of this term, one which historically forced the *abandonment* of ontology for semantics itself, is complex.[6] The dissonant "conceptual" remainder of Nature becomes divided again between what was once called the logic of denotation and the logic of connotation, the result providing a certain irreducible "degree zero" in the "object-language" of rational semiotics. The dissonance that results—as Kant was again perhaps the first to see—could not simply be reduced by appeal to the sciences, either physical or exact. Instead this dissonance revealed a nature that belies all our attempts to be its "law-giver"—a domain that remains, to use Schelling's term, "right outside the limit of the empirical" and thus virtually excluded from the strict demonstrations governing the physics of enlightenment (Natur:37).

Nature in this other sense was already divided by Kant between concept and intuition, the conscious and the unconscious (CJ:§49), and could not be constructed. Its epistemic "constitution" would always be deficient, a representation whose mirroring always lacked bridging principles for what exceeds the limits of representability—the remnants of a subject matter which the ancients had decreed to be the most fundamental 'object' of enquiry. For this other 'nature', which is not an 'object' of representation, there would be no 'phenomenology' in the Kantian sense because it would not give rise to a "figurative synthesis" or schematism that might adequately trace the application of pure concepts to it. Here nature remains always beyond such "application" *sensu stricto:* hence Kant's precedent in exchanging the "lawless speculations" of ontology for transcendental analytics. Still, it was Goethe who had seen the "double function" in Kant's 'delimination': "Kant limited himself intentionally to a certain field and ironically pointed beyond it."[7] As "ironical" as his work might be, however, even Kant was unprepared for the irony awaiting it. The 'counterfactual' that would soon arise, that this other 'semantics' of nature, whose transcendental analogies remain 'figured' beyond all analysis, might in fact remain strictly indisociable from the semantics of 'right', 'law', and 'constitution' itself, would then doubtless further complicate such analyses. For the latter's intelligibility—if not the theoretical exposition of its concept, then at least the 'archaeology' of its ruins—thinkers are still wont to conceptually recur to the development of the Greeks *Physis,* "the history of the concept of nature." Yet such a genealogy itself is not without a certain (but always ironical) complicity with modernity itself, for it seeks the justification of a concept neither in intuition (sensible or rational) nor in deduction, but through its "birth certificate" in the philosophemes or mythemes of the ancient systems.

Vico had perhaps been the first to thus transform the articulation of the natural law by a kind of "return enquiry" into its origins; he thereby intended to overcome not only Hobbesian reductionism, but the limitations of the rational (and mathematically based) reconstructions of those like Grotius, Selden, and Pufendorf who had, he claimed, confused the end result of history with its sacred origin.[8] Similar confusions of ends and origins would doubtless motivate numerous histories and genealogies in Vico's wake. Surely, for example, Marx belongs here as much as Darwin. Even Nietzsche's quarrel with the naïveté of the utilitarians would not be far off. Accounts of the history of the concept of nature in general would similarly attempt to trace the origin or *arché* of this concept, with the hope of overcoming the quarrels in which it had become engulfed. Tracing the descent of this *arché* however would surely be complex, of necessity articulated not only through its ancient semantic markers but equally through modern transformations as arcane as 'ether' and 'phlogiston'.

Accordingly, while originally linked to proper names as ancient as Homer or Lucretius, the history of the concept of nature would encounter transformations as decisive as the modern explanations of Newton or Einstein, as much as it would such seemingly anachronistic retrievals as those of a Winckelmann and Rousseau, or Schiller and Hölderlin. The opposition between nature and myth would as a result be no less complicated than that between being and *logos*, which doubtless itself attests to the Romantic preoccupation with nature, a preoccupation that signaled that neither nature (nor myth) had simply been exhausted in being theoretically reduced or epistemically represented. The Romantics in this regard were perhaps only the last to take the semantic plenitude attached to Nature's *'transcendens'* seriously, an excess attested to even in the diversity of its artifacts. Consider, for instance, the paintings of Casper David Friederich (linked from the outset with Fichte)[9] or Goethe's metaphorics of the *Urphänomenon* of nature or Schelling's attempt to replace Newton with a certain *Schwärmerei* that both acknowledged. Whether it was through Schelling's modern 'analogical' articulation of electricity or Goethe's retrieval of the mystic illuminations of color, both hoped, after all, to discover a speculative meaning which might escape the impending abysses of physicalism. And it is not at all accidental that the "destiny" of the excessive semantics attached to "speculation" and the idea of 'nature' should share a common itinerary, nor that both would seem particularly "untimely," to use Nietzsche's term, in its lapse.

Even the return to the Greeks here would be complicated by this distance. Herder himself before Nietzsche had claimed that the origin of the poetic was not to be found in the rational constructions (and self-confirmations) of neoclassicists but in a more primordial, Dionysian ecstacy they had omitted, the "delirious rapture of the Bacchantes who, struck by the lightening of wine, sang with foaming mouths of the birth and deeds of its inventor."[10] If Winckelmann before him had not yet been this enraptured, he had openly asserted in fact that "Nature, after having passed step by step through cold and heat established herself in Greece"—and that, consequently "the only way for us to become great or, if this be possible inimitable (*unnachahmlich*) is to imitate the ancients (*die Nachahmung der Alten*)."[11] But the complex logic of such a retrieval is even grammatically apparent, its reciprocal rejoinder divided before the repeatable itself. What even Winck-elmann provided, after all, as Schlegel already argued, was a "first basis for a material knowledge through the perception of the absolute difference between the ancient and the modern."[12] Schlegel realized too, however, that in this difference "Winckelmann . . . was the first to demonstrate how to establish an art through the history of its genesis." It is precisely in this double gesture that "there remained a tradition whose contention was to return to the ancients and to nature."[13]

But Winckelmann's position thereby also becomes especially significant, granted the nostalgia regarding traditionism—and the scepter of histori-cism—which descends from it. Herder himself described Winckelmann as an *Originalgenie*, as inimitable as the Greek masters themselves. It is perhaps the complexity of the synthesis of the ancient and the modern that was original. Consistent with Montesquieu's *Spirit of the Laws* (not without its own links with Vico) both Winckelmann and Herder link the rise and fall of nations and cultures not only to politics but equally—and not inconsistent with the transformation of law in modern explanatory science—to geography and climate. But in this respect the Greeks themselves are beyond us precisely insofar as their time and place are both different and inaccessible. To imitate the Greeks now could only mean to imitate Greece inimitably in Dresden, as Winckelmann put it. Others after him would soon repeat this theoretical alternative. Still, while the ground of such an inimitability may lie in a historical encounter with Greece, it also depends upon a natural origin, as he had learned from Hume and Schaftsbury. But this "encounter" itself was not simply a regressive "enquiry" into the passions but an encounter with a nature which in fact could only be enlivened through the *humaniora* them-selves. Indeed, as has been seen, the complexity of this encounter with the Other provides something of a transcendental logic for the *humaniora*. The complicity between the return to the passions and the return to the ancients, these two *archaí*, will be inevitably overdetermined, and not least of all by the figure of nature itself within theoretical modernity.

The time, in any case, in which a speculative discourse on nature seemed an obvious topic for rational exposition now seems entirely remote. Accord-ingly, the fact that Emerson, for example after Coleridge, Wordsworth, and Schelling—wrote address after address on the topic of nature now seems as anachronistic a matter as the steam engines with which nature characteris-tically and mysteriously received metonomyic opposition in his work. And, the same can be said for the complicity of such discourses on nature with the denunciations of the impact of science and industry on the human that are to be found in Carlyle, William Morris, and Marx—which seemingly separates them in turn from Bentham, or Mill, or Helmholtz's attempts to submit the moral sciences to quantification, or, finally, Bergson, Dilthey, and Husserl's radical attempts to distinguish a science of the human from it. All these moves might be dismissed as parts of the dispersion of the nineteenth century's excesses, a period whose omissions from standard accounts satisfies the syntagm "exclusion from the canon" as much as anything perhaps. And yet this dispersion complicates even the seemingly most "uncomplicated" accounts—empirical or otherwise. Surely it is not at all absent even from Strauss's attempt to escape the necessities (and the ancestry) of history by a retrieval of the Greeks and natural right: "Through the discovery of nature, the claim of the ancestral is uprooted; philosophy appeals from the ancestral to the good, to that which is good intrinsically, to that which is good by nature" (NR:91). What seems especially peculiar in this regard however is the tendency of nineteenth-century thinkers—and those they influence—to sift through the ruins of their predecessor's thought. To use another of Kant's figures, theoreticians everywhere continued to undertake "all kinds of mole-tunnels that reason has dug in its futile but confident search for treasures and that make that structure precarious" (A319/B375–76).[14] Such precarious-ness is doubtless still witness—like all search for deferred treasure, as has been seen—to a lingering fascination, or even nostalgia that accompanies the concept of tradition as such.

There can be, in fact, no "canon" of nineteenth-century philosophy, or for its concept of "nature"—or the natural rights that accompany it. Paradoxi-cally though, perhaps nowhere is the legacy of Hegel more evident than in this fact alone: our historical canon typically culminates the modern period with Kant and Hegel, just as Hegel's own lectures on this topic did. And we should add to this legacy both Hegel's elevation of history in general and his dissolution of nature before the figures of Reason. Hence his difficulty in even "hearing" Schelling's protests on behalf of nature, that existence exceeds such rational reduction, or that in nature "we have an earlier revelation than any written one."[15] It is not so accidental that both nineteenth-century com-mitments to the "excess" of nature and that of history—Spirit's fall into time, as Hegel put it—would emerge together, nor that both would overdetermine the reemergence of the concept of tradition. Moreover, it is not accidental that the legacy of this rational dispersion remains still poignantly divided between those who follow Mach, Schlick, and the early Carnap in submitting the appearance of nature to the atomistic figures of physicalism, and those in the wake of Husserl and Heidegger, who still appealed to a transcendence seemingly inseparable from its conceptualization. Nature had been, after all, irrevocably divided between the manifest image of lived experience and its scientific reduction. Both the necessities of the new science of physics and those at stake in the exploration of history would find both impact and support. Moreover, this impact becomes perhaps especially localized in the complicated account of corporeality from Fichte to Schopenhauer and beyond. The unwieldy *topos* of the 'lived body' reconstituted the human body's privilege in the 'divine' cosmogony in the same moment that it attested to the disintegration of the corporeal beyond modern identity. If, as has been argued, the appearance of the lived body provided the concept of the political with a certain criterion of applicability—even the appearance of freedom—like all images it could do so only ambiguously.[16] For this image was divided, like the very term 'incarnation' which appears so often in its discourses, between the ancient transcendences and the modern necessities. The problem of the lived body thus took on an overdetermined status in the detraditionalizations of modernity, a problem with both historical and theoretical overtones. It was not accidental that Marx too had attempted to liberate "human sensuousness" as "embodied time" precisely through a defence of Epicurus and Lucretius.[17]

The penumbra of Romanticism's commitment to "nature" is indeed as complex as all of this, articulated in modernist epistemic paradigms (and dispersed through the latter's dissolution of the passions) all the while openly retrieving both the medieval's accounts of transcendence and the ambiguities which had already threatened the ancients' invocation of atomic play and purpose, primordial *chaos* and cosmic harmony. Kant's third *Critique*—and in particular its reelevation of Longinus's account of the sublime (which Kant received from Burke himself)—would be provoked by nothing so much as this encounter with the *chaos* of nature. To speak fairly, however, Kant was perhaps less convinced of its sacred implications—'the transcendence' of the sublime—than of the theoretical dissonance it portended (CJ:99). If, on the other hand, Rousseauian intuitions concerning the (noble) *sauvage* more robustly prefigure Romanticism, coming replete with a certain exoticism which had accompanied modernist thought from the outset, they do so precisely to the extent that Rousseau himself had simply revolted both against the elevation of Reason and against as well the splitting of the natural universe accompanied by modern science and Hobbes's substitution of liberty (as compatibilist freedom from exterior compulsion) for the Good. There was, as Rousseau realized, a certain tragedy in all this, a certain "denaturing," to use his term, by which the human and citizen, politics and morality would now be inexorably opposed. This contradiction extends not only backwards to Hobbes, but onward to Kant and Fichte, and ultimately even to Freud's *Psychopathology of Everyday Life,* which Walter Benjamin rightly saw as "reallegorizing" perception once more and revealing "a different nature" than the space hitherto consciously explored.[18]

And yet, if the passions will now need not only to be educated but also liberated, as Rousseau and Freud suggest, if, that is, culture and civilization will now be recognizably at odds with one another—it was partly because Reason could no longer recognize itself in them. Moreover, if for the Romantics the passions themselves more primordially articulated a natural law outside the "promulgated law," it was first and foremost because modernity had come to condemn the passionate as egoism. And finally, if "Nature" consequently seemed implicitly revolutionary, it was first and foremost because desire, like the *ordo naturae,* had been transformed into an object to be manipulated and ordered from without. Despite deep problems in post-Nietzschean attempts such as those of Lacan's or Klossowski's to claim a certain affinity between Kant and de Sade, here, in any case, such complicities would indeed be difficult to deny: both depended on the pulverization of the passions which transformed them into an object to be manipulated and controlled before the law, thus radically disrupting the bond between nature and order, *physis* and *logos,* the *lex naturae.* The result, devoid of origins, ceded to obligationism a certain "will to will," to use Heidegger's Hobbesean term. The problem was what could ordinately be recognized as an end. Notice however—as Nietzsche's French interpretors surely did—the Sadean caveat here: "All man-made laws which would contravene Nature's are made for naught but our contempt."[19] The irony, as Lacan saw—and it is testimony to their modern allegiances—is that notwithstanding the gulf that divides Kant and de Sade, they agree about the "compulsions" of nature. We have already traced the dialectics by which Kant reinstated a nature otherwise than modern physicalism. But regardless of how one ultimately views such claims, those who first attempted to overcome the Enlightenment did so first and foremost by a retrieval—or refiguration perhaps—of antemodern objectifications of nature. Moreover, the complications attending this retrieval would neither be left behind nor readily dissolved.

If even now the biocentric retrievals of "deep" ecologists once again appeal to the phenomenologies of Romanticism and indeed phenomenology itself "for the development of consciousness of a non-instrumental, non-utilitarian content of the immediate experience of nature," they often do so in ignorance of the antinomies in which phenomenology itself developed.[20] In this regard one might, for example, claim that Goethe's color analysis, which retains the remnants of the link between expressivism and manifest image that accompanied "lived experience," can be seen as protophenomenological in its description of nature. And yet it also remains true as

Einstein put it, that "the greatest achievement of Newton's mechanics lies in the fact that its consistent application had led beyond . . . phenomeno-logical representation."[21] Moreover, claims that explanation always required transcending the given of immediate consciousness spawned not only at-tempts to turn such intuitions hermeneutic but equally, from Edward von Hartmann to Geiger to Lacan, the demand for a "phenomenology of the unconscious" to recapture what escaped such immediacy. Yet such claims seemed in principle not to suffice: phenomenology, lacking in (explicit) explanatory criteria, would always result in what Kant called a merely negative science.[22] Doubtless Einstein's criticism of the phenomenological left out its intrinsic scepticisms regarding the apparent (hence its *epoché*) and owed more to Mach than to Husserl. If Husserl's and Heidegger's "phe-nomenologies of nature" prove fertile nonetheless, their contribution re-mained always oblique before Schlick's and Carnap's own attempts to reduce *Konstitutionstheorie* by purely extensional definitions. And yet as the "phe-nomenological" moment in Wittgenstein attested, the problem—or the pseudoproblem—seemed always to be misplaced. As Wittgenstein saw, "If I say 'For me the vowel *e* is yellow' I do not mean: 'yellow' in a metaphorical sense—for I could not express what I want to say in any other way than by means of the idea 'yellow'." It was perhaps a question of distinguishing between the limits of language and justification strictly construed and those which, by a kind of dissonance with the respect to the latter, always ex-ceeded it. As Wittgenstein realized, if I am not strictly *justified* in such usage, this doesn't mean that I don't *use* it by right.[23] And yet the most passionate appeals to or retrievals of the narratives of original experience and factical or everyday life—or ethically or politically to primitive life, to the *sauvage,* the uncivilized, etc.—would seem always complicated thereby.

2. The "Natural Histories" of Reason

Still, such retrievals and especially the retrievals of post-Kantian thought, many of which stand in the background of such considerations, would again be complex. The dissonance of the elements attests to this complexity demarcating both these texts' adherence and rupture within the modern. Granted their theoretical commitments regarding the paradigms of objectiv-ity itself, any account of nature in those post-Kantian retrievals we identify under the rubrics of German Idealism would need to be inscribed in terms of the science of nature. But, unlike other considerations having do with German Idealism, 'science' here would not simply be a matter of rigorously organized knowledge (*Wissenschaft*), that is, systematic construction—but likewise empirical method. Hence doubtless the complication which attended the complicity and investments regarding speculation and *mythos* in its texts: in the same moment in which there could no longer be a simple relation between *empeiria* and *theoria*, there could no longer be the simple elevation of the mythic itself—both *mythos* and *logos* would now instead remain inextricably complicated in the ruins of theoretical modernism. It was this complexity, the problem of a criterion which might distinguish knowledge from fiction that had, after all, incited the question of the critical system. The wonder perhaps is that Nature ever again became a problem granted those commitments. Granted, that is, the closure which obtained between science and determinate objectivity, it is perhaps startling that nature in any other sense ever intruded.

Even those perhaps most sympathetic to German Idealism would be confounded by its interpretive preoccupation with nature—even to the extent that they would continually downplay it. For Philippe Lacoue-Labarthe, writing in Heidegger's wake—but knowing full well Heidegger's own commitments to its accounts of nature—it was not "physics" or *Naturphilosophie* that was decisive for the speculations of German Idealism but aesthetic and literary invention.[24] On the other hand Stanley Cavell (equally connecting his work to Heidegger), having correctly seen Emerson's reliance upon German Idealism and thus having stressed its *Naturphilosophie*, proceeded as if its metaphysical speculations concerning the subject could be divorced from the affirmation of allegories of ordinary nature. Cavell focused instead upon the affirmation of the ordinary over against Kantian skepticism regarding the thing in itself.[25] And to the extent that Cavell saw all this in light of the so-called analytic-continental divide, the difference in the "interpretations" at stake seemed still (oddly) to divide the wake of post-Kantian philosophy less, say, between the poetics of Hölderlin and Emerson (or the aesthetics of Friederich and Constable), than by its trajectories through Husserl's categorical intuitions or Frege's grammars.[26] For Heidegger, on the other hand, at stake in the systems of German Idealism were its speculations concerning both mind and nature, *logos* and *physis*, and the jointure (*systema*)—and perhaps even the 'body'—that links them.[27] Moreover, as the treatises on *Naturrecht* in German Idealism continually attested, the articulation of this *systema* was not without ethical or political impact. Even here, however, it seemed anything but clear what such a *systema* might mean.

The problem always seemed to be one of reconciling natures—although again, even the demand for such reconciliation seemed uncanny in the wake of the physicalist reductions of theoretical modernism. And while this reconciliation, *inter alia* a reconciliation between the ancients' and moderns' conceptions of nature, seemed preeminently a matter of "re-readings," as Cavell thought, for reasons that will become evident, it was already apparent to the authors of German Idealism that it must be more, that it must be a question of reinterpretation (and thereby that the problem of interpretation had become a universal one). And yet of course the question of the unity of these other "natures" intervened continually. Even after Kant's defense of freedom (theoretical, transcendental, or practical), the name of Spinoza continually emerged in this respect along with a reconsideration of nature, from Jacobi's 1785 book on Spinoza to Freud's admonition that we respect Nature too little, and beyond.[28] It is doubtless not insignificant that Freud himself found his early origins in Goethe. Provisionally, and again invoking Schelling, it can be said that what occurs in this countermemory is nature as a *plenum* irreducible to representation or the figures of certainty, confronted with an event in which, beyond all critical opinion, "Nature speaks to our mind or our mind to Nature" (Natur:41). And while it is a matter speculative enough, Schelling too provisionally claims that the ordinary understanding grasps it better than philosophers.

> Whoever is absorbed in research in Nature, and in the sheer enjoyment of her abundance, does not ask whether Nature and experience be possible. It is enough that she is there for him; he has made her real by his very act, and the question of what is possible is raised only by one who believes that he does not hold the reality in his hand. (Natur:9)

From the outset it must recognized, then, that the Kantian question of criteria established on the basis of modern proof-theoretical necessity had been explicitly set aside. Such constitutive necessity was transformed into the speculations of reflective extension, in an endeavor to decipher in the depths of "sacred obscurity," an event "which lies right outside the limits of empirical research into nature." Indeed in one sense the claim is that science itself made such speculations possible: this unity, the unity underlying the concept of force, and hence even mind and matter, are one. The first to have recognized it, Schelling again thought, was Spinoza, whose system "was the first bold outline of a creative imagination" (Natur:15). Indeed, two years previously he had claimed that "Spinoza's solution [to the transition from the nonfinite to the finite] is the only possible solution though the interpretation it must have in his system can belong to that system alone."[29] To this solution Leibniz added, he claimed, the principle of individuation, preparing the way for a "higher" account of Nature itself. And while nature had always been compared to a work of art, henceforth art itself (as even Proust and Heidegger still attested) would emerge from Nature, but only by complicating the issue of *individualität* itself; the latter would never, after all, be simply the remnant of an *individuum*. Here as Schlegel put it, "Every fact must have a strict individuality, be both a mystery and an experiment, that is, an experiment of creative Nature."[30]

While those before Kant had attempted to provide a unified theory of scientific phenomena, and Kant himself had demarcated the limits of scientific objectivity, those in his wake more specifically articulated the domain of nature in terms other than the empirical and mechanistic paradigms which had dominated the scientific revolution. Here, beyond the question of (representational) possibility of the object, to use Kant's term, Schelling recurs by an *ekstasis* which lies beyond the *Entzweiung* of finite representation to its origins, no longer "lost in mythology and poetic fictions that were founded on that conflict between spirit and matter" (Natur:15). To use Bergson's similar argument—and he too was never far from this archive—here the legacy of Kant's critique of metaphysics returns ironically in the recognition that "if metaphysics is possible, it is through a vision and not through a dialectic."[31] In one sense, this retrieval of a plenitude which belies all objective representation, and on which all objective representation depends, was prefigured in Spinoza's third form of knowledge. But here, as will be seen, Spinoza's retrieval of expressivism and his affirmation of nature were of a piece. Although Schelling contested Spinoza's dogmatism by means of Leibniz and then by neoplatonism, it was doubtless because of what he (and post-Kantian thought in general) had seen at stake in Spinoza's third form of knowledge as a liberation from finitude. But in any case, that the question of the bond between nature and consciousness was fundamentally ethical in import was a claim made by post-Kantians from Fichte and Schelling to Heidegger, or the later Merleau-Ponty in appealing to nature as the solution to the origins of finite order.

Even the adherents to the strictest descriptions of consciousness and its legacy would inevitably end in the puzzle of nature, as Husserl would attest in his later works. The lectures collated in his *Erste Philosophie* already pivotally reveal his proximity to Fichte in this regard.[32] Later, while still similarly opposed throughout to what Kant called dogmatism, reducing consciousness and its contents to external form, Husserl claimed that phenomenology would require precisely, as Schelling too had argued, a kind of "natural history of our mind." And here, it might be said, is precisely its almost unavoidable repetition of the conceptual space opened by German Idealism, the account internally divided in a certain attraction and repulsion before nature.

3. Symbol, Expression, and Hieroglyph: Ciphering the Nature of the Self

Schelling's own account of a nature that "speaks to us" through "symbolic language" if only we interpret the revelation of its *symbolische Dartstellung* seemed radically opposed to his predecessor's critique of revelation. Yet in one sense, both Kant and Fichte had authorized and prefigured such a possibility as well as its difficulties. Indeed Kant himself in the third *Critique* argued for a "symbolic" resolution to the theoretical antinomies erupting from the ruins of the ancient systems, thus introducing to his heirs both the problem of the origin of the self and the question of the nature or drive (*Trieb*) which underlies it. Kant however—unlike the Fichte in third part of the *Wissenschaftslehre*—never saw it simply as a conflict over natures. Instead 'nature' (both constitutively and determinately) had been univocally invested in its mathematical projection, and its teleological variants at best had been regulatively and analogically extended in reflective judgment, as the Transcendental Dialectic and the third *Critique* had intimated. Schelling would demand more, but he did not simply deny Kant's limits. Rather for him Nature's 'symbolics', as fully hieroglyphic—and hermeneutic—as the definition of the symbol itself dating to the patristics, had been construed too restrictedly: "It is true that chemistry teaches us to read the *letters,* physics the *syllables,* mathematics *Nature;* but it ought not to be forgotten that it remains for philosophy to interpret what is read" (Natur:5). Schelling's refusal of dogmatic readings here would no doubt be portentous, depending all the while upon a distinction between the spirit and the letter that had accompanied the itinerary of German Idealism. This distinction appeared explicitly in Fichte's lectures on the difference between "The Spirit and the Letter within Philosophy" (1794), in which he called for an extension of reflective judgment in the exposition of the pure I.[33] Kant, while omitting the self from his restrictions, recognizing that to make the self simply an effect within the chain of causes would amount, to use his terms, to the "euthanasia" of reason, had instead claimed—consistent with the *ordo cognoscendi* he had set forth—that we have at best an "indeterminate intuition" of the self's existence.

Those writing in Kant's wake—Reinhold, Schulze, Maimon, and finally Fichte himself—raised anew the question of the nature which is exhibited (or exhibits itself) in the self—and finally the dispersion of the natures contested in its antinomies. Fichte's concern with the *Tat* of the self led him directly to transform the indeterminate empirical intuition by which

Kant had understood the 'I think' and its equivocity as something 'between' the facts of consciousness and its 'nature'. While Kant had signaled a sense of immediate (and precategorial) intuition of the existence of the "I think" (*Existenz*) (albeit as *expressing* an indeterminate perception *unbestimmte Wahrnehmung* [B423]), the parameters of the third *Critique* itself suggested to his progeny the possibility of an indeterminate development of this self-perception in the form of reflective articulation or exposition—and an account of the spirit's extension beyond the letter of the literal.

By this exposition of the self, however, pace the limitations of Kant's semantics (which grants this precategorical sense of the "I think" *Bezeichnung*, but not *Bedeutung*) apperception had been openly linked with nature. Fichte's 1794 review of Schulze's *Aenesidemus* had already attempted to expand upon Kant's account of synthetic a priori intuition in this regard, explicating the event (*Tat*) in which the faculty of representation stands before itself as an event of real self-positing (poised that is, between content and act, *Tatsache and Tathandlung*). Moreover, it further articulated this relation between act and content itself as a unifying act. This transformed Kant's account of a priori synthesis by providing what Kantian synthesis did not: namely a "single principle" which would extend from the manifold of space and time through to the recognition of an object. The unity of reason itself would thereby be derived as "a practical philosophy [which] emerges by going through in descending order the stages which one must ascend in theoretical philosophy"—explicating in turn the striving (*Streben*) of the self as performative.[34] This conception of the unity of reason in apperception outlined in advance the trajectory of the *Wissenschaftslehre*, articulating further the primacy of the presentation itself as a faculty of synthesis—or as Kant had defined it, the faculty of transcendental imagination, which makes possible the joining of sensibility and intelligibility, the 'joining' of the *systema* itself.

The 1794 *Wissenschaftslehre*, consistent with these principles, would provide their epistemic elaboration. Fichte's 1796 *Rechtslehre* began the task of applying this system to the historical world, deepening and extending the structure of his 1794 *Wissenschaftslehre* in the process, as recent scholarship has shown.[35] In his 1798 *Sittenlehre*, Fichte further extends this development, and both the questions of inner human nature and external nature now become more explicitly posed (and in the language of the *Wissenschaftslehre* itself *mutually* opposed) in reciprocal interaction. Still, in the end—consistent with the resources of reflective judgment—the transcendental ego becomes constituting and limited with respect to both. Fichte would never surpass the limits of the possibility of thought in the way that Schelling had in the

above passage. Moreover, again consistent with the logic of reflective determination, while Kant's own account of the antinomy was a theoretical matter,
Fichte's was phenomenological: "I find myself in related opposition" or later,
"I find myself with an organizing nature" (SE:23f., 114f.). And, as this *Trieb*,
the ethical becomes rationally articulated as the need to unite oneself with
nature as a whole, consistent again with the *Aenesidemus's* self-explication
which would make "the intelligible dependent upon itself and thus to bring
to unity the ego which represents the intelligible and the self-positing ego."[36]
The result would be momentous and far-reaching. Indeed it would not be
long before Novalis would proclaim Fichte the Newton of the laws of inner
world.[37]

Of all the texts which emerge within this conceptual backdrop, the *Science
of Ethics* most directly and most decisively (and surely most portentously,
granted its influence) concerns itself with the problem of the junction
between Nature and the self. While the *Wissenschaftslehre* had revealed
Fichte as the first theoretician of the modern self, linking the problem of
evidence to the invocation of the first person, the realism of such a science
remained in doubt so long as the problems accompanying the ancient analogies of Nature had been left unrelated to the "I," pace standard attempts
to distinguish Fichte's thought from the bygone era emphasizing reason's
bonds with nature.

It is surely not unimportant that Fichte's "abandonment" of such bonds
would be claimed to provide the most "enlightened"—or in any case the
most extreme—instantiation of modernity's commitment to the rationality
of freedom and the republican idea. The point however is that its internal
transformations would not occur unambiguously, since they were linked
from the outset to a certain rational eschatology that could appear against
the ancient backdrop only under the complications of voluntarism.[38] In
1794, a year after he had defended the French revolution against Burkean
objections—Fichte fully transformed the Boethian paradigm of providence
and fortune that had ruled the rationality of history before him by writing
in his lectures concerning the vocation of the scholar: "Thus what Rousseau
and the ancient poets place *behind* us under the names 'state of nature', and
'golden age', lies *ahead* of us instead" (VS:182).[39] Instead, in the wake of
Rousseau's almost unconscious commitment to spontaneity, Fichte appeals
(as did Hobbes's commitment to the sure increase of science) to "the constant advancement of culture and in the equal and continuous development
of man's talents and needs."[40] Hence the conclusion: "Act! Act! That is what
we are here for."[41] And yet all of this still seemed obscure against the
philosophical problems of the critical system, not least of which was the

problem of the noumenon, the limits of human understanding, and reason's involvement in nature. By 1797, having more fully articulated the problematic of transcendental spontaneity in the *Wissenschaftslehre,* he had become perhaps even better theoretically equipped to confront the problem of nature. And, as becomes apparent, that this confrontation occurred in relation to ethics was by no means accidental.

Especially in the *Science of Ethics* it becomes clear that the question of the self is intrinsically and inevitably linked to the question of the *nature* of the self, and through what his commentators would term a certain *rehabilitation* of nature against Kant,[42] the Fichtean self becomes explicitly (and "speculatively" [SE:18]) linked thereby to Nature—transforming the question into one which complicates the account of both nature and the self in its wake. Beyond the epistemic constraints of modernist theory—whether it had led to the elevation of physics or to the elevation of art and the *homo aestheticus* (which already loomed on Fichte's horizon)—the question of the Good again raised the problem of the transcendentals that Kant's transcendental deduction had suspended. Here again the paradox, to invoke the ancient predicates, of a "good beyond the true" helped to limit anew the paradigms of philosophical modernism, renewing its investments in subjectivity and the primacy of practical reason.

First and foremost, as with all critical thought, is the question of origins, and in particular the status of the event which invokes the origin of the self. As with Kant's indeterminate self-intuition, such an impulse which underlies or invokes the self is to find its explanation in external nature ("and is originally in fact explained from that other nature" [SE:117]). Yet the latter cannot suffice to account for it. While I can grasp myself as participating in a causal series ("through which alone time, and identity of consciousness in the progress of time arises for us" [SE:116]) such a series cannot explain, Fichte maintains, the working (*Wirksamkeit*) of the links themselves. For these we will need the reflective and not determining subsumption in order to grasp the self-determination of the link itself (SE:115–16). It is precisely as this 'working' that "my nature is described as an impulse" (*Trieb*) (SE:117).

My particular nature, for Fichte, thus becomes articulated as a self-determining link in the whole of reciprocally determined nature(s). And Nature in general, Fichte claims, consistent again with Kant's teleological judgment, is such an organic whole and is posited as such (SE:119). Still, it too remains merely posited ("My nature is not *all* nature" [SE:117]). If as *Trieb* I am impelled to the realization of my freedom, the very idea of the mystic completion of that project is *Schwärmei.*[43] Such delusions of totality and immanence were fatal, accounting neither for the finitude of reason (the need for "moderation") nor for its positive accomplishments within its limits. It is just such fantasies regarding completeness that Kant had already called the euthanasia of pure reason. And Fichte had reaffirmed this diagnosis: "The utter annihilation of the individual, and submersion of the same in the absolute and pure form of reason, or in God, is most certainly the final end of finite reason, but it is also not possible in any time" (SE:159).

If the idea of such a completion is itself not only mystical but illusory, its vision reerupts within the transcendental standpoint, where the distinction between my impulse and my tendency, like two Spinozaistic modes, dissolves in indifference as expressions of true substance:

> My impulse (*Trieb*) as a being of nature, and my tendency (*Tendenz*) as pure spirit: are they two difference impulses? by no means. From the transcendental point of view, both are one and the same original impulse (*Urtrieb*), which constitutes my being, only regarded from two different sides. For I am subject-object, and in the identity and inseparability [*Unzertrennlichkeit*] of both consists my true being [*wahres Seyn*]. (SE:135)

Still Fichte (unlike Schelling in his account of symbolic presentation) remained committed to the division of these modalities, precisely insofar as the impulse in question itself originated from and remained limited and checked from outside.[44] Time itself is the event of this opposition, a relation to the beyond (*ein Aussereinander*), even if this beyond is the beyond as posited, and hence desubstantialized before reflection. Indeed, in a sense, Fichte's account of the ethical becomes then fully desubstantialized, the reciprocal determination of specific (and hence real) relations between self and nonself; this ineluctable circle of determination and appropriation became thereby a morality of impulse and enactment, or (*qua* reflected) of feeling and yearning. The explication of its *Urtrieb* presented remnants of the ancients' co-natus and concupiscence. Here indeed Fichte had appended the original idea of its absolute being (*Absolut Seyn*): of striving or endeavor (*Streben*) and the restriction not of this endeavor, but of real existence (*wirklichen Daseyns*). This, he immediately claims, distinguishes his account from Stoicism which identifies the infinite ideas of the self with real being (SK:245n). It is of course the same remnants of Stoicism to which he objected in Spinoza's account, which is similarly "refuted by showing that it cannot account for the possibility of consciousness" (ibid).

From quite early on Fichte had projected a certain "Spinozaism in reverse." But the account remained throughout Spinozaistic in the sense that, as Spinoza's *Ethics* claims in Book III: "Everything insofar as it is, endeavors to persist in its own being."[45] Leibniz would perhaps more precisely characterize this view as the ruins of neoplatonism in *expression*. Both would moreover see the problem as intimately corporeal; for Spinoza the idea of body is prior to that of idea, while for Leibniz perception can proceed without apperception. The Fichtean self would transform both, however.

We shall need to steer clear of readings which would make Fichte's account of this self-impulse egoistic *simpliciter* in its claims. It is important in fact to recognize its implicit neoclassicism in the elevation of absolute self-sufficiency as "our final end and aim" (SE:240)—even perhaps its elevation of "the heroic character" (SE:200). Indeed the impulse to self-sufficiency is described as the opposite to such egoistic reduction. This impulse results instead in a free determination that underscores "a genius for virtue" (SE:195) which appears *un*Hobbesian even while remaining Hobbesian in language. Even the specific duty of the artist in this regard remains parasitic upon the ends of nature, life, and growth (SE:368). The claim to freedom for freedom's sake (SE:161) remains always intrinsically linked to Nature's teleologies and in this respect remains always mimetic with respect to Nature's energetics: to be precise, an energetics of self-realization of the ideal to which (and this is its other side) we are all "slaves" (SE:368).

Fichte's position on the relation of self and nature thus provides a complex synthesis in its reinstitution of *energeia, physis,* and even *techne*. Indeed Fichte declares, "I am the tool of the Moral law in the sensuous world" (SE:275) articulating this synthesis in the Kantian remnants of system, nature, and self, and resulting in an account of personhood as genetic individuality.[46] Accordingly, Fichte presented a critique of ethical judgment which articulated such judgment in the harmony between the power of judgment and the moral impulse (SE:185), a certain *Ich steh hier* that for reasons now clear relies upon Kant's third *Critique's* harmony of the faculties, one discovered by "the free reflecting power of judgment" (SE:176). Unlike matters of aesthetic judgment, where reason does not demand satisfaction "but merely expects it as a favour of nature" (SE:177), Fichte declared, in moral experience there cannot arise the pleasure of the aesthetic's "surprise" but "merely a cold approval of that which was to be expected"—albeit one through which the indeterminacy of the possible is overcome, "the free power of the imagination floats between opposites." Hence now "the power of imagination is necessitated as through all reality; I cannot view the matter in any other way" (SE:177). As was the case with Kant himself, this characterization of the "required cognition" will then be related more to the sublime than the beautiful, but in either case will need to be distinguished from simple self pleasure, which must be distinguished even in aesthetic matters from the ideal of the beautiful (SE:370).

4. Fichte, the Incorporation of Right, and the Body of Natural Right

In this regard Fichte's account will perhaps more closely resemble Schafts-bury's anti-Hobbesean impact in the moral realm, thus paralleling that of Schaftsbury's effect on Kant and German Idealism in the aesthetic realm, where he argued that the egoistic character of Hobbes's extreme case is only one possibility among others. The failure of the fruition of benevolence, indeed its corruption, and a corrupt imagination, are claimed by Fichte first to be the result of corrupt *education*, since it is only through "the general influence of society upon us, that we are first cultured for the use of our freedom." This is true because the impulse to higher freedom cannot come from within but must come from without and hence we must come "in contact with exemplary men" (SE:215). Thus "if Society were better we also should be better" (SE:194). Secondly, this failure in benevolence is attrib-uted to a distraction and thoughtlessness (*Zersteuung und Gedankenlösigkeit*) in which the wavering of the imagination is allowed to continue despite the power of judgment, and the determinedness of the act thus escapes, result-ing in our erring conscience and guilt (which is not imputed to nature) (SE:204–205). Here consequently, habit and the process of habituation will be intrinsically dangerous, and each person "will have to fight against it all his lifetime." While what "the history of all men" reveals is that "through education they receive that which all previous mankind has established up to their time," to act solely under the dictates of traditional authority is to act "necessarily unconscientiously" (SE:185).

It might be said that the history which Fichte analyzes is not a history of the perdurance of the good, but, to speak Kantian, of the inclination to stray. The history which Fichte describes is a history, of necessity *gewis-senlos*. Indeed the regularity and order of most of humankind is nothing but this tendency to repose and habit (SE:211), a moral *vis inertia* (SE:210), which is Fichte's gloss on Kant's account of radical evil. Here it pivots around the historical event in which "morality may at times, and perhaps, to a great extent, be clouded, and man thus sinks down to be a mere machine" (SE:145). If, as has been seen, Fichte's search for self-sufficiency will still require the *phronimos*, and if this search will require habit, he will also require its rupture. Society in general involves a certain leveling. Laziness, "reproducing itself infinitely through long habit and so changing into utter impotency to be good, is the true, inborn evil which has its ground in human nature" (SE:212). As Plato's *Meno* already saw, we will be lucky if a statesman passes on to a statesman any virtue in ruling: hence, the inherent dangers of the social.

The *Sittenlehre* also recognizes the "problem of the other," the *thou,* but does so by explicitly citing Schelling's 1796 *Naturrecht,* where Schelling (perhaps in turn under the influence of Fichte's 1794 *Wissenschaftslehre*) had distinguished the physical from the ego by means of its *resistance.* Schelling claimed that where physical power finds resistance there is nature, and he is still Kantian at least in this respect, for "in nature there can be no *moral* resistance to me" and "where my moral power finds resistance, there can no longer be nature. I shudder and stop. I hear the warning: Here is *humanity! I may* not do more" (SE:236). In this, as has been claimed, Boethian providence has once and for all been left behind and the ego itself assumes the stance of the *nunc stans,* i.e., in Fichte's terms "each one becomes like God" (SE:271) in undertaking a freedom for the sake of freedom, while each ego demands the imposition of the freedom in determining the totality of nature. Both Schelling and Fichte equally envisage a *totality* of reciprocally interacting free agents. "True virtue consists in acting, in acting for the totality, in which acting each forgets himself utterly" (SE:271)—the now fragile remainder of modern Stoicism. Indeed Fichte's own *Rechtslehre's* account of recognition (*Anerkennung*) mirrors the *Anstoss* which originates reflection by claiming that it is just this event of recognition which makes possible, or solicits, the higher impulse, the ethical impulse. The *Rechtslehre* itself, in other words, claims both that the soliciting or call (*Aufforderung*) presupposes that "the subject can understand and comprehend it" and must consequently have for its ground or origin one capable of comprehending, that is, an intelligence—and hence that the soliciting or impulse is already intersubjective or 'communitarian' (SR:27). Only the Other can call my freedom into being. This is not simply a transcendental condition of freedom or rationality, for the Other is as much an origin as a condition—only freedom can call freedom into being. Indeed one might see in it a post-Cartesian version of Aristotle's account of the friend as "another self." Moreover, the process in which my freedom is called by the Other is itself further identified by Fichte as the process of education itself (*Erziehung*) (SR:61). It would take a Sartre, however, to see its limits in raising all the problems associated with *comprehending* the Other and comprehension itself, divided between the reflective and the unreflective (*l'irreflechi*).

Still, while Fichte linked recognition and its *Anstoss* as the ground of intelligibility to that of the second person or the Other, Fichte's argument concerning recognition as a question of obligation likewise pivotally turned on the cosmological significance of the lived body, a question of how freedom became embodied or incarnated a metaphysics of 'the same'—and in the first place, a self-extended form of corporeality. The metaphysics of self-realization as the instantiation of freedom dictated that the "whole sensuous world is to be brought under the rule of reason, and to become its tool in the hands of rational beings" (SE:315). Such a conception required, Fichte realized, a subservience of the corporeal in general and the human body in particular: that "each human body is tool for the promotion of the final end of reason" (SE:296). And insofar as my body is so viewed, so too is every body and it is precisely here again that respect for the *thou* again necessarily arises:

> But each body is also such a tool. Hence I must have the same care for each body, if I really am impelled only by the moral law. Here we meet for the first time the proposition: take as much care of the welfare of your fellow-men as of your own; love thy neighbor as thyself; a proposition which will hereafter be regulative in all positive duties against others. (SE:296)

If Fichtean conscience is dependent upon the call of the Other, it returns in the form of respect for the Other as *embodied*—a matter to which we shall return. And yet the instrumental models which dominate Fichte's ethical thought inevitably will intrude upon such cases. Moreover, the ethical and epistemic ambiguities which would haunt such an ethics of self-sufficiency are already in place. In fact, the ethics of obligation and vocation now divide themselves ambiguously between the mythemes of self-mastery, the determination of totality and a self-forgetfulness which acknowledges oneself as a part of the totality. In either case, however, the simple identity of cognitive and the conative is to be precluded; Fichte continues the Kantian distinction between "is" and "ought." Still it remains ambiguous; if passivity (or dispersion) is the source of evil in human nature and ordinary (natural) self-determination is our highest vocation, what prohibits instead the sheer release of 'force' itself from being virtuous by contrast to the laziness of the ordinary man (*das gewöhnlich natürlich Mensch*)?

> This is the position of the ordinary natural man. Ordinary, I say; for the extraordinary (*aussergewöhliche*) man, whom nature has specially favoured, has a powerful (*rustigen*) character, although from a moral point of view he is no better. He is neither lazy, nor cowardly, nor false; but he tramples overbearingly

upon everything around him, and becomes master and subjugator of those who choose to be slaves (*die gern Sklaven sind*). (SE:213–214)

Self-determination, self-sufficiency does not of course simply imply over-reaching. Hegel will equally find similar limitations on the master, albeit not by means of the ambiguities of judgment and habit but through the concrete historical event of conflict itself. The absolute of the Fichtean self, however, had recoiled from such a solution, seemingly relying instead upon the veracity of its own 'inner' resources.

5. Reason and the Disenchantments of Authority: Communicability and Alterity

It is true, nonetheless, that Fichte did not simply indemnify consciousness with self-veracity—and yet ambiguity returns here as well. First, there is the requisite of conscience: "conscience never errs and cannot err" (SE:183) and "certainty and conviction can never relate to the judgment of others, and conscience cannot allow itself to be absolutely governed through authority" (SE:185). But then the other sense of objectivity of knowledge, the iterability of truth claims, intervenes. While Fichte claims that "the person who acts solely on the strength of anthority acts necessarily unconscientiously," he recognizes (as has been seen) that such knowledge cannot simply come from within because of the intersubjective character of truth. Indeed it requires the need for "reciprocal communication" (SE:255), since "the more extended this intercommunication is, the more does truth (objectively considered) gain and I likewise" (SE:260).

Indeed in this sense the impulse to self-realization repeats itself at the epistemic level—"all are *desirous* to infuse their convictions into all others, and the union of all for this purpose is claimed the *Church*" (SE:254)—since "only through intercommunication can I attain security and certainty" (SE:259). Elsewhere with regard to communication, Fichte would appeal to "the drive to make the people round us as like ourselves as possible"—claiming in turn that "only the unjust egoist wishes to be the sole representation of his kind."[47] We perhaps see why, in this conjunction of communicability and objectivity, reason demands that even though "it is quite possible that philosophizing individuals do not agree on a single point," for the sake of truth "each one is to influence *all* who probably diverge considerably in their individual opinions" (SE:254). The symbolic extensions of the Dialectic of Kant's *Critique of Practical Reason* would thus become determinately institutional. We have noticed the indeterminacy and plurality—in fact the plurality of the symbol itself—from the outset. This institutionalization of the symbolic insures the rational requisites of communication and objectivity: the 'church' is in effect a space of symbolic or discursive exchange and argument, at the same time providing commensurability between self and Other. What Fichte would not allow at the ontological level—a symbolic *Darstellung*—he provides at the level of the social, albeit as an objective medium which underlies rational exchange.

It is precisely here, moreover, that Fichte saw himself to be completing Kant's account of the practical, claiming in the 1798 *Wissenschaftslehre nova methodo* that the Kantian system is unfinished insofar as the notion of *communication* is not fully achieved.[48] Such an achievement would fully equate objectivity, truth, and communicability—while for Kant's reflective account this idea of reciprocal communicability remained merely regulative in character. Hence perhaps the effect of Romantic objections to Kantian claims such as Schlegel's regarding the rationality of the fragment and the genre of the *Athenaeum:* "Of all things that have to do with communicating ideas, what could be more fascinating than the question of whether such communication is actually possible."[49]

Elsewhere Schlegel had claimed that Fichte's shortcoming lay in not "characterizing" himself, that is, in not providing an exposition of the self, the passage from individual to concept: in not providing, in short, the schema of the Absolute. Schlegel's own "fragmented" exposition was surely an attempt to provide just that. His defense of the fragment in the above statement is in fact a response to Schleiermacher. What Schleiermacher and Schlegel were in agreement about, however, was that Fichte's notion of communicability presupposed precisely what it sought to prove, and both attempted to provide the possibility of such a medium. In the case of Schlegel, this explication of the unity of finite and infinite became articulated in the disequilibrium of the fragment: in the case of Schleiermacher, the interplay of parts and whole in the hermeneutic circle. Both are of a piece 'hermeneutic' in this regard and mark the (reciprocal) emergence of modern 'hermeneutics' and linguistics.[50] While Fichte still wrote an essay on the origin of language, organized on the basis of an already presupposed communicable objectivity, these writers sought to articulate its very possibility, the origin itself in a sense having been dispersed in the diversity of the 'ordinary' or the 'natural' language and the heterogeneity of its rhetorical, argumentative, and ideological forms.[51] At stake therefore was less the simple assertion of communicated understanding, or the consensus of 'conventional' or 'standard' usage, than the acknowledgment of the lapse in 'commonality'—to use Schleiermacher's figure, the general problem of misunderstanding, and the ensuing task of interpretation. Notwithstanding Fichte's recognition of the potential differences that ambiguate transcendental consciousness, Fichte himself however remained faithful to the formal universals of Kantian objectivity, without sufficiently grasping the dialectics that underwrote its transcendental analogies—leaving him thereby perhaps still closer to Hobbes than to the humanists he sought to emulate.[52]

Even Fichte himself in one sense acknowledges the internal limitation Kant found in the hermeneutic status of the symbolic, however: while the categorical imperative itself remained syntactically determinate (a determinate formula, as he put it), the narratives to which it symbolically gave rise remained dialectical in status; *reflective* and not simply constitutive in origin. The 'performative contradiction' it focuses on is neither simply syntactic (logical) nor symbolic (teleological). And Fichte's attempt to institutionalize the "church of reason" would in fact similarly acknowledge such limits. In addition to the church of reason, Fichte argues on behalf of a "forum of common consciousness" where scholars may investigate beyond even these limits, that of a society of learned public or scholars (SE:261)—Fichte's first attempt at articulating the requirements of a "free university." Beyond the limits of conceptual intercommunicability, beyond the limits of epistemic certainty, the requisites of the rational required a domain of free enquiry into truth. This idea tacitly anticipates an objection which would be at stake in Schelling's *On University Studies*. While Schelling had at one time himself claimed that nature itself was amoral, in accord with his own elevation of *Naturphilosophie* (and the hermeneutic problems associated with its symbolics), he was later openly critical of (perhaps even motivated by) the desubstantialization this amoralist interpretation had effected, wondering what *kind* of action was called for.[53] Schelling had not gone as far as Jacobi or Jean Paul in condemning Fichte for nihilism, but simply for insufficiency. But that the debates over the question of nihilism had their origins here was surely not insignificant.

In another form, however, it has been suggested that such considerations still rest on the philosophy of history itself: Schelling's *Abfall*, in articulating our separation from origins, relied on the priority of the past, while Fichte's remained "eschatological." Hence their differences emerge regarding not only the deduction of the finite but of the integrity of consciousness itself, whose content Fichte had sought to defend—a content whose internalist abstractions Schelling from the outset found transcendentally incomplete (and illusory). And while Fichte's position was open to such objections, a forum for critical discussions had surely been offered precisely to provide the rational conditions for such considerations, where beyond the certainty of institutional objectivity, the question of the transendence of truth would be broached.

Its obverse unfortunately was equally evident in Fichte's account, however, in the ambiguous and unstable concept of the 'nation' as a boundary for such truth. The nation was both, on the one hand, a space of legitimacy which replaced the king's "two bodies," and, on the other hand (as Fichte's discourses on the German nation and his praise of Machiavelli had noted) the natural kind which would unite a geographical contingency in terms of co-mmunity. Heidegger's 1930s' discourses on the speculative character of the German people would doubtless continue the "lineage." In this respect a concept of the nation and the people (*Volk*) still contained the inheritance of Herder on natural language and natural culture, spirit and nature that predominated in Fichte's thinking.[54] And yet obviously, it was a legacy fraught with both ambiguity and danger. The ambiguity reaches a certain climax in Fichte's claim that "Each one becomes like God" in the moral universe when he adds: "precisely because his whole individuality is annihilated and destroyed" (SE:271). Reciprocally, when the community of communication is fulfilled both "church and state fall away" (SE:266). Here the diremption between individual and individuum, certainty and truth, subjectivity and objectivity, "the learned and the unlearned public," is again leveled off—and annihilated. Indeed, anticipating the reductivist projections of "revolutionary" discourses to come, Fichte declares that the state itself falls away as "a *legislating and compulsory* power." Hence "all have the same conviction, and power."

Kant's third *Critique,* as has been seen, had similarly postulated a movement from compulsion to sociability through "reciprocal communication of ideas" (CJ:231). Such a transition for him was made possible however by the *humaniora,* a practice conjoining sympathy and communication. But Kant idealized this emergence as promoting (republican) harmony without dissolving difference—especially when, he thought in the future, we "will be even more remote from nature" (CJ:232). Fichte thought otherwise, fully postulating the idea of rational immanence and transparence between reason and history, spirit and nature. As a result, "each one with all his individual power, and as well as he were able, modifies nature for the use of reason" (SE:266). The model for totalitarian dissolutions of individuality—and thereby the reflective judgments which are inevitably connected with them—is still unmistakable here, affecting both Fichte's model of the rational as abstract universal form and its account of nature (as *manipulandum*). Moreover, the result becomes pointedly concrete in the account of their bond itself, the lived body, where Fichte often receives high praise on standard accounts.

Fichte's emphasis on the body has been purported to provide a new solution to Kant's third antinomy overcoming the last vestige of (teleological) dogmatism in the appearance of the body as the schema of freedom.[55] And yet, while the importance of this introduction of the lived body as a central feature of the *Naturrecht* is undeniably significant, its significance cannot be divorced from the ambiguities it inherits from the detraditionalization at stake in theoretical modernity itself. As Bakhtin realized, beginning as early as Rabelais, the emphasis upon the body was itself emancipatory, presenting

> the human body, all its parts and members, all its organs and functions, in their anatomical, physiological and *Naturphilosophie* aspects alone. . . . It was important to demonstrate the whole remarkable complexity and depth of the human body and its life to uncover a new meaning, a new place for human corporeality in the real spatio-temporal world. In the process of accommodating this concrete human corporality, the entire remaining world also takes on new meaning and concrete reality, a new materiality; it enters into a contact with human beings that is no longer symbolic but material. Here the human body becomes a concrete measuring rod for the world, the measurer of the world's weight and of its value for the individual. . . . This new picture of the world is polemically opposed to the medieval world in whose ideology the human body is perceived solely under the sign of decay and strife. . . . Between the word and the body there was an immeasurable abyss.[56]

Kantorowicz's analyses have further shown that the Middle Ages had figured corporality through a certain Christological *pros hen,* instantiating its transcendence in the figure of the king's two bodies.[57] The modern reduction of this transcendence however did not in fact simply dissolve its legacy, as Lefort notes.[58] The Kantian "immeasurable abyss" between concept and being that perhaps Bakhtin still cites is not simply resolved in a physicalist reduction, even if such a reduction remains an ever-present tendency of philosophical modernism after Hobbes. And this doubtless was a sign of theoretical modernity's inherent danger. If indeed theoretical modernity liberated the *topos* of the human body from what Bakhtin describes as the "false associations established and reinforced by tradition" that "distort the authentic nature of things," it also facilitated modernist instrumental construals by which transcendence itself might originate in a constitutive will (or the will of the people), as a voluntarist (spiritual) accomplishment, or perhaps even as the willful expression of an original natural kind.[59]

In one sense all this too might be thought to be a Stoic remnant: Marcus

Aurelius, for example, claimed that "nature has so mingled the intelligence with the composition of the body, as to have allowed you the power of bringing under subjection all that is your own," that "whatever presents itself is material for virtue, both rational and political" and in this all are "godlike."[60] The reason that oversees the body for Fichte, communicable objectivity, as has been seen, too has been detached from any 'natura' of which it is not the (conventional) measure. But the dangers that lurk here too have been similarly evident. What Fichte called the "articulated body" could equally be all too easily subsumed beneath a more "natural" *logos* and community, that of spirit and race, simply dissolving the difference (and the ambiguity) that both unites and distinguishes word and body—as became evident in its aftermath in the subsequent genres of nationalist discourses.[61] On the other hand, rather than appealing to such immanences, democracy, as Lefort argues, became precisely the institution of this ambiguity: while transcendence was never simply beyond democratic 'incorporations', neither was transcendence ever simply instantiated or simply individuated within them. Its "measures" always lay also "beyond" it. The question is whether and in what sense, to use Merleau-Ponty's terms, there remains a "good ambiguity."[62] But, in any case the pivotal role of the lived body in the question of "the body politic" and the "incorporation" of the political remains clear, and Fichte should be credited with having already seen it. The 1794 lectures on the *Vocation of the Scholar* already claim this *topos* to be decisive as a propedeutic to natural right:

> Among the questions which philosophy has to answer we find two in particular, which have to be answered before, among other things, a well-founded theory of natural rights [*Naturrecht*] is possible. First of all by what right does a man call a particular portion of the physical world "his body"? How does he come to consider this to be his body, something which belongs to his I, since it is nevertheless something completely opposed to his I? And then the second question: How does a man come to assume that there are rational beings like himself apart from him? And how does he come to recognize them, since they are certainly not immediately present to his pure self-consciousness? (VS:153)

Fichte's response, however, could not but eliminate the (good) ambiguity articulated between individual and universal, ego and community—in the same way that it had the distinction between (and the attempt to unify) nature and self from the transcendental standpoint. While, as has been seen, the rationality of the judgment articulated the interplay between imagination and understanding, a matter in which the individual is the precondition of the ego, this interplay remained ambiguous—"not absolutely fixed" (SK:185). Beyond the "wavering" of conscience there remained only nothingness, as Fichte put it in a proto-Sartrean formulation. What began with an emphasis on individual conscience in Fichte continually ends in its annihilation. The problem, as has been seen, lingers within the society of intercommunication which Fichte claimed could provide the correction for the epistemic shortfall in which truth might be "falsified by individuality" (SE:258). There remains in this society the threat of false authority and all that had been identified as the *vis inertia* of institution and history.

The problem, it might be said, is that while institutions might promote such a consciousness, nothing can enforce it—nor guarantee the good judgment underlying such institutions, of course. Hence perhaps Fichte's concern at one point that "it seems impossible to communicate morality" (SE:329). And, while Fichte would not simply give this threat the last word—we have seen too his commitment to freedom, to invention and the interplay of reason and imagination—that this tension is its remainder should not be surprising granted the models of its origins. Fichte, after all, had extended Kant's account by means of the theoretical fertility—albeit indeterminate exposition—of reflective judgment, again all in endorsing once more the "spirit" of philosophy. Like the individual origins of the ego itself, however, reflective judgment begins *problematically,* the universal always extended beyond it; the indeterminacy now, however, returns under the guise of the *Wechsel* between transcendental self and individual, universal and institution, symbolic schema and discursive judgment. As Fichte himself reemphasized, the function of reflective judgment "arises only however where subsumption is not possible; and reflective judgment *prescribes itself its own law,* namely, the law to reverse the law of subsumption" (SE:117). But this "reversal" never overcomes the lack of determinacy that had incited it from the outset: freedom is always more ventured than possessed, always more a matter of interpretation than proof. Neither freedom nor nature are "mastered" in the end—even when the evidence it imparts is as undeniable as it is fragile. And this has more than simply "theoretical" significance.

In all this the complexity of the relations between authority and knowledge, institution and consensus, and again last (but not least) master and slave perhaps becomes doubly evident. Fichte from the outset introduced the latter figure by reference to Rousseau's claim that "Many a person who considers himself to be master of others is actually more of a slave than they are. He might have said with even more accuracy, that anyone who considers himself to be the master of others is himself a slave."[63]

6. Schelling, the Speculative Turn and the Nature of Reason's 'Unconscious'

Fichte's own role in this uneasy transformation of the reflective venture is evident. The *Sittenlehre* paradoxically attests to a passage beyond the demonstrative requisites of modern rationality and a (speculative) "nature" that finite articulation more relies upon than conceptually subsumes. As has become evident, however, rather than recognizing the status of this reliance, in Fichte's account nature remained cognized simply as the manifold of Reason's construction. As such his account fully attests to an ambiguity in the concept of 'objectivity' itself—divided between 'absolute' truth and 'constituted' object, between 'transcendence' and the 'transcendental'. In this, however, Fichte had in a sense here interceded—epistemically, metaphysically, and logically—between the early philosophy of the will that the 1794 *Wissenschaftslehre* (and the early Schelling) had drawn from Kant's priority of practical reason and the *Naturphilosophie* which followed him.

Fichte had already glimpsed the problem of nature as the foundation of ethics and articulated the *fluctuatio* and analogies of imagination crucial to its grasp. As Schelling would immediately attest in his own *Naturphilosophie,* Fichte's philosophy "was the first to restore the validity of the universal form of subject-objectivity"—in this regard, too, the first to complete the undeveloped presuppositions of Spinoza's commitments to *Naturphilosophie*. Yet for Schelling "the more [Fichte's account] developed the more it seemed to restrict that very identity" (Natur:54). In all this, Schelling declared, Fichte's philosophy lacked speculative power, remaining portentously silent about the meaning of all that remained *unconscious* before it—in ways in which even Kant himself had not been, Schelling declared. If Fichte's turn to the lived body had purportedly "liberated" law from the "dogmatism" of Kantian dialectic, Schelling sought the "exposition" of life itself precisely in such symbolics. To return to Schelling's figure, "Nature in its purposive forms speaks figuratively to us, says Kant; the interpretation of its cipher yields to us the appearance of freedom in ourselves" (Natur:215-16). However, for Schelling conceiving nature would ultimately require a transformation of both the ciphering and its symbol, submitting consciousness to all that exceeds it, all that from the standpoint of finite intuition remains simply "unconscious." For Fichte, on the other hand, the discovery of transcendental imagination meant that "taken in themselves my words are empty noise" to be filled out by the spirit.[64]

Kant's critical account had itself been similarly divided, as has been seen: nature had been divided between general philosophy of nature and mathematical construction. This makes nature, on the one hand, causal series and abyss, on the other, organic totality: on the one hand, the realm of freedom, and yet, as the later writings on history demonstrate, Hobbesian or Machiavellian cunning which provided rational counterbalance to human weakness. The third *Critique* simply truncated this division, divided perhaps between the teleologies of Aristotle's harmonies and Burke's monsters. The latter doubtless forces to prominence the heterogeneity of the natural, of a world more at home with Democritus, Empedocles, and Lucretius than with Plato: hence perhaps Schelling's preoccupation with the work of Le Sage, "Lucrece Newtonien" (Natur:161). And this disequilibrium doubtless explains why Schelling could find chemistry, physics, and mathematics to refigure the lexicon, the letters, syllables, and Nature of the Absolute anew. What is at stake however ultimately in all these cases is the distinction between "what is" and its ratiocinative articulation: and *Naturphilosophie* is not limited therefore (ontically) to this or that motion or matter but concerns the possibility of "matter and motion as such" (Natur:166–67). The continual invocation of Spinoza, as Leo Strauss rightly recognizes in this regard, is important precisely as prefiguring such an original synthesis of elements, which neither disregards the ancient's science of being nor forgets its dissolution within the advance of the science of the modern. Hence: "Spinoza restored the dignity of speculation on the basis of modern philosophy or science, of a new understanding of 'nature'. He thus was the first great thinker who attempted a synthesis of premodern (classical-medieval) and of modern philosophy."[65]

It is clear that Kant's followers, Fichte included, had from the outset been fascinated with Spinoza. But Fichte's fascination was still tempered by Kant's theoretical discoveries in the Antinomies, and in a way, consequently, ambiguously divided between individual and universal, nature and spirit, the heroic and the overreaching—all the while relying in these conflicts upon Kantian reflective judgment and its organic metaphors. Hence perhaps the hope that state, society, the church, and religion as educational systems, "institutions arranged by pre-eminently good men with a view to cultivate the moral sensibility of others" (SE:215), might provide resolutions, notwithstanding the dangers of the *vis inertiae* and leveling he ascribed to the habits of tradition and inheritance. It is clear too, however, that these extend beyond Kantian investments in the philosophy of history.

For Schelling, however, throughout these ambiguities, the latent truth in Spinoza remained "unrecognized" (Natur:53)—reduced, by the claim of dogmatism, to a mere theory of objectivity and then reduced once more by the Kantian limits on finite subjectivity. While Fichte had endorsed Schelling's elevation of Leibniz over Spinoza, it still remained for him ensconced within the axioms and the mysteries of (finite) intuition. But, against all Fichte's (Kantian) reservations concerning the illusions of finitude, Schelling had glimpsed the neoplatonist resonances in such intuition:

> Philosophy has higher demands to fulfill and is called upon to lead mankind, which, whether in faith or in unbelief, has long enough lived unworthily and unsatisfied, at last to vision. The character of the whole modern era is idealistic; its dominant spirit, the return to inwardness. The ideal presses mightily towards the light, but is still held back by the fact that Nature has withdrawn as mystery. The very secrets which the ideal harbours cannot become objective save in proclaiming the mystery of Nature. (Natur:54–55)

The mystery of external objectivity is to be unveiled as *natura naturata*, a symbol, as Schelling puts it, of *natura naturans* (Natur:50), the "secret bond . . . through which Nature speaks to our mind or our mind to Nature" (Natur:41). Here beyond all "sacred obscurity" which attributes the organization of nature to an external agency, the idea of life itself as "self-organizing matter" is finally to emerge (Natur:35). And he is just a few years from adding Bruno to Spinoza in this regard, when all will be symbol and hieroglyph, when act will finally "return" to nature. And to Fichte's Hobbesean limitations on self-realization as domination, Schelling in effect reminds us that Spinoza's ethics are not simply an ethics of 'empowerment' but—beyond such ceaseless "desire of Power after power" (Lev:II.11)—an ethics of beatitude: knowledge is not only the *eros* of finite desire or *Trieb* but of *co-natus*. And perhaps even more to the point, Schelling's account of the symbol had surpassed Fichte's account of the symbol itself here. While Fichte's account of the church as symbol, as has been seen, had guaranteed the coherence requisite for finite communicability and extended objectivity, for Schelling nature itself as symbol elevates the finite into the infinite, into the unity of nature and ideal (Natur:50). If Fichte had relied upon the transitions of symbolic institution, he would not guarantee such institution, but at most *believe* regarding it. For Schelling, Kant's claim that the "I think expresses an indeterminate perception" would now need to be *read* or construed fully within the protocols of *expressivism* itself, demanding a hermeneutics (an account of the spirit and the letter) beyond the pure form of reflective immanence.

7. The Scepter of Spinoza and
the *interpretatio naturae*

It is not accidental in this regard that Spinoza's *Theologico-Political Tractatus* was intended to furnish a model for interpretation in general, or for retrieving the problem of *interpretatio naturae* (and the book of nature). But notwithstanding his considerable debts to materialism, neither the self-preservation nor nature at stake could be understood in the Hobbesean sense. Spinoza, after all, had staunchly attempted to think together the confluence of freedom and necessity, without simply losing the classical predicates that had accompanied teleological accounts of nature. He did so, however, fully aware of the analogies connected with the question of the "law of nature"—theological, juridical, and scientific.[66] Against Hobbes's materialist reduction of the natural law to power, Spinoza had himself begun the project of refiguring the ethical through modern narratives. It is thus not surprising that Trendelenburg's 1860 *Naturrecht* paired Spinoza's and Aristotle's definitions of virtue.[67] But in this regard two points should be made. First, if freedom and necessity continue to be interwoven in a way that equates right and power, Spinoza still distinguishes what we ought to do and what we are "inclined" to do with power, in sharp contrast to Hobbes or those in his wake. For Spinoza, it is not just the fear of coercion which answers the question "why be moral"; rather it is the search for the good and enlightened understanding. Second, rather than simply suspecting sacred narrative (or any narrative that remains irreducible to the causal account of science that Hobbes invokes), Spinoza turns hermeneutic with respect to them. Fichte's emphasis upon what Spinoza had already identified as the wavering of imagination perhaps only reemphasized such a hermeneutics of what exceeds the limits of the finite[68]—an event which, beyond the drive to dominate it, would always complicate the exhibition of nature.

As has become evident, beginning with Fichte's attempt to reverse Spinozaism from the standpoint of a transcendental account of nature, the very concept of power and force itself had begun to be refigured in articulating the hermeneutics of desire as energetics. The impact of Schelling's transformation of *Naturphilosophie* and its 'natural history' extends this 'counter memory'. Moreover, its impact is far reaching. Coleridge, for example, openly used Schelling's texts. Shelley and Wordsworth were also influenced (and probably in turn influenced the early Newman and his account of evidence and tradition). Last but not least there is Emerson, whose own essays on Nature still reflect Schelling.

The conflict concerning the potentials of finite intuition between Fichte and Schelling becomes perhaps most pointed in the correspondence of 1801 following the latter's *System of Transcendental Idealism*. Fichte's response to Schelling was as historically informed as it was prophetic. Fichte reproaches Schelling for starting with Being in place of starting from an act.[69] What was at stake in the unfolding of the Absolute was the question of whether one could speak of Being or nature apart from its (finite) epistemic origin. But to this Schelling could only reply that it is just here that the true annihilation of the finite occurs out of which nature emerges.[70]

For Schelling this originated a transformation in the genres of practical reason, however. Schelling would not write a *Tugendlehre* or a *Pfülliglehre*: for him the question of morality was transformed (along with the question of Being itself) into philosophy of religion, a question of the sacred, of myth, and of history. As he put it in a piece that he was preparing in the background to the correspondence with Fichte:

> Thus the genuinely speculative question remains still unanswered, namely, how the absolutely one, the absolutely simple and eternal Will, from which all things flow, expands into a multiplicity and into a unity re-born from multiplicity i.e., into a moral world.[71]

To Fichte's (Kantian) question about epistemic access—the question of critique and judgment—there seemingly remained little response. And yet, those on the other hand who followed Fichte's version of the symbolic—and there are many, including Bradley, Green, Meade, and at one point Habermas—perhaps missed the underdeterminacy and *Wechsel* on which Fichte's requirement of the communicable and the legitimate depended, mistaking its commitment to the requisites of objectivity and communicability for mere consensus in intersubjectivity. Whatever else we will ultimately have to say about the problem of Nature, it will not be reducible to its concept, nor will its shared experience be *equatable* with consensus, nor can the claim to truth be identical with constituted, rule-governed objectivity. These reductions forget the Humean legacy in Kant's account of the noumenon and further forget the Copernican turn's transformation regarding the ancients' *transcendens* in the venture (and illusion) of dialectic.

Throughout, as has been seen, Fichte staunchly appealed to the certainty of the first person with an almost proto-Nietzschean gloss declaring that "I become like God" and that the certainty of judgment is guaranteed in a priori synthetic intuition because it is my act: "The philosopher contemplates himself, scans his act directly, knows what he does, because he—does it" (SK:36). The argument was doubtless thoroughly modern, not simply in its "Cartesian" commitments to epistemic certainty but equally in its commitment to an act (*Tat*) that would found historical reason over against the vagaries of *fortuna*. In this regard, it was an argument with antecedents both in Hobbes and Vico. But, as has been seen, Fichte also demands equally that we acknowledge the requisites of communicative rationality for its objectivity, acknowledging the problem of errancy and the moment in which truth becomes "falsified" by individuality, the 'I' in this regard 'falling away' from the state. This disequilibrium is undeniable in Fichte's text, a disequilibrium never simply surpassed. Thus its obscure legacy in places may seem surprising. For example, Bradley and Green doubtless still reflected Fichte's commitment to intersubjective objectivity in their appeals to fulfilling "one's station in life," (in ways, for example, that Heidegger's critique of *Das Man* would find both naive and now corrupted).[72]

This disequilibrium bequeathed an ambiguous legacy to philosophers committed to an analysis of the first person, distinguishing the idea of evidence from truth. The result, as became evident in Kierkegaard and his followers from Heidegger to Sartre, would be the affirmation of the moment of individuality (of "my nature" which is "not the whole of nature") as prior to the concept and requiring the suspension of the ethical as universal. Hence emerges the complications concerning the absolute accompanying what Kierkegaard called "individual virtue." Hegel had already seen it in the *Differenzschrift:* "If the community of rational beings were essentially a limitation of true freedom, the community would be in and for itself the supreme tyranny" (Dif:145). For Fichte, freedom remains indeterminably divided between the modern antinomies of power, between objectivism and subjectivism, unlimited self-will and mechanistic automatonism. The state, on the other hand, must everywhere remain, for Fichte, a potential coercion whose function was to prevent the possibility of violation (SR:377). Indeed, he proclaims, "the source of all evils (*Übels*) in our present states, as they are constituted, is *disorder,* and the impossibility to produce order" (SR:386).

What is true of 'natural right' becomes even further emphasized in the *Sittenlehre,* where suppression of natural individuality by the state now becomes exchanged for "suppression of nature by oneself," a suppression that is even more *unnatural,* Hegel claims (Dif:150). In this respect Hegel had seen—pace Fichte's liberation of freedom—that the suppression of nature results in an account in which the state had become, precisely to the contrary of Fichte's intention, a mere machine (Dif:149). Fichte's internalism would always be fraught by this disequilibrium between the affirmation of spontaneity and the need for order, freedom and constraint, 'genius' and 'instrumentalism', ultimately impacting, as we have seen, Fichte's political theory. The 1806 *Addresses to the German Nation* would accordingly still find its starting point in the imagination's "power to create spontaneous images," but (pace Kant or Schelling) it would also abandon liberalism, claiming that "the new education must consist in this, that it completely destroys freedom of will in the soil which it undertakes to cultivate and produces on the contrary strict necessity in the decisions of the will."[73] Reason would doubtless require still other resources than those of reflection and act to grasp the bond between freedom and nature. Against Fichte, even in his elevation of the Greek *polis,* Hegel himself would rely first upon the Christian conception of love, then on the realization of nature that he had learned from Schelling—but in either case an ethics of *eudaimonia,* manifested as has been seen, in Hegel's own account of *Natural Law,* where philosophy would (no less ambiguously perhaps) intervene to mediate the relation between positive law and substance, resulting in the unity of individual, community, and nature.

8. Life as the Schema of Freedom

Fichte's strong claims about the Absolute contained lingering Hobbesian commitments (ultimate epistemic foundations require ultimate coercion, political and epistemic modalities being intrinsically glossed as of a piece). In Fichte's wake, however, what becomes deemphasized is precisely what Hegel still took to be one of the proofs of such an Absolute, namely Fichte's own recognition (implicit in the problem of conscience, and explicit in the analysis of obligation) of unalterable ethical implications, the very ones by which Fichte had also refused to abandon the individuality of conscience. Granted the finitude of judgment which had been discovered in the *Wissenschaftslehre* (granted, that is, "the unattainable idea of determinability" [SK:194]), beyond Kant's "formalism," the issue of interpretation in the moral sphere had emerged and, in this sense, the problem of casuistry. Fichte had already claimed in this regard that the moral impulse is a "mixed impulse," a freedom which is solicited only by "counterbalance" to, and in conflict with, natural necessity (SE:159f). It is precisely this which constitutes its ambiguity and which brings it into contradiction, generating the need to surpass it speculatively. For Kant and for Fichte, however, as Hegel acknowledges, it is this ambiguity which demands casuistic reasoning—and perhaps, it should be added, what from the beginning philosophy has acknowledged as "mixed forms" of governance, political and individual.

Kant had already said in his own casuistics that the problem of application inevitably "leads to questions which call upon the faculty of judgment to decide how a maxim is to be applied in particular cases" (Tugend:71). He was led as a result to acknowledge the limitations of ethical judgment—and to exclude its ambiguities from moral science, thus excluding both the remnants of classical *phronesis* and the modern or Baconian problem of application as experimental appropriation or interpretive "accommodation." Despite those who would like to broaden Kant's commitment to formalism and rigorism—and the necessity of such interpretations has already been apparent—it still remains true that casuistics, for Kant, is "neither a science nor a part thereof" but is "interwoven fragmentarily and not systematically with ethics" (Tugend:71). Following Kant, Hegel himself claimed in the *Differenzschrift* that Fichte explicated two sources (if not models) for such judgments, namely, art and religion, but he left their implications vague (Dif:151–52). But precisely refusing Fichte's "mixed epistemic results," Hegel also in the end refused to tolerate the contingencies of application, as the opening of the *Philosophy of Right,* as we have seen, reiterated. Instead of the heterogeneity of jurisprudence, all principles instead were to be exposed and deduced from a single source. But latently, it might be claimed, Hegel's critique (like Schelling's) was that the Fichtean genius of virtue had been unable to decipher the speculative (or interpretive) 'excess' which made such particular applications of the universal possible—and that if both art and religion were excluded, the result was lifeless formality. When Hegel explicitly makes this argument in his early *Naturrecht,* in any case, it finds its principle in the *Differenzschrift:* on this account "reason is nothing but the death and the death-dealing rule of formal unity" (Dif:142). Hence the claim emerges that in Fichte "the principle of speculation, identity, is wholly set aside" (Dif:142). Rather than setting aside the 'past' at stake in the transcendental origin for the sake of rational eschatology, as Fichte had, in order to grasp the unity of nature and spirit, Schelling claimed that it would be necessary to articulate the history of reason and its modern detraditionalization out of original diremption, collapse, and ruin—their *Abfall.*

If Fichte's account of an *Urtrieb* reflecting the unity of nature and spirit had itself incited Schelling beyond modern dualism, already in this respect raising the question of Being, Hegel would not rest with the disequilibrium, the *Wechsel* and *Entzweiung* between subject and object that it bequeathed. Nor would he in the end rest with Schelling's positive (and mutually implicatory) identity, demanding ultimately that *realization* be more than a revelation or metaphysical expression. Instead the antinomy between being and act itself must be sublated, as his own transcendental logic would seek to demonstrate.

It is doubtless true, too, as is often claimed, that Hegel's own account of nature remains—like Fichte's—similarly impoverished. Just as Hegel's *Phenomenology* would in the end deny the Romantic's elevation of art as insufficient and too vague—again lacking in the demonstration of realization, as he put it in criticizing Schelling (or Schleiermacher's doctrine of intuitive religion as insufficiently subjective)—his own account of nature would also have to be similarly surpassed. It is true that Hegel's *Philosophy of Nature* would still grasp Nature as an inert (representational) Now, and separate it (as a moment of alienation and externality [*Ausserlichkeit*]) from matters pertaining to remembrance, fear, or hope, since these were simply a matter of subjective imagination.[74] But it would be a mistake to simply think that Hegel had therefore never been committed to the "solution" of nature itself. In the 1790s, the Tübingen fragment demonstrated Hegel's own proclivities for "Mother Earth"—as he called it—every bit as much as do other works and other authors.[75] Indeed, the significance of the earth lingers on in Hegel's continuing affirmation of the Empedoclean elements as the moment of developed difference and individual determination.[76]

It would be false, then, to claim that the *Idea* had simply been purged of its "natural" significance in Hegel's move beyond Schelling. The same can be said for Hegel's account of Spirit and the recognition of the essential moment of intersubjectivity with respect to Fichte; the point in both cases for Hegel is again the ultimate unity of Being and act, Nature and Spirit. And the fact remains that Hegel too criticized the limitations of Kant and Fichte on the basis of Spinoza. Unlike their earlier accounts of transcendental infinity based upon the (quantitative) infinite series of extension, Hegel appeals to Spinoza's letter XXIX and its account of an *infinitum actu* "because the nature of the fact surpasses every determinateness" (WdL:250). The problem was that Spinoza had not thought of the task of liberation and dispersion with respect to the fact—that is, for Hegel, Spinoza's substance remained "fixed" or "inert."

German Idealism, and those who have been influenced by it, was in this regard infatuated not only with Nature but with the cleavage which both separates and joins us to it. But as is now evident, ancient mysteries were also always at stake in the question of this relation: as Lucretius too put it: "the earth is sodden, sure, sensations can all out of nonsensations be got."[77] And yet in these idealizations of Nature the Empedoclean "chaos" perhaps also reigned supreme. This is true not only in what the Idealists found in the heterogeneity of their Kantian origins, as has been seen, but in what they bequeathed to its followers—or so was the claim of Marx, whose dissertation began precisely at this point. Rousseau's account of the *sauvage* had now in fact been transformed into a certain reading of the ancients' attachments to nature. Although such readings were never just nostalgic— recall that even Winckelmann never doubted the possibility of a retrieval of the ancients in which "Dresden will henceforth be the Athens of artists"— the notion that the ancients provided at least a remedy for the moderns became a widely affirmed polemic that ultimately circulated around the topic of nature itself.[78] Indeed, by the time such polemics had reached Hegel, he defended Empedocles every bit as much as he did the ancients' account of the elements: "The ancients were right in saying that all things were composed of these four elements; but the elements they had before them were only 'thoughts' of such Elements."[79] Notwithstanding his own critique of the analogues of imagination, we need to grasp once more, Hegel claimed, the laws at work within such thoughts as well as the different levels of discourse in which they operate: "People want to put everything on the same level."[80] And while the point (as undeveloped as it is) remains a critical one, recognizing that levels of discourse (as well as discourses and traditions themselves) will need to be distinguished, for Hegel its implications were clear: it is in just this sense that, *rightly understood*, Empedocles has already provided an outline (albeit abstractly) of the philosophy of nature (HP:346). From the outset then the *Philosophy of Nature* was intent upon distinguishing itself from mechanics precisely in order to think *otherwise* than from within its limits, but also in recollection of an experience of nature prior to it. Here the distance between Kant and Hegel could not be greater in its passage through Spinoza.

What the legacy of Spinoza and the transcendental standpoint bequeathed to this project of recovery was the fecundity of the event of nature as naturing. To cite Empedocles or Lucretius in this regard (alongside the *natura naturans*) is no doubt both paradoxical, yet not perhaps simply without warrant. Lucretius's own "hymn to nature" had been lingering since its appropriation within Democratian atomistic science in the Renaissance. If his arguments against the dangers of religion had at one time been dismissed *tout court*, they now would gain certain force and enter into naturalist rejections of religion as well as naturalist "affirmations." And, pace Straussian attempts to deny that reason was at stake in the conflict between reason and enlightenment[81] for those writing around 1800 on the topic of *Glauben und Wissen*, it could not be denied that it was reason itself that had been divided. Hence even Schelling's account of revelation

(*Offenbarung*) would demur from pious opinion: "we require to know, not how such a Nature arose outside us, but how even the very *idea* of such a Nature has got *into us*" (Natur:41). Schelling assumes after all that the effects of the Copernican turn itself were certain. If speculation inextricably surpassed the dichotomy between self and nature, it did so without embracing either conjunct *simpliciter*. Moreover, idealist retrievals of the ancient archives on nature that scientific modernism had excluded were not as simple, say, as Winckelmann's similar neoclassicism in aesthetics—even if he had provided a catalyst for a retrieval of classical "nature" as well. The tension between Stoicism and Lucretius, for example, was as difficult here as it would be everywhere in the wake of the Enlightenment. However, Lucretius inexorably takes on a liberating edge in the Idealist's reclamation of nature as the "soil" of freedom. As Schelling puts it in reference to him: "The complete destruction of all that is spiritual, the reduction of nature to a game of atoms and of emptiness, which he practices with genuinely epic lack of concern, is replaced by the moral grandeur of his soul which in its own 'happy genius' turn elevates him above nature"—recognizing Lucreticus as a precursor of Spinoza.[82] Indeed here it becomes evident most of all that nature could be both 'home' ground and a dispersion that itself *liberates*. Life itself, as Schelling's own 1796 *Naturrecht* proclaimed, might then provide "the schema of freedom."[83] In this heterogeneous synthesis connecting freedom and necessity it becomes perhaps fully prominent. German Idealism was consciously a return to the ancients, but it was so precisely within a modern effect whose legacy would remain fully unwieldy. And nowhere is this effect more prominent than in the idealist's constant elevation of nature and the mixed influence it imparts. Recall that Bergson himself, five years before the heterogeneous discovery of *durée* in *Time and Free Will*, had published his own commentary on Lucretius.[84]

9. The Idealistic Dissolution, an Uneasy Legacy, and Straussian Historicism

Nature would thus be in fragments according to such views; its cosmological harmonies are internally disrupted, the result verging, to use Kant's term, on mere "rhapsody." In these ruins the philosophy of nature would also betray its "Hölderlinian moment," one which has continually contained portentous implications for those seeking to retrieve ancient appeals to nature, both theoretical and practical. Hence the complexity of attempts to use Kant's intellectual synthesis to grasp nature, divided between the various semantic, lexical, and syntactical components of Kant's *Elementlehre*. If Hegel could claim that "Aristotle is still further on than the moderns, since he had not the conception of elements which prevails at the present time, according to which the element is made to subsist as simple," nevertheless for Hegel too, Aristotle's account was restrictedly empirical—it was neither for him sufficiently experimental (i.e., critical), nor did it recognize the (critical) conflict of the inner and the outer (HP:156, 177). Here in the end, the conflict becomes unsurpassable and the dispersion at stake, the idealist's moment of transformation, is laden both with the overtures of freedom and the epiphanic possibilities of imagination. It is in just this regard, as Hölderlin would put it, that "the idealistic dissolution overcomes the limitations of the old."[85]

We will miss the originality of this moment, then, if we miss its complexity. If those in the tradition of *Naturphilosophie* or those in Spinoza's wake had appealed to nature as an *Urgrund* or *Urtrieb* resolving the complexities of reason, they would likewise inevitably have recourse to its withdrawal and to the "inner" reserves which facilitated its transgression—a transgression that would transform both freedom and necessity, nature and spirit. In this regard, Schelling again remains instructive. If the *Naturphilosophie* had turned to the inner and to a nature which "necessarily and originally should not only *express,* but *even realize* the laws of our mind" (Natur:42) the *Identitätsphilosophie* a few years later had seen the organic equilibrium of inner and outer as itself the self-transformation of character, not an exclusion of passion but instead the power of beauty in relation to passion.

> Otherwise the enterprise of moderation would merely resemble that of the shallow moralists who, in order to cope with man, prefer to mutilate nature in him and have so thoroughly eliminated everything from his action that people gloat over the spectacle of great crimes in order to enliven themselves with the sight at least of something positive.[86]

Here doubtless character would remain connected with the ancient accounts of grace (*Charis*) and *dignitas*—the expression of excellence—albeit one fully ordered to the task of beauty, of moderation, equilibrium, and expression.[87] And like beauty, it too is claimed to have its foundation and vitality in nature.[88] Still, Schelling is quick to point out that such claims can only hold for the highest, not the lowest of natures, "for the soul must not be called upon to moderate those passions which are merely the revolt of inferior passions."[89] The link between ethics and will, character and power would doubtless be complicated, underwritten by a certain disequilibrium inherited from the Hobbesian account of liberation and complicated in the "analogies" of freedom itself. But the legacy it bequeathes, as we will see further, will be equally complicated, divided again between instrumentalism and expressionism.

The idealist's intuitional appeal to nature, to a dispersion or chaos untamed by theory was, once more, not simply the invocation of fate or the dissolution of the human, but instead construed as the occasion of human excellence. Schelling had from the beginning been concerned not simply with the plenitude of nature but with the resources of the will with respect to it. By 1809, he had made the metaphysics of nature as such a philosophy of the Will, or the problem of the will as primordial being, albeit by linking the *grace* which he had sought previously now to the ontological principle of love. Ontology had become central now, as it had in his contemporaries, in the later Fichte and Hegel. But that it bequeathed an uneasy account of both dispersion and liberation is unquestionable.

In fact, we can stipulate again the breadth of its legacy. For example, the 1807 text of Schelling's quoted above can be found cited again in Coleridge, who in turn disseminates it to the Anglo-American reception of Romanticism. As Emerson put it in this regard, "We value in Coleridge his excellent knowledge and quotation perhaps as much, possibly more, than his original suggestions."[90] And Emerson too reinstitutes the complications of nature, relying again upon its "harmonies" and "dissonances." He does so, however, without losing sight of the 'good' at stake: "a beautiful form is better than a beautiful face: a beautiful behavior is better than a beautiful form." It is the latter, the question of "the moral quality radiating from [a person's] countenance" that is bound up, as will become further apparent, in the interpretation of character.[91]

Yet Emerson's essays on nature still openly repeat the logic we found in the German Idealists, invoking in its own accounts of nature and character both the harmonies of the Greeks' *Cosmos* and the play of transcendence at work in the "schoolmen's" distinction between *naturans* and *naturata*. In fact he praises both while at the same time attesting to both nature's *plenum* and its ruins in discontinuity and alterity. It is obviously wrong either to see in Emerson's account the simple remnants of his Unitarian Deism or his Empedoclean chaos: it too is both at once. As the essay "Experience" attests, if he too had raged against the physicist's materialism, he likewise realized that "we thrive by causalities" and that "life is a series of surprises" because "we find ourselves in a series of which we do not know the extremes."[92] Here again "I am a fragment" and character is just the moral order seen through the medium of an individual nature—again a matter of a natural power which "cooperates" with space and time in self-sufficiency.[93] The result thus remains then paradoxical: while Emerson is committed to the fecundity of nature, he invokes "the universal impulse to believe" on its behalf (as proto-Nietzschean as it is proto-Jamesian), and holds that despite all that civilization had done to distance and defile it, still "the umbilical cord has not been cut." And yet Emerson admits too its (Hölderlinian) deferral: "nature is always elsewhere."[94] Hence "scepticisms are not gratuitous or lawless, and the new philosophy must take them in, and make affirmations outside them, just as much as it must include the oldest beliefs."[95] This is the task of the midworld. As he put it in the essay, "Self-reliance," "I will have no covenants but proximities."[96]

For Emerson, the excess at stake in nature belies terms such as "Fortune, Minerva, Muse, Holy Ghost—these are quaint names too narrow to cover this unbounded substance."[97] As the essay on "Nature" too put it, all "literature, poetry, science are the homage of man to this unfathomed secret," and "one can hardly speak of it without excess."[98] Tropes for nature are tropic *tout court*. Pierce also would describe it well in characterizing the intellectual background against which he broke:

> I mean Cambridge—at the time when Emerson, Hedge, and their friends were disseminating the ideas that they had caught from Schelling, and Schelling from Plotinus, from Boehm, or from God knows what minds stricken with the monstrous mysticism of the East.[99]

Nonetheless he too admitted that after long incubation the immanence of nature, and the importance of Scotus in particular, returned in his own work "modified by mathematical conceptions and by training in physical investigations."[100]

If we see such commitments to nature, moreover, simply as transcendental "quietism"—and the latter as the remnant of the "unhappy consciousness" of Stoicism—we forget the radicalism which accompanied Spinoza's gesture from the outset—as well as Emerson's political activism in his rile over racism, for example. The account of moderation it entailed was both powerful and unstable at once, as the logic of conscience had dictated before it from Fichte to Schiller and beyond. The connection between nature and liberation would in fact be reinvoked time and again—not again in simply grounding right antecedently but instead in Spinozaistically confronting the necessities which imprison us. Time and again Rousseau's *sauvage* would transfer its liberations into the political realm, opening the way for the "revolutionary" retrievals of nature itself. Even Marx, after all, as has been seen, attempted to find in Empedoclean theory the overcoming of inert materialism and the beginning of revolutionary theory.

This affirmation and its energetics also in the end privileged Emerson for Nietzsche—or at least such is what Nietzsche's best interpreters have thought. The result then allows Nietzsche to be the culmination of a certain antimetaphysical naturalist tradition. "From Lucretius to Nietzsche, the same end is pursued and attained. Naturalism makes of thought and sensibility an affirmation. . . ." Against false philosophy and myth, "Lucretius reproached Epicurus' predecessors for having believed in Being, the One and the Whole."[101] Here nature exists precisely as a heterogeneity and things exist 'one by one', without any possibility of their being gathered together all at once. "The multiple as multiple is the object of affirmation, just as the diverse as diverse is the object of joy," as Deleuze put it. Consequently, Deleuze suggested that identity must be thought of as the effect of difference, which is in turn, pace Schelling, "the first potency." But if Deleuze originally found this affirmation in Lucretius before Nietzsche, it is once again Spinoza whom he too credits with its modern expression and who thus opens the way for an "ethics of difference" modeled upon the possibilities of the body.[102] Both Spinoza and Lucretius are claimed to "denounce all myth" and set "the image of positive Nature against the uncertainty of the Gods."[103] Still, such investments in the liberative potential of nature as difference, and thereby against myth and "everything that is the cause of sadness" always faced the contingency of fate itself, as Lucretius's own invocations of Venus attested. The problem of the sacred and the multiplicity of myth haunts the potencies of difference as much as it did those of identity. Against the affirmations of its positivities we can reassert Schelling's critique: such affirmations always assume that the question, "What *kind* of affirmation?" has been resolved. For the latter we will not be able to dissolve the *problem* of myth, of narrative, and interpretation so readily.

Strauss, on the other hand, has emphasized the role of Lucretius's hymn in his classic account of the three waves of modernity. The invocation of Lucretius occurs, as Strauss points out, for example, in Montesquieu, "a last vestige of the poetry underlying modern prose"—precisely in prefacing a discussion on population in the *Esprit des lois*. Indeed the only other such poem in Montesquieu is one by the author himself prefacing a book on commerce—in both cases, Strauss claimed, at work is a "serpentine wisdom which corrupted by charming and charmed by corrupting."[104] The point for Strauss is again twofold: if the moderns invoked the ancients, they did so with distinctly *non*ancient results. Montesquieu in fact provided the *parcours* to Strauss's second wave of modernity, leading to Rousseau, who "bore both German romanticism and the romanticism of all ranks in all countries." This second wave would provide "a return to premodern thought" but with a result "more alien" to the ancients than its predecessor (e.g., Rousseau returning from the world of commerce to that of the citizen and virtue, Kant returning from the ideas of Descartes and Locke to Plato, Hegel from the world of reflection to the higher vitality of Aristotle).[105] The result in all these cases however would finally dissolve the distinction between the natural and positive laws—thereby succumbing, for Strauss, to irrationalism. The preceding wave began with Hobbes and the third wave, or historicism, which finally truncated the antinomy itself of natural and positive law altogether, Strauss associated with Nietzsche. In this third wave nature was seemingly now void of all rationality, an "estrangement from man's deepest desire" and the "oblivion of eternity."[106] Of course it is just this "estrangement" that Deleuze claims Spinoza and Nietzsche, following Lucretius, greeted as liberation.

There is, it might be argued, a certain historicism in Strauss's three-wave account and its own ensuing charge of irrationalism. Indeed, the justificatory motivations for such transformations—which we have followed out, especially with regard to the critical transformations of post-Kantian thought—are missing from Strauss's argument.[107] The complexity of the transformations involved in articulating the relation between 'spirit' and 'nature'—epistemic, political, and metaphysical—is omitted. In this regard, Strauss's thought doubtless participates in the very history he describes, setting off a series of antinomial and decisionist choices. Much more would need to be said in order to render its dispersions intelligible, much more concerning, on the other hand, the analogies in which nature will be constituted, the 'aesthetic' model of its discovery, the hermeneutic model of its justification, and the ontological status of our "being in it." To see the modern's technical investments, on the other hand, as simple decline would be short-sighted and overly nostalgic—a nostalgia Strauss's appeal itself to "the discovery of nature" perhaps owes to the Romantics, and about which more too will need to be said. What such views fail to recognize is that the narratives of the ancients are no more self-evident than were those of the moderns. Neither form of affirmation of nature—ancient or modern—can escape the problem of interpretation. And that doubtless is the point: that the complexity of their development has not yet really been thought together.

Deleuze too is adamant here, however—and he is so precisely in confronting (while affirming) Strauss's analysis of natural right. For Deleuze,

Spinoza's liberation, recognized again to be a liberation of the possibilities of the body, stands firmly on Hobbesian ground as a rejection of the rules of authority, precedent and perfection.[108] While

> reason does of course on its own account involve a *pietas* and a *religio*, and there are of course precepts, rules or 'commands' of reason. . . . They are not duties but norms of life relating to the soul's 'strength' and its power of action.[109]

Still, short of exchanging one authority for another—nature as perfection, versus nature as 'life' or 'action'—we will need to further grasp the complexity of the event. We have already stressed not only Schelling's own attempts to link Lucretius and Spinoza but also the remnants of the *interpretatio naturae* in Spinoza and its resulting distance from Hobbes's mechanical account of the mechanics of political action. It was perhaps just this that Schelling had recognized both in criticizing the impoverishment of the (Fichtean) emphasis upon the act and in holding that life itself is "the schema of freedom." And yet Schelling refused to align self-affirmation with the mere "pious opinion" (Natur:41); instead he explicated how "such a Nature got *into us*" through a hermeneutics of nature and the speculative potentials of transcendental imagination. Ethical difference as a result remains more than simple affirmation figured within the complications of transcendental schematism itself, an exposition of the passage from intuition to concept. This was the complexity at stake in the origins of post-Kantian thought: its narratives (and phenomenologies) were divided between freedom and nature, the imaginary and the real, the new science and the old.[110] Hence arises the problematic status of its "idealistic" turn inward, divided, in turn, between the dogmas of pantheism and mechanism.

10. At the Limits of Enlightenment

Even here, however, Fichte's own encounter with the question of nature—a question that, in its resistance, becomes crucial to the *Wissenschaftslehre's* claims to 'realism'—provides a precedent for this division. Beyond the figure of mathematical constraint, nature itself ushers in this more "ancient" resistance. Against the ancients' confidence in the 'world', the 'transcendental' turn to the inner, to the remnants of the self as *intus,* required a turn to a reflective stronghold free from epistemic and metaphysical challenge, a reflective and ecstatic release from external necessities. And yet Fichte also (aptly) worried that if our thoughts are completely freed from such necessities, nothing prevents our thoughts from being dreams, a matter which plagued all his and perhaps all other phenomenologies of the absolute which followed.[111]

From the outset, however, Fichte's formulation of the "transcendental concept" of a drive (*Trieb*) that underlies the striving (*Streben*) of consciousness, required him to articulate a semantic domain that divided not only all "philosophy of consciousness," but also all the "philosophies of the unconscious" which were parasitic upon it. The result has appropriately been described, to speak Deleuzian, as an "antilogos" — an event divided between freedom and necessity, the known and the unknown, the voluntary and the involuntary. To base their unity on the philosophy of consciousness involves a clear paradox, as Schelling suggested:

> To say that necessity is again to be present in freedom amounts, therefore, to saying that through freedom itself, and in that I believe myself to act freely, something I do not intend is to come about unconsciously, i.e., without my consent; or to put it otherwise, the conscious, or that freely determining activity which we deduced early on, is to be confronted with an unconscious.[112]

Fichte, however, would never go so far, nor would he opt for Schelling's immediate proposal that the work of art could resolve this conflict, a proposal that aestheticizes both Knowledge and Nature, the conscious and the unconscious. As has become clear, Fichte had nonetheless recognized the revelatory problem of its event.[113] The 1795 third part of the *Science of Knowledge* from the outset articulated the complexity of this new semantic field. Concerning the drive of the self (*qua* finite and realistic) Fichte claimed, Reason must "encounter in itself something heterogeneous, alien, and to be distinguished from itself" [*etwas heterogenes, fremdartiges, von ihm selbst zu unterscheidended in sich antreffen*] (SK:240). Hence, the striving (*Streben*) of the self as *actus*, as autodetermination (*Selbstbestimmung*), as drive must be articulated through the concept of limit and the not-self. This requires an "explanation of how the self is able to feel itself *driven towards something unknown* [*als getrieben nach irgend etwas unbekanntem*]" and in which precisely as a "drive toward something unknown . . . reveals itself only through a *need*, a *discomfort*, a *void*" [*durch in Bedurfniss, durch ein Misbehagen, durch eine Leere offenbart*] (SK:261, 265). But this splitting, again, was of the order of belief, not knowledge, as evidential as it might remain at the limits of the empirical. The result would be a play of ideal and real, of the knower and the unknown, of self-determination and the undetermined which would articulate a *heterogeneity* at the heart of the self itself. Yet as has been seen, this "intrasubjective difference" did not detract from Fichte's claim that the self is like a mathematical point (SK:241) and does not succumb to dispersion, even though surely the entirety of the *Wissenschaftslehre* itself points to a certain 'counter-factual' which threatens its *Ursache*—that such dispersion might be insurmountable and in any case could not be ruled out. Hence would arise Fichte's own preoccupation concerning the risk that intuition is a dream and thought the dream of that dream.

Nor was Fichte alone in grappling with the division within the event of the self implied. If Fichte's practical philosophy more fully attends to the complexity of this domain, Schiller had already glimpsed its rudiments. Hegel claimed (and Heidegger concurred[114]) that

> it is Schiller who must be given credit for breaking through the Kantian subjectivity and abstraction of thinking and for venturing an attempt to get beyond this by intellectually grasping the unity of reconciliation as the truth and by actualizing them in artistic production. (Aesth:61)

Still Schiller himself again cited Fichte in this regard, specifically the *Vocation of the Scholar*, if not for his aesthetic resources, but for the principle that "the ultimate vocation of every finite, rational being is absolute unity, constant identity and perfect harmony with itself."[115] Even here, however, the matter is complex: Fichte's *Sittenlehre* itself concluded by claiming that the Nature at stake in his analysis has "two sides" (SE:368), as has been seen. The unified intuition which overcomes its diremption is seen as an aesthetic intuition—albeit one that disregards the diremption more than resolves it. If such an aesthetic sense is a preparation for virtue, as has already become clear, it is not virtue itself. Instead duty crushes all natural inclination, and the aesthetic furnishes in this regard only its preparation insofar as "the fine arts lead man back into himself, and make him at home with himself" (SE:368-69). That is, "they tear him loose from given Nature" (SE:368). Hence again Hegel's claim that the "necessary viewpoint of [Fichte's] *Ethics*, far from being aesthetic is precisely the one that reveals distorted, fear-ridden, oppressed forms, or ugliness" (Dif:154). Schiller had demanded otherwise regarding both the aesthetic and nature. Indeed, Schiller's twelfth letter would perhaps be ever more pointed than Hegel in declaring that "thought may indeed elude it for the moment, and a firm will may triumphantly oppose its demands, but Nature once rebuffed soon returns to claim her rights. . . ."[116] Schiller claims that, divided between what he called the sensuous and the formal impulse (*Trieb*), humans "are urged by two contrary forces which, because they impel us to realize their object, are very properly called impulses."[117] The formal, the timeless, here too receive the final word, but precisely because in deciding for the moment it decides for eternity. "Consequently it embraces the whole time series which is as much to say it annuls time and change; it wishes the actual to be necessary and eternal, and the eternal and necessary to be actual; in other words, it aims at right and truth."[118]

In this way man would be enabled to overcome the sundering of the *Naturstaat*, where "an unavoidable exigency had thrown him there before he could freely choose his station"—precisely because "the work of blind force possesses no authority before which Freedom need bow."[119] In Schiller, in other words, the intellectual *Formtrieb* (more clearly Reinhold's term) and the *Sinnlichen Trieb* are united and sustained through the interplay or *Spieltrieb* that would unite nature as blind force and nature as idea through the reconciling of energizing Beauty.[120] But as is now clear, these relationships also involve both a transformation of Rousseau's elevation of the *sauvage* and Schiller's own nostalgic view of the Greek "Bygone Golden age of Nature."[121] Both in any case stood behind his aestheticization of reason and the account of the state as work of art.

Still, for all Schiller's importance here (and it is considerable)[122] the 'counterfactual' remains, as does the question of nature's revenge on any reason that seeks to escape it. Reflective judgment, like the aesthetic model it prefigures, relies upon the benevolence of imagination, on the harmony of the faculties and the rationalization of *phantasia*. Freud would declare that we must respect nature more—not by regarding it as a "reserve," however, but precisely as insurmountable. Instead, 'nature', as Hölderlin would see, would itself be the site of a certain *caesura* of the speculative.[123]

As recent interpreters attest, we should tread carefully here. Gadamer would insist, for example, that the Romantics' *Spieltrieb* was in the end not subjective, i.e., not simply a conative faculty, but rather an ontological event irreducible to such a subjective effect (TM:101ff.). It has been claimed that Hegel completes the Copernican revolution that began in Winckelmann's retrieval of the Greeks, albeit fully on modernist principles, namely in pronouncing the death of art. In the same way Hegel also dissolved Schiller's transformation of Winckelmann in retrieving "the golden age of nature" in his metaphysics of Spirit's *Realisierung* and its 'desubstantialization' of the object. Still, the 'completeness' of spirit seems always to elude the system, which relied narratively upon the very "plasticity" and *Witz* Hegel sought to domesticate. Similarly the completion of Spirit's *Realisierung* relied upon the *plenum* of nature to overcome what Hegel had early on called transcendental philosophy's Voltairean abhorrence of nature in Kant and Fichte which merely "soars above the wreckage of the world," a kind of "sublime hollowness."[124] Neither nature nor art would be so simply subsumable and here

Hegel's own expositions too always presupposed a presence which always eluded presentation, reduction, and consequently certainty.

Indeed most primoridally and in a moment that sounds more like medieval physicists such as Grosseteste than Hegel's own predecessors, his own philosophy of nature sought its initial substantialization in the self-manifestation of light:

> In the oriental intuition of the substantial identity of the spiritual and the natural, the pure selfhood of consciousness — self-identical in the abstract forms of the True and the Good — is one with light. When so-called realistic thinking [Vorstellung] denies that identity is present in Nature, it can be referred among other things to light, to this pure making manifest which is nothing but a making manifest.[125]

While Grosseteste might seem to be an appropriate antecedent for such a physics, he does so by a metaphorics that extends behind him to Plato and onwards to Descartes, to Hegel himself, and beyond Hegel, to Heidegger's attempts to articulate "the lighting of Being" beyond "categorical representation on the part of subjectivity" (LH:211). But Hegel's account of nature as a transmutation of forms through the metaphysics of light now also became figured through the development of the pure ego understood as the event of this "pure manifesting" or "enlightening." Still, this reliance on pure ego already presupposed a nature beyond the ego (or pure self-presupposition) that always accompanied such idealist Naturphilosophie. At most it seemed, as Kant had seen in the third Critique, such claims would be "problematic." As Hölderlin insisted in his own Empedoclean retrieval, if nature still remained connected with the holy, it also "manifested" the site of a certain tragedy of the spirit, which, instead of revealing the intelligibility of a pure light, revealed a being who belonged to the "twilight," for whom, as Hyperion ponders, "twilight is our element."[126] Hence, as Heidegger would claim, "When Goethe says 'nature', and when Hölderlin speaks the same word, different worlds reign" — one in the fulfillment of nature, the other, in the withdrawal and dispersion of nature, a concealing on its way to "the tragedy of beings as such."[127]

Even here, however, we again encounter the complications deriving from Fichte's legacy. Fichte had similarly articulated the Wechsel of light and darkness, seeking the synthesis of their opposition in the productive imagination, and in that very opposition he sought the condition under which a theory of human cognition could be established (SK:201). While such a unification belies finite reason, the synthesis itself is compared to this twilight in which it can be seen that "darkness is simply a minute form of light—that is precisely how things are between the self and the non-self" (SK:138). But in so understanding this event, Fichte had not encountered the problem of *withdrawal* that such a "twilight" indicated—beyond the reconciliation of opposites and the domination of "nature" by enactment. The matrix in question, as has been seen, had throughout been divided in an uneasy economy between nostalgia for a mythic golden age, the culmination of its modern proof-theoretical replacement, and a meditation on the "dispersion" at stake in their midst—and divided in turn between memory, judgment, and *Witz*. It was evident in any case that no simple solution to these divergent demands could be had. And consequently all that remained both unknown and unconscious behind pure ego of idealism had not been considered—as those after Nietzsche and Freud would insist.

The Freudian meditation on nature, and on the nature of the self in particular, is similarly overdetermined. Indeed, the account of the subject gives rise, as poststructuralists saw as well as anyone, to a self that is heterogeneous—to use Lacan's terms, "decentered and divided from within," the historionics of *Trieb* itself divided between sublimation and desublimation. The history of the "series" in which Fichte had posited the self is divided between sense and non-sense, a conceptual inheritance whose different sides are exemplified in Kant and Freud, divided between 'liberation' and 'perversion' before the law. And yet the Romantic vestige is not thereby dissolved; its logic of sense still remains consonant with Emerson's "elsewhere." But if Emerson glimpsed this excess, and even its withdrawal before the beyond (transcendence as "self-reliance" itself), we will have to add to Emerson's emphasis upon reliability Poe's horror, again the 'counterfactual' to Romantic beautitude, in order to fully comprehend the ruins of *Naturphilosophie*. It is doubtless here, as Walter Benjamin realized, that Baudelaire, for example, would found the poetry of modernity.

Still, if Baudelaire had learned his genre from Poe, he could not, as Benjamin also perceptively recognized, simply identify himself with Poe. In particular, he could not identify with Poe's fascination with the secret and in particular the detective story:

> Baudelaire wrote no detective story because, given the structure of his instincts, it was impossible for him to identify with the detective. In him the calculative, constructive element was on the side of the asocial and had become an integral part of cruelty. Baudelaire was too good a reader of the Marquis de Sade to be able to compete with Poe.[128]

All this seems to be missing from Emerson's affirmations, who doubtless did not feel Poe's denials of Emersonian beatitude. If for Baudelaire, in any case, Poe had understood "the funeral cortege of modernity," it was de Sade who had explained to him its evil—but only again, as Lacan saw, in its proximity to Kant's own account of evil, as a propensity to stray that always accompanies the instruments of reason. The passions in both Kant and de Sade had been pulverized; if Hobbes is correct that ratiocination is calculation or computation[129] then reason itself is now, to speak Kantian, instrinsically divided between its predisposition to the Good and its propensity to stray. As Cavell has noticed, the analysis at stake in the irony of Poe's horrors doubtless has something to do with the skepticism about the ordinary that accompanies analysis in general—and hence prohibits "reconstruction or resettlement of the everyday."[130] We might wonder however whether the everyday will be so readily domesticated as to yield to either 'reconstruction' or 'resettlement'—whether the *question* of analysis (as much as the *question* of dwelling) already indicated a rupture that required a reinterpetation which, precisely in its 'deconstruction' of the 'dogmas' of analysis, precluded such reconstruction, let alone resettlement. Both Emerson's ecstacies and Poe's horrors will need in this regard to be thought together. This much remains true: Reason's transcendental 'purity' could now be grasped only in terms of this division, the errancy of its event, and to use Kant's term for Reason's respect before its own "self-conceit" (*arrogantia*) and "humiliation" which arises in default (CprR:76). As Kant also realized, however, the phenomenologies of pure reason, theoretical and practical, would always stumble before this need to identify their interpretation with adequation, ratiocination with intellection, the conditional with the unconditional, and the fragmented and the dispersed with totality (A298/B354).

As much as he may have initially sought to separate *strenge Wissenschaft* from such considerations, the final writings of Husserl had come to a similar conclusion. First of all, they called for a deepening of the science of phenomenology in light of the "unquestioning tradition of modern *Technisierung*," claiming of its investments in instrumental rationality that "a one-sided rationality can certainly become an evil" (K:46, 291). There is a sense in which all of Husserl's critique of modernity could be viewed as posited against the 'perversion' that underlies the (Hobbesian) reduction of the rational to subjective 'calculability'. Instead, consistent with his attempts to return the variety of rational forms back to the evidential insights of lived experience, Husserl was led to articulate anew the bodily organism on which all transcendental 'egological' experience rests—"an *intrinsically first Nature* which is not yet Objective nature"—and to reinterpret its lifeworld and even its earth.[131] This latter sense of the earth, the earth (and the region) on which we dwell, challenged the pure iterabilities of modern objectivity—not least of all phenomenology itself. Indeed, Husserl claimed, by appealing still to an "earth [that] does not move" perhaps "phenomenology has supported Copernican astrophysics—but also anti-Copernicanism according to which God had fixed the earth at a place in space."[132] Here phenomenology, again, would participate in the retrieval of premodern narratives of the 'lived'. At the same time this preobjective origin remained both intentional object and even the correlate of a "nature in itself"—all of which had been occluded in positivist "overcoming" of the manifest image and yet upon which it irreducibly depends (K:305). It is this world of "pre-logical validity," a proto-objectivity of "persons, the apparatus, the room in the institute," that makes up the "prescientific world" upon which even Einstein depends—and even in his own "*epoché*" of the manifest image (K:125f). And yet the "coincidences" of this second scientific *epoché* inevitably decenters the intentional correlates of the first, raising the scepter of a certain *Hexenkreis*, a vicious circle of mutual but inadequateable dependencies. Hence the problem of the correlation returns with respect to the link between such theoretization and the preobjective lifeworld, raising anew the problem of the excess in which individual and universal is 'constituted'—and raising thereby Kantian and hermeneutic suspicions anew. The latter emerge not only with respect to the criteria by which theoretical expositions might be vindicated, but equally in the question of whether all the "conditions" of finite "intuition" had been encountered—or perhaps could ever be encountered from the egological framework. Schelling had queried with regard to Fichte, as Heidegger would with respect to Husserl, whether the egological framework had not in the end rendered its discourse incommensurable with the 'transcendence' (and withdrawal) of nature. But then the question arises, can nature still be thought? Can the excess of nature be grasped beyond such calculation? And, can the notion of the *reliability* of nature make sense in this disequilibrium in which its withdrawal remain incalculable? And finally, what sense can the ancient harmonies of nature have after the "idealistic dissolution"?

11. Heidegger's 'Physis'

Here in any case is where we might directly rejoin that other contemporary meditation on the remainder of nature itself, formulated more specifically in relation to the archive we have now delineated. Heidegger's thinking, perhaps more than any other contemporary work, maintains its link with the archive of *Naturphilosophie,* developing especially in the later works, against a certain "type of thinking that is about to abandon the earth as earth."[133]

We can focus in this regard on his 1940 essay, "On the Being and Conception of *Physis* in Aristotle's *Physics* B1," which had prefaced its account by articulating the conceptual development of this "*Grundwort* that designates fundamental relations that Western historical man has to beings, both to himself and to beings other than himself."[134] Heidegger returns in this discussion to the history of the concept of nature, rejoining others such as Vico, Schelling, or Nietzsche in linking the rationality of nature to an interpretation of the diachrony of the received views. Heidegger notes first that the Romans had translated *physis* by the word *natura. Natura* itself is traced to *nasci,* to be born, to originate, which in Christian thought became a matter of what is bestowed upon humans—a condition in which, left to themselves, the passions are able to bring about the "total destruction" of our humanity. He then claims that Nietzsche makes the body his key to the interpretation of the world and thus secures a new and harmonious relation to the sensible. Finally, Heidegger claims, nature becomes the name for everything elemental and everything human, even as "above the gods." Here, however, (beyond Nietzsche) Heidegger cites Hölderlin, claiming that in construing nature as that which is "*above* the gods and 'older than the ages' in which beings always come to be . . . 'nature' becomes the word for 'Being'."[135] The most primary ontological questions, then, become those regarding 'nature' without ever fully grasping what is at stake in this connection, a jointure that is prior to both 'history', 'matter', and 'mind' and yet "sustains" them all. Heidegger's interpretive translation thus grasps the problem of *physis* in terms of the problem of Being. Here, too, Heidegger returns to the ancients to discover an account of Being antecedent to the split between subject and object upon which German Idealism had foundered, an account neither reducible to representation, nor simply concealed from it in occlusion: "for the Greeks however 'Being' means becoming present, coming into the unhidden."[136] The account of *logos* in turn is linked in Greek mathematics to relation or proportion (*analogia*), where the latter signifies less a correspondence than a gathering together of the incommensurate, of which words themselves are but fragments.[137] Heidegger's later works thereby attempt to provide an articulation of this event antecedent both to calculation and to the reductions of theoretical modernism—and thus antecedent to the physicalistic reductions of modern physics and the reductions of representation and phantasmagoria in subjective idealism. The basic terms of Aristotle's physics, e.g., place, motion, form, matter, essence, or the elemental defy their modern

physicalistic reductions as much as their semantic plenitudes defy the "philosophy of language."[138] As such, they would escape all transcendental subjectivity and even Heidegger's own prior attempts to break out of such
representationalism through *Being and Time's* fundamental ontology—which
doubtless still affects these later interpretations.

But to grasp the latter we doubtless should first preface Heidegger's account with a caveat. It would be misleading to think that Heidegger's earlier
work in *Being and Time* could not be similarly read in connection with these
issues, nor in proximity to the archive we have traced through German
Idealism. Dasein's thrown projection cannot be separated from the archive
we have traced: it refigures the Fichtean *Trieb* and its denaturalization, but
the articulemes of *dominating* the *Umwelt* were left behind in the same
moment that the Absolute ego was replaced by Dasein's original relation to
Being. The hermeneutic circle then "intentionally" articulates a prior relation to idealist reflection, openly attempting to surpass the subject-object
dichotomy. In effect, Heidegger's emphasis upon the (hermeneutic) link
between intentionality and the question of Being thereby openly denies
Hobbes's dissolution of the significance of abstract terms or second 'in-
tentions' like "Entity, Intentionality, Quiddity" (Lev:101). Rather than focusing on Hobbes or Spinoza in his later works, however, as has been seen,
Heidegger focused upon Leibniz in tracing his concern with the modern
transformation of *mathesis* vis à vis classical thought. Here the problem of
nature became openly subsumed by the universal calculus, the *ars analytica*
that fully *equated* the problem of the individual and the singular.

But Heidegger also did not simply abandon the legacy of the Spinozaistic model of reflected necessity. It returned in his later thought under
the guise of that other form of dangerous necessity, the seduction of
history, accompanied by concerns about the moderns' exclusion of the
passions. This historical necessity in *Being and Time* already perniciously
appears under the guise of a certain false tranquility (*vis inertiae*) accompanying the "hustle" (*"Betriebs"*) of modern everyday life (the *They* or
'public interpretation') and whose failure becomes manifest only through
the privileged mood of anxiety, in which once again an "unknown" would
erupt within the horizon of cognition. While Fichte had cognized the
basis of cognition in a *Trieb* and this in turn as a feeling in which the self
"is driven out abroad from itself," both then active and passive (SK:260),
Heidegger reiterates this primacy of the passions by the articuleme of a
Stimmung in which Dasein reveals that it has been delivered over in its
being (BT:173). Both he and Fichte concur, to use Heidegger's term, that
"the possibilities of disclosure which belong to cognition reach far too

short a way compared with the primordial disclosure belonging to moods, in which Dasein is brought before its Being as 'there'" (BT:173). Both Fichte and Heidegger, moreover, emphasized the problematic character of the received practices or public interpretation. And both, too, are cognizant of this event of originary feeling as a sort of *antilogos* which reveals the passivity of thrownness, its *Geworfenheit*. What in fact this *Stimmung* reveals is not simply emotional, nor psychological, but equally historical; as an epistemic event, it is fully mystified before its institutions, prohibiting human "authenticity" in the very moment that we depend upon those institutions as part of our being (*Mitsein*). Hence arises the question of Dasein's inauthenticity, its fate, and its tragic destiny.

While *Being and Time* itself was not silent on the problem of nature, then, it still reveals Heidegger's proximity to idealist reflection—to Fichte and to Husserl—even while criticizing both. Like Scheler before him, moreover, Heidegger had linked the problem of the passions to the Senecan and Augustinian *cura*, even to the latter's *ordo amoris*. Scheler too had articulated the relation between soul and body as a *Wechsel* of levels.[139] To this, explicitly building upon both Scheler and Augustine, Heidegger had added a specifically ontological level to the Augustinian account of transcendence. He also added an historical dimension to the *Umwelt* itself, one again in which Dasein's state of mind (much like the feeling of the alien or the heterogeneous in Fichte's *Anstoss*) reveals the factical character of human finitude. Only on the basis of this original 'attunement' to our being-there can analysis "so to speak, 'listen in' to some previously disclosed entity as regards its being" (BT:178-79). And this figure of 'listening' itself characterizes Dasein's being called forth with respect to the truth of Being, a 'call' that comes *"from me and yet from beyond me and over me"* (BT:320). In this "anxious" call of Being the legacy of post-Kantian thought and perhaps philosophy itself is still remotely intact, divided between the self and the beyond; Dasein's original *Stimmung* is the attunement of this "exchange" itself. Hence nature itself is parsed as a moment in the "reciprocal rejoinder" of Dasein's historicality. Here Heidegger once again takes up the figure of "natural history" that had provoked both Schelling and Husserl before him:

> And even Nature is historical. It is *not* historical, to be, sure, in so far as we speak of 'natural history', but Nature is historical as a countryside, as an arena that has been colonized or exploited, as a battlefield, or as the site of a cult. These entities within-the-world *are* historical as such, and their history does not signify something 'external' which merely accompanies the 'inner' history of the 'soul'. (BT:440)

The later Heidegger—*inter alia,* ever more cognizant of both the conceptual limitations of phenomenology and more suspicious of the voluntarist
connotations of the egological framework—recoils from this historicity in
order to provide his own archaeology of a nature yet more "primitive," one
which beyond, but within the duplicity of the *Stimmung* itself indicates an
event prior to activity, prior to interpretation, prior to cognition, and even
prior to self-reflection. Here Heidegger more openly encounters the heterogeneity and the 'antilogos' implied in reflection and interpretation itself,
that zero point of meaning which eludes the self as archimedian point of
enacted modern subjectivity. Heidegger's insight here had been anticipated
by Scheler with respect to the passions again:

> 'Modern' man eager to 'control', wanted first in the case of outer reality, to
> recognize as real in the psychic life only what could be controlled. He was
> inclined to recognize only the associative-mechanical side of the soul as the
> true soul, and hence his eyes became blind to its non-mechanical side.[140]

This blind spot at the basis of reflection came increasingly to the fore in
Heidegger's thought—but equally elsewhere in Husserl's wake, e.g., in
Sartre's concerns with the '*irreflechi*' involved in consciousness or Merleau-
Ponty's return to the "nascent *logos*" of the lived body. Indeed it led
Merleau-Ponty also to speak in the later works of a need for a psychoanal-
ysis of objective knowledge and a new account of the philosophy of nature.
    Merleau-Ponty had in this regard doubtless more explicitly faced the
implications of the 'Soul' as 'besouled' in the lived body's adherence to
nature, as the legacy of Fichte's achievement. If it is true, as Sartre quotes
Merleau-Ponty as saying, that "nature is in tatters," it was still for him
impossible to simply deny our (bodily) adherence to nature.[141] And, significantly, Merleau-Ponty too returned in this regard to meditations on
Schelling: his final work took its title, *The Visible and the Invisible,* from
the preface to Schelling's *Ideas for a Philosophy of Nature* and its search
for "the secret bond that couples our mind to nature or the secret organ
through which Nature speaks to our mind or our mind to Nature"
(Natur:41). Despite the rupture in the philosophy of reflection as a result
of its dependence on the unreflected, Merleau-Ponty was led to articulate
a final *factum,* a reciprocal envelopment or *chiasmus* for the Fichtean
Wechsel, whereby the visible requires a new ontology. This 'elemental'
ontology again raises "pre-Cartesian themes" that reaffirm our bond with
the visible—that I am "of it" (*en est*).[142]
    For Merleau-Ponty this link between the visible and invisible again implied

a more fundamental fact of nature (*Naturfactum*), namely that "all corporality is already symbolism."[143] Correlatively, spirit, as "the problem of the other is a particular problem of the problem of others, since the relation with someone is always mediated by the relationship with third parties."[144] Intersubjectivity involves not a logic of opposition, but rather, as Fichte's solicitation (*Aufforderung*) had only partially seen, "the problem of the initiation to a symbolics and a typicality of others of which the being for itself and the being for the other are reflective variants and not the essential forms."[145] Here, however, Merleau-Ponty, in accord with his symbolics of the lifeworld, rediscovered the itinerary of Schelling at the limits of the philosophy of consciousness: "What resists phenomenology within us—natural being, the 'barbarous source' Schelling spoke of—cannot remain outside phenomenology and should have its place within it."[146] But at the same time the link between reason and reflection too, as has become evident, cannot but be internally disrupted.

Now Heidegger similarly—and increasingly—articulated this prereflective moment upon which all reflection relies in a meditation upon the 'earth': first as figured within a rift or struggle (*Riss*) (between world and earth, disclosure and withdrawal); then second, in overcoming the illusion of opposition itself in a narrative of the fourfold (*das Geviert*), where the earth while withdrawing in the interplay of mortal and gods, sky and earth, is still emphasized for its sustaining and reliable character—precisely in this withdrawal. Here Heidegger (doubtless stoically) regathers the ruins of nature in an account that acknowledges the danger which modernity has inflicted upon the earth, while at the same time acknowledging its sustaining power, the 'lighting' of Being that first affords a view, and thereby a *Nomos* whose dispensation itself is "capable of supporting and obligating" (LH:238).

This account of the reliability of nature would, however, necessarily elude the antinomies that had divided the philosophies of nature, history, and tradition in Kant's wake between past and present, the I and nature, self and Other. And perhaps nowhere does this become more glaring than in Heidegger's new emphasis upon Leibniz, articulating, as we have seen, the impact of the new scheme on the old, a meditation combining the legacy of *techne* and *mathesis*, within their modern *destiny*. It is precisely here that Heidegger can no longer see his history of the concept of nature, as Schelling saw his own, to be *completing* modern science: hence the (fragmented) narratives of Heidegger's later works. If Heidegger sees himself as gaining a more primoridal access to the "systematicity" of Being as the "jointure" of Being and beings, he no longer sees such a system as harmoniously resolving the conflict between 'nature' (Being's semantic excess) and the modern (mathematical) science of physics.[147] The passage between the ancient science of being and the moderns' systematic demonstrations would now be openly in conflict, an *Auseinandersetzung*. And moreover this move openly impacts on the legacy of the transcendental histories it inherits.

Schelling's transcendental history, as has been seen, viewed itself as the culmination of modern metaphysics, fulfilling Herder's historical transformations of Leibniz. Indeed the 1800 *System of Transcendental Idealism* already viewed transcendental history as itself a "revelation" of the Absolute: "Man through his history provides a continuous demonstration of God's presence, a demonstration, however, which only the whole of history can render complete."[148] In such claims Schelling already anticipates both a philosophy of revelation and a philosophy of mythology. The *Abfall* out of which finite existence proceeds is then a matter of aligning oneself with a history always already (factually) beyond the human: the recapturing of an Absolute in which nature, history, narrative and the calculations of human judgment might in the end coalesce.[149] As such, however, Schelling's logic of identity remained confounded by the logic of transcendental illusion, inevitably verging upon a metaphysical "naturalism" whose origins could not be indicated.

Fichte, on the other hand, granted the inevitably dialectical (and incomplete) character of such intuitions, could view such commitments only sceptically, replacing their transcendence with the immanence of rationality itself and hence the immanence of subjective enactment. While, as has been seen, Schelling's transcendental historicity, like all return to origins, must inevitably temporalize itself out of the (illicit) guarantees of the past, Fichte's history would invest itself in a transcendental eschatology—as he put it, pace Rousseau: "a golden age" which is the "state of nature" that "lies ahead of us." In this regard it is precisely temporality that divided German Idealism against itself—as well as its deductions of the finite. Still, the transcendental illusions that accompany Fichte's and Schelling's demonstrations, which are divided between the certainty of Being and the certainty of enactment, have perhaps become readily apparent—and Heidegger's emphasis upon the *aporiae* of time did not fail to encounter them.

Being and Time's account of authenticity likewise privileged the future, enough so in fact that Merleau-Ponty's already Schellingian intuitions concerning nature in the *Phenomenology of Perception* led him to criticize the possibility of Heidegger's privilege of the future ("it is always in the present that we are centered").[150] While our decisions open up a dimension of the new, granted the need for critique and the ambiguity of time itself, such historical decisions "afford us only a temporary reprieve from dispersion."[151] But Heidegger's emphasis upon the 'shattering' of Dasein against its own death had acknowledged this dispersion, of course. The later works' privileging *physis*, on the other hand, seems at first glance to bring Heidegger into closer proximity to Schelling—and to lead to an ethics more fully conceived in terms of the integrity of the 'entity' itself. Hence there arises the emphasis in his Schelling lectures on the account of love and reconciliation as "letting-be" in a time in which "all compassion and forbearance [*Nachsicht*] have been burnt out."[152] And yet at the same time, against Schelling's speculative "Leibnizianism," Heidegger univocally criticized any attempt to reconcile the sensible and the intelligible. If he granted that behind Schelling's treatise lay Aristotle's question of the Being of all beings and constituted an attempt at an answer to the question of the *ti to on,* here too Heidegger claimed that the ontological difference—the difference between the beings and being—would not be reducible. As Fichte put it in replying to Schelling in 1801, we cannot simply start with being but only with the (ontic) difference of vision, act, and intuition.[153] And yet the modern technical construction of *mathesis* upon which, we have seen, Fichte still modeled the act of the self, had confused model and Being. This equation of historical act and construction, moreover, is one to be found in both Vico and Hobbes before him. As Vico put it:

> History cannot be more certain than when he who creates the things also narrates them. Now as geometry when it constructs the world of quantity out of its elements, or contemplates the world, is creating it for itself, just so does our science, but with a reality greater by just so much as the institutions having to do with human affairs are more real than points, lines, surfaces, and figures are.[154]

But we do not create history, and we are not certain of our own acts, as Fichte thought, simply because we 'enact' them: Being and Act, after all, are not the same. It is false that "all being is to be derived from doing" (SE:59). Against these antinomies, Heidegger's account of the resulting "ruins of beings" would ultimately approximate Hölderlin more than Schelling: the reliability of "nature" now might be sustained only in acknowledging its withdrawal before both the ancient speculative narratives and the reductions of the modern sciences.

Even so, how is such a withdrawal to be thought and how can it avoid the antinomies in both transcendentalism and historicism? The 1941 Schelling seminar provides Heidegger's answer in an extended passage that re-counts our argument:

> In spite of all the criticism, does not the danger of historicism or actualism remain? It does not. Historicism brings the past to the present and explains it in terms of what lies further back in the past. It flees to the past to find something to hold onto and counts on escapes from the present. It wants "restoration" or else "eschatology." Mere "relativizing" does not constitute the essence of historicism.
>
> Actualism is the reverse of historicism. Through it relativism is seemingly overcome. It calculates the present value of the past. The "future" is the pro-longed present in a forward direction and is that present in its rigidification. The calculating game between origin and future turns out to be servitude to the uncomprehended present.
>
> We are not concerned with the historical explanation of the past, relevant to the present, but with historically coming to grips with what has been (*Gewesenen*) still presencing.[155]

Heidegger's historical account here becomes based upon what still presences in its withdrawal from the present. Its experience, as he puts it elsewhere, "cannot be forced"—it can be reduced neither to future nor to origin, but only to the possibility of what still presences between them in the "jointure of Being." And it is precisely in attending to what still "calls" through this difference beyond all calculability and demonstration that Heidegger would still explicate the "reliability" of nature.

12. 'Physics', the Boundaries of Theory, and the Ineluctability of the Calculable

Still, it will most certainly be asked, what of that other narrative, 'physics' itself, and what of the other side of the critical project—that of general natural science and mathematics? If the earth remains fractured by the calculable, if "nature hates calculators" as Emerson suggests, what then of the legacy of calculation? Fichte had claimed of the reality that the divided status of feeling "revealed," that it was only a belief (SK:264). It may be true, as Merleau-Ponty still put it, that "what we are finally as *naturata* we first are actively as *naturans*," but what of its status? Heidegger's gesture toward the earth is equally lacking in any certainty that could provide a counterexample to Hume's scepticism.[156] Why would one give up the certain for the sake of the uncertain? Does indeed Heidegger think that the discourse on the 'earth' could itself be simply substituted for a discourse on nature as infinite mathematical substitutability? Does Heidegger's appeal to the poetics of the earth falsify this other discourse? And does Heidegger's own *Seinsgeschick* fall prey in the same way as have other critics of modernity we have discussed—even Strauss—to the very historicism it sought to overcome? Will we be able to confront the failure of modernity until we can think the impasse of its reciprocal rejoinder, its *Erwiderung* with the ancients more fully? All this we will need to return to later, the "mixed legacy" of Kant's solutions—perhaps the antinomies of dogmatism and scepticism, as Schelling put it very early on. And surely Heidegger too remains "Schellingian" in his own resolutions in this regard. But he did so not without surpassing his own "Fichtean" tendencies and the lingering subjectivism or metaphysics of *Being and Time*.

The 1941 Schelling seminar notes show Heidegger's denials:

> According to Fichte the ego throws forth the world, and according to *Being and Time* it is not the ego that first throws the world, but it is *Da-sein* (human being), presencing before all humanity, which is thrown.[157]

We should be cautious perhaps. Fichte's lectures concerning the *Scholar's Vocation* equally claimed that "what Rousseau forgot is that mankind should approach this condition [of the state of nature] only through care, effort and labor" (VS:182). Yet Fichte's last word was the spontaneity of the self and the transcendental imagination for which nature would always be an object, and reason bound by no law external to itself. But what would be more external than nature, which is, to use Hegel's term, *Aussersein* itself? As has been seen, in *Being and Time* as well nature remains a *mise en scène*. Heidegger could perhaps agree with Fichte's phenomenology that "I find myself as active in the sensuous world" (SE:2), but he could not follow his instrumentalism. If Dasein's rationality begins similarly in the facticity of our (practical) circumspections, what Heidegger's account revealed were their levelings and deficiencies: indeed Being itself became most authentically revealed only in the aftereffects of such "break-downs." It was not Hobbes but Aristotle who had the last word—and indeed increasingly so. If, as the Marburg lectures reveal, Aristotle's practical philosophy became the articuleme for Dasein's Being-in-the-World—and this in turn the articuleme for fundamental ontology (hence the status of nature as *mise en scène*)—by 1940 the *Grundwort* 'nature' now finds its "standard" in the *Physics*: "Aristotle's *Physics* is the hidden, and therefore never adequately studied, foundational book of Western philosophy."[158]

Moreover, in his 1940 discussion of the *Physics*, Heidegger himself for-
mulates the modern objection to such commitments and responds with the
most archaic of analogons:

> Nevertheless the following objection could be raised at this point. Say that two
> doctors suffer from the same disease under the same conditons and that each
> one treats himself. However, between the two cases of illness there lies a period
> of 500 years, during which the "progress" of modern medicine has taken place.
> The doctor of today has at his disposal a "better" technique and he regains
> health, whereas the one who lived earlier dies of the disease. So the *arché* of
> the cure of today's doctor is precisely the *techne*. There is, however, something
> further to consider here. For one thing, the fact of not dying, in the sense of
> prolonging life, is not yet necessarily the recovery of health. The fact that men
> live longer today is no proof that they are healthier; one might even conclude
> to the contrary.[159]

The healthy, as Aristotle already realized, cannot be functionally defined,
any more than the *relata* at stake in Dasein's Being-in-the-World can be
grasped extensionally (BT:121f.)—both involve always already a reference
to what lies beyond them, a *'pros hen'*. Nor can *techne* by itself internally
provide this standard—a standard which, Aristotle claimed (as he did with
respect to all such cases) the demand for proof is comical or ridiculous.[160]
Still, as with all things comical, the ironical and tragic are never far off.
Modern proof-theoretical reasoning could only deny such a *petito principii*.
If Heidegger rightly provides a critique of functionalism or instrumental
rationality, he would not be able simply to dispense with it.

Here too Heidegger believed in general that we lie in the legacy of Hegel's
rationalism. Hegel's own *Naturphilosophie* had begun by attempting to ex-
punge itself from Nature's ruins, making *Aufgehoben* not only the moderns'
physics, but the ancients' speculations: emanation, revelation, and last but
not least, Schelling's intuition "which is usually nothing but a fanciful and
sometimes fantastic exercise of the imagination on the lines of analogies,
which may be more or less significant, and which impress determination
and schemata only externally."[161] As Heidegger put it, to seek in analogy an
explanation is to surrender Being to the oblivion of beings.[162]

Hegel's resolution, on the other hand, would provide an exposition of
both the empirical content of Nature and its Notion (*Begriff*), certain that
both might coincide in full *adequatio,* an account expressivist and demonstrative, theoretical and practical at once. This was to be the biconditional
of Dialectic. Not only did Hegel's endeavor posit the hope of vindicating
certainty, but equally the hope that, in Nature's dispersion, as Hölderlin had
also said before him, we might find both the fecundity of the ancients and

the liberation of the moderns, the unity of freedom and necessity. To Hegel, Kantian and Fichtean restraint concerning what ought to be, as distinguishing it from what is, represented an immature way of looking at the world. Schelling's belief that the world was ruled by divine providence represented the view of the religious mind. The "man's way of looking," as Hegel put it, no longer needs to distingush between *posse* and *esse* confident in the unity of the will and Good (L:§235). But this unity could not be guaranteed without succumbing to historicism and that was perhaps the ultimate lesson of Hegel's commitment to tragedy.

The point perhaps instead is the complexity of the event itself, one which doubtless reveals Spinoza's legacy despite himself. Having raised the possibility of this unity, we can also find in Spinoza's speculative synthesis of the ancients and the moderns a synthesis that divides reason from within—in the play of analogies in which the *nomos* now will be constituted, nature will now inevitably be at risk. As Spinoza had put it, "the word law seems to be applied to natural phenomena only by analogy, and is commonly taken to signify a command." Nonetheless, as much as any modern, he remained adamant too that it not only applies "universally," for we have *deduced* it from human nature, but also that it "does not depend on the truth of any historical narrative whatsoever."[163] But the notion of law itself will always be figured in this regard and theory-laden as well; its bonds with historical narrative will never simply be dissolvable—in this sense always augmented by what Vico called "a metaphysics sensed and built up by the imagination."[164] On the other hand, Heidegger's own (translative-interpretive) account of nature, it will be claimed, while aware of the complicated history in which the law becomes 'written' through modern demonstration, neglects its inevitable (modern) involvement in our evaluative procedures and the calculation of nature. If the accounts of "modern natural science" had inevitably robbed us of our place (*topos*)—both ontological and juridical in the end—we will still—ineluctably—need to calculate its implications.[165]

Heidegger's limitations concerning the politics of the written law, it will be pointed out, are legion. Even beyond his own political failures in the 1930s, in his later works he was still too quick to equate democracy, technological rationality, and subject-centered metaphysics (see LH:220) and to contrast with them the virtues of heroic (and tragic) decision.[166] Here too it may be decisive that Heidegger centered his attacks on modern "technocracy" (directly in any case) neither from the republican tradition that stemmed from Machiavelli, nor from the moralist tradition that stemmed from Montaigne—nor even from the humanist accounts of science stemming from Bacon or Boyle—but from the *poiesis* of Romanticism. In fact, the account of the complications of the rationality at stake would perhaps have required all of these in ways Heidegger had not (explicitly) seen. All had, in any case, provided better answers than Hobbes's to the concern that, especially with regard to the natural law, we will encounter the perils of interpretation. It is true too, nonetheless, that what Heidegger ultimately valued was a transcendence that withdrew from the calculations of modernity—a space that was not "spatial." Indeed in the 1942–43 *Parmenides* lectures, Heidegger claimed that the ancient *polis* itself had this character, being "as little political as space itself is spatial."[167] Heidegger staunchly continued to argue for an account of the *polis* that acknowledged its narratological status, perhaps still privileging its Greek account of the "sacred" in this regard. Yet what he discovered in the Greek *polis* was the recognition that the *polis* is precisely *not* political, but rather an opening from which and in relation to which the political always emerges at risk. "Politics" in this sense—the same sense of irony to which we alluded at the outset—is always the institution of what is essentially unpolitical. Its laws are not "simply fabricated by human reason" and the political remains unidentifiable with the mythemes of the nation or the state or even Herder's *Volk*—and any ontic tradition, consequently.[168]

This means, however, that Heidegger's (later) account must inevitably break with the jurisprudence of positivism in its "Romantic" or "scientific" forms. Romantic jurisprudence, in accord with the naturalism that descends from Herder's account of tradition, had ultimately and almost unavoidably sought—pace Fichte's account of habit as *vis inertiae*—to institute custom itself as the "true natural right," in a search for a fully new mythic mythology of law.[169] Against this, "politics" and the proclamation of right instead remain always the problematic *incorporation* of the political, defused beyond such pure natural bases.[170] In this regard the event of the *polis*—the *espacement* of the political—is already the problem (and the promise) of such incorporation and its modern failures, both theoretical and historical.

It would not be accidental, consequently, that the Spinozaistic problem of the body combining the conflicting narratives (or modes) contested in modernity would be pivotal in this regard—nor perhaps that phenomenologists like Scheler, who had introduced the problem of embodiment into the narratives of phenomenology, would see Heidegger's discussion of care in *Being and Time* as already presupposing the body.[171] The paradigms complicating Fichte's account of *Naturrecht* and incorporation—divided both between ancient and modern forms of reasoning and narratives—had not simply been dissolved, nor resolved. Still, if Heidegger had grasped the complexity of those relations, his own account in this regard may still seem to be burdened with the legacy of the speculative's opposition to the empirical. In discussing the objection above, for example, his own reduction in one sense seems glaring: modern medicine, indeed modern therapy in general, does in the end *grasp* our health "better"—or at least more rigorously in the most undeniable of senses, that of certainty. Yet it should also be acknowledged that the progress of scientific practice never itself occurs, however, without speculative reduction, nor does it compensate for the apparent departure of "certainty" resulting from the detraditionalization implied in challenging the 'excess' or transcendence out of which both our narratives and our 'values' concerning 'health' (as being and possibility) become meaningful. It is just as a result of this instability that the conflict between faith and knowledge, *Glauben und Wissen,* arose at the heart of Romanticism. Such reactions to the science of Enlightenment occur, as we have seen, always at the same time while still portending something "right outside the limits of the empirical." Hence also the antinomies between Romantic metaphysics and scientific positivism emerge in their attempts to reduce truth simply to transcendence or to calculable nature.

13. Narrating Insufficiences: A *Topos* That Is Not 'Spatial'/A *Polis* That Is Not 'Political'?

The narratives in which nature gets articulated remain figured between (reciprocal) insufficiencies. No law simply determines its object, no experience exhausts 'nature's' withdrawal; in this regard 'nature' remains a semantic marker fully captured neither by 'explanation' nor 'understanding'. To think that the concept of nature itself had been thereby dissolved, or left behind, or might be recreated—to think that we might have to "overcome" nature or that it might now be more properly grasped elsewhere as a mytheme obsolete in the technics of reduction and substitutability—is indeed to misunderstand the semantics of 'nature' as a mere 'operator' in the matrix of theoretical construction. There remains a transcendental illusion in such theory construction. And, first and foremost such confusion postulates that any theory of the natural is simply a construction, or that nature is simply an *object* of knowledge. The hope, which Fichte internalizes, of prescribing freedom for freedom's sake, without regard for external criteria, is a dream, the very dream by which, we have seen, Fichte's *Vocation of Man* threatened his account of *Wissenschaftslehre* from within: reflection, disembodied and detached from nature, would simply be "the dream of that dream." Hence Schelling had recognized the problem of all that remains both 'excessive' and 'unconscious' before reflection and for which we require the art of interpretation, one consigning an ambiguous legacy to those who would articulate reflection and nature, justice and its institution in his wake.[172] As Merleau-Ponty had seen with regard to the body, reflection is always dependent upon a body that *transcends* consciousness—and justice too would necessarily be *embodied* or "incorporated." If justice then always exceeds ontic (or refective) specification, it nonetheless depends on the frail inventions of human consciousness for intelligibility. Indeed, as Merleau-Ponty recognized: "Justice and truth, whose source men think they possess insofar as they are consciousness, are in reality based upon lawcourts, books, and traditions, and are therefore fragile like these and like them are threatened by individual judgment."[173] And saved by such judgment, of course. And it is just in this sense that both Merleau-Ponty and Lefort would continue to see democracy as the institution that both preserves the withdrawal of truth and the virtue of human engagment. Without denying the "claims" of either consciousness or nature, the point is that neither consciousness nor nature can be abstracted from the narratives and histories that articulate their intelligibility—as the treatises on *Naturrecht* of German Idealism attest. Hence the excess of freedom. But freedom too requires, as Kant knew, both a narrative and a law.

In this regad, Vico's appeal to narrative—even "Vicoan" appeals to the *Grundwörter* in figuring the experience of modernity otherwise—remains insurpassable. We will not create history, but (the creation narrative itself notwithstanding) we will narrate it. And such narratives (the narrative of explanation notwithstanding) will also be narratives (or models) of what 'exceeds' theoretical reduction—and even narratives of all that such theory relies upon. Fichte could see such reliance only as dogmatism. Schelling, appropriately, already in the 1790s had written on the *Philosophy of Mythology*, one his 1800 *System of Transcendental Idealism* would proceed to accommodate. But the conflict between the critical and the dogmatic was neither a conflict between *mythos* and *logos* nor between narrative and reason. 'Science', after all is both a system of narratives and a system of their critique. The opposition between dogmatism and purely critical thought is once more abstract.

When Fichte equates freedom itself with the immediate fact of consciousness, and thus distinguishes it from the law of the categorical imperative, he forgets Kant's account of the *factum* of reason and its hermeneutics of principles (SE:58–59). Just as Being cannot be equated with doing, no more can meaning: both possess us as much as we possess them. Experience is not "a box strewn about with letters of the alphabet"

in which only "the human spirit . . . brings a sense to this chaos."[174]
Fichte's *Formtrieb* had deluded him here. Being will be equatable neither
with its meaning nor freedom, nor with our labors to grasp it. (SE:73).
Fichte had declared (in a certain proto-Kierkegaardian fashion), that it is
"by not going beyond this appearance of freedom in us, that appearance
becomes reality for us" (SE:58).[175] But it is equally true that freedom
begins, Fichte acknowledged (and as we have seen, Kant acknowledged
before him) precisely in realizing that things "might have been otherwise"
(SE:112f.). Indeed this recognition is the linchpin of post-Kantian accounts of both freedom and rationality. But to grasp both we will require
again the affirmation of the complex relation between interpretation and
principle, Being and narrative. Neither Kant before him, nor Schelling
after had been so naive about the narratives and histories in which consciousness is embodied—even those, as Schelling put it "of which scarcely
the memory has survived, and whose greatness we deduce only from their
ruins." Schelling nonetheless equally appealed to intuition (rather than
act) for his hermeneutics of nature, since he thought that, apart from such
an intuition, philosophy "has no other way than to strive to orient itself
historically and to take as its source and guiding principle the *tradition*."[176]
But in this respect he too seemed only to reassert the antinomies between
form and content, syntax and semantics.

At one point Heidegger's 1941 Schelling seminar openly questions Schelling's intuitional claim that "we have an earlier relevation than any written
one—nature," denying both its Leibnizian backdrop and its claim to the
given.[177] Schelling's *symbolon* that would unite the sensible and the intelligible remains, to use Kant's terms, the symbol of the logicians: devoid of
the complexity, the *doppel Geschaft* Kant's own account of the symbol had
articulated. The *interpretation* of this event or its "exegesis," to use Schelling's terms, will be more complicated, since its appeal to what lies beyond
the narratives of tradition is by no means a simple intuition, nor is its
intuition beyond narrative itself. The antinomies between tradition and
revelation would not be so readily resolved: hence the transcendental illusion of Schelling's "naturalism" that seeks to unite revelation and mythology. The hermeneutic relations between the 'symbolic' and the 'unconscious'
would be more complex.[178] On the other hand, Heidegger's own appeal to
Being (or to Being's appeal) was perhaps never itself free from such attachments to myth—notwithstanding his own claim that

> the great beginning of Western philosophy . . . became great because it had to
> overcome its greatest opposite, the mythical in general, and the Asiatic in

particular, that is, it had to bring it to the jointure of a truth of Being, and was able to do this.[179]

But this presupposes (beyond Heidegger's Occidentalism) that such a "beginning" was not itself mythical, that interpretation might be free from the *Auseinandersetzung* of narrative—and that theory and myth are ever simply so dissociable.[180]

One of the various *mythoi* in which we articulate nature is as an object for instrumental manipulation, practical or otherwise—and of these "modes" of nature, not the least is nature as *explanandum*. Even the opening afforded by Kant's reflective judgment itself, as we have seen, emerges concomitantly in this respect—not only in retrieval of the ancient teleologies of nature but also in the transition beyond the "ancient" pure elements to which phlogiston theory still appealed.[181] Even those still most deeply committed to nature in the humanist sense gain conceptual access to this domain only against the underdeterminacy and pluralistic limits of contemporary theory.[182] Contemporary "deep ecologists" who criticize modern experimentalism for the sake of a more robust account of nature do so not without acknowledging the rigors of experimentalism—and not without acknowledging the dangers, the transcendental illusions involved in mistaking myth for theory. In this respect even to bemoan the figure of experimental control is still to rely on it for the demonstrative requisites that accompany it.[183] More direct attempts to conjoin anarchy and ecosystem suffer, consequently, from the same lack of principle governing all transcendental illusion.[184] The attempt to retrieve the all-embracing intuition of Nature à la Spinoza cannot simply depend on intuition, on pain of succumbing to what Fichte had already identified as dogmatism. This is true even when such intuitions accompany the (correct) recognition that "History is littered with the remains of cultures that upset the equilibrium [of Nature]."[185] Or, to rephrase the problem, the terms 'Being' and 'Nature' are not equivalent: their relation is always as ambiguous as the link of our embodiment which conjoins them. Hence the risk even in Fichte's own Spinozaistic claim that would again dissolve the differences between being and act, pure form and content, the syntactics and semantics, the iterability and idealizations of representation: "All our philosophical assertions are 'bodies' [Köper] and nothing more. And we hand these bodies over to you in order to help you develop philosophy out of and through your own self."[186] If such thinking and its significance will inevitably be "embodied," the tropics of such embodiment (or appropriation, which lingers here also) will never simply be substituted either for assertion (or propositional meaning). Such embodiment instead is just the opening of critique.

Like the link between knowledge and power, the articulemes of the control of nature doubtless begin in modern arrogance. However this "arrogance" marks (and accompanies) the demise of transcendental authorities — including, it will be claimed, even appeals to Nature itself. Knowing, after all, was always defined as a disposition or capacity of the soul, as one of its powers: still outstanding remains always the question of its ends and their interpretation. Like the problem of certainty itself, the link — and the danger at stake — between power and knowledge emerges only in relation to the fundamental uncertainty and demise of transcendental authorities at the origin of the modern age and this age's urge to right the tradition's wrongs. But it is precisely in this sense, as we have seen, that the account of nature continued to have ethical and political significance. The account of the ancient bonds modernist thought refigured was not simply dissolved in the emergence of a successor theory. Even Bacon had acknowledged as much, indeed understanding that experiment itself is a kind of care, and that even the nature we 'test' is a kind of garden cared for.[187] This is not to say that we understand it better some other way, e.g., by 'living' it, or that the concept of our natural bond or natural contract with things escapes such vagaries. If we 'constitute nature' we do not just construct it. To reinvoke the Kantian metaphorics, if reason is the "lawgiver" of nature it is not its "creator." Nor, it will be objected, need anything be nature's creator for that matter. The point is that 'nature' will always be figured in the tropics of theory. As Gadamer admitted, even Vico, who "lived in an unbroken tradition of rhetorical and humanist culture, and had only to reassert its ageless claim," now deliberates only within a "sphere of knowledge" in which "there is a *querelle des anciens et de modernes*" (TM:23, 21).[188]

This is to say that nature will be both fragmented and hermeneutic through and through. And yet this — as the later Heidegger would insist — still misses the point, which is that it is hermeneutic precisely with respect to that which exceeds it, makes it possible, and even perhaps 'speaks' through it — while hermeneutics and even the word 'interpretation' would almost lead us to say the opposite, that at the limit of the empirical is the act which 'constitutes' it and not its own immersion in Being itself. Still, the antinomy between interpretation and nature is again abstract and contrasts with Heidegger's own itinerary. *Being and Time*, after all, had already spoken of Nature as "the very soil of history" (BT:433). And, as we saw too, even interpretation itself relies upon a certain *lumen naturale* not to be contrasted with the historical, whose possibilities it articulates and from which Heidegger declares "it must nurture itself" (*sich nähren müss*) (BT:194). Thus the *lumen naturale* becomes outlined in the very interplay of understanding and interpretation, the remnants not only of the modern *Wechsel* of subject and object but also the ancient link between things divine and things human, things ethical and things "physical," a link which care itself could only hope to bridge.[189] This was perhaps Heidegger's point in the end—and it was surely not, as has been suggested, an attempt in bad faith to smuggle values back in by a kind of reification that Fichte's critique of revelation would have recognized as mere religion.[190] Notwithstanding his shortcoming, however, beyond the demonstrative failures of modern instrumentalism, Heidegger attempts to think both the human and the values at stake 'otherwise', their narratives refigured in the very dispersion of 'nature'—and ultimately Being itself. The *lumen naturale* of *Being and Time,* as Merleau-Ponty saw again, is in this regard precisely the opening of 'another nature' than that of the sciences (ancient or modern).[191]

But we need to stay clear about the implications of this for the antinomy between freedom and necessity and the dispersion of the natures it portended. What Merleau-Ponty perhaps saw regarding this appeal to nature and the elemental, as Lefort realized (and perhaps Heidegger never sufficiently saw), was the specific ambiguity in the dispensations of Being. Merleau-Ponty grasped an insight clearly at stake in the various treatises on *Naturrecht*—beginning with Kant—that emerge in classical German thought: although freedom is never simply reducible to its positive institutions, neither can freedom be simply analyzed or interpreted apart from the institutions—political, juridical, and conceptual—of law. Whatever else justice might be, it remains a human affair, one which depends upon human intervention for intelligibility. Moreover, against what he called Kantian "optimism" concerning democracy, Merleau-Ponty was not led to postulate, as did Fichte (or Hegel), its immanence. We need to distinguish—as Kant did himself obliquely—between the letter (*littera*) and the spirit of the law.[192] It is in just this sense that Merleau-Ponty worried in 1945 that "we know today that formal equality of rights and political liberty mask rather than eliminate relationships based on force."[193] The ontological difference interrupts such calculability without dissolving it: the 'equity' of justice, its *analogia,* always exceeds the politics of equality—precisely as its condition. And it is just in this respect that both require interpretation. If, as has been seen, the recognition of the ambiguous relations between 'natural' right, liberty, and power descends from the republican and humanist tradition since Machiavelli, never did it simply entail the denial of human rights (nor the institutions that realize them); rather it entailed an insight into the complexity of their articulation and the task of interpretation itself.

For the articulation of rights, which means negotiating the antinomy between freedom and nature, we must be even more attentive to the specificity of their interpretative status, and in particular to the hermeneutics of freedom and the dangers inherent in the institution of freedom's law. When a modernist like Spinoza connected the genealogy of law with divine command, he had in fact refigured the past of both obligationism and physical necessity by the schemata of mathematic necessity: a refiguration that became demonstrably exposed in Kant's dialectic, which itself, as has been seen, ultimately by an "episyllogism" refigures the purely ethical with its sacred past.[194] While such an ideal—the ideal of absolute necessity— might demonstrably hold for the natural laws at stake in Descartes, Newton, or Spinoza's (or Kant's) physics, the speculations which obtain in the juridical domain always proceed with reference to a 'nature' that remains staunchly dissonant to this (modern) concept of demonstrable necessity. This remains true, of course, even if, as Kant perhaps rightly thought, the categorical imperative might provide one of its evaluative criteria. A "pure" ethics might well exist even if humans did not, but by comparison with these new necessities, however, its interpretation will occur always with reference to a *pros hen* that has withdrawn. The relations between *physis* and *logos* will remain equivocal and fragile—and in this regard consequently both plural and human. Doubtless in this regard the speculative legacies of German Idealism remained divided between the "excess" of nature upon which it relied and the allegories through which freedom might ultimately be liberated. But it did so perhaps in venturing a virtue through which the jointure of freedom and nature need not be dissolved, precisely in the recognition that their appropriations remain always at risk, always expropriated.[195] At stake was an event both beyond representation and irreducible to calculability and mere use—in the same way that all human care had been from the outset.

4. Hegel, the "Plasticity" of Character, and the Prose of the World

The philosopher must possess as much aesthetic power as the poet.

—1790 *System Fragment*

Do as the sculptor does with a statue he wants to make beautiful; he chisels away one part, and levels off another, makes one spot smooth and another clear, until he shows forth a beautiful face on the statue. . . . Never stop sculpting your own statue, until the godlike splendor of virtue shines forth to you.

—*Plotinus Ennead,* I.6.9.

Fortune reigns in gifts of the world, not in the lineaments of Nature.

—*As You Like It,* I.ii, 37–39.

1. Shakespeare's Characteristic of Modern Individuality

In his 1802–1803 Lectures on the *Philosophy of Art,* Schelling remarked in analyzing modern dramatic poetry through the figure he thought to be its exemplar that there was nothing that Shakespeare did not touch upon that he did not touch in its individuality, "whereas antiquity touched it in totality."[1] It was in fact precisely the characteristic of modern drama to detotalize in this sense, to disperse from the highest to the lowest, youth as well as age, the king as well as the shepherd, in the exploration of individuality. The point of this dispersion, however, was not lament but simply the free explication of difference itself. "Whereas that ancient lyre enticed the whole world with *four* strings, the new instrument has a thousand strings; it splits the harmony of the universe [*es zersplatet die harmonie des Universsums*] in order to create it, and for that reason," Schelling asserted, "it is always less calming for the soul."[2] And yet, by dispersing totality this way, rather than enforcing the lament for the lost unity so common to all Romanticism, Shakespeare "lends his tragedy the densest richness and pregnancy in every part, including the dimension of breadth."

It cannot be said, however, that this explication of individuality was intended, as "postmodern" writers might be inclined to say, as a simple affirmation of difference for its own sake. Indeed, as Schelling immediately adds, "the intention of the *whole* remains clear and then descends into an inexhaustible depth in which all viewpoints can immerse themselves." What is excluded is the lament in which the individual would ultimately be subsumed beneath its fate. Instead, in accord with his Tübingen colleague's post-Kantian commitment to a rational retrieval and transformation of 'natural law', Schelling thought the result of Shakespeare's art was the free development (and fulfillment) of rational individuality in its richness and profundity.[3] As Hegel would later put it, in a remark with complex relations to both nature and law: "That which is original and natural, does not exist as original and natural, rather it must be first sought out and won" (HP:40–41). It is precisely the richness of this venture which, for Schelling, marked Shakespeare's greatness: "If we now summarize our findings and express succinctly Shakespeare's relationship to the sublimity of the tragedy of antiquity, we must call him the greatest creator of *character*."[4] In this regard Emerson would not be off the mark in claiming that Shakespeare is the "father of German literature" nor perhaps that his works received only thereby adequate critics.[5]

Schelling had claimed that poetics cannot be universal "without drawing all the elements of present culture—science, religion, art itself—into its sphere," resulting in something like a "universal mythology." Indeed the prominence of Shakespeare in the *mythoi* of the German *Aufklärung* was evident from the outset.[6] As early as 1773, Herder's essay on Shakespeare emphasized the latter's dramatic originality in contrast to the univocity of the ancients. "Whereas in Sophocles' drama the unity of a single action is dominant, Shakespeare aims at the entirety of an event, an occurrence." While Sophocles makes a single tone predominate in his characters, Shakespeare, in other words, employs the full wealth of *everyday life*: "Shakespeare uses all the characters, estates, walks of life he requires to produce the concerted sound of his drama."[7] Still, for Herder the significance of this characteristic individuality remained dramatic; he did not recognize that what was at stake was not simply a mimetic event and that its occurrence, not simply "pathetic" but also epistemic, was lacking. That Shakespeare's "everyday" involved an event in which even "the four strings of the moral universe"—or four character types—might be put in question, remained unthought. Unlike Schelling, and indeed unlike Aristotle,[8] for whom the account of tragic character remained essentially connected with moral purpose, Herder restricted the concept of character itself to a realm of *Vraisemblance* in ways that his Romantic successors would reject.

2. Kant and the Signs of Character

Such in fact already was the case with Kant, the figure Hölderlin would claim to be his colleagues' Moses—both in these and other matters.[9] Kant's

Anthropology likewise culminates with the problem of character, or more precisely with the question of characterization—the problems of discerning "man's inner self from his exterior." Granted Kant's premises, i.e., Kant's standard recognition of the conflict between the passions, and also the conflict of narrative *Standpunkten* for their exposition—granted, in short, both the moral and theoretical conflict between freedom and determinism discovered in the *Critique of Pure Reason's* third antinomy—this task is no easy one. Before Kant, Hume had been concerned with action as a sign of character, because it is "only as a sign of some quality or character that any action can be virtuous or vicious," i.e., as the result of some durable and largely unchangeable quality of the soul which we find agreeable or disagreeable.[10] Even though Kant seems to disagree *tout court* with Hume at this point on how action is evaluated, his account would nonetheless agree with Hume's in retaining its connection with the most literal sense of the word 'character', claiming that first and foremost the problem of 'characterization' was, to use Kant's term (taken over from Lambert and extended to Pierce, Husserl, Saussure, and Morris), a "semiotic" matter, that is, the distinguishing of *characters* or signs.[11] Nonetheless the complicated requirements of such a project of semiotic characterization have already become manifest to us as they were to those in Kant's wake. Kant's Copernican turn would not easily accommodate simple accounts of meaning and reference, even if his own account of both seemed to have been adequated in the validity conditions of the first *Critique's* Transcendental Aesthetic, which linked the warrantability of concepts to *sensibilia*. Signs, or mere "characterization," as Kant puts it in the third *Critique,* are merely *designations* (*Bezeichnungen*) of concepts, containing nothing whatever that belongs to the intuition of the object: they are, if you will, the bric-a-brac of nominalism—or empirical imagination. Significative relation to an object, on the other hand, had indeed become more complex for Kant, granted the Copernican turn. Any account of such a relation, as has been seen, will be articulated either by means of schemata, as the transcendental schematism had imparted, or by means of symbols, i.e., analogical presentations, in which, as has become evident, "judgment performs a double function [*ein doppeltes Geschäft*]" (CJ:227).

Now it is significant here too that such symbolic exhibition is immediately distinguished by Kant himself from the "wrong" (*unrecht*) usage of the term by recent 'symbolic' logicians, which "runs counter to the meaning of the term," since the latter substitutes an algebraic relation for a (real) relation to an object. Even Husserl, as will be seen, had acknowledged the significance of Kant's transformation at this point. Still, the complexity of the matter doubtless remained more unthought than even Kant himself allowed, granted the complexities of the narratives and ontologies at play in the critical tribunal. And nowhere, as has become evident, does this become more complicated than in Kant's attempts to step beyond the axiomatics of the transcendental aesthetic in exhibiting the symbolics of the moral realm—which has in turn immediate impact upon the problem of characteristic and character. Not only does Kant's account openly invoke and transform the question of the 'is' and the 'ought', it also reinterprets the relationship between characterization, the symbolic, and the algorithmic sign—the determinate formula of the categorical imperative. Accordingly, when the *Anthropology* proceeds to confront the issue of human character, it still remains a matter of a *doppel Geschäft*, or movement between the character a person "has" and what he or she ought to be.

Initially, in fact, Kant divided the possibilities of characterization in a binary fashion: "on the one hand we say that a certain man has *this* or that (physical) character or, on the other hand, that he *has* character simply (moral character)" (Anth:152). According to the first, Kant claimed that examining what is characteristic in human nature, we indicate what can be made of a man; according to the second, "what man is prepared to make of himself [*sich selbst zu machen*]." Kant's characterization in the first sense reinvokes Schelling's four strings of the ancient lyre, i.e., a characterization whose protocols are drawn from the classical typology: the sanguine, choleric, melancholic, and phlegmatic temperaments.

In the second sense, however, the ascription of character to the person as a property of his or her will is an exceptional matter—one which is categorically distinct from merely playing a role. The *pathos* which emerges in such recognitions remained categorically distinct, it being "a rare thing, which inspires respect and admiration" (Anth:157). Granted the conflict of narratives, granted the antinomies of Reason, and that freedom cannot (strictly speaking) be *known,* it might be said that such recognition is a genuinely rare event. Yet its possibility had been, if not assured, at least safeguarded within the critical system. What was in question, then, remained a moral matter, a question again of what human beings make of themselves. As such it formed something of the culmination of the anthropological project, understood not simply as the theoretical articulation of the play of nature (*Spiel der Natur*) but as actually having participated (*mitgespilt*) in it (Anth:3).

In all this, however, the account seemed to be simply in accord with the most ancient accounts of *mimesis*. Indeed "mere characterization" as a "means for reproducing concepts," as the third *Critique* elaborated, adjoins mimetic (*selbst mimische*) and algebraic signs and dispenses with the problem of the *Mittel* which complicates the relation between 'subject' and 'object', sign and signified. Recall that it was precisely the problem of the *Mittel* which the critical system had brought to issue in the Copernican turn and the withdrawal of the noumenon. And, in dividing Reason by way of the Antinomies, thus disrupting the links of pure characterization, it likewise transformed its moral characterization into tropes, making the practical realm, beyond strict categorical subsumption, symbolic in content. As a result, the moral act or deed (*Tat*) became a dramatic event through and through.

If Kant's retrieval of Stoic 'natural law' had in fact recodified the legal standing of individuals (*personae*) before the law both in accord with the politics of modern egalitarianism and in parallel with the nomothetics of modern science, those in his wake would rearticulate this archive. Moreover, Kant's works reencountered the multifariousness of its archive. In the account of personality in the first *Critique*'s Paralogisms Kant had, following Leibniz, refigured the character of perduring individuality. But Kant's works on practical reason also retrieved and refigured the account of character itself from the ruins of the ancient systems in two different ways: first regarding what the Stoics had called *decorum*, that is, the appearance of virtue, and second with respect to the 'play' (*Spiel*) of character itself. Here in fact Kant reencounters the ancient account of person as *persona* (mask) and character itself—as dramatic role—and history, as has been seen, as a dramatic event, a *mise en scène*, or stage. Thus the dramatics of "personality" in the sense of role comes to light. As again the *De Officiis* puts it, itself retrieving the most ancient accounts of *persona* as dramatic mask:

> Everyone, therefore, should make a proper estimate of his own natural ability and show himself a critical judge of his own merits and defects; in this respect we should not let actors display more practical wisdom than we have. They select, not the best plays, but the ones best suited to their talents. . . . Shall a player (*histrio*) have regard to this in choosing his role (*scaena*) upon the stage and a wise man fail to do so in selecting his part in life?[12]

Shakespeare's refiguration of the stage as world in this regard surely again refigures the Stoic's ethos. The wise person will be like a good histrionic artist (*hypokrites*).[13] The difference, as Shakespeare's *As You Like It* demonstrates, is that the gifts of the world have overtaken the gifts of nature, a matter in which he interfaces with both Machiavelli and Hobbes. Hegel will confront the diaspora of nature and freedom even more directly, the artistic interplay between faculty and quality, nature and individual, the universal and the particular, which Hegel referred to in general as *Qualierung*. Kant, having split the appearance of virtue from the realm of knowledge, had in fact intensified the split between nature and freedom and had thereby re-intensified the problem of character as dramatic appearance, reconfiguring its relation to classical *mimesis*, appearance, iterability, and the Good.

3. Mimesis, Characteristic, Virtue

We can begin to record this transformation in Kant and his successors by attending to the complexity of Kant's account in the *Anthropology*, where Kant's account of character took on the attributes of pure practical reason. Character has an intrinsic worth, is an end in itself, demands respect, and occurs autonomously insofar as a person "binds himself to definite practical principles that he has ascribed to himself irrevocably by his own reason" (Anth:157). Yet in spite of the fact that the person of character arouses admiration and respect in the spectator (like Aristotle's account of the moral teacher), it remains irrevocably true that any account of character must be split from the category of *mimesis*.

This split with *mimesis* is doubly effected and inextricably linked with the modern question of legitimation. Mere imitation, mere habituation, knowl-edge by rote, mere iterability, remains a matter of custom—perhaps even tradition—which is not in any case justified on its own terms. Morality on its own thus becomes, to use Kant's term, experimental: it goes beyond *mimesis* positively, as the exploration of the extension of knowledge, and negatively, as the invocation of the limits of reason through critique. In both cases, the nature of the Good must be a "precarious" one. It will pertain to the essence of the Good in its deepest sense that it be profoundly question-able. If not before, then certainly after Kant, ethics, epistemology, and on-tology will be inextricably bound together.

Granted this twofold rupture with *mimesis*, character will demand not simply freedom, or spontaneity, but equally originality. In fact, Kant claims, "character is precisely originality in one's way of thinking"—and only as such is it determinate (Anth:158). Granted its link with *Originalität*, moral-ity cannot be wholly separated from the aesthetic—nor, as will be seen, can its semiotic characteristic be separated from the symbolic; nor, finally, can reason be simply distinguished from *Witz* (CJ:§59).

From the beginning, what was at stake involved a *Spielraum* that puts character in question. To invoke Kant's modern categories, character must involve an apodicticity that remains inerradicable, requiring a firmness of will which "explodes," but without adequating the precarious state of instinct. This notion of character will, consequently, at the same time refigure the ideal of greatness of soul, magnanimity, and fortitude. The adequation in which act and intention, virtue and its expression might be accomplished remains nonetheless always deferred, always underdetermined, always, to use Kant's term, "undecidable" and in need of interpretation. The good will arises always and only in a *Spielraum* of unknowing, since its realization escaped finite capacities for demonstration or verification. Hence the tragedy which underwrites any science of imperatives emerges—a tragedy sufficient to elicit from Schelling the scepter of Oedipus at its heart—perhaps wholly, initially, on Kantian grounds.[14] Indeed when in the third *Kritik* Kant instantiates the purposiveness of the Good in the figuration of the human, a union of "great imaginative power" (*grosse Macht der Einbildungkunft*) in which the ideas of Reason find bodily expression (*Körperlichen Ausserung*) again, a certain modern reinstitution of Cicero's *decorum* (as the manifestation and characterization of virtue)—the virtues that result remain fully in accord with the economics of tragedy.[15] The resulting virtues are those of goodness of heart, purity, strength, and finally peace (CJ:§17).

By Descartes' time the Greek virtue of magnanimity had already reemerged from its conflict with Christian humility—in fact its reemergence was in a sense coextensive with the emergence of modern subjectivity, as can be witnessed in Hobbes' or Descartes' remodelings. But cut off from the nature—or providence—that might ground it, modern 'magnanimity' remained profoundly unstable. While the ideal of magnaminity can be projected, it remains the case, as Kant claimed, that "the sole proof a man's consciousness affords him that he has character is his having made it his supreme maxim to be truthful, both in his admission to himself and in his conduct toward every other person" (Anth:160–61). Even if there is a science of morality, there is no pure science of human characterization—neither intrinsically nor extrinsically. And this may be the proper way of understanding the odd section on physiognomy—the inference of character on the basis of appearance, its *persona*—which follows Kant's discussion of character in the *Anthropology*.

In any case, such is the trajectory of Kant's text, if not his demonstration. Physiognomy, he immediately remarks, is "the art of judging what lies within a man" (Anth:164). Hence already, it could be claimed, the problem of *recognition* (*Anerkennung*) and the troubling appearance of the Other's 'face' emerges. Expression is the continual reinvocation of this *mitgespielen*, the transcendental illusion (*Schein*) which undercuts the scientific claim of physiognomy, since expression is itself always already theatrical, and in this sense mimetic: "the face put into play."[16] And yet as Hegel also realized in the *Phenomenology's* account of physiognomy, all that one says regarding the face is in the end "idle chatter, or merely the voicing of one's own opinion" (Phen:193), since it always relies upon the contingent external artifact of its expression. Accordingly, as Sartre would claim in reinvoking this archive, human suffering is not fully revealed on the animated face of others; it comes through "better yet in portraits, in the face of a statue, in a tragic mask."[17] But, for Hegel this was precisely its downfall: "the face or outward appearance is not the individual's *in itself* but, on the contrary, can be an object for handling" (Phen:195). Hence, there emerges, as Sartre realized, "the drama of suffering:" expression remains ambiguously divided between the inner and the outer, while the deed (*der Tat*), at least for Hegel, does not (Phen:193).

4. From Token to Type: Schlegel and the Explication of Character

Although he is usually thought to be so distant from Kant on these matters, Hegel in fact initially remains—both axiomatically and textually—in immediate proximity. Early in the third part of the *Encyclopedia*, Hegel treats the topic of character under the aspect of the singularization or "deuniversalization" of the soul. Again the account becomes differentiated in terms of talent, disposition, temperament, and physiognomy—in short, those features also at stake in Kant's *Anthropology*. The accompanying notes to the *Encyclopedia* §395 in fact specifically single out Kant and his treatment of the four temperaments, pairing them once more with the four cardinal virtues (prudence, justice, temperance, fortitude.)

Hegel adds, however, that these natural 'particularities' become "not so important as was formerly supposed" precisely because "in a highly developed culture [*in der Zeit grösserer Bildung*] the various accidental mannerisms of conduct and action disappear" (PS:52). Not so with character, however, which for Hegel remains always that which specifically distinguishes individuals. Hence, it is only in the realm of free mind or spirit that character will reveal itself as fully determinate, once again in a being possessing a will which has a "substantial, universal, content . . . making him a beacon for others" (PS:53).

Lacking character, then, "a man remains indefinite." Character demands, to reinvoke Kant's terms, the articulation of freedom, a certain "explosion" from the precariousness of the instincts—or, to use Hegel's, "the formal element of energy with which a man, without letting himself be diverted, pursues his aims and interests" (PS:53). Hume had claimed, almost by a Newtonian trope, that it is even impossible for the great person to change his (or her) character.[18] Kant had left the purity of maxims indemonstrably asserted within grounds that escape the finite. Hegel, on the other hand, having fully distanced himself from Humean necessity, sees this event of characteristic determination as the cunning of reason itself. It involves again, to use Herder's term, an event, a "realizing [of] great aims," which would provide "the absolute unity of the content and the formal activity of the will and thus possess a complete truth." (PS:53) Consequently, if Hegel initially had aligned himself with Kant, here the distance between them again seems almost incomprehensible, indeed almost separated by an incommensurability that ultimately concerned characterizations of appearance (*Erescheinung*) and its illusion (*Schein*) itself.[19]

Friederich Schlegel had in a sense, extending Kant beyond himself, prepared the way for this explication of the figural investments of character. Similarly undertaking the analysis of character under the auspices of physiognomy, his account had transformed the ancient genre of the character sketch inherited from Theophrastus by means of La Bruyère and Shaftesbury (and nascently Hume and Kant). Rather than a description of types, the task of characterization was now to become part of the artist's responsibility to explore the possible. In fact, in accord with his aesthetic demurral before the Beautiful for the sake of the *characteristic* and the *interesting,* Schlegel had argued that a novel should become famous when, through "absolute imaginativeness," it "develops a thoroughly new character interestingly."[20] The task of characterization then became an explication which would not simply explain and conserve what exists in a person but which would itself invent character, at least indirectly, as it directs, orders, and provokes.[21]

Jean Paul was right to assert that the task of such characterization was one of symbolical or allegorical individuality, although he himself failed to recognize the rationality at stake therein—or its problem perhaps—one whose *theoretization* had accompanied post-Kantian thought at least since Wilhelm von Humboldt's 1794-97 *Das achtzehnte Jahrhundert.*[22] It has been claimed directly in fact that to tie the rational to such individual characterization is to abandon justification for psychology, insofar as doing so deflates the importance of the social and traditional backdrop of concept formation—and thereby to abandon ultimately the standpoint of agency (and judgment) for that of the spectator.[23] But such claims of course miss the complexity of its hermeneutics just at that point at which the latter emerges from the experience of detraditionalization itself. They miss the interplay of such characterization in its passage between past and future, the real and the irreal, this 'is' and the ought. They miss, in short, the task of allegorical transformation and individuation—and thereby its inherently critical (and evaluative moment). Schlegel would in fact claim that such characterization involved not simply a higher individuality but the cultivation of friendship, dialog, and a new or higher urbanity.[24]

Such "characterizations" were inherently at stake in the (reflective) judgments of the rational in general, as those after Kant had recognized. It is in just this sense that, for Schlegel, the author him- or herself had become the explication of character. Here in fact lie Schlegel's reservations with regard to Fichte's Absolute *Ich*, namely that "Fichte has not characterized himself," and hence has not articulated transcendental schematism itself, the passage from singular intuition to concept.[25] Notwithstanding Fichte's emphasis upon transcendental imagination it is "impossible to imagine . . . without character."[26] It is in just this sense, moreover, that Schlegel's commentators rightly saw that "the closest English equivalent to Schlegel's *Charakteristik* is interpretation"[27]—articulating thereby, as we have seen, the 'hermeneutic' transformation of transcendental schematism beyond the subsumptions of determinate judgment. Equally however it would be mistaken not to capture the ethical significance of this new Typic: "Manners are characteristic edges," themselves instantiating the possibilities of character; "every human being who is cultivated and who cultivates himself contains a novel within himself."[28] While Kant had seen that the issue of manners in general pertained to issues of singularity (*Sonderbarkeit*) he left the matter unexplored, articulating the latter only through contrast with method (*modus logicus*) and determinate principle. Rather than explicitly articulating a realm of interpretive exposition, such singularity had still been relegated to a *modus aestheticus,* and the latter had been reduced to feeling (CJ:187). Here Schlegel's fragmented attempts (*essais*) would find precedent neither in Aristotle, nor Hobbes and Kant, but in Montaigne, divided between the ancients and the moderns, tradition and the experience of detraditionization, in which manners have become, to use Hobbes's terms, both "dangerous" and too "various" for reason to rely upon them. As a result of the experience of detraditionalization, there emerges the crucial link between experiment and transcendental imagination to which the fragment attests.[29]

For Schlegel, criticism depended upon the possibilities of original exposition, a fundamental comprehension by which one understands the spirit of a work, one which "if one expresses it in precise terms, is to characterize it, constituting the proper task and intimate essence of critique."[30] Criticism as ex-position, consequently, also becomes itself experimental, precisely as original characterization, the exposition of human potential—or to speak, as

Schelling did, of Being's *potency*. And yet if such criticism opens new possibilities of meaning, it does so only because the spirit of the work itself arises (always and only) in the expressive interplay between the finite and the infinite, the known and the unknown. The resulting *combineatoire,* the effect of this interplay, consequently remains still (ironically) ideal. The instantiation of character is limited by the specificity of the *Wechsel* upon which its inventions depended. Its effect could be achieved, that is, only through the vehicle of irony, the interplay of the demonstrable and the indemonstrable: 'narrative' and 'abyss', 'wit' and 'chaos'. Accordingly, as Schlegel's *Fragments* too claimed, "true virtue is genius" and "virtue is reason transformed into energy."[31] Hence, eschewing classical friendship as much as the aesthetic ideal of Proust would later, he claimed, "individuality is precisely what is original and eternal in man,"[32] and "to give the brotherhood of artists a particular purpose would mean substituting a shabby institute for an eternal union, or debasing the community of saints into a state."[33]

Hegel similarly affirms it in the *Encyclopedia:* genius completes both talent and what "the individual mind has been given by Nature" insofar as "genius creates a new genre" (PS:52). Still, as Kant had demanded, genius requires critique, taste—that is, the ability to not only produce, but judge originally (CJ:§48). In language harkening back upon the second *Critique's* problem of the Typic, Kant claims, "taste is basically an ability to judge the [way in which] moral ideas are made sensible . . . by means of a certain analogy in reflection" (CJ:232). Mere inward originality would not then be enough.

Hegel had also recognized, however, granted the critical demands which adhere to morality, that "one cannot say that there is a genius for virtue; for virtue is something universal to be required of all men" (PS:52). Although both Hegel and Kant remained in agreement that virtue required a kind of originality, and thereby the importance of analogy in its extension—as Hegel put it, that "analogy is the instinct of reason" (L:326)—virtue likewise required legitimation, the venture of the universal. As will be seen, this is a venture which, consequently, disarticulates mere dramatic originality from the ethical.

5. Hegel and the Crisis of Legitimation:
The Justification of Character

If Hegel, in the demand for critique over against originality, openly recognizes that dramatic-mimetic and "ethical" ends *need not* coincide, it is also true that he would never be willing simply to disconnect them *tout court.*

Equally, he asserted, "character and an ethical end *may* coincide" (Aesth:1226). Moreover, while this possibility of ultimate *adequation* for ethical concepts seems to be precisely what escaped Kant's (and Schlegel's) account, thus transforming Kant's idea of magnanimity into being ideal, Hegel also remained no less committed to the demand that the aims in question be "inwardly justified." Still, in a move which reflects (without repeating) Kant's denial that the purity of moral intent could not be adequately—or empirically—distinguished from a delusion covering self-interest (but not of course Kant's commitments regarding the formal determinacy of the categorical imperative), Hegel claimed that maxims which remain *simply* a matter of inner interest and are *only* justified 'inwardly' result in mere "self-will" (*Eigensinn*) (PS:53). They are either a matter of mere arrogance, or as the *Phenomenology* had suggested, simply a case of the unhappy consciousness, devoid of connection with its own substantiality (Phen:§2–8). Even these forms of self-will are perhaps not without *any* effect, however. Precisely as a "parody of character," they have, he acknowledges—ironically—"a disturbing influence on social intercourse" (PS:53).

Against Kant, however, if Hegel remains committed to the necessity of inward justification, he is equally committed to the denial that mere inwardness might be enough. He remains committed, that is, to what he calls elsewhere "the right of the objectivity of action" (PR:82), i.e., the right and the necessity of the 'energy' in question "to evince itself as known and willed by the subject as thinker." Indeed, the *Encyclopedia* would go so far as to evince this right as an obligation: "Every person should be required to show character" (PS:53)—precisely in order to reveal its inner content justifiably universal. Virtue and its inner perception remain distinct (HP:II.204). Modern civil society has disrupted the direct connections between sign and signified, virtue and nature. Hobbes and Machiavelli have intervened upon Aristotle's notion of natural beneficence. And, to invoke a figure which haunts modern theoretical and historical certainties, the good life has now been threatened from its origins with a potential—metaphysical, logical, and historical—"fight to the death."

If the demand for expression is to be parsed as a moral right, however, it remains devoid of epistemic and natural guarantees. Consequently it is a *tragic* necessity—granted the gap between intention and outcome—and, it is the right of tragedy. Moreover, Hegel evokes such a 'right' in his analysis of tragedy (Aesth:1212). Once again, Shakespeare's work is cited as the exposition of this right and as exemplary for modern tragedy. Even when pathos in fact overtakes particular passion, it still remains possible for the agents to "contemplate and see themselves objectively like a work of art. He

[Shakespeare] makes them free artists of their own selves" (Aesth:1227f.). What Hegel admires in Shakespeare's characters in this regard is their fulfillment of individuality, precisely insofar as "he actually gives them spirit and imagination." Hegel likewise acknowledges from the outset, however, that the event of realization is not simply a fate thrust upon freedom. The actualization of the "world-stage" does not result in an outcome which might "be inserted by a sort of dialectical machinery (*Räderwerk*) into the individual's own character" (Aesth:1229). It is precisely here that we approach Shakespeare's "unapproachable height":

> In this again Shakespeare is differentiated from the ancients: The heroes of Greek classical tragedy are confronted by circumstances in which, after identifying themselves with the one ethical 'pathos' which alone corresponds to their own already established nature, they necessarily come into conflict with the opposite but equally justified ethical power. The romantic dramatis personae, on the other hand, are from the beginning in midst of a wide field of more or less accidental circumstances and conditions which it is possible to act either in this way or in that. (Aesth:1226)

Hence emerges the problematic of the "plasticity" of the ethical, a concrete individuality developed precisely in the midst of the dispersion of the possible. To emphasize this plasticity, as will be seen, will require articulating both the venture and the equivocity of the speculative in its attempt to exhibit the intelligibility of the singular, thus explicating character "in the modern sense of the word" (Aesth:1209).

The account of a *plastische, freie Tugend*—an ethics, that is, which extends beyond moral ambiguity (*moralischer Zweideutigkeit*)—may be found as early as Hegel's 1809 discussion of classical education, the *humaniora* (IV:319). The problem, however, as he realizes in the later *Aesthetic,* is that even granted the privileged status of the Greeks within *humaniora,* they lack precisely the specificity of the individual: even "at its plastic height in Greece, tragedy remains one sided . . . leaving undeveloped the individuality of the dramatis personae and the depths of personal life" (Aesth:1222). As a result, the question of justification remains undeveloped, occurring only as an event of corruption. Homer, Hegel claims, resolves conflict not by individuation, but by invoking an undifferentiated force in opposition to individuals, which is "ultimately dissolved again ironically" (Aesth:1210). The *persona* of ancient tragedy remains (as the word originally indicates) a mask. From the outset, for Hegel, the Greeks lacked the recognition—or the hope, in any case—that fate could be mastered, that history might be more than necessity, that rationality might not simply be fallible in this regard, and that individuality might itself be differentiated precisely in this process.[34] And granted Hegel's concerns for formal accounts, even Aristotle is condemned in this regard. If Aristotle had argued for constancy of character, Hegel claims, he had not argued for the legitimacy of its individuation, and in this regard had not therefore sufficiently recognized the plasticity of character itself. No virtue ethic in the classical sense demanded the legitimation of determinate virtue. Consequently, for Hegel, in accord with his post-Kantian recognition of the semiosis and underdeterminacy of form, the doctrine of the mean remained *merely* formal, i.e., indeterminate (HP:II.206).[35] Here, Hegel's account of (qualitative) virtue must be related to his account of quantitative indifference and alterity—and also distinguished from his predecessors (Kant, Schelling), whose account remained, he was convinced, formal. As Hegel stated with respect to the differential calculus, the problem is that such "analytic" coherence will not suffice: there remains the problem of *application* (*Anwendung*) (WdL:295), a problem of the sign's "meaning" (*Bedeutung*) and original "function." In short, application always raises the question of the status of formal concepts before the singular and the impoverishment of all symbolism before the demands of the rational (WdL:325). The rational in this respect remains hinged upon the disarticulation of *the singular* before the concept—not simply a matter of formal indifference and construction, but a matter of qualitative instantiation of a rational difference. To invoke the term Hegel borrows from Jacob Boehme, a figure (like Shakespeare) privileged by Hegel at the opening of modernity, beyond simple formal coherence the rational always depends upon this differentiation—again, the event of *Qualierung* (WdL:114).

Lacking this individuation—historically, linked to the inwardness of the Romantic—the Greek's plasticity of consciousness remained undirempted, the difference between intention and event undeveloped (Aesth:1214). Consequently, if tragedy itself could still be recognized as a universal theme, the Greek's idea of fate became for Hegel—like their fourfold differentiation of the passions—if not simply deemphasized, then at least (to speak Wittgensteinian) "de-ossified."[36] In one sense Hegel himself realized that the ossification of Greek typologies was their greatness: to have foregone the vacillation of deliberation and irresolution, or to use Kant's terms, to have demonstrated the possibility of the integrity of character. And yet in this regard the Greek ideal of character still remains unified in notion only, still undeveloped in consciousness. The "preservation of their character remains empty," merely cold resignation (Aesth:817).

Even in the most exemplary forms of artistic expression—those of Romantic art and the Christian ideal of love—Hegel claims that this 'beyond' cannot simply be characterized as absent. *The Aesthetics* claims that the elevation and reconciliation of love, for example, should "not be painted as a purely spiritual 'beyond' but as actual and present . . . [one expressed] above all in the Madonna's love for her child" (Aesth:819).[37] The plasticity in question cannot remain simply abstract, devoid of individuality; it is precisely the 'plasticity' of *persona* in the other sense, defined from the outset by Boethius as "*natura rationalis individua substantia.*"[38] And, Hegel initially concurs with this formal characterization, at least to the extent that he could define characterization itself as an actualization of constituent traits existing, to put it logically, as "predicates inhering in them *qua* the subject of the predicates" (Aesth:237).

6. Person, *Sittlichkeit,* and Natural Law

Still, this would not suffice for Hegel. The notion of the person so distinguished remains once more a mere persona, "a sheer empty unit" (Phen:291). The notion of character cannot be understood by means of mere "congeries of traits," or merely in terms of the categories of substance and predicate. To think it can is to lose sight of the paralogisms affecting all abstract accounts of the soul (indeed all formalism), the indeterminacy of form and the "floating center" of the propositional (Phen:38). As the *Phenomenology* puts it, the limited plasticity of formalism always remains "monochromatic" and its differentiation still arbitrary (Phen:9). Such formalisms lose sight of the underdeterminacy which incites the complex grammar of the speculative proposition, the event of what Hölderlin had called *caesurea,* a counter rhythmic rupture demarcated in tragedy's recognition of the limits of representation.[39]

The *Phenomenology* had already confronted the issue of the underdeterminacy of laws and the level of understanding in its famous account of the inverted world (Phen:§155ff.). The section on Reason as testing laws rediscovers this indeterminacy in the practical sphere, claiming once again that such laws remain in themselves too underdetermined, even tautological. While it is surely too strong to claim, as Hegel does, that "the criterion of law which Reason possesses within itself fits every case equally well, and is thus in fact no criterion at all" (Phen:259), it is sufficient that this criterion itself fails critical tests. If Kant purported to provide univocal criteria satisfying necessary conditions, i.e., a determinate formula for moral maxims, their intelligibility (as has been seen) always required symbolic exposition, that is, analogical (and indeterminate regulative extension) for sufficient articulation.

The hermeneutic problem of determinacy explicitly dates at least to the *First Philosophy of Spirit* (1803) in which the interrelation between singularity, determinacy, and meaning had became explicitly formulated. Consciousness itself, as the middle 'term' between concept and intuition, began by being defined semiotically: "consciousness as this existing middle of its concept is thus just a sign in general in which something intuited, wrenched out of its context, is posited as connected to another, but [only] ideally, because it still subsists in turn in its context" (FPS:220). Determinacy itself is (initially) the problem of the singularity of sensation—an event for which "other being is something else outside it" (FPS:218). The *Phenomenology* would repeat this analysis in its opening pages, in which both the semantics of natural language became disarticulated against the realm of the singular and meaning became exhibited as an excess over singularity. Meaning both is and is not singular—it is the particular 'this' of the universal. The immediacy of singularity consequently reveals itself only in this excess: "it is not what we mean by 'being' but is 'being' defined as an abstraction, or as the pure universal." Being remains, Hegel recognized, in accord with protocols which were ancient, a *pros hen* beyond the difference of singularity (Phen:60–61), thus beginning the *Phenomenology of Spirit*'s Homeric quest for realization—or what the *Logic* would call the increasing "impregnation" of the copula (WdL:663). Here again, however, the difference at stake in determination would be recognized in the claim that "the individual is also not a particular, for particularity is of wider extent than individuality" (WdL:640). For similar reasons Hegel held that all induction is implicitly— and imperfectly—analogy (L:326).

Now Kant had similarly (and provisionally) recognized the distinction between the transcendental and the empirical, claiming of sensation that it is the "element in the appearances . . . that can never be known *a priori* and that therefore constitutes the distinctive difference between empirical and a priori knowledge" and "cannot be anticipated" (A167/B209). Indeed sensation in this sense marked the epistemic difference between the empirical and transcendental ego in general, demarcating 'this' particular apprehension (and this desire) from categorical purity. And, as has been seen, it is this excess which authorizes and limits Kant's risk in the Typic. Kant affirmed the possibility of sufficient justification through the determination of *a priori* syntheses, although he also recognized the indeterminacy afflicting hopes to complete determination.

But it is just such sufficiency that Hegel challenged regarding the understanding, which his sections on reason as lawgiver and as testing laws called into question. Moreover, Hegel portentously himself refers to a debate regarding the right to private property which had been prominent since Maimon's 1795 *Die ersten Grunde des Naturrechts*—one which would culminate in Marx's own attempt to strip such claims of their semblance of determinacy entirely, and would in effect argue for the need for a "hermeneutic of suspicion" for the ideology of determinacy itself.

For all its fecundity, Hegel's challenge regarding the issue at stake can now be bluntly stated. The point is that the ideal demands not simply 'syntactic' but 'semantic' exposition, the interplay of *mimesis* and *semiosis,* and thus the legitimation of individuation itself. Indeed we can affirm the suggestion of Theodor Litt that the concept of tradition in Hegel becomes inseparable from the this process of individuation.[40] This requires not merely the categorical subsumption of particulars, but also speculative and analogical extension of concepts to their motivational forms. Once again, coherence will not suffice for the rational—no more in practical than in speculative matters. Indeed, mere coherence, like mere firmness of will, remains at the level of *understanding* as opposed to reason: necessary but not sufficient. Although "without understanding, no firm character is possible" (PS:226), it still remains true that the *rationality* of the ethical had not thereby been vindicated. It is in this sense that Hegel remarks that talk about virtue readily borders on empty rhetoric and virtue becomes manifest only in exceptional circumstances (PR:107–108).

Hegel had become convinced that it would require a more robust sense of coherence than Kant's *bestimmt formal* of the categorical imperative to give the *logos* of virtue. In one sense, this recognition prepared the ground for his retrieval of the ancients against the moderns. We have already seen, in fact, how such a classicism informs Kant's moral theory from the beginning in its attempt to refigure the ancient codes in accord with the requisites of modern systematics: with Kant, the ancient inheritance of natural law had been transformed in accord with the pure syntactics which had accompanied the transformation of nature into a system of laws. For Hegel, however, the retrieval would take the form of an even more complete retrieval of ethical life or custom (*ethos*) as a whole, which would extend not only beyond the simple "tautologies" of positive law (NL:114), but also reaffirm the excess which accompanies singularity— the event in which "everyone is absolutely identical as both universal and particular" and hence a life form which "expresses reality or living custom" (NL:116). It is no accident that Hegel quotes Aristotle's *Politics* precisely in this regard:

The state comes by nature before the individual; if the individual in isolation is not anything self-sufficient, he must be related to the state in one unity, just as other parts are to their whole. But a man incapable of communal life, or who is so self-sufficient that he does not need it, is not part of the state and must be either a beast or a god (NL:113).[41]

Hegel had fully transformed the accounts of natural law that had preceded him by means of the ancients. Against Kant and Fichte's formal cosmopolitanism (which were in the end based, Hegel already believed, on private, bourgeois interest and the shallow virtues of possession and private property [NL:114]) and against Schelling's indifferent substantialism, Hegel appealed to the living custom of the ancients—and, as has been seen, he appealed to them by name.

That Hegel appealed at all to *Naturrecht* may appear curious. Granted Hegel's commitments to the historicity of rationality, granted his view of nature as accidental, or external in any case, to consider the decisive role played by natural law in the development of the system seems incongruous. Still, this misses the logical and historical context of the generation of the system itself. Historically, in Hegel's time the genre of *Naturrecht* was a common one, including treatises by Kant, Fichte, Schelling, Maimon, Schleiermacher, von Humboldt, and others. Moreover, this still omits Hegel's contribution to the genre in the retrieval of the Greek polis as a model for ethical life. In doing so, Hegel likewise retrieved what Aristotle already in the *Rhetoric*, for example, recognized as the distinction between written or positive law and unwritten law—a distinction appealed to earlier in the origins of the conceptual articulation of tradition, by Tertullian and Iranaeus.[42] For example, consistent with this concept of tradition, the former claimed that mere custom is but the interpreter of reason, but in God all things are alike natural and rational—a distinction formalized by Aquinas's differentiations between first principles and second, and divine and human law, in the *Treatise on Law*.

Hegel, of course, belongs in a complex way to the modern development of this tradition. As with Hooker and Grotius, who had retrieved Aquinas for the modern age, for Hegel, it is the light of reason itself that reveals the natural law of things.[43] Like Pufendorf, who had already emphasized the category of the individual in modern accounts of natural law, Hegel would affirm the priority of individuals in the articulation of rational institutions. Unlike Hooker, Grotius, and Locke, however, Hegel did not hold that 'natural law' is simply independent from its historical institutions, nor did he think that the rights of the individual are simply distinguishable from their instantiations. Nor would Hegel concur, as Suárez had before him at the outset of the modern age and Bradley had at its end, that the instantiation of right implied mere obligationism. But in all these matters Hegel still does not simply distinguish himself from the 'tradition' of natural law; rather it is precisely this complexity regarding nature and institution, *physis* and *nomos*, being and time which in the end unites him to it. We will need to take seriously the fact that Hegel saw himself as still working under the title of natural right throughout his career.

Now, however, the problem of 'natural law' is also inseparable from the law of freedom, as he had learned from Kant, Fichte, and Schelling. Nonetheless, it is precisely in the retrieval of the *polis* as living custom that the concept of nature becomes "explicit" (to use Hegel's expressionist term) in concrete conditions for freedom's flourishing, and the transition (*Übergehen*) from the "in itself" to the "for itself." The problem is again overcoming the dispersion of modern civil society, in which the customs have become dead and, as Hegel put it in relation to Fichte's *Rechtlehre*, human flourishing has become transformed into thinking that "disunity and division [*Entzweiung*] constitutes the essence of man" (Dif:150).

7. The (Tragic) Education of Character and the Prose of the World

It is against this disunity that Hegel continually appeals to the Greek *polis* as a model, all the while reaffirming the importance of the *humaniora*. But precisely insofar as the *polis* would again provide the *eudaimonia* of human nature, it does so by a gesture through which Hegel's expressionist and analogical metaphysics underwrote and regulated the history which he had uncovered. This is a complex history in which *historia* and *physis*, the before and after, the old customs (*Sitte*) and the new are gathered together, resulting in a complex interchange between the history in which they emerge and the good that is revealed and legitimated—readmitting the distinction between positive law and ethical substance. The *Philosophy of Right* consequently begins by denying the opposition between positive and natural right or law, as a simplistic "opposition" which "perverts their difference" and correlates law, understood from the philosophical point of view, with *Naturrecht* (PR:16).

Hence, fully aware of the experience of detraditionalization, Hegel also retained his debt to the moderns, denying the simple affirmation that natural law could be founded on antecedent conditions—a denial also found in Kant's claim that such customs still lack the universal. It is

possible for traditional communal life to wither and withdraw. The problem then still remains one of distinguishing historical flourishing from its
opposite: the need "to distinguish properly what is dead and without truth
from what is still living" (NL:130). And it is precisely here, in the account
of the rationality of character, that he transformed both Aristotle and Kant
at the same time. Hegel, however, appealed to the transitions of *Bildung*
and historical achievement for criteria to guide customs of communal life,
appealing once more not only to the moral teacher of custom but equally
to the process of *Bildung* itself as the source of the justification of such
an ethos.

According to Hegel, what had been missing in the quarrel between the
ancients and the moderns, granted the underdeterminacy at stake, was
precisely the recognition of this rational concretization of ethical form in
custom, the disarticulation of the singular—and thereby, the opening of
reason through which understanding attains content. What is lost in all of
this (to readopt the genre of the tragic) is what Aristotle called *discovery*
(*anagnorisis*) and Hegel called education (*Bildung*), i.e., an event separating
formal individuality (and deductive form) from determinacy, undercutting
formal individuality from within—the diremption, the oscillation effected
through the force of circumstance and the play of possibility or alterity.[44] If
Novalis had already claimed then that the past's intelligibility is always
tragic, that "every representation of the past is a tragic drama in the veritable
sense," Hegel would add in this regard, attempting at the same time to
refigure the genre of tragedy itself, that the tragic is precisely the order of
the intelligible.[45] "Education is the absolute transition from an ethical substantiality which is immediate and natural to the one which is intellectual
and so both infinitely subjective and lofty enough to have attained universality of form" (PR:125). If, as Aristotle proclaimed, *mimesis* (like metaphysics) begins in wonder—if, moreover, it is only by *mimesis* that we learn—it
is also true that the affirmations of mere perception (*doxa*) will not suffice
for education.[46] At the theoretical level, concretization will be required; at
the ethical level, the emergence of the heart (HP:I.413). While without
understanding there can be no firmness of will, then without education
there is mere obstinacy of will, merely "self enclosed minds" (Aesth:584).
Hence, as has been seen, it is precisely the advance of Shakespeare's account
to have articulated a 'world-stage' of action in which (formally) "it is possible to go this way or that," thus fracturing the search for univocal *Er-
klärung* that had driven philosophical modernism. It is just in this regard
that what Shakespeare's tragedies enunciate is what the *Aesthetics* had seen
as the *prosa der Welt*:

> This is the prose of the world, as it appears to the consciousness both of the individual himself and of others: a world of finitude and mutability, of entanglement in the relative, of the pressure of necessity from which the individual is in no position to withdraw. (Aesth:150)

And as has become evident, what is true generically, even "naturally," is true generally regarding the immediate actuality of spiritual interest:

> The individual as he appears in this world of prose and everyday is not active out of the entirety of his own self and his resources, and he is intelligible not from himself, but from something else. For the individual man stands in dependence on external influences, awe, political institutions, civil relationships, which he just finds confronting him, and he must bow to them whether he has them as his own inner being or not. (Aesth:149)

Thus by articulating modern individuality as a world-play of conflicts between individuals rather than eternal forces, Shakespeare became for Hegel the tragedean of the everyday, of civil society or "the system of the ethical order, split into its extremes and lost" (PR:123)—and thereby, the passage between the ancients and the moderns. For the ancients, Hegel realized, insofar as this order involves the 'splitting' of intention and object, theory and practice, self and interest, its event could only appear "as an invasion of ethical corruption," since it marks the diremption of the self between intention and outcome, narrative and irony (PR:123). Instead, the justification of virtue would involve not only the affirmation of a narrative and its intelligibility but the question of its emplotment, its invention or figuration, transformation or refiguration.[47] Rationality could not be bound by the limits of iterable truths, but would further require "knowing how" both when to venture—and when to give them up.

The Romantics, on the other hand, for Hegel, while emphasizing irony, missed the 'plasticity' (the experiment, and thereby, the rationality) of character. The ironical instead simply exchanges *Bildung* for the unhappy consciousness, Romantic adventure for nihilism.[48] If "the modern doctrine of irony too has its justification in a certain respect," namely in the oscillation of the self in its diremption as a necessary condition of deliberation (indicative of the lingering significance of Fichte), this notion of irony remains fully indeterminate and aloof—"soaring above the wreckage of the world," as he puts it elsewhere (FK:174).

While the modern world is a world dirempted, the totality of the ancients is dirempted into plurality, and the ironical or unhappy consciousness of the moderns turns away in horror, like Novalis "driven into a void with no specific interest" (Aesth:158). Hence Hegel's single condemnation of the characterization of a dramatic persona which would waver (as he condemned Aristotle's), and his defense of Shakespeare from accounts which would transform his characters into ironic ghosts.[49]

In place of the play of impersonal forces and "one-sided" characters of the ancients, Shakespeare exhibits characters of "free imaginative power and gifted spirit" (*menschen von freier Vorstellunskraft und genialem Geiste*), thereby "extending and elevating" them beyond the collisions of their own situations. In this regard the 'prose of the world' became for Hegel an occasion for the (modern) adventure of spirit—and hence for "the particular circumstances and situations which stir [*anregen*] character" (Aesth:585–86). The contingent forces of the fates then might be overcome by the resources from within, perfecting the force of *Vorstelleung* itself by means of "a depth and wealth of Spirit," the force of imagination (*Einbildungskraft*)—and the wealth of speculation. Hegel had denominated the imagination as the faculty of speculation early on precisely in opening the experiment and the extension of the possible (FK:80). In one sense, the waverings and dispersals of imagination already outline Benjamin's destructive character which "sees nothing permanent . . . but for this reasons sees ways everywhere"—or perhaps hearkens back to Hölderlin's creative dissolution which in the language of tragedy is "forever creative . . . the genesis of the individual out of the infinite."[50] And yet for Hegel such dispersal among possibilities was the way to the fulfillment (rather than the destruction) of nature and character. Thus the critical role of the "plasticity" of the speculative—with respect not only to the practical, but equally to the intellectual virtues.

The plasticity of this prose moreover resonates perhaps with a certain Bakhtinian overtone. Bakhtin had privileged Dostoyevski's novels in an analysis of the polyphonic, dialogic, and heteroglossic moments, contesting epic monologism in the affirmation of the plasticity of the everyday itself. In fact its exploration, Bakhtin also claimed, had already appeared in both Dante and in Shakespeare, and in the process of the emergence of the novel, whose prosaic practices in this regard break with "the absolute past and tradition."[51] Poetics, on the other hand, "depersonalizes days" and formalizes the heterogeneity of the prosaic reality of the novel.[52] Precisely in this regard the novel "is by its very nature, not canonic. It is plasticity itself. It is a genre which is ever questing, ever examining itself and subjecting its established forms to review,"[53] a "radically new zone for structuring images."[54] But if Hegel would thus seem contradictory here—credited both with acknowledging that the novel should become for the moderns what the epic was for the ancients[55] and for providing the paradigm of the monological—here this plasticity itself had been at stake in the very possibility of the speculative itself.

8. On the Exposition(s) of the Speculative

The importance of the problem of the "plasticity" of speculation, as has been evident, had already been prepared in Kant's undermining of *mimesis*. Kant's move, differentiating universality and iterability, already had invoked the need for both originality and experiment. The extensions of rational tradition would involve, even in the perdurance of identity, a synthesis (and development) of identity and difference—in Kantian terms, a heterogeneous synthesis—in Hegel's terms, an investment within the 'plastic' or figurative synthesis of the speculative in its exposition of the singular.

From the beginning of the system—or the *Phenomenology of Spirit*—Hegel had himself appealed to the resources of this plasticity of expression in extending beyond the abstractions of understanding. It was that work's first word in a sense, and its appeal—its *hermeneuein*—which justified the claim that the formalism of the Enlightenment was now "old fashioned," now "belonging to a bygone culture" (Phen:28). Against it Hegel's preface invoked the *plasticität* of exposition and its rhythm, one which relied upon the 'floating center' of the speculative proposition in extending beyond the abstractions of reflection. Moreover, if this *plasticität* was Hegel's first word in the *Phenomenology's* "detailed history of the education of consciousness," it was perhaps equally his last. The 1831 preface to the *Science of Logic* again expresses hope that "an abstract perfection of exposition . . . might be dispensed with relying instead upon the plasticity of discourse." And given that "a plastic discourse demands a plastic receptivity and understanding on the part of the listener" (WdL:40), both in the saying and the said, the speculative relied on what always exceeded the requisites of strict demonstration for its adventure beyond the rigidification of pure form. Never perhaps would Hegel be closer to—and yet distinguished from—Schleiermacher's hermeneutic.[56]

The lectures on *Aesthetics* in which Shakespeare's account of character had taken on such prominence, also risked this figuration, once again a matter of spirit's *plasticität*—and again axiomatically, it might be claimed. In his most critical discussion of human figuration and "exteriority," i.e., the artist's *Vorstellung* of sculpture, Hegel described this event explicitly as "the miracle of spirit's giving itself an image of itself in something purely material" (Aesth:710). Schlegel before him also had spoken of the *plastisch* and physiognomy as of a pair, understanding them once more in terms of the ironical. However, far from claiming, as is "frequent in modern times" that "the man who is by nature beauteous and noble, is better than he who acts from duty" (HP:II.205), Hegel had recourse to originality as the opening of rationality in the moment of *Bildung,* the adventure (and the experiment) of spirit's extension beyond the limitations of the moral. This extension relies upon the underderminability of the "moral," relying upon the potentiality of its ambiguity in order to extend beyond it—in order, that is, to fulfill this plasticity in arriving again at a "solid and cultivated objective language" (Aesth:1215).

Still, as has become evident, Hegel could not rest with simple inner intention or decision for the rationality of moral action, since he was committed both to the underdeterminability of moral claims (in themselves) and to the fallibility of individual decision, denying in advance, it might be claimed, the agonies of Kierkegaard and Abraham's "purely personal virtue."[57] Hegel again approaches Burke in the affirmation of a historical account of the rational and the latter's own conservative reception of natural law. As Burke stated:

> Where the great interests of mankind are concerned through a long succession of generations, that succession ought to be admitted into some share in the councils which are so deeply to affect them. If justice requires this, the work itself requires the aid of more minds than one age can furnish. It is from this view of things that the best legislators have been often satisfied with the establishment of some sure, solid, and ruling principle in government—a power like that which some of the philosophers have called a plastic nature; and having fixed the principle, they have left it afterwards to its own operation.[58]

Although both Hegel and Burke concurred that the abstract individual could not provide such a principle, Burke remained committed in the end to the past in a way that Hegel was not: "We are not the converts of Rousseau; Helvetius has made no progress amongst us. Atheists are not our preachers; madmen are not our lawgivers. We know that we have made no discoveries."[59] Hegel, on the other hand, in articulating virtue as 'plastic' once more remained committed nonetheless to the necessity (and virtue) of individual innovation and decision, to the necessity of decision within the possible. He remained, that is, Kantian regarding the past—even if *unlike* Kant he took both the encounter with the historical to be decisive and the decision itself to involve a complex interchange between necessity and contingency. There remains a certain disequilibrium, to use Hegel's term, in the speculative problem of *plasticität* and the force and power at stake within its faculty, the imagination (*Einbildungskraft*)—a disequilibrium which would be as manifest here as it would in the concept of force generally, always the possibility of the inverted world. From the outset, as has been seen, Hegel saw the link between the indeterminacies of scientific explanation and law and those of justice (PS:§158). Beyond the strict algorithmics of justice, here too judgment itself arises in the indeterminacy of freedom, and becomes more an art of discernment, the *techne diacritike,* than the construction of modernist *mathesis.* Hegel's advance here also involves a complex gesture regarding the status of the *humaniora.* As the *Philosophy of History* put it, "art received a further support and experienced an elevating influence as the result of the study of antiquity" (PH:409). The link Hegel drew between art and the *humaniora* is doubtless indebted to Winckelmann's account of the plasticity of ancient sculpture as well as to Creuzer's and Schelling's studies on myth and symbol, in which finite and infinite found harmonious presentation (*Darstellung*). Philosophically, however, Hegel's gesture remains intelligible only within the legacy and transformation of Kant's protocols.

Shorn of ultimate determinacy outside its application to schematized manifolds, Kant realized that Reason would need to proceed not simply by determinate judgment, in which the particular would be known in advance, but reflectively. As Kant put it in the first introduction to the third *Critique:*

> The reflective judgment thus works with given appearances so as to bring them under empirical concepts of determinate natural things not schematically, not just mechanically, like a tool controlled by the understanding and the senses, but artistically.[60]

Before such a judgment the figures of Newton and Euclid, who had dominated the Copernican turn, could no longer hold sway. The rational mechanics of subsumptive judgment would be abandoned before the fecundity of (artistic) discernment, the subsumptive mechanism of the 'understanding' for the inventions of imagination. It was no accident then that Hegel's *Faith and Knowledge* had recognized the imagination as the faculty of speculation, nor that Kant's third *Critique* culminated its argument in speculations on the fecundity of the symbol, an event involving an indeterminate plurality of possible construals but no univocally adequate concept, for which the plasticity of the symbol provided the unity of identity and difference. And symbolism functions this way, as has been seen, by what the *Religion* would finally admit to be a schematism of *analogy,* with which (as a means of explanation) "we cannot dispense" (Rel:58n). Although the third *Critique* would not say it so explicitly in logical terms, it said it even more directly in claiming that the symbol provides a means, if not of revelation—as Kant's successors would claim—then at least of "exhibition" (*Darstellung*) (CJ:227). And while both schematic and symbolic presentation are "exhibitive," the difference is that the former is demonstrative while the latter is 'analogic'. Although this contrast again reveals Kant's deductive investments, because 'demonstration' is strictly limited to 'objective' subsumption, Kant's followers recognized what had been accomplished. The 'objective' or 'schematic' subsumption remains, after all, finite—and in the latter sense, at least, subjective: both types of presentation indeed strictly remain, as he put it elsewhere, presentation by an *aspekt*. By thus interlacing the univocal and the equivocal, the symbol nondemonstrably refers to a unity beyond it, precisely, that is, to an equivocal *pros hen*. The question will always be the rationality of its conjecture or discovery, that is, its interpretation. What Kant's distinction between reflective and determinate judgment pointed to, without denying the validities of either, is the distinction between the rigors of construction and exhibition themselves.

In this respect, as Gadamer put it, Kant's symbolics in the third *Kritik* do "justice to the theological truth that had found its scholastic form in the *analogia entis*." In this it reinstitutes an account dating from Chrysippus's Christian transformation of neoplatonism that had, by means of a certain anagogic function, joined the finite and infinite. Gadamer also realized, however, that the truth of symbolic analogy was that it had critically acknowledged the noumenon: "it keeps its concepts separate from God" (TM:75). Kant's own account of the sublime similarly instituted this distance by acknowledging an extension, an indeterminacy which always in this respect placed its 'plasticity' (indemonstrably) at risk. Here, as Gadamer realized, pace the metaphysics of genius and its elevation of the symbol, by virtue of the very indeterminacy which underwrote the extension of the symbolic itself, the latter became subject to a vacillation interfacing those of allegory, of *distensio,* dissonance, the disruption of tradition, and the untimely (TM:72–80). No one in fact articulated this disequilibrium between symbol and allegory more emphatically than Walter Benjamin, precisely, again, in refusing all attempts at symbolic idealization:

> Whereas in the symbol destruction is idealized and the transfigurized face of nature is fleetingly revealed in the light of the redemption, in allegory the observer is confronted with the *facies hippocratica* of history as a petrified, primordial landscape. Everything about history that, from the very beginning, has been untimely, sorrowful, unsuccessful, is expressed in a face—or rather in death's head. And although such a thing lacks all 'symbolic' freedom of

expression, all classical proportion, all humanity—nevertheless, this is the form in which man's subjection to nature is most obvious and it significantly gives rise not only to the enigmatic question of the nature of human existence as such, but also of the biographical historicity of the individual. This is the heart of the allegorical way of seeing, of the baroque, secular explanation of history as the Passion of the world; its importance resides solely in the stations of its decline. (Trau:166)

While Benjamin's work articulated both allegory and the event of mourning attending it, Hegel, in inaugurating his own theoretical meditation, did so by exchanging the ambiguities that attended Kantian systematics (with its underdeterminacy of form) for the tropes of tragic form. This recovery of the tragic would not be limited simply to providing the opening of the ironical, but extended to providing its denouement, its *discoveries,* its *catharsis,* and ultimate *clarification.* That is, Hegel transforms underdeterminability into epistemic conflict, into an event in which the deed itself "becomes the negative movement, or the eternal necessity, of a dreadful fate which engulfs in the abyss of its single nature divine and human law alike" (Phen:279). We can witness the result in the critical close to §140 of the *Philosophy of Right* where this provision becomes perhaps most explicit. If *Bildung* is seen as overcoming the diremption (and conflict) in civil society, Hegel remains steadfast regarding his unswerving commitment to tragic form. Here again we find him arguing against Schlegel, and reinvoking the *Phenomenology's* figure of the unhappy consciousness:

> The *tragic* destruction of figures whose ethical life is on the highest plane can interest and elevate us and reconcile us to its occurrence only insofar as they come on the scene in opposition to one another together with equally justified but different ethical powers which have come into collision through misfortune through their opposition to an ethical law. Out of this situation there arises the right and wrong of both parties and therefore the true ethical Idea, which, purified and in triumph over this onesidedness, is thereby reconciled in *us.* (PR:102)

9. What Belies the Machinery (*Räderwerk*) of Dialectic: Beyond the Algorithmics of Character

Despite its fecundity, however, it is clear that Hegel's interest in tragedy remained mixed. Having from the outset rejected the tragic account of fate, it could not have been otherwise. Interested in the underdeterminability of moral claims, he became committed to conflict—or collision—as the critical tribunal for the resolution of such claims, ultimately still exchanging the plasticity and rhythm of the speculative for the formal algorithm of their resolution. He was interested, that is, in the question of how an agonistic of claims that are different but equally justified might be brought to resolution, i.e., how, through being adjudicated by an *uns,* "the right and wrong of both parties" might emerge—and how there might result (as the *Aesthetics* puts it) the exposition of a complication which "preserves the justification that both have [their] inner rationality" before "eternal justice" (Aesth:1215, 1197). In a sense this is just an account of Hegel's dialectic itself. Unlike ancient accounts of dialectic, always ancillary to deduction, Hegel's dialectic would itself deliver ultimate truth and justice. Its model, in this regard, often enough missed, is perhaps less ancient dialectic than medieval dialectic, "the science of sciences" alone "capable of knowing," whose "conclusions lead us to an apprehension of our being and of our origin."[61] The latter, however, always remained ultimately figured toward a *pros hen* that escapes the finite, hence relying upon the sacred figures of theology. Similarly, the figure of tragedy would not replace such dialectic but at most serve once more as its trope.

Hegel's own account of the *plasticität* of character could no more serve as a guarantee for such critical resolution, "the cancellation of the conflicts as conflicts." Its agonistic was one which mapped the matrix of the intrinsic failure of the antagonists and the justificatory shortfall of their claims. What is perhaps most apparent in this regard is that Hegel did not believe in the tragedy his extension traded upon in its very undecidability. Hence emerges the significance of comedy as its dialectical suppression.

Granted the question which spurs the tragic—the underdeterminability of the moral and the conflict of interpretations—there is after all a certain transcendental illusion to the resolution of the tragic. Hegel, like others after him attached to it as a philosopheme, doubtless succumbed too often to its illusion. Insofar, that is, as the negative infinite of tragedy became determinate, insofar as the excess explored by consciousness was held to be ultimately and finally resolved in the adjudication of a transhistorical or transnarratological *uns,* the singularity of death itself became dissolved through a symbolic investment which would in the end turn, to use Benjamin's terms, both its "enigmatic question" and the biographical fate of the individual determinate. Hence emerges, as Benjamin saw, Hegel's reduction of the allegorical moment in Shakespeare. Those in the wake of the *Sturm und Drang* movement, "which discovered Shakespeare for Germany, had eyes only for the elemental aspect of his work, not the allegorical. And yet what is characteristic of Shakespeare is precisely that both aspects are equally essential" (Trau:228). Hence the enigmatic question of the allegorical would be lost in the fundamental resolution of speculative determination, and the difference between individual and universal thereby dissolved. The significance of the singularity of death—not simply the "ineffability" of death, but precisely the fraility of human life—would be denied. The singularity of death could not be the dissolution of speculation (one does after all speculate about death), if it would provide a transcendental subreption for the specular image itself, the event in which the individual itself will not be subsumed.

We have seen that what Hegel himself had claimed to have found in Shakespeare's emphasis upon individuality and the "fragmentary prose of the world" was a dialectical development that could not be reduced to a caculative machine or *Räderwerk*. Nietzsche would similarly claim of tragedy that it belied such a reduction: refusing "the enormous driving-wheel of logical Socratism" that dissolved tragic indeterminacy into "logical schematism."[62] Such a schematism was linked to philosophy's ('Socratism's') refusal of the Dionysian, its link to justification always for Nietzsche a sign of the attempt to dissolve what the Appollonian essence cannot determine. Notice however, that what Nietzsche and Hegel agreed upon was that such indeterminacy could not be reduced to logical schematism: what they disagreed about was whether justification had *any* role to play as a result. But what they still agreed upon—even in this difference—was that justification would be an all-or-nothing thing, a matter of "logical despotism."[63] While Nietzsche's logical Socrates is a Socrates devoid of irony, Hegel still claimed the philosopher could provide the mediation of the chorus. But it is precisely such reductions, denying the interpretations of both principle and allegory, that must be resisted.[64]

In citing the Kantian sublime in the *Logic*, Hegel could not but dissolve the difference between Nature as conceived in the first *Critique* and that of the second *Critique*. Hegel could not but wish for a substantial freedom which united both in the same act, so that "Nature is determined by the ego, sense by the will of the good" (WdL:231–32). But this presupposes not only a resolution to the third Antinomy, but also that the laws of each 'nature' might be reducible to the (teleological) laws of the other. Moreover, it presupposes that the specific difference of the singular—the difference which intervenes between the empirical and transcendental ego—can be reduced to a mere (conceptual) particular. And, when the *Logic* came to the question of teleology and the question of its own interpretation of the singular, Hegel was specific in this regard. After consistently claiming that Kant's account of determinate (or subsumptive) judgment was (improperly) abstract, Hegel proceeded to view reflective judgment as its logical replacement, and thereby (almost unawares) proceeded simply by the logic of the very substitution which he himself had criticized. The dubious result was the "*End,*" a *concrete universal,* "which possesses in its own self the moment of particularity and externality and is therefore active and the urge to repel itself from itself" (WdL:739). Despite all Hegel's criticism of formalism, the analogy of the Good thus becomes transformed into a syllogism (that is, the syllogism of "immediate realization") precisely in the (ironical) moment in which "mediation sublates itself" (WdL:818–19, 823)—the reduction of *physis* to *ergein.*

In thinking all this Hegel had to forget the Copernican turn, and he had to forget the difference at stake. Moreover, when it came to the genre of tragedy, he had to transform the death of this singular into a determinate epistemic event. The tragic threat of a fight to the death (or an epistemic conflict) had indeed provided the penumbra of modern political theories, which had been valorized from the outset by the withdrawal of Nature (and the natural law). Yet while the tragic might provide an articuleme for such conflict, it could not provide its simple replacement, let alone resolution.

Perhaps ironically, Kant saw the risks of tragedy in this regard even better than Hegel himself—and despite the latter's charge that he had never grasped the ambiguity of the moral, i.e., that Kant never understood the tragic and the question of its underdeterminability. Although Kant in his "Idea for a Universal History" could understand history as a narrating of the appearances, and even see it as a "great world-stage" or a theodicy in which "natural urges . . . drive men to new exertions of their forces and thus to the manifold development," he could not turn such conflicts determinate.[65] Even if his critical philosophy of history led him to proclaim by a certain *hubris,* notwithstanding his own desubstantialization of the natural law, "Thanks be to Nature, then, for the incompatibility, for heartless competitive vanity, for the insatiable desire to possess and to rule,"[66] it precluded the possibility of substituting the algorithms of tragedy for those of moral intention, *salva veritate.* Too much intervened: the difference in time-order, appearance, justification, the withdrawal of truth itself. Accordingly, in the third *Critique,* which provides consistently scant discussion of tragedy, Kant declares that many people believe they "are improved by the performance of a tragedy when in fact they are merely glad at having succeeded in routing boredom (*Langweile*)" (CJ:134). Kant had perhaps already realized that if this dispersion is the opening of tragedy, nothing would safeguard its resolution.

10. Between Individual and *Individuum:*
Beyond 'Socratism'

This is not, of course, to say that Hegel's venture had ever simply given up the rational. Never did he declare it to be the case, as Schelling had argued in 1795, that rationally "there is nothing left but to fight and fall."[67] Nor did he ultimately follow—even if he always depended upon—Hölderlin's attempt to assuage this conflict by claiming that the end of true character, the destiny of man, was merely to trace out this tragic dispersion, to "multiply, propel, and disperse the life of nature" and hence to attain harmony precisely in this dispersion.[68] Instead, for Hegel, the underdeterminability whose extensions the ethical tragically relied on, turned out to be an illusion, a matter inevitably to be resolved—although this was arguably something his "experimentalism" precluded in principle (a contradiction that provides his own account of the tragic with a certain philistine and comic edge). Just before his final words on dissolution of the Romantic form of art, and after having transformed the Romantic character and its adventure into the course of the world and its requirements of "family, civil society, state, laws, professional business, etc.," finally affirming the narrative of the *Bildungsroman* in the aesthetic, Hegel states:

> But in the modern world these fights are nothing more than 'apprenticeship', the education of the individual into the realities of the present. . . . However much he may have quarrelled with the world, or been pushed about in it, in most cases at last he gets his girl and some sort of position, marries her, and becomes as good a Philistine as others. The woman takes charge of household management, children arrive, the adored wife, at first unique, an angel, behaves pretty much as all others do; the man's profession provides work and vexations, marriage brings domestic affliction—so here we have all the headaches of the rest of married folk. We find its right significance, wherein the fantastic element must experience the right corrective. (Aesth:593)

In this respect, as the *Phenomenology* proclaims, "the 'way of the world' is not as bad as it looked; for its reality is the interdependent reality of the universal" (Phen:235). And the classical account of virtue, which was already "downplayed," is called more radically into question. Irigaray has aptly argued with respect to Hegel's account of tragedy that its dialectic of the 'equality' of sexual difference was already mythic—"already the effect of a dialectic produced by the discourse of patriarchy."[69] Notwithstanding the alleged purity of the brother-sister relation, Antigone gains access to the dialectic "only by devoting herself to the cult of his death."[70] In the above passage we witness even more blatantly its modern inversion, one which everywhere accompanies Hegel's cynicism. But the point is that such a dialectic will be neither tragically resolved nor comically dissolved—anymore than the pain of the allegorical can be symbolized. To think so is to confuse the need to (historically) refigure the symbolic realm with the (mythic) negations of its ideal purges. But here even those most ancient virtues of friendship and *filia*, which elsewhere seem to reappear in Hegel's elevation of the family, are all of a piece presented as animated by "vain hope."

Emerson would soon articulate the (Schlegelian) change which lies nascent in Hegel's failure—as would Bakhtin, even more disturbed by the political effect at stake. In *The Conduct of Life*, with Shakespeare's metaphor still lingering, Emerson claimed:

> Society is the stage on which manners are shown; novels are their literature. Novels are the journal or record of manners, and the new importance of these books derives from the fact that the novelist begins to penetrate the surface and treat this part of life more worthily.[71]

Bakhtin would see the novel as the breakdown of genres, the literary now fragmented in the collapse of tradition. What Emerson saw was that—pace Burke—something else had emerged for which "neither Aristotle, nor Leibniz, nor Junius, nor Champollion has set down the grammar-rules of this dialect, older than Sanscrit; but they who cannot yet read English can read this."[72] Emerson would also dwell upon the importance of invention in the dispersion which results, criticizing precisely the artificiality of prior genres: "The novels used to be all alike, and had a quite vulgar tone. The novels used to lead us onto a foolish interest in the fortunes of the boy and girl they described."[73] Against this (and by a certain vindication of Schlegel), Emerson declared, in "the 'new novel' it is truth and friendship which are at stake, and the novel is its exploration."[74] It is in just this regard that Bakhtin would declare that, beyond the ancient canon, the novel, accordingly, "is plasticity itself."[75] The result again is "the fuller development and the freer play of character as a social and political agent."[76] If such "development" remained also devoid of justification in Schlegel, as Hegel had rightly seen, it was not simply devoid of rationality. In fact neither Hegel nor Schlegel had sufficiently seen individual judgment's involvement in such development as irreducibly crucial to its rationality.

Such development, as Hegel's cynicism in the above text notes, only arises as an interplay and conflict between role and individual. Further, as Hans Robert Jauss has shown in citing Heloise or Montaigne, "in literature, on the other hand, the 'I-you' relation of friendship or love is celebrated as a role-independent relationship."[77] While admitting that such an event would appear to the sociologist—as much perhaps as it would to Hegel—as a "purely literary or mystical mode of experience," Jauss nevertheless claimed that it was "perfectly well known to us from everyday life." Still, for the same reason that it eludes sociological reduction and the rule-governed constraints of role-playing—just to that extent it eludes simple conceptual individuality. Here the *individuum* and the individual cannot coincide. Hence then emerges the complex development of the individual as the 'inner', the intimate—and the contested.

That the issue could turn on such topics may seem startling. Yet it might seem no less startling if it turned out that on this point Hegel's political theory rejoins (while separating itself from) Aristotle. In one sense, in any case, the modern problem of ethical recognition itself belongs to the virtue of friendship in Aristotle's sense. Such (reciprocal) recognition or goodwill, *along with* decision, is what friendship adds to love.[78] It is recognition and certainty that are at stake when Hegel abandons his earlier ethical accounts and the account of the *ethos* itself based upon love. Hegel's later "cynicism" may well respond to modern necessities and to the complications by which the modern (and civil society) has intervened on his earlier (idealized and Romantic) account of the ethical community as a community of *agape*.[79] As has become apparent, this complication forced him to a second reciprocal rejoinder with the past and the *humaniora*, with the Greek *polis*—as the new solution and yet here too not without modern effect.

If Aristotle and the ideal of the Greek *polis* had now replaced Hegel's earlier views, they arrived with the death throes of modernity itself—and in particular those opened by Hobbes. Following Hobbes's demand for certainty—or as Strauss put it, Hobbes's concern for the extreme case—the struggle for recognition would be correlated first with the master-slave dialectic and the fight to the death, and then correlated, *not* with friendship but with Absolute Knowledge, a move which translated the *ethos* into a matter of subject-object identity. If Hegel had gone beyond Kant here by realizing that right is a matter of recognition and more than simply rational coherence among atomized agents, the result still threatened a dissolution of individuality and the ensuing diminution of friendship. Moreover this same dilemma even affects the investment of classicists in the Greek ideal itself. Recall again that when Winckelmann sought to make of Dresden "the Athens of artists," it was not simply nostalgia, imitation, or identification, nor even an attempt to prove the reiterability of the ideal. Rather, the ideal only became evident in this encounter with temporal difference. It suffices

to say once more—and perhaps Nietzsche was the first to stress its complications—that it would not be Athens, it would be Dresden.[80] Any account
of the rationality at stake would require an account of this encounter, the
difference at stake, and the problem of application.

It was not insignificant, then, that Hegel's *Philosophy of Right* began with
the problem of recognition but immediately dissolved the question of application (PR:16). As Gadamer would realize, the question of application
was really the remainder of *phronesis,* the problem of *epagoge* and the Good:
he described it in Hegelian tones as the problem of the "concrete" (TM:21).
It is precisely the question of application that should have lent substance
to Hegel's account of rationality. Rather than the simple tragic venture on
which he modeled it, rationality requires the relevance of judgment, prece-
dence, and both articulation and innovation. And in this respect it cannot
have been accidental that, lacking all reference to a common law tradition
that might foster such an account built on the interplay between precedent
and relevance, Hegel's *Philosophy of Right* begins by excluding the problem
of such "application" at the outset. His critique of formalism and substantialism had established the outlines for just such an account by recognizing
the limitations of the formal as a problem of its meaning (an excess beyond
the particular) and its application. Any positive account of such ambiguities
was precluded by Hobbes's (deductive) demands. And they precluded,
moreover, the very itinerary that Hegel's speculative extension had opened
up: i.e., the possibility that the *humaniora,* rather than providing a model
for the immanence of subject and object (the *parousia* of the good infinite),
would make possible an interpretation of what escapes those limits, along
with invention and translation in their breach.

The ambiguity of character for Hegel would, nonetheless, again be resolved in the metaphysics of the deed (Phen:193). In other words, despite
all that he had seen concerning the intricacies of fact and theory, intention
and event, institution and significance, the iterabilities of nature and culture,
possibility and necessity, he still claimed that "ethical self-consciousness
now learns from its deed the developed nature of what it actually did"
(Phen:283).

However, the legacy of the account of plasticity of the speculative becomes overdetermined. What is at stake in such events is not simply deeds,
but *words* and deeds, *theory* and practice, expression and the expressed.
Although he had emphasized the figural investment of (experimental) imagination in the symbolic investitures of Spirit, Hegel always underestimated
the indeterminacy which had incited his brief against formalism. As a result,
the formal difference between positive law and natural law, and the differ-

ence between the primary and the secondary principles (the 'promulgated' or 'positive' principles) of the law, the difference between the 'divine' and the 'human' law, and the difference between the ontic and the ontological were erased, reduced to the reductionist protocols of Objective Spirit. And if we are to believe critics such as Lacoue-Labarthe, who see Hegel's legacy as pervasive in German political theory—up to and including Heidegger—the difference between nature and act (*physis* and *ergon*) and nature and law (*nomos* and *physis*) were always endangered by a mimetology Hegel, for reasons we have made evident, already called into question.[81]

11. Allegory and the Disenchantments of Justice

Hegel's account of the "plasticity" of human reason, and all that Hegel had discovered in the *Bildung* of the Spirit, then became transformed by a certain transcendental subreption into the simple plasticity of substance itself—one malleable enough that the *Natural Law* compares it to the heating of a metal and its transformation into liquid (NL:132). Certainly not of necessity, Hegel often grants the figurative plasticity of symbolic investiture the privileged status of the *parousia* of the Absolute itself, its *Darstellung*. The excess of community it had sought in the Greeks became transformed into immanence.

As Benjamin rightly points out, in Creuzer, Hegel's Heidelberg colleague,[82] the spirit of Winckelmann speaks in the account of the artistic symbol as plastic, resolving the tension between the finite and the infinite as "the symbol of the gods, which miraculously unites the beauty of form with the highest fullness of being and which, because it receives its more perfect execution in Greek sculpture, may be called the plastic symbol" (Trau:164). As has been noted, Hegel reinvoked such symbolism in his own account of Greek sculpture as expressing the outward character of the great virtue of individuality itself: "a totality in itself and that totality's unity and harmony as an individual" (Aesth:476-77). Indeed, as such this account formed something of a culmination of the *Aesthetics* itself, beyond the equivocal indeterminacy which Hegel saw in the symbolic—but not simply dispersed within the inner life of the Romantic—in short, the paradigm of objective Spirit. The latter found its most appropriate form in the sculpture of human figures, providing insight into "the perfect plasticity of gods and men preeminently at home in Greece" in the age of Pericles. "In the beautiful days of Greece men of action, like poets and thinkers, had this same plastic and universal yet individual character, both inwardly and outwardly" (Aesth:719). This ideal could in the end be underwritten only by a grand synthesis, involving a sort of pantragicism on the one hand, but equally a sort of incarnationism on the other—resulting in a disequilibrium that still divided thinkers in his wake, e.g., Nietzsche and Kierkegaard.[83] It is not accidental that Hegel himself invokes sculpture for the figure of virtue's plasticity in his analysis of tragedy. The immanence of figurative plasticity thus fully embodied, fully naturalized would turn the embodiment of virtue into a sculpture (Aesth:1195)—an object, in short a cadaver. It is not accidental, on the other hand, then that Benjamin would see allegory precisely here "expressed in a face—or rather in death's head."

The figures of such a classicism, underwritten by the codes of ontotheology, as Benjamin realized, "could not but scorn allegory." Indeed this is precisely what Hegel did, criticizing Winckelmann's text on allegory as both immature and confusing symbol and allegory (Aesth:400). Justice for the ancients, *Dike*, should not, Hegel claimed be identified with allegory: "she is universal necessity, eternal justice, the universal powerful person, the absolutely substantial basis of the relations of nature and spiritual life" (Aesth:400). All but succumbing to historicism, Hegel claims (as he had of the rationality of the ancient state) that "it does not matter in the least whether individuals as individuals want law and justice to prevail or not; law and justice prevails in and by itself, and even if they did not want it to, nevertheless it would" (Aesth:183). And while it is the virtue of civil society to subdivide such power in the "most varied possible way" (Aesth:183), the subordination of the individual subject and individuality remains intact. The difference between individual and *individuum* remains unintelligible on this account—one upon which the 'mourning' of allegory implicitly relies as much as Schlegel's fragmented exposition in venturing beyond it.

A cursory glance at Winckelmann, by contrast, shows him tactfully to be acknowledging this difference internal to the aesthetic, even in reintroducing the neoplatonist account of ideal as its model. It will not suffice simply to identify Hegel's appeal to the figural, to plasticity and the plastic ideal as merely dogmatic or metaphysical in the pejorative sense. Indeed from the outset, Winckelmann himself had noticed the aesthetic's exclusion within philosophical modernism. In affirming the grasp of the particular contained in the aesthetic, Winckelmann explicitly denied that its truth might be captured *more geometrico,* and he links the ideal to an interplay between spirit and nature. Beauty is a matter of expression—expressionism of the ideal.[84] Hegel's critique of formalism, of course, initially falls into place here as does his retrival of the ancients. Hegel's emphasis on ethical life depends on an event in which, rather than internalizing predetermined rules, the *phronimos* becomes an exemplification of virtue—albeit of rule-governed or at least *replicable* virtue.

Hegel's *Differenzschrift* credits Fichte's *Science of Ethics* with already blinkingly recognizing the possibilities that underlie the possibility of fulfilling a science of the ethical—only to fall short before the split that divided reason from its object, the finite and the infinite (Dif:141f.). Schlegel had perhaps read Fichte better. This "aesthetic" model however was never simply absent from the ethical—as is clear from not only Aristotle's *phronimos* but also, as has become apparent, in Cicero's transformation of *persona* through *honestum* and its manifestation in the appearance of virtue [*decorum*], which as Cicero relates, can be more readily felt than expressed.[85] Still, he was clear both that this appearance of virtue was real, that it shines forth in the aspect (*aspectus*) of the act and that the distinction between *honestum* and decorum perceptible in every act can be made theoretically better than it can practically. Nor could the aesthetics of "plasticity" and the category of genius that accompanied it simply be reduced to a metaphysical subjectivism, the voluntarist 'will-to-will'. Indeed, far from being capable of such reduction, the inventive works of genius, as Kant realized, remain always beyond such calculability, the interplay of conscious and unconscious, the subjective—always ventured in the hermeneutic *indeterminacy* of reflective judgment. Whatever else the judgment of taste may be regarding such plasticity (and it is obviously never devoid of institution and tradition) it is not merely a matter of taste, but judgment—and beyond the opposition that divides imitation and lawlessness, the rulelike and the "unruly."

In Cicero's account, it remained already obvious that the idea that the plasticity expressed and exemplified in individuality could never be simply equated with or deductively derived from the universal that it instantiates. The plasticity of virtue relies upon the 'virtue' of expressivity in default of the limits of demonstrable rule and practice. What is virtuous differs by circumstance and becomes apparent in the event, which is always a historical matter and subject to its risks, fate, and destruction. Hegel's idea of a justice that "will be whether or not individuals want it or not" made justice itself then both historicist and symbolical. It is not accidental that Gadamer saw the decline of tradition with the Baroque precisely where Benjamin had focused upon its violence. Hegel nonetheless had sought what even Gadamer would not—to invest the rationality of tradition as the symbolic (and immanent) violence of *Dike* itself. And yet how could the allegorical not but inevitably haunt, challenge, and itself scorn the exuberance of self-sufficiency in which the symbolic had emerged? The allegorical demands instead that the passion of the world not be transformed into comedy—that the venture of the figural could not be transformed into simple epistemic *Darstellung*. 'Reality' could not be grasped through such a *Realizierung* in which speculation and the mimetic impulse might be united in an event of will. What the 'speculative' denoted instead was an event that could no longer be understood through a pure mimetology precisely in the same moment that it could no longer be thought as a "pure malleability or pure plasticity."[86] The (interpretive) rationality that accompanied the aesthetic could not be transformed into such absolutes without transcendental (and speculative) illusion. Neither virtue nor speculation could be so readily reduced or identified, either as 'self' or substance.

It was not accidental that the Schlegels identified the Beautiful, not with the immanence of the symbol, but with the transcendence of allegory—nor that the allegorical still retains its link with the question of tradition. Moreover, it is not accidental that the search for a new mythology that always accompanied the elevation of the symbol's *Darstellung* failed—attesting again as Gadamer saw more to the disintegration (*der Zerfall*) of community than to its mythic future (TM:88). If Romanticism's commitment to imagination doubtless remained insurpassable, it was equally inextricably bound to the tragedies of *Realpolitik* from which it emerged, divided both between the exclusions of the past and its own inner hopes (dividing in turn narratives in its wake between the *Kunstslerroman* and the *Bildungsroman*). As Wilhelm Friederich Schlegel had put it, Romanticism remained inevitably divided in this regard between the treasures of the past and its exclusions, possibility and necessity, the real and the irreal: both "believing in tradition and always straining at new insanities."[87] The problem was always their relation—and the complexity of the justificatory moment that resulted, as Hegel saw. But Hegel's emphasis upon objectification over against individuality in the end only dissolved both the complexity and the ambiguity of *Realpolitik*, in effect reinstating the aesthetic hope for an indisputable immanence in the event of historical realization itself—but paradoxically only by dissolving, as much as had the search for a new mythology, the bonds of community themselves.

Hegel's great-souled individuals, dispersed in the experiment despite Aristotle's admonitions concerning gods and beasts, stand again beyond all community and venture the world-spirit in order to dominate it. While the *Nichomachean Ethics'* treatise on friendship was not itself unequivocal, since Aristotle himself was divided as to whether friendship was a virtue or "like virtue," whether it derived from or sustained virtue, and whether it encompassed the Good or the Good was its *pros hen*, Hegel was not. Hence the paucity of Hegel's account of friendship—which (like the other classical virtues) turns out in his version to be "not so important as was formerly supposed" (PS:52). While Hegel cites Greek proper names as the finest models (Achilles and Patroclus, Orestes and Pylades) their importance has indeed diminished in modernity: the bonds of friendships do not become articulated "in the most varied possible way," but dissolved in the moment in which each "fends for himself."

> In the friendship of adults . . . a man's affairs go their own way independently and can not be carried into effect in that firm community of mutual effort in which one man can not achieve anything without someone else. Men find others and separate themselves from them again; their interests and occuptions drift apart and are united again; friendship, spiritual depth of disposition, principles, and general trends of life remain, but this is not the friendship of youth, in the case of which no one decides anything or sets to work on anything without it immediately becoming the concern of his friend. It is inherent essentially in the principle of our deeper life that, on the whole, every man fends for himself, i.e., is himself competent to take his place in the world. (Aesth:569)

12. Friendship, Self-sufficiency, and Community: Interpretation and the "Many-sidedness" of Character

The question remains then the status of such a friendship, and what to make of its breach, its *Entzweiung*, to speak Hegelian, when the transcendental illusions of such self-sufficiency have been unmasked. It is not accidental in this respect that one of the most significant debates on the status and inter-action of friendship and the political occurred in the wake of Hegel, between Leo Strauss and Alexander Kojève. Nor is it surprising that Kojève would appeal to friendship in the failures of subjective certainty, while Strauss would appeal to natural right: in a sense they divided up between themselves the ruins of Hegel's thought, the ruins of 'subject' and 'substance'.

Indeed the problem in this debate became what to make of self-sufficiency (both moral and epistemic); what, in the end, to make of the rationality of the self once this historicity of the rational has been encountered. Here Strauss's concerns with historicism led him to privilege anew the reflective stronghold of the individual philosopher over against the community, while Kojève, staunchly post-Hegelian in this regard, indeed recalling Hegel's criticism of self-certainty (*Gewissheit*), retained the latter's commitment to recognition and the process of historical verification as the emergence of truth. Strauss, on the other hand, (aptly) continued to see such Hegelian concerns in light of the ancient scepticism attached to the political impact of friendship.

> Friendship as the classics understood it offers no solution to the problem of subjective certainty. Friendship is bound to lead to, or to consist in, the cultivation and perpetuation of common prejudices by a closely knit group of kindred spirits.[88]

The problem however, Kojève claimed, was a modern one of reciprocal recognition and particularly the danger to which the inhabitants of various "gardens"—"academics," "lyceums" and "Republics of Letters"—are exposed from what is called the "cloistered mind": justice will inevitably be a human institution, a function not of the first or second person but of the third.[89] It is true enough that Aristotle (directly, in any case) faced neither the problem of the individual nor consequently the modern problem of *recognition*. It is also true that for him friendship in the end was based upon similarity. But it is true too that he did recognize that what friendship in general adds to love is something like mutual recognition and that the community would require friendship not simply among similars but among persons with major differences: he called it the friendship of the citizen—that is, the friend of the many.[90]

Doubtless it is unclear what Aristotle has thereby bequeathed under the circumstances of this debate. Hobbes in a sense has fully trumped its terms. If Hegel has, as a result, to use Findlay's term, become our Aristotle, debates generated by Strauss and Kojève represent the antinomy in Hegel's Aristotelean inheritance: either, we simply equate Being, Truth, Man, and History, where Being simply is Becoming (or as he sums it up, Being is essentially temporal); or, on the other hand, we appeal to the unproblematized (and ahistorical) premises of a pregiven nature.[91] The problem with the former is that it equates Being with certainty—precisely insofar as it *equates* Being with anything—while the problem with the latter is that in the end it forgets the underdeterminacy which threatens all axiomatic enumerations, especially those of 'nature'. Neither Being nor Becoming are so simply separable, as perhaps Hegel realized. But, it is also true that neither Being nor Truth are so simply adequatable or 'equatable', which Hegel (along with Kojève and Strauss) did not realize in the end. And the ruins which result—which will be haunted by many in Hegel's wake (phenomenologists, critical theorists, poststructuralists et al.)—will not be simply resolved. Being will not be a function of a posit or a certainty, nor will the task of its articulation, its legitimation, its "axiomatization" simply be discardable. As Kojève put it to Strauss in a letter: "If there is something like human nature then you are right about everything. But to deduce from premises is not the same as to prove these premises. And to infer premises from (anyway questionable) consequences is always dangerous."[92] If Strauss and others[93] are right in seeing Kojève's objection to the Hobbes-Machiavelli background to Hegel, it will not be readily overcome: the natural beneficence upon which the ancients relied has "withdrawn," as Hegel knew. Neither the risks nor the necessity of attempting Being's exposition are readily irradicable; they arise respectively from the necessary and sufficient conditions of the rational. Reason requires exposition and Being exceeds our categories, which may always turn out to be not only inadequately but inappropriately applied. Hence arises the necessity of critique—as Kant realized in relation to dialectic in general; but hence also the indispensibility of dialectic in revealing the ultimate nonself-sufficiency of reason.

Such self-sufficiency is again denied to Hegel, and indeed, in the epistemic sense, to Aristotle, who even in the guise of contemplation turns to what Kojève suspects to be a theistic or ontotheological conception of truth. At stake instead, Kojève claimed, is not a question of subjective evidence but a question of dialogue and verification that always falls short of *episteme*.[94] The philosopher, the greal-souled person, far from being an independent mind who should "exclusively give thought to his own recognition of his own worth" always requires friends, not only for the goods of communal life but for the rigors of recognition itself. Here the requisites of reciprocal exchange within the context of practice again intervene on the fallibility of conscience. In mere epistemic 'self sufficiency' and devoid of the rigors of recognition, the philosopher and the tyrant become indistinguishable and the threat of madness becomes an ever-present accomplice.[95] Strauss's own response, on the other hand, was straightforwardly platonist: "But one cannot know that one does not know without knowing what one does not know. . . . It is impossible to think about these problems without being inclined toward a solution, toward one or the other of the very few typical solutions."[96] From this vantage, Kojève inevitably sounded like a relativist and an historicist. And yet Kojève was aware of the extent to which Strauss's epistemic issue had turned Plato into a modern.[97] But both in the end missed the full complexity of the matter—again both with regard to nature and law.

Strauss is doubtless right that for Hobbes "virtue is no longer conceived to be a state but solely an intention."[98] Hence "he no longer believes in the existence of an 'objective' principle according to which man must order his

actions—in the existence of a natural law."[99] Only the remnants of magnanimity and courage in the fear of death overcomes modern suspicion, epistemic and political—an account Strauss argues, that lingers still in the the
master-slave dialectic of Hegel's *Phenomenology*, "prefacing his analysis of
the premodern forms of self-consciousness."[100] The difference of course is
that in Hegel, the struggle to overcome suspicion has become much more
complicated—not simply epistemically and politically but equally morally
(and not least of all by Hegel's complicated retrieval of Aristotle).[101] In the
Phenomenology the "struggle for recognition" *is* a moral one, an historical
event, even if it remains shrouded in the epistemics and the deed (*Tat*) of
self-consciousness.

But to claim of this struggle and the self-identity it yields that it is
irretrievably historical in nature only raises Straussian ire anew. Here it is
not Hobbes but Bacon who becomes Strauss's foil: Bacon's own attention to
"history, poesy, and daily experience" was also undertaken because of a
certain disavowal of objective virtue; instead of seeking the nature of the
good Bacon sought maxims for the creation and protection of virtue in
history.[102] This move, both Bacon and Strauss agree, is Machiavellian—and
Strauss suggests that it shows "the origins of the modern interest in history."
Still, even if Strauss is right about this, the new historicist interest occurs
precisely to venture the possibility of virtue when certainty has become
problematic—not to deny virtue altogether.[103] As thinkers like Lefort and
Pöggler saw better, the dialogue with Machiavelli was not simply a reduction
of either knowledge or the political realm to mere power, but rather a
dialogue concerning a history in which all three had become problematic.
At stake in this dialogue consequently was the interplay (*Wechselspiel*) between history, nature, and power itself, one that neither precluded nor
guaranteed either *politeia* or *arete*, but interrogated the extent of their remainder. Hence again the reciprocal rejoinder in the attention to historicity
itself: to "save" virtue, it engages in a complicated retrieval (and critique)
that became necessary in the default of traditional authorities—that is,
because a certain *detraditionalization* that has already taken place.

If it is true that everything begins in the deed, as Fichte had already put
it—nothing in the requisite sense gets decided there. Instead, 'natural law'
(and virtue) would be not so much expressed or simply created anew—let
alone 'realized'—as *ventured*. The unity of the virtues, like the unity of the
narratives in which each virtue is inscribed and the unity of the self which
articulates and is explicated though them, is always both historical and
always yet to be made, a reciprocal relation between retention and protention. This does not mean that such virtues, even if they remain open to an

inextricable indeterminacy, are simply arbitrary or even conventional, nor, that the "ancient" virtues have no relevance. This is rather the problem that underlies the problem of application and critique, the *techne diacritike,* as Arendt recalled.[104] But we might just as well name it under its modern guise, under the problem that it had become, beginning with Bacon and Hobbes and formulated by Schlegel and Schleiermacher—it is the problem of the art of interpretation. Even if manners are a form of characteristic exposition, as Schlegel claimed, manners are never merely conventional, since, on the one hand, it is the *being* of the self that is 'characterized' and since, on the other hand, as Mead would soon put it, such manners always express "the nature of community"—and implicitly a certain respect for the "generalized other."[105] It is just the indeterminacy in the difference at stake, however, that turns such articulations of character and their practices interpretive—as Hobbes already nascently realized. Hence arises the extension and the complication of the event which underlies their "experiment."[106] Yet as Hegel also saw we would need other resources than the mathematical and other forms of reason than the calculative for its reconciliation. Still he did not realize the extent to which it likewise belied a return to self or overcame the subjective. It is this venture, which Hegel aptly found in Shakespeare, Montaigne, and Boehme, that summons both the resources and the profundity of character, that is, its "plasticity." It is just in this respect that Hegel rightly claimed that it is "the many-sidedness [*Vielseitigkeit*] alone that gives living interest to character" (Aesth:238). Moreover, Gadamer would not be wrong then in claiming that it is precisely this kind of multisidedness, and the "multifariousness (*Vielfachhiet*) of voices" it implies that constitute "the nature of the tradition in which we want to share and have a part" (TM:284).

Strauss was surely right to see that "the quarrel between the ancients and the moderns eventually (and perhaps even from beginning) concerns the status of individuality" (NR:323). However it concerned the status of the singular given the withdrawal (but not the dissolution) of 'substance'. Now perhaps it is clear: both Being and the Good can be articulated "in many ways"; both truth and virtue are in this respect always already plural, i.e., interpretive—and it is precisely as such that their appeals gain warrant. What Hegel realized, which Strauss did not sufficiently, was that epistemological crises that arise in their differences could no longer simply be solved by a return to origins—even if "returning" is not simply to repeat. The origin does not repeat itself. Instead, even in *memoriae,* access to origins would now depend—without being reducible to—a speculative venture, that is, the (interpretive) fecundity of individuality itself. And this venture, divided within the deed (*Tat*), as Schlegel had already nascently seen, is the dividing of character itself—dividing it between the conscious and the unconscious (*Unbewusstsein*), between the known and the unknown, freedom and nature, and dependent upon the figural for its reprise. Hence emerges the rational 'fertility' of classical German thought's turn to the sources of the self, the lingering resources of the inward turn of individuality, the *intus*—precisely its reciprocal rejoinder with a history that had become problematic. But all this complicates Hegel in ways standard rejections too often miss in their simplicity.

What simple rejections of Hegel's historicism miss, again, is Hegel's venture in default of tradition. Granted: the rational cannot be an all-or-nothing matter, nor can tragedy provide—even in the fight to the death—resolution or mediation. In glossing Hegel's venture through the problematic of character, the exposition of individuality, and his experiment regarding the "plasticity" of virtue, however, we can still see the extent to which he remains less the heir of Hobbes and more of Bacon (and Vico). In this light his attempt perhaps is less to control or simply to calculate the actual than to articulate the venture of the possible. The prose of the world (and of the world-historical) is not so much the emptying of transcendence as it is the articulation of another order, an exposition of transcendence 'otherwise'—a transcendence before which Hegel himself, admittedly, often played the role of Oedipus in his attempts to regain a science of the Absolute. But perhaps at long last we can see both the fate and the interpretive grace ventured in Hegel's having "one eye too many," and thereby a path beyond the tragedies of modernism and historicism. The exposition of individuality might then become less a simple struggle undertaken under the fear of death and in default of tradition than the possibility of recognition, a reconciliation ventured in the ruins of friendship in precisely the sense that it lies beyond the modern ruins of both 'subject' and 'substance'.

13. The Care for Self and the Remnant of Decency

The symbolic connections revealed in the concepts of law, nature, virtue, and community in post-Kantian continental thought surely reveal the effects of the fragmentation of tradition. At the same time, they reveal their investment in modern theoretics and the idea of system, and as a result, their own ideological investment.[107] But to end the matter there would be to miss what is most at stake in this reciprocal rejoinder with the past. Beyond the experiments of modernity and the requirements of calculable reason are revealed an experience of individuality and freedom, of a "nature" not simply reducible to mechanics and a reason still capable of relying upon its own lived experience, the resources of imagination, and the reliability and discretion of individual judgment. While this doubtless reflects a modern Romanticism—opposed to the ideology that accompanies the reduction of meaning to rule governed practice, the "view from nowhere"—this experience is equally a refiguration of the ancients. The very idea of decency or the equitable (*epeiekes*) and the decent person in Aristotle still lingers in Kant's concerns in the *Critique of Judgment* and those that it influences: the decent person is precisely the one who is not only capable of 'following a rule' but both knowing when to go further and when to depart from the rule.[108] Both are at stake in interpreting a rule: the art of 'knowing how' to apply, to invent, and to refigure the rule in accord with what is required in the figurative discernment of the particular. The decent person requires both imagination and communication; both indeed are what makes it possible for his or her judgment "to make up for the defects in the written law of a community's written law or code."[109]

But in this regard, as the very notion of the decent person itself exemplifies, and as recent scholarship has underlined, the renewed emphasis on the art of judgment itself provides a certain return to the ancients' idea of philosophy as a way of life. We reencounter this idea in the explication of (individual) form—and even the invention and "characterization" of oneself as the Romantics put it. As Pierre Hadot has insisted and Foucault has reemphasized in his discussion of the care of the self, it is just this ancient emphasis upon the 'practices of the self' that is lost after the ancient world and that must be recovered to sustain the ethical.[110] This claim is surely part of the retrieval of the ancients in Romanticism—and it is even perhaps 'existential'. Kierkegaard, after all, had insisted on nothing else in *Fear and Trembling*.[111] Beyond such existential readings we should insist, however, upon the complexity of the reciprocal rejoinder of the experience at stake, a venture or an attempt (*experiri*) divided between past and future—and ambiguously divided thereby between the ontic and the ontological.[112]

The fragmentation of individuality itself reveals the complications of this effect: divided, to use terms which originate with Goethe, but with steady effect after him, between lived experience (*Erlebnis*) and experience as systematic knowledge (*Erfarhung*).[113] This word '*Erlebnis*' attests to the fragmentation of tradition itself, still divided as Gadamer points out between positivism and pantheism (TM:64). It attests to the legacy of Plotinus in any case, as Hadot would argue. Gadamer himself (like Heidegger before him) claimed that "seen philosophically, the ambiguity we have noted in the concept of *Erlebnis* means that this concept is not wholly exhausted"

(TM:67).[114] Indeed we can trace its recent legacy. Here too we confront that ancient inheritance upon which Hadot and Foucault deliberate. Hadot himself recalls in this regard the Plotinian trope concerning the figural and its admonition that, like the sculptor, one should never stop sculpting oneself until the radiance of virtue shines forth.[115]

In one sense this "vision" is already at work in Aristotle's account of *praxis*. While *techne* results in a product beyond or external to it, *praxis* involves precisely the (qualitative) production of oneself: doing well.[116] And yet in this lies the evidence that the Foucauldian idea of a "techniques of self" and the freedom at stake in it must fail: the self is not reducible to techniques at one's disposal.[117] It is instead 'always already' beyond itself. If the ancients' 'fixed' references to this 'beyond'—i.e. to nature, the *polis*, the *Kosmos*, the Good—now seem problematic, we can still perhaps see the 'transcendence' in the very ambiguity of the 'life' that remains. Or, in any case, this is what Heidegger thought in construing the ambiguity of life through Aristotle's account of Being as what "can be said in many ways" (*pollachōs legomenon*).[118] It is doubtless just this ambiguity that remained at stake in Heidegger's own retrieval of Seneca and Augustine: Heidegger explicitly refigures the ambiguity in the concept of life through the figure of 'care'—resulting in an individuality neither arbitrarily or totally at its own disposal nor simply 'ordered' passively from without, but instead exists as the task that now opens in the question of the self. The problem was how to evaluate the remnants of such 'transcendence' within the 'leveling' of modernity.

What is equally clear, however, is that such differentiated individuality could be equated neither with the mystic ineffable nor could its inventions be reduced to the solipsistic. The (modern) problem of legitimation had both incited the problem of the self anew and accompanied its own theoretical refigurations—as the sculptured figures of "plasticity" and the "speculative" themselves attest in the exploration of the possible. Moreover, the question of legitimation was present even in the most extreme attempts to distinguish the experience of individuality from the question of certainty. Even Kierkegaard's account of the "justified hiddenness" or a "new interiority" in *Fear and Trembling* still attested both to the question of legitimacy and the problem of the 'poetic plasticity' of individuality.[119] But what is attested to again, beyond Romantic individuality, is not simply the distinction among law, virtue, and community, but their problematic and interpretive venture—one doubtless united in the remnant of 'care' itself.

Strauss at one point claimed that "recognition of the other must remain subordinate to recognition of the truth."[120] There are those who would invert this thesis, and would claim that the requisites of recognition itself force the abandonment of (our) truth for the sake of a good that lies "beyond" it—the ethical. But both these exclusive theses assiduously deny the complicated relations of meaning in which the Truth and the Good would now emerge, relations that are particularly problematic in the detraditionalization out of which modernity emerges. In the ruins of tradition, paradoxically, the love of truth itself could no more be separated from the care for the Other than it could from the care for self. Indeed the divided inheritance of the modern self lies perhaps precisely in this 'dia-logue' of care itself—and equally perhaps, only in such differentiations, which are the remainder of tradition.

NOTES

Introduction

1. Martin Heidegger, *History of the Concept of Time*, trans. Theodore Kisiel (Bloomington: Indiana University Press, 1985), p. 138.

2. Friedrich Nietzsche, *The Gay Science*, trans. Walter Kaufman (New York: Vintage Books, 1974), para. 289.

3. For a discussion of the second beginning and its "other history" see the analysis of Michel Haar, "'Achèvement de la métaphysique' et 'nouveau commencement'," *La fracture de l'Histoire* (Grenoble: Jérome Millon, 1994), chap. 11.

4. See Michel Foucault, *The Order of Things*, trans. A. Sheridan (New York: Random House, 1970), chap. 2, "The Prose of the World." This chapter, as will become evident, provides Foucault's analysis of the archive from which the 'circular' epistemologies of modern 'hermeneutics' emerge.

5. An important analysis of Boethius's role in the emergence of the 'modern' philosophy of history and indeed the emergence of the republican tradition itself is provided in J. G. A. Pocock, *The Machiavellian Moment* (Princeton: Princeton University Press, 1975), chap. 2. Similar affirmations can be found in a wide variety of contemporary scholarship, including Claude Lefort's important analysis of Machiavelli with respect to those close to Heidegger or that of Seyla Benhabib regarding the Frankfurt School. See the latter's "Autonomy, Modernity, and Community" in *Cultural-Political Interventions in the Unfinished Project of Enlightenment*, ed. A. Honneth, T. McCarthy, C. Offe, and A. Wellmer (Cambridge: MIT Press, 1992). Also see Claude Lefort, *Le travail de l'oeuvre Machiavel* (Paris: Gallimard, 1972).

6. See Hannah Arendt, *On Revolution* (New York: Penguin, 1987), pp. 42–43.

7. Jürgen Habermas, *Justification and Application: Remarks on Discourse Ethics*, trans. Ciaran P. Cronin (Cambridge: MIT Press, 1993), p. 119.

8. See Kant (A835/B863).

9. (NR:86). Compare Luc Ferry's attempt to argue against both Strauss (and Heidegger) on behalf of the republican idea, thus avoiding a return to the ancients in *Rights — The New Quarrel between the Ancients and the Moderns*, trans. Franklin Philip (Chicago: University of Chicago Press, 1990), part 1.

10. Francis Bacon, *Novum Organum*, book I, section XXVI, *The Works of Francis Bacon*, vol. 8, ed. James Spedding, Robert Ellis, and Douglas Heath (Cambridge: Cambridge University Press, 1863).

11. Bacon, "Of the Advancement of Learning," *The Works of Sir Francis Bacon*, vol. III, book II, p. 435.

12. See Leo Strauss, *The Political Philosophy of Hobbes*, trans. Elsa M. Sinclair (Chicago: University of Chicago Press, 1952), pp. 92–93.

13. See Francis Bacon, "Of the Advancement of Learning," *The Works of Francis Bacon*, vol. VII, p. 439, 433. Bacon's elevation of application thus contains

in embryo the Kantian problem of judgment—or the problem of appropriation that developed in his "Romantic" followers, Novalis and Schlegel. While neither of the latter saw this connection, Coleridge perhaps did. See, for example, Elizabeth Sewell, "Bacon, Vico, Coleridge, and the Poetic Method" in *Giambattista Vico: An International Symposium,* ed. Giorgio Tagliacozzo and Hayden White (Baltimore: Johns Hopkins University Press, 1969). Finally, while again both Novalis and Schlegel would downplay the connection between issues of application and issues of legitimation Hegel doubtless did not, as will become evident.

14. Francis Bacon, "Novum Organum," *The Works of Francis Bacon,* vol. VIII, book I, section XIX–XXI. Compare in this regard Gadamer's account (TM:23, 348).

15. Michel de Montaigne, "Of Experience" in *The Complete Works of Montaigne,* trans. Donald M. Frame (Stanford: Stanford University Press, 1965), p. 816.

16. Claude Lefort, "The Question of Democracy" in *Democracy and Political Theory,* trans. David Macey (Minneapolis: University of Minnesota Press, 1988), p. 10. Montaigne already recognized such a 'reinterpretation' with respect to the essay on experience: "Our opinions are grafted upon one another. The first serves as a stock for the second, the second for the third." Likewise (as with Hobbes) it is experience itself which breaks out of the circle: "It is more of a job to interpret the interpretations than to interpret the things" (*Of Experience,* p. 818).

17. Aristotle, *Politics,* 1281a.

18. Friederich Schlegel, "Critical Fragments" (§83) in *Philosophical Fragments,* trans. Peter Firchow (Minneapolis: University of Minnesota Press, 1991), p. 10.

19. *The English Works of Thomas Hobbes,* vol. IV, ed. Sir William Molesworth (London: John Bohm, 1840), p. 49.

20. See George Herbert Mead, *Mind, Self and Society,* ed. Charles Morris (Chicago: University of Chicago Press, 1934), pp. 260ff. For a discussion of the impact of surrealism in these matters, see for example Sartre's discussion in *What Is Literature?,* trans. Bernard Frechtman (Gloucester, MA: Peter Smith, 1979). The complications that attend Sartre's relation to surrealism remain still largely unexplored. While Sartre himself viewed the surrealists' *merveilleux* as a revival of the *epoché* of Carneades and Philo, he criticized surrealism for its abstract nihiliation "on the ruins of subjectivity"—one that remained ideal, i.e., irreal, totalized, and thus confusing means and ends. Nonetheless Sartre's proximity to all this still lingers: epistemically in the privilege he accords *l'imaginaire,* ethically in the importance of *générosité,* ontologically in the emphasis on the prose and the freedom of the everyday—a topic to which we shall return. Notwithstanding this critique of surrealism Sartre in fact admitted, "I recognize in no uncertain terms that surrealism is the only poetic movement of the first half of the twentieth century." See *What Is Literature?* pp. 172–73; 190–91.

21. Aristotle, *Nichomachean Ethics,* 1159b.

22. See Jean-Paul Sartre, *Being and Nothingness*, trans. Hazel Barnes (New York: Washington Square Press, 1966), pp. 479–80.

23. Emmanuel Levinas, *Totality and Infinity*, trans. Alphonso Lingis (Pittsburgh: Duquesne University Press, 1969), p. 21.

24. Leo Strauss, *Studies in Platonic Political Philosophy*, ed. Thomas L. Pangle (Chicago: University of Chicago Press, 1983), p. 210.

25. Montesquieu, *Spirit of the Laws*, vol. XI, §4 in *Selected Political Writings*, ed. Melvin Richter (Indianapolis: Hackett, 1990), p. 181.

26. Max Scheler, *Ressentiment*, ed. Lewis A. Coser, trans. William W. Holdheim (New York: The Free Press, 1961), p. 166.

27. Jean-Paul Sartre, *Saint Genet*, trans. Bernard Frechtman (New York: Pantheon, 1963), pp. 24–25.

28. Herman Weyl, *Philosophy of Mathematics and Natural Science*, trans. Olaf Helmer (Princeton: Princeton University Press, 1949), p. 112.

29. Martin Heidegger, "The Anaximander Fragment," in *Early Greek Thinking*, trans. David F. Krell and F. Capuzzi (San Francisco: Harper & Row, 1984), p. 26. It is worth recalling that it was Hannah Arendt who perhaps first saw this work, following Heidegger's own failure of will in the 1930s to outline another ontological speculation on the possibility of the justice and the political. See Hannah Arendt, *The Life of the Mind/Willing* (New York: Harcourt Brace Jovanovich, 1978), pp. 188–89.

30. Maurice Merleau-Ponty, "A Note on Machiavelli," *Signs*, trans. Richard McCleary (Evanston: Northwestern University Press, 1964).

31. Boethius, *Consolation of Philosophy*, trans. V. E. Watts (Harmondsworth: Penguin, 1969), chap. IV, §VII, p. 144.

32. It does so, however, standing on Hobbes's abyss, while denying the apparent antinomies (and decisionism) of Strauss's formulations: because "men can know what is good" they had to choose "between natural right and the uninhibited cultivation of individuality" (NR:5).

33. Martin Heidegger, *Nietzsche*, vol. II, trans. David Farrell Krell (San Francisco: Harper & Row, 1984), p. 28.

34. See Maurice Merleau-Ponty, *The Prose of the World*, trans. John O'Neill (Evanston: Northwestern University Press, 1973), pp. 112–13. As will become evident, it is not accidental that Merleau-Ponty's admonition concerning the frailty of the evidence of the phenomenological would occur in a defense of the 'prose' of the everyday and democratic politics.

35. See Martin Heidegger, *Nietzsche*, vol. I, trans. David Farrell Krell (San Francisco: Harper & Row, 1979), p. 143.

36. Ibid., pp. 146–47.

37. Ibid., p. 144.

38. Carnap, who had attended Husserl's lectures in Freiburg, continually made reference to Husserl's work—not only (frequently) in the early *Logical Structure of the World*, but also as late as 1947 he was invoking Husserl's

Wesensschau in regard to solutions for problems concerning the foundations of logic in correspondence with Quine. See Rudolf Carnap, *The Logical Structure of the World and Pseudoproblems in Philosophy,* trans. Rolf A. George (Chicago: University of Chicago Press, 1969) and letter to Quine, April 13, 1947 in *Dear Carnap/Dear Van* (Berkeley and Los Angeles: University of California Press, 1990), pp. 405–406. The latter is again further evidence of what recent histories have referred to as the central European origins of analytic philosophy.

39. The impact of Heidegger's thought upon Husserl thus is fully evident. All these terms are operative in Husserl's 1931 manuscript C 17, 9 *Beilage* III.

40. Heidegger, *Nietzsche,* vol. I, p. 130.

41. A particularly pointed example of such failures, as David Krell points out, occurs in the *Nietzsche* lectures, regarding the July 1940 British attack on the French fleet at Qran. See Heidegger, *Nietzsche,* vol. VI, trans. Frank Capuzzi (San Francisco: Harper & Row, 1982), pp. 144–45.

42. Jacques Derrida, "Force of Law: The Mystical Foundation of Authority," trans. Mary Quaintance, *Cordozo Law Review* 11, nos. 5–6 (1990): p. 971.

43. Ibid.

44. Ibid.

45. See Aristotle, *Politics,* 1308b.

46. Hence emerges Derrida's infamous 'notion' of *différance:* a 'concept' reducible neither simply to an internal nor external difference, neither qualitative nor quantitative, intensional nor extensional. Still the logic of such a difference neither precludes the universal nor hands the rational over to the ineffable, as is evident from the account of justice itself: "justice always addresses itself to singularity, to the singularity of the other, despite or even because it pretends to be universality." See Derrida, "Force of Law," p. 955.

47. See Jacob Klein, *Greek Mathematical Thought and the Origin of Algebra,* trans. Eva Braun (New York: Dover Publications, 1968). Klein's analysis obviously remains close to Heidegger at this point concerning the effects of the *renovatio* that incited theoretical modernity (p. 153).

48. See ibid; chap. 11.

49. Nietzsche, *The Gay Science,* trans. Walter Kaufmann (New York: Random House, 1974), para. 373.

50. Martin Heidegger, *The Metaphysical Foundations of Logic,* trans. Michael Heim (Bloomington: Indiana University Press, 1984), p. 184.

51. See for example the following text from the Nietzsche lectures, testifying both to Heidegger's proximity to and distance from Nietzsche in precisely the moment that it undertakes a (historical and hermeneutic) "reciprocal rejoinder" with premodern accounts of Being's *transcendens:*

> The essence in which the many dovetail must be one and the same thing for them. But from that it by no means follows that the essence itself cannot be changeable. For, supposing that the essence of truth did change, that which changes could always still be a 'one' which holds for 'many', the transformation

not disturbing that relationship. But what is preserved in the metamorphosis is what is unchangeable in the essence, which essentially unfolds in its very transformation. The essentiality of essence, its inexhaustibility, is thereby affirmed, and also its genuine selfhood and selfsameness.

See *Nietzsche*, vol. I, pp. 147–48. This account of the legacy of analogy surely spurs Heidegger on from the outset. It is surely the 'equivalent' both to his critique of the metaphysics of 'logistic' and the epigram for the *Scotusbuch's* conclusion taken from Novalis:

"We seek for the unconditional and everywhere meet the conditional."

It is not at all accidental in this regard that Heidegger preserves the young Romantics and the art of 1800 from Nietzsche's critique of Romanticism (p. 132). Indeed Heidegger's 1929–30 lecture course on *The Fundamental Concepts of Metaphysics* still takes its "lead" from Novalis. See *The Fundamental Concepts of Metaphysics,* trans. William McNeill and Nicholas Walker (Bloomington: Indiana University Press, 1995), §2.

52. Aristotle, *Nicomachean Ethics,* 1143a.

53. Jacques Derrida, "Afterword: Toward An Ethics of Discussion," *Limited INC,* trans. Samuel Weber (Evanston: Northwestern University Press, 1998), p. 149.

54. Emmanuel Levinas, *Totality and Infinity,* trans. Alphonso Lingis (Pittsburgh: Duquesne University Press, 1969), p. 246.

55. Doubtless, to use Manfred Frank's term, such an account would refigure an event and a tradition distinguishing the individual from a subsumptive *individuum* that remains "heretical" with respect to all these philosophemes (and yet not simply detached from them), both in accounting for the belonging-together, the community of such singularity—and its rationality. See Manfred Frank, *What is Neostructuralism?* trans. Sabine Wilke and Richard Gray (Minneapolis: University of Minnesota Press, 1989), pp. 362–63.

56. Emmanuel Levinas, *Totality and Infinity,* p. 80.

57. See Umberto Eco, "Ür-facism," *The New York Review of Books* LXII, No. 11 (June 22, 1995): pp. 12–15.

58. Søren Kierkegaard, *The Concept of Irony,* trans. Lee M. Capel (Bloomington: Indiana University Press, 1971), pp. 272–73. See Theophrastus, *Characters,* chap. 1. We shall return to the problem of characterization in a later analysis.

59. Friederich Schlegel, "On Incomprehensibility," in *German Aesthetic and Literary Criticism,* ed. Kathleen M. Wheeler (Cambridge: Cambridge University Press, 1984), p. 36.

60. See Kierkegaard, *The Concept of Irony,* p. 313. To claim that irony need not require the resolution of religion surely does not entail that it precludes the religious, of course, though it may well entail that no religious claim will be simply free from 'irony' thus understood, i.e., as interpretation. As will become evident, this too is an effect of Kant's categorical imperative.

61. This is, I take it, an effect of Heidegger's account of the hermeneutic circle (BT:194).

62. Here I refer to the distinction between politics and the political in the work of Claude Lefort, one which surely bears the trace not only of Heidegger's 'concept' of the ontological difference, but before him the play of irony itself. See Claude Lefort, "The Question of Democracy" in *Democracy and Political Theory* (Minneapolis: University of Minnesota Press, 1988):

> The political is thus revealed, not in what we call political activity, but in the double movement whereby the mode of institution of society appears and is obscured. It appears in the sense that the process whereby society is ordered and unified across its division becomes visible. . . . This observation is in itself an invitation to return to the question that once inspired political philosophy: what is the nature of the difference between forms of society? Interpreting the political means breaking with the viewpoint of political science, because political science emerges from the suppression of this question. (11)

63. Hence as Benjamin knew too, even the German *Trauerspiel* that so fascinated him always lives from its own (rational) limit—that even "the dizziness of its own bottomless depths" would be unavoidable "were it not that, even in its most extreme of them, it had so to turn about that all its darkness, vainglory, and godlessness seems to be nothing but self-delusion" (Trau:232). From the outset the allegorical was a venture on behalf of the enigmatic that had turned away from such finality. Such "internal limitations of allegorism" surely, however—no more than those of formalism—condemn it to self-contradiction, but rather specify the conditions of rationality. Moreover, as will become evident, the internal limitations of allegoricism and formalism will not in the end simply be disconnected. It is not accidental that the protocols of both Benjamin and Heidegger interface here from the outset: their difference doubtless *inter alia* involves a difference regarding the fragmented remainders of the figures of allegory and the *pros hen* of analogy themselves. Both interface likewise in articulating this loss of immanence through the figure of primordial guilt. But it is important to recall, unlike many "lapsed" idealists, that primordial guilt must be distinguished both from epistemic fallibility and the view that all persons are "equally" guilty. The latter, as Arendt realized in criticizing Heidegger, is tantamount to "proclaiming universal innocence." See Arendt, *The Life of the Mind*, p. 184.

1. Traditionis Traditio

1. I borrow my title here, if not the project itself, from Gérard Granel. See his *Traditionis Traditio* (Paris: Gallimard, 1972).

2. In effect this paradox arises within a conflict concerning the concept of the transcendental itself as it passes from the ancients (where the transcenden-

tals, Good, unity, truth, and Being all remained harmoniously—and analogically and thus, equivocally in unity) to an account, in accord with the requisites of modern certainty (epistemic and logical) that restricted the transcendental to "the origin, the scope, and the objective validity of such knowledge" (A57/B81). Hence arises the inevitable diminution in the role of transcendent 'knowledge' itself, where it became restricted to the logical realm of the 'indemonstrable' and the epistemic realm of the 'inadequate'. It is just this constellation that prepares the elevation of epistemology (and the philosophy of science) to first philosophy and the substitution of analysis for ontology, again in accord with the *ars analytica*.

3. In fact Gadamer had received the problem from Heidegger and had encountered it in the celebrated Aristotle lectures of 1922, "Phenomenological Interpretations with Respect to Aristotle": "The confusing ambiguity of the word 'life' and of its application must not become grounds for simply getting rid of the word." See Martin Heidegger, "Phenomenological Interpretations with Respect to Aristotle: Indication of the Hermeneutical Situation," trans. Michael Baur, *Man and World*, vol. 25, 1992, p. 361. See Gadamer's account in *Philosophical Apprenticeships,* trans. Robert Sullivan (Cambridge: MIT Press, 1985), pp. 46-47. Both however explicitly related the concept—and in particular, grappling with the complexities of intentionality and *transcendens*—to a certain 'annexing' of more classical issues in ontology and philosophy of mind. The explication of ambiguity that accompanies the application of this concept is an explication in this regard of the remnants of the ancients (and in this case Aristotle) within theoretical modernity; the ambiguity itself attesting to the continuing effect (discontinuity and 'detraditionalization') of the *querelle des anciens et de modernes*.

4. The concept of tradition is in this regard no more anomalous than that of the 'concept' of analogy with which it is intertwined—as classical discussions of the 'analogous' character of analogy itself demonstrated. Both venture the economics of unity and diversity, identity and difference, and a *pros hen* that always stands midway between equivocity and univocity.

My own treatment here depends not only on such classical resources but on more recent discussions of interpretation, analogy, and tradition that further truncate the paradoxes of its logic. These occur basically in the wake of Kantian (and Nietzschean) criticism of reflective and regulative (teleological) principles in recent continental philosophy, further problematizing the unicity of its *pros hen*—evident for example in the works of Heidegger, Gadamer, Sartre, Derrida, and Foucault. Kant had seen that, notwithstanding the fact that all our knowledge may be dependent upon receptivity, by means of productive imagination we "restructure experience; and though in doing so we continue to follow analogical laws, yet we also follow principles which reside higher up, namely in reason"—a fact which makes transcendental constitution both analogical (and rational) through and through. See Immanuel Kant, *Critique of Judgment,* trans. Werner S. Pluhar (Indianapolis: Hackett, 1987), para. 49. Still he recognized also that all such analogy remains indemonstrable, and ultimately regulative in import—its claims always dialectical and potentially illusory. Or as Heidegger would put it after his discussion of Aristotle, analogy will not be reducible to a system. For further discussion see my *Extensions: Essays on Interpretation, Rationality, and the Closure of Modernism* (Albany: SUNY Press, 1992). A similar discussion can be found in Courtine's discussion of the after-effect of ontology in the modern age. See Jean-François Courtine, *Suarez et le système de la métaphysique* (Paris: P. U. F., 1990), part 4. For a discussion of the nineteenth-century tendency to such inventions see *The Invention of Tradition*, ed. Eric Hobsbawm and Terrence Ranger (Cambridge: Cambridge University Press, 1983). When later Heidegger describes the hermeneutics of *Being and Time* as the "attempt first of all to define the nature of interpretation on hermeneutic grounds" he remains equally on traditional grounds. See *On the Way to Langauge*, trans. Peter D. Hertz (San Francisco: Harper & Row, 1971), p. 11.

5. See Martin Heidegger, *History of the Concept of Time*, trans. Theodore Kisiel (Bloomington: Indiana University Press, 1985), p. 13.

6. See F. H. Bradley, "The Presuppositions of Critical History" (1874), *Critical Essays*, vol. I (Westport, CT: Greenwood, 1970), Collingwood, *The Idea of History* (Oxford: Oxford University Press, 1946), p. 135. The former, as Mink realized, is a too often neglected piece that marks the first significant attempt at the critical interpretation of history in English and marks in this respect "a monadnock in the landscape of British intellectual history." See Louis O. Mink, *Mind, History, and Dialectic* (Bloomington: Indiana University Press, 1969), p. 266. Gadamer's account in *Truth and Method* of the logic of question and answer at stake in hermeneutics attests openly to its connection with this idealist legacy, one which he likewise finds in Croce ("who influenced Collingwood"). See TM:370.

7. See Martin Heidegger, "My Way to Phenomenology" in *On Time and Being*, trans. Joan Stambaugh (New York: Harper & Row, 1972), pp. 74ff.

8. See Martin Heidegger, *The History of the Concept of Time*, p. 19.

9. Further discussion of Foucault's complicated relation to hermeneutics will emerge in the second volume of this work.

10. See Aristotle, *Metaphysics*, 980bff; *Physics*, 221a.

11. *The Invention of Tradition*; also see Stephen Toulmin and Jane Goodfield, *The Discovery of Time* (Chicago: The University of Chicago Press, 1965).

12. Walter Benjamin, *Reflections: Essays, Aphorisms, Autobiographical Writings*, trans. E. Jephcott (New York: Harcourt Brace Jovanovich), p. 334.

13. Friedrich Nietzsche, *On the Genealogy of Morals*, trans. Walter Kaufman, R. J. Hollingdale (New York: Random House, 1967), p. 109.

14. Friedrich Nietzsche, *On the Advantage and Disadvantage of History for Life*, trans. Peter Preuss (Indianapolis: Hackett Publishing, 1980), p. 60.

15. Martin Heidegger, "The Concept of Time in the Science of History,"

trans. Harry Taylor and Hans W. Uffelmann, *Journal of the British Society for Phenomenology,* January 1978–79, p. 10.

16. Schelling's account of the tautegorical status of myth can be found in the *Philosophie der Mythologie,* where interestingly it is footnoted to Coleridge who in turn had been greatly influenced by the former's *Naturphilosophie.* For further discussion of the 'symbolic' character of the tautegorical in Schelling, see Marc Richir, "Qu'est-ce qu'un dieu? Mythologie et question de la pensée," preface to F. W. Schelling, *Philosophie de la mythologie,* trans. Alain Pernet (Grenoble: Editions Jerome Millon, 1994).

17. See Bertrand Russell, *Critical Exposition of the Philosophy of Leibniz* (London: Allen & Unwin, 1937). Ludwig Wittgenstein, *Tractatus Logico-Philosophicus* (London: Routlege & Kegan Paul, 1960). Given this underdeterminacy, it is little wonder that Russell's Leibniz book ends itself in the elevation of practical reason—every bit as much as would Wittgenstein's *Tractatus.*

18. For further discussion of the judgments of predication and relations, and the status of internal and external relation, specifically as they impact issues of interpretation and significance, see the discussion of Husserl and Russell in Jules Vuillemin, *Leçons sur la première philosophie de Russell* (Paris: Armand Colin, 1968), pp. 61ff.

19. T. S. Eliot, *Knowledge and Experience in the Philosophy of F. H. Bradley* (London: Faber and Faber, 1964), p. 141.

20. Ibid., p. 165.

21. Recent attempts to reduce Eliot to a precursor of pragmatism in this regard miss the complexity of the analogies that underwrite the logic of interpretation. See for example the otherwise excellent study of Richard Schusterman, *T. S. Eliot and the Philosophy of Criticism* (New York: Columbia University Press, 1988), chap. 8. Although Schusterman rightly relates Eliot's work to the influence of Russell and compares its account of interpretation and the mutations of objectivity to Gadamer, insofar as he does so against Bradley's idealism and by accommodating both to recent pragmatism, he equally misses the complexity of both and the complications that attend the logic of analogy upon which they depend—missing, as do many similar readings, the specificity of the *Seinsfrage.* What is true, however, is that recent emphasis upon Eliot's relation to Russell is symptomatic with respect not only to twentieth-century aestheticism, but equally the origins of "analytic" philosophy and the complex (Hegelian) archive from which they emerge.

22. T. S. Eliot, "Tradition and Individual Talent," in *The Sacred Wood* (London: Methuen & Co., 1960), pp. 47; 50.

23. J. N. Findlay, *Meinong's Theory of Objects and Values* (Oxford: Oxford University Press, 1963, p. xiii). Compare Eliot's discussion of Russell and Meinong in chapter iv of *Knowledge and Experience.* It is significant to note that as late as 1927 ("Shakespeare and the Stoicism of Seneca") Eliot continued to invoke both Meinong and Husserl and phenomenology as the theoretical

backdrop to his poetics. See his *Selected Essays 1917-1932* (London: Faber and Faber, 1932), p. 138. Later we will be forced to confront more broadly the reception of Stoicism in twentieth-century thought. Heidegger, for example, cites Seneca as a precursor to (and in confirmation of) his own hermeneutics of care. See *Being and Time*, p. 243.

24. Eliot, *Knowledge and Experience*, p. 99.

25. See Edmund Husserl, *The Phenomenology of Internal Time-Consciousness*, trans. James S. Churchill (Bloomington: Indiana University Press, 1964), §13. As Paul Ricoeur had noticed in his famous commentaries of the early fifties, the structure of internal time consciousness is analogical in character. What he did not (explicitly) realize until more recently is that its analogical structure is aporetic, the invocation of a *pros hen* whose unity (and unification) remained always 'regulated', deferred, and underdetermined. As Ricoeur realized, "recourse to analogy creates as many problem as it solves." Hence he came to juxtapose it with Kant's account in the transcendental analogies—one that acknowledges the problem of the noumenon (or the problem of ontological difference). See Paul Ricoeur, *Husserl: An Analysis of his Phenomenology*, trans. Edward G. Ballard and Lester Embree (Evanston: Northwestern University Press, 1967), p. 126; and *Time and Narrative*, vol. 3, trans. Kathleen Blamey and David Pellauer (Chicago: University of Chicago Press, 1988), section 1.

26. See Josiah Royce, "Recent Logical Inquiries and their Psychological Bearings" in *The Basic Writings of Josiah Royce*, vol. 2, ed. John J. McDermott (Chicago: University of Chicago Press, 1969), p. 661.

27. See Gilbert Ryle, Review of Martin Heidegger's *Being and Time*, in *Heidegger and Modern Philosophy*, ed. Michael Murray (New Haven: Yale University Press, 1978). A discussion of the sceptical reception of the Göttingen circle to Husserl's increasing turn to transcendental idealism (under the influence of neo-Kantianism and Natorp in particular) occurs in Herbert Spiegelberg's *The Phenomenological Movement* (The Hague: Martinus Nijhoff, 1984), p. 168.

28. Edmund Husserl, *Ideas Pertaining to a Pure Phenomenology and to a Phenomenological Philosophy* [1913], trans. F. Kersten (The Hague, Martinus Nijhoff, 1982), §23.

29. See Edmund Husserl, *Logical Investigations*, vol. 2 [1902], trans. J. N. Findlay (London: Routledge & Kegan Paul, 1970), Sixth Investigation, §20. On the importance of this text for Heidegger's *Being and Time*, see the commentary of Jacques Taminiaux, "Heidegger and Husserl's Logical Investigations: In Remembrance of Heidegger's Last Seminar (Zähringen, 1973)" in *Dialectic and Difference*, trans. James Decker and Robert Crease (Atlantic Highlands, N.J.: Humanities Press, 1985), pp. 91–114. Moreover, in this regard, as will become evident, in exposing the functionalism and *Seinsvergessenheit* of instrumental rationality (and in the 'fall' of *Zweideutigkeit* itself, a leveling of the positive reliability of the ancients' account of Being's plurality), the analysis of *Das Man* would betray the legacy that Hobbes had first codified theoretically. Also see

in this regard Taminiaux's "The Hobbesian Legacy," *Philosophy and Social Criticism* 13 (Fall 1987): pp. 1–15.

30. Maurice Merleau-Ponty, *The Visible and the Invisible*, trans. Alphonso Lingis (Evanston: Northwestern University Press, 1968), p. 40.

31. Jacques Derrida, "Plato's Pharmacy" in *Dissemination*, trans. Barbara Johnson (Chicago: University of Chicago Press, 1981), pp. 74–75.

32. Ibid., p. 109.

33. Eliot, "Tradition and Individual Talent," p. 49.

34. See T. S. Eliot, "Leibniz' Monads and Bradley's Finite Centres" [1916], reprinted in *Knowledge and Experience*, pp. 204, 207. The importance of Leibniz's monadology for both Husserl and Heidegger should be similarly kept in mind on this issue.

35. Herder's account of tradition emerges in his *Outline of a Philosophy of the History of Mankind* [1784], trans. T. Churchill (New York: Bergman, 1800), a work that Kant reviews. Both will be further analyzed in the discussion of Kant that follows.

36. *History and Truth*, introduction to "Savonarola" cited in Piers Gray, *T. S. Eliot's Intellectual and Poetic Development*, 1909–1922 (Sussex: Harvester Press, 1982), p. 96.

37. Josiah Royce, *The Problem of Christianity* [1918] (Chicago: University of Chicago Press, 1968), pp. 291–95.

38. Ibid., p. 336. The Pauline background of Heidegger's account of interpretation and time, dating from lectures in the early 1920s, should not be forgotten.

39. See Richard Wollheim, "Eliot and F. H. Bradley: an Account" in *Eliot in Perspective*, ed. Graham Martin (New York: Humanities Press, 1970), p. 171.

40. See G. E. Moore, "The Refutation of Idealism," *Mind* XII (1903). On Brentano's criticism of Husserl see *The True and the Evident*, ed. Oskar Kraus, trans. Roderick M. Chisolm, Ilse Politzer, and Kurt R. Fischer (New York: Humanities Press, 1930). For Ingarden's views, see "Bermerkungen zum Problem Idealismus-Realismus," *Festschrift, Edmund Husserl zum Geburtstag gewidmet. . . . Jahrbuch für Philosophie und phänomenologische Forschung, Supplement* (Halle: Niemeyer, 1929). Compare Heidegger, BT:246ff.

41. Eliot's own conservative options were recognized by him to be "regional" from the outset. See T. S. Eliot, *Notes Towards the Definition of Culture* (New York: Harcourt, Brace and Company, 1949), chapters 3 and 4.

42. At one point, Heidegger described the "Carnap-Heidegger" contrast as the "most extreme counter-positions" in contemporary thought. See "The Theological Discussion of the 'Problem of a Non-Objectifying Thinking and Speaking in Today's Theology'—Some Pointers to Its Major Aspects," in *The Piety of Thinking*, trans. James G. Hart and John C. Maraldo (Bloomington: Indiana University Press, 1976), p. 24.

43. See Heidegger's own attempt to provide an analysis of just such an

account of the meaning that "the word 'humanism' has as such" and, correspondingly, his attempt to "redefine" this word in "Letter on Humanism"
(LH:224).

44. See T. S. Eliot, *After Strange Gods: A Primer of Modern Heresy* (London:
Faber and Faber, 1934), p. 24. On the concept of 'traditionalism' in contrast
with the logic of tradition, cf. Edward Shils, *Tradition* (Chicago: University of
Chicago Press, 1981), p. 19. Finally compare Gadamer's similar remarks on
'traditionalism', denying the conception of tradition-in-itself (TM:281).

45. Ludwig Wittgenstein, *On Certainty*, trans. G. E. M. Anscombe and G. A.
von Wright (New York: Harper & Row, 1972), §564.

46. To insist that interpretation is unavoidable is obviously *not* to deny the
possibility of analysis so much as it is to insist upon its limits. It is to insist
that analysis will not simply be a logical matter. Nor is this simply to deny
determination—or the various forms of realism that have accompanied analysis.
Rather it is to insist that the problem of the relevance (and the genealogy) of
such issues accompanying underdeterminacy is inescapable.

47. Emmanuel Levinas, *Otherwise than Being or Beyond Essence*, trans. Alphonso Lingis (The Hague: Martinus Nijhoff, 1981), p. 42.

48. Emmanuel Levinas, *Totality and Infinity*, trans. Alphonso Lingis (Pittsburgh: Duquesne University Press, 1969), p. 80.

49. Ibid., p. 46.

50. Hans Blumenberg, *Work on Myth*, trans. Robert Wallace (Cambridge:
MIT Press, 1985), p. 163.

51. Ludwig Wittgenstein, *Philosophical Investigations,* trans. G. E. Anscombe
(New York: Macmillan Company, 1953), §198; 201.

52. It will be objected that this gloss of interpretation as 'active' overly
restricts Heidegger's account, and especially restricts it to *Being and Time*. This
is doubtless true. It is equally true, however, that the later Heidegger's deepening
of this account depends on the rational and evidential opening that *Being and
Time* institutes, precisely in the interplay of *Interpretation* and *Auslegung*.

53. See, for example, Richard Rorty, "Overcoming the Tradition: Heidegger
and Dewey" in *Consequences of Pragmatism* (Minneapolis: University of Minnesota Press, 1982).

54. Royce, *The Problem of Christianity*, p. 337.

55. Wittgenstein, *Tractatus Logico-Philosophicus* (London: Routledge, 1960),
6. 4ff.

56. Ludwig Wittgenstein, *Zettel*, trans. A. E. M. Anscombe (Berkeley and
Los Angeles: University of California Press, 1970), para. 326.

57. Wilhelm von Humboldt, *Linguistic Variability and Intellectual Development*, trans. George C. Buck and Frithjof A. Raven (Coral Gables: University of
Miami Press, 1971), pp. 127-28. The importance of von Humboldt for the
tradition of hermeneutics has been stressed since Hans Lipp's 1938 *Untersu-
chungen zu einer Hermeneutischen Logik* (Frankfurt am Main: Klostermann,

1959). Recent research has renewed this task. See for example, Jean Quillien, "Pour une autre scansion de l'histoire de l'herméneutique" in *La naissance du paradigme herméneutique,* ed. Andre Laks and Ada Neschke (Lille: Presses Universitaires de Lille, 1990), pp. 69–117.

58. Ferdinand de Saussure, *Cours de linguistique générale, Edition critique pour Rudolf Engler* (Wiesbaden: Otto Harrossowitz, 1967), pp. 264, 285.

59. Ferdinand de Saussure, *Course in General Linguistics* [1915], trans. Wade Baskin (New York: McGraw Hill, 1959), pp. 74, 124, 92.

60. See Ludwig Wittgenstein, *Culture and Value,* trans. Peter Winch (Chicago: University of Chicago Press, 1980), p. 77:

> Tradition is not something a man can learn; not a thread he can pick up when he feels like it; any more than a man can choose his own ancestors. . . . Someone lacking a tradition who would like to have one is like a man unhappily in love.

61. Ludwig Wittgenstein, *Lectures and Conversations on Aesthetics, Psychology, and Religious Belief* (Oxford: Oxford University Press, 1970), p. 5.

62. cf. Antoine Berman, *The Experience of the Foreign,* trans. Stefan Heyvaert (Albany: SUNY Press, 1992).

63. See Richard Rorty, "The World Well Lost," *Journal of Philosophy* 69 (1972): 649–65.

64. See for example, Richard Rorty, "Private Irony and Liberal Hope," in *Contingency, Irony, Solidarity* (Cambridge: Cambridge University Press, 1989).

65. As will become evident, our account differs from Rorty, *inter alia,* with respect to his account of irony, his account of language and his account of the ordinary or common. Against Rorty it must be asserted that the asking of the 'metaphysical' question, 'what is?' as *problematic,* is ironical. The *assumption* that it has an answer (corresponding to our vocabulary)—or doesn't have an answer (as Rorty's account claims)—is dogmatic. Compare Rorty's account in *Contingency, Irony, Solidarity,* pp. 74–75. Thus the *ordinary* is not the same as our common vocabulary, but always exceeds it. Hence the importance, at least since Bacon (as we have seen) of experience as indicating what exceeds our common vocabulary, its experience of "detraditionalization," in which 'Being' has become problematic. It is just in this sense that Schlegel claimed that for irony every fact is both "a mystery and an experiment." See "Athenaeum Fragments" §427, *Philosophical Fragments,* trans. Peter Firchow (Minneapolis: University of Minnesota Press, 1991), p. 87. In this sense, however, the ordinary is already 'divided' against itself, to use the language of German Idealism—or to use Kierkegaard's, the ordinary is already 'extraordinary'.

66. I have further traced the legacy of this difference and its *Erweiterung* (which is in fact Kantian in origin) with respect to the problem of interpretation in my *Extensions: Essays on Interpretation, Rationality, and the Closure of Modernism.*

67. Merleau-Ponty, *The Visible and the Invisible*, p. 168.

68. See Peter Slojterdijk, *Critique of Cynical Reason*, trans. Michael Eldred (Minneapolis: University of Minnesota Press, 1987).

69. Edmund Husserl, "Philosophy and the Crisis of European Humanity" [1935] (K:291).

70. Ibid., p. 287.

71. Husserl, *Ideas Pertaining to a Pure Phenomenology and to a Phenomenological Philosophy,* book 1, trans. F. Kersten (The Hague: Martinus Nijhoff, 1980), p. 374.

72. Blumenberg, *Work on Myth*, pp. 166–67.

73. G. W. F. Hegel, "Prefatory Lectures on the Philosophy of Law," *Clio* 8, no. 1 (1978): p. 66.

74. Blumenberg, *Work on Myth*, p. 163.

75. Ibid., p. 169.

76. Ibid., p. 162.

77. Ibid., p. 166.

78. Ralph Waldo Emerson, *Representative Men* (Boston: Houghton Mifflin: 1891), p. 187. Emerson, too, it should be noted, connected all this to an ontology of life: "the history of the universe is symptomatic and life is mnemonical," ibid., p. 36. Still he was equally aware of the internal tension of tradition. His essay, "Self-Reliance," proclaims "What have I to do with the sacredness of tradition?" And, the essay on "Memory" itself acknowledged that we "cannot overstate our debt to the past, but has the present no claim?" Indeed, taking up the logic of traditionality itself, he proclaims, "time hides no treasures."

79. Blumenberg, *Work on Myth,* 128.

80. Karl R. Popper, "Towards a Rational Theory of Tradition," *Conjectures and Refutations* (New York: Harper & Brothers, 1965), pp. 126–27. Still, Popper's attempt to distinguish first-order and second-order tradition, *mythos* and *logos,* was not without its own positivist penumbra.

81. Eliot, *After Strange Gods,* p. 19.

82. From the outset, like others articulating the notion of tradition, Eliot linked the problem of finite knowing to the unconscious: "Experience, we may assert both begins and ends in something which is not conscious." See *Knowledge and Experience in the Philosophy of F. H. Bradley,* p. 28.

83. Claude Lefort, "Novelty and the Appeal of Repetition" in *The Political Forms of Modern Society,* trans. David Macey (Minneapolis: University of Minnesota Press, 1988), p. 124.

84. Those writing in the wake of Heidegger's political aestheticism were doubtless right to emphasize the dangers in too closely linking *techne* and *poiesis* in mythicizing the West. Cf. Philippe Lacoue-Labarthe, *Heidegger, Art and Politics,* trans. Chris Turner (Oxford: Basil Blackwell, 1990), pp. 84–85. Here we should insist not only on the *lacunae* of Heidegger's accounts of *poiesis* and the political as masterfully analyzed by Lacoue-Labarthe, but also the *lacuna*

affecting even these analyses themselves insofar as they miss both the specificity of aesthetic rationality and its emergence within the modern. That such aesthetic paradigms need not have been linked to the totalizations of facism is evident from their link to (Romantic) liberalism and its emphasis on authentic *Individualität*, a link whose remnants doubtless remain still nascently present in Heidegger's Dasein. See for example Wilhelm von Humboldt, *The Limits of State Action* [1791–92], ed. J. W. Burrow (Cambridge: Cambridge University Press, 1969). Ironically, this work perhaps influenced English political thought (it is cited for example by both Mill and Arnold) even more than German thought.

85. Heinrich Klotz, *Filippo Brunelleschi: The Early Works and the Medieval Tradition,* trans. Hugh Klein (New York: Rizzoli, 1990), p. 156.

86. See Robert Jan van Pelt and Carroll William Westfall, *Architectural Principles in the Age of Historicism* (New Haven: Yale University Press, 1991), p. 290.

87. Klotz, *Brunelleschi,* p. 77.

88. See in this regard the analysis of Peter Murray, *Piranesi and the Grandeur of Ancient Rome* (London: Thames and Hudson, 1971).

89. F. W. J. Schelling, *System of Transcendental Idealism,* trans. Peter Heath (Charlottesville: University of Virginia, 1981), pp. 211–12. It is no accident that the context for the emergence of Schelling's considerations concerns first the emergence of universal history, secondly, the universal state, and, third, the task of the creation of a new mythology.

90. Claude Lefort, "The Death of Immortality?" in *Democracy and Political Theory,* trans. David Macey (Minneapolis: University of Minnesota Press, 1988), p. 270: "The idea of permanence alone cannot account for another idea which seems to emerge with humanism: the idea that works of art are contemporaneous *within* a time-difference."

91. Arendt's characterization of the Renaissance as "a first attempt to break the fetters of tradition . . . by going to the sources themselves to establish a past over which tradition would have no hold" is thus too abrupt. It again misses the logic of juxtaposition and refiguration at stake in traditionality. The latter becomes explicit in the Renaissance as much as does the former's ruptures. The point is that both belong together. The schematics of origin and overcoming doubtless in this regard betray her allegiance to Heidegger's (and Nietzsche's) metaphysics more than the fecundity of her own meditations on foundation. See Hannah Arendt, "Tradition and the Modern Age," in *Between Past and Future* (New York: Penguin, 1968), pp. 25–26.

92. In fact this pairing of 'innovation' and 'renovation' is very broad in extent in the early Renaissance. As Jacob Klein has shown, it is at work even in mathematics (Vieta) and the sciences (Galileo). See Jacob Klein, *Greek Mathematical Thought and the Origins of Algebra* (New York: Dover Publications, 1992), p. 153.

93. Lefort, "The Death of Immortality?" p. 270.

94. Philippe Sollers, "Dante and the Transversal of Writing" in *Writing and the Experience of Limits,* trans. Philip Barnard with David Hayman (New York: Columbia: University Press, 1983). This multiplicity should not perhaps be construed in a merely formal sense, adhering instead to the very specificity of language itself. It is the latter which makes it possible for Sollers to link Dante's 'fluctuation' to Mallarme's attempts to return language to its essential rhythm while noting as well its link to "what we call *music*" and its "significant convergences" with the *Ars nova* of polyphony.

And, while such apparently oblique (even musicological and aesthetic) issues seem irrelevant to discussions of the rationality of tradition, they doubtless become less so against the background of claims like Adorno's that Stravinsky's use of Russion folk music is regressive and irrational, or Wittgenstein's (purported) concerns regarding the status of tradition in African art (and its "use" in modern art). See Theodor W. Adorno, *Philosophy of Modern Music,* trans. Anne G. Mitchell and Wesley V. Blomster (New York: Seabury Press, 1973); Ludwig Wittgenstein, *Lectures & Conversations on Aesthetics, Psychology and Religious Belief,* ed. Cyril Barrett (Berkeley and Los Angeles: University of California Press, 1967), pp. 8–9. Moreover such issues become even further relevant perhaps before claims like Habermas's that poststructuralists like Derrida (and presumably Sollers) had abandoned "the tradition that was shaped from Dante to Vico, and kept alive through Hammann, Humboldt, and Droysen, down to Dilthey and Gadamer" that protested "the primacy of the logical over the rhetorical." See Jürgen Habermas, *The Philosophical Discourse of Modernity,* trans. Frederick Lawrence (Cambridge: MIT Press, 1987), p. 187. I am inclined to suspect, for reasons that will become further evident, that only the poststructuralist emphasis upon difference is able to capture the rhetorical tradition in question and the specificity of the (political and epistemic) liberalism it receives from Humbolt—and finally that this is precisely the status of its 'hermeneutics'. That is, rightly understood, only such a hermeneutics (which emerges in Humboldt and Schlegel) is sufficiently grounded to be open both to the past *and* to the Other.

95. See Umberto Eco, "Two Models of Interpretation" in the *Limits of Interpretation* (Bloomington: Indiana University Press, 1990); and *The Aesthetics of Thomas Aquinas,* trans. Hugh Bredin (Cambridge: Harvard University Press, 1988).

96. Hugh of St. Victor, *Didascalicon,* III.VIII.

97. From the outset Dante's extension of sacred poetics was perceived to hold dangerous consequences. His account of the "universal community of the human race"—setting up, for the first time, above the Christian ideal of a universal church, a single universal temporal order—secularized the Church's ideal of a universal Christendom (in the same way, it might be argued, that it had secularized its poetics of transcendence). See Etienne Gilson, *Dante, The Philosopher* (London: Sheed & Ward, 1952), pp. 166–67. As Gilson noted,

however, Dante himself should be defended against charges of "Averroism." Dante's account of the intellectual potentials of the whole of humankind must be understood *not* as the Averroist possible intellect—as a *de facto*—unity based upon an actual structure, a single intellect in all humankind, but as a possibility that remains ideal, a potential of a *multitudo*. The modern objectivities that would soon follow may well be more suspectible in this regard.

For Dante, the opening of the vernacular was the opening of the light of reason (*De Vulgari Eloquentia* I. 18). The poet's gift is one in which the language of the people is unveiled. "I let that which it has within itself as something possible and hidden come out into the open" (*Convivio* I. 9). Still, the complex relation between the sacred, the vernacular, and the "nation-state" are also already lingering in the background. It is the Italians who are united by the light of reason while the German's High Court of Justice is a king (*De Vulgari Eloquentia,* I. 18). Nonetheless, as the opening lines had attested, if the vernacular is privileged, it is both individual (and more natural) and universal (because the whole world employs it) [I. 1].

98. Having claimed that "the very concept of a philosophical tradition, subject to many changes and variations but basically uniform and continuous, seems to have been formulated by Renaissance Platonists," Kristeller notes that the concept of *philosophia perennis* itself was coined by Augustinus Steuchus, a Catholic theologian of the sixteenth century strongly committed to the platonic and pseudoplatonic tradition in philosophy. See Paul Oskar Kristeller, "Renaissance Philosophy and the Medieval Tradition" in *Renaissance Concepts of Man* (New York: Harper & Row, 1972), pp. 152–53.

99. Lefort, "The Death of Immortality," p. 272.

100. See the analysis of S. N. Eisenstadt, "Post-Traditional Societies and the Continuity and Reconstruction of Tradition," *Daedalus* 102, no. 1 (Winter 1973): 1–27.

101. Arendt, *On Revolution* (New York: Penguin, 1987), p. 201.

102. Cicero, *Of the Laws,* Bk. II, cited in Edmund Burke, *Reflections on the Revolution in France,* ed. J. G. A. Pocock (Indianapolis: Hackett, 1987), p. 79n.

103. Ibid., p. 207.

104. Ibid., p. 197.

105. See PH:409.

106. Blumenberg, *Work on Myth,* p. 183.

107. Yves Congar, *Tradition and Traditions,* trans. Michael Naseby and Thomas Rainborough (New York: Macmillan, 1967).

108. Irenaeus, *Against the Heretics,* trans. John Keble (Oxford: James Parker & Co., 1872), book III, section 3, p. 206 (translation altered).

109. Tertullian, "The 'Prescription' of Heretics," *On the Testimony of the Soul and On the Prescription of Heretics,* trans. Rev. T. H. Bindley (London: Society for Promoting Christian Knowledge, 1914), chaps. XXI; XXIX.

110. Irenaeus, *Against the Heretics,* pp. 208-209. It is important to add that the issue was neither disconnected from nor precluded by the problem of intertranslatability: "While the languages of the world differ, the meaning of the tradition is one and the same." I. 10, pp. 33-34.

111. David Gross, *The Past in Ruins: Tradition and the Critique of Modernity* (Amherst: University of Massachusetts Press, 1992), p. 8.

112. Burke, *Reflections on the Revolution in France,* p. 28.

113. See Hobbes, *Leviathan,* chap. 44 (Lev:III.44). See Friedrich Nietzsche, *On the Genealogy of Morals,* trans. Walter Kaufman (New York: Vintage Books, 1964), pp. 48ff. Nietzsche's criticism here is a criticism of both Tertullian and Aquinas for their ethical subjectivism or ethics of resentiment. Interestingly enough, Brentano, writing at the same time, attempted an extended defense of Aquinas, whose views, he noted, "have often been presented as though they were pure subjectivism." See Franz Brentano, *The Origin of our Knowledge of Right and Wrong,* trans. Roderick M. Chisolm (London: Routledge & Kegan Paul), p. 87.

114. Hannah Arendt, *The Life of the Mind/Willing* (New York: Harcourt Brace Jovanovich, Inc., 1978), p. 210.

115. Ibid.

116. Ibid.

117. Michel Serres, *Rome: The Book of Foundations* (Stanford: Stanford University Press, 1991), p. 40.

118. Arendt, *On Revolution,* pp. 197, 280.

119. St. Jerome, cited in Lewis Mumford, "Augustine: Salvation By Retreat," *Interpretations and Forecasts* (New York: Harcourt Brace Jovanovich, 1972), p. 147.

120. See T. S. Eliot, "Virgil and the Christian World" in *On Poetry and Poets* (New York: Noonday Press, 1969). What Arendt claims Virgil had to teach the modern revolutionaries was precisely the continuity and *traditio* of reestablishment itself: the foundation of Rome "was the resurgence of Troy"—hence a rebirth, "the first, as it were, of the series of re-nascences that have formed the history of European culture and civilization." Arendt, *The Life of the Mind,* pp. 211-12.

121. T. S. Eliot, "Virgil and the Christian World," *On Poetry and Poets,* pp. 141-43. It was just such 'humility' of course that Eliot had found before him in Newman's concept of faith vis-à-vis tradition—and which Newman in turn had found in Burke and Shaftsbury. See Newman's *The Idea of a University* (Notre Dame: University of Notre Dame Press, 1982), chap. 8.

122. Arendt, *The Life of the Mind,* p. 211.

123. Ernst H. Kantorowicz, *The King's Two Bodies: A Study in Medieval Political Theology* (Princeton: Princeton University Press, 1957).

124. See in this regard the analysis of Marc Richir, *Du sublime en politique* (Paris: Payot, 1991), chap. 2.

125. See Cornelius Castoriadis, "The Greek *Polis* and the Creation of Democracy," in *Philosophy, Politics, Autonomy* (New York: Oxford University Press, 1991).

126. Serres, *Rome: The Book of Foundations*. For Serres's discussion of the impact of mathematics in the quarrel between the Orients and the moderns, see *Hermes I: La Communication* (Paris: Minuit, 1969), p. 46. Commentators have only recently identified the importance of Serres's early work in the development of poststructuralist thought.

127. The issue regarding the impact of post-Gödelian theory on Husserl's transcendental logic (always modeled upon Hilbert's classical formulations of determinacy and decidability) remains to this day controversial. The *locus classicus* of such debates remains Jean Ladrière, *Les limitations internes des formalismes: étude sur la signification du théorème de Gödel et des théorèmes apparentés dans la theorie des fondements des mathématiques* (Louvain: E. Nauwelaerts, 1957). It is evident, however, that such considerations stood in the background of many poststructuralist 'deconstructions'. See for example Jacques Derrida, *Edmund Husserl's Origin of Geometry: An Introduction,* trans. John P. Leavey, Jr. (Stony Brook: Nicholas Hays, 1978). A more recent discussion of the issue is John Scanlon, "'Tertium non Datur': Husserl's Conception of A Definite Multiplicity" in *Phenomenology and the Formal Sciences,* ed. Th. M. Seebohn, D. Föllesdal, and J. N. Mohanty (Dordrecht: Kluwer Academic Press, 1991), pp. 139–47.

128. Serres, *Rome: The Book of Foundations,* p. 126. Compare Husserl's similar claims concerning the Greek origins of the theoretical attitude (at the expense of "Indian" or "Chinese" philosophies) in his *Vienna Lecture.* See *Crisis:* 280f.

129. Ibid.

130. Burke, *Reflections on the Revolution in France,* p. 81.

131. Michel Foucault, "Nietzsche, Genealogy, History" in *Language Counter-Memory Practice,* p. 147.

132. Arendt, "Tradition and the Modern Age," *Between Past and Future,* p. 28.

133. Blumenberg, *Work on Myth,* p. 131.

134. Burke, *Reflections on the Revolution in France,* p. 148.

135. Arendt, "Traditon and the Modern Age," p. 26.

136. Serres, *Rome: The Book of Foundations,* pp. 232, 95.

137. Ibid.

138. Martin Heidegger, *The History of the Concept of Time,* §15.

139. Cf. Aristotle, *Metaphysics,* 993a. This fallibility also led Aristotle to recur to the epistemic community of investigators as much as the *Ethics* had taken recourse to the community for moral virtue: "No one is able to attain the truth adequately, while, on the other hand, we do not collectively fail, but every one says something true about the nature of things, and while individually we contribute little or nothing to the truth, by the union of all a considerable amount is amassed."

140. Hans Robert Jauss, *Aesthetic Experience and Literary Hermeneutics,* trans. Michael Shaw (Minneapolis: University of Minnesota Press, 1982), p. 69.

141. Blumenberg, *Work on Myth,* p. 96. That the problem of interpretation is as much logical as it is metaphysical or existential is a point too often missed.

142. See my "On the Rationality of the Fragment," *Extensions* (Albany: SUNY Press, 1992), chapter X. Compare Michel Serres's similar remarks in "Leibniz retraduit en langue mathématique" in *Hermes III, La traduction* (Paris: Minuit, 1974).

143. Blumenberg, *Work on Myth,* p. 106. At least since 1912, Heidegger criticized *Logistik* less for its simple inadequacy than for "concealing meaning and meaning changes of judgment: both of which would ultimately be irreducible to function." See Heidegger, "Neu Forschungen über Logik," *Gesamtausgabe* I: 42. 'Significance' instead is the hinge between intentional and extensional logic, between quality and *quantitas,* or intensive and extensive magnitude, to use Kant's terms. As this hinge itself it is to use Hegel's term, an event of *Qualierung;* as the *determinatio* of this between itself, i.e., as *underdetermined* it is interpretation. And finally, as the event that accompanies this distinction itself it is, as will be seen a certain *Vorausspringung* that is neither universal nor particular: 'Dasein'.

144. Blumenberg, *Work on Myth,* p. 171.

145. Lacan's Freudian reading of Saussure in effect again maps the dispersion between intentional and extensional features of discourse, the conflict between expressivity and denotation now turned ontological, the very metaphorics or metonymics of expressivity articulated now as an algorithmics of desire. The result, on the one hand, is a signifying function, a 'connotation' irreducible to the intentionality of consciousness—and yet not simply detachable from the 'subject'—and on the other hand, a meaning irreducible to its referents—and yet not without extensional effect and 'truth', or at least the Freudian truth. Perhaps the most informed discussion of this matter, especially again in terms of *rapprochement* with Heidegger has been provided by Lacoue-Labarthe and Nancy. See Jean-Luc Nancy & Philippe Lacoue-Labarthe, *The Title of the Letter: A Reading of Lacan,* trans. François Raffoul and David Pettigrew (Albany: SUNY Press, 1992).

146. T. S. Eliot, "Ulysses, Order, and Myth," *The Dial* (Nov. 1923), p. 483.

147. Eliot, *The Sacred Wood,* p. 50.

148. Samuel Beckett, "Dante . . . Bruno . . . Vico . . . Joyce," *Our Examination Round His Factification for Incamination of Work in Progress* (Paris: Shakespeare and Company, 1922).

149. Serres, *Rome: The Book of Foundations,* p. 186.

150. See Claude Lefort, *Le travail de l'oeuvre Machiavel,* ch. VI. Compare Serres, *Rome: The Book of Foundations,* chap. 4, "Suffrage: Multiplicity Assembled."

151. Maurice Merleau-Ponty, "A Note on Machiavelli," *Signs,* trans. Richard McCleary (Evanston: Northwestern University Press, 1964), p. 221. That Merleau-

Ponty saw such considerations to be of a piece with the complicated epistemic and ontological issues of 'phenomenology' is doubtless not accidental. Elsewhere I have more specifically traced the complex emergence of phenomenology within the itineracy of philosophical modernism. See my *Extensions*, chap. 8, "On the Right to Interpret: Beyond the Copernican Turn."

152. See Martin Heidegger, "Vom Wesen und Begriff Der *Physis*, Aristotles, Physik B, 1" *Wegmarken, Gesamtausgabe* Band 9 (Frankfurt am Main: Klostermann, 1976), p. 244.

153. J. N. Findlay, *Hegel: A Reexamination* (London: Allen and Unwin, 1958), p. 353.

154. Chaucer, *Boece*, II. 2. 93.

155. Ibid., I. 4.

156. See Boethius, *The Consolation of Philosophy*, V. V.

157. Again see Lefort, *Le travail de l'oeuvre Machiavel*, p. 470. Also see, for example, J. G. A. Pocock, *The Machiavellian Moment: Florentine Political Thought and the Atlantic Republican Tradition*, chap. 7.

158. Ibid., p. 400.

159. Here Lefort's and Strauss's readings of Machiavelli could not be further apart, granted Strauss's reduction of Machiavelli to a nihilist for whom "all legitimacy has its roots in illegitimacy." Compare Lefort's critique of Strauss, *Le travail de l'oeuvre Machiavel*, pp. 259–60. Against it Lefort continues Merleau-Ponty's caveat: "Machiavelli does not ask that one govern through vices—lies, terror, trickery; he tries to define a political *virtue*, which is to speak to these mute spectators gathered around him and caught up in the dizziness of communal life" (*Signs*, p. 217). For further discussion of this issue see my "Merleau-Ponty, the Ethics of Ambiguity, and the Dialectics of Virtue," in *Merleau-Ponty in Contemporary Perspective*, ed. Patrick Burke and Jan Van der Veken (Dordrecht: Kluwer, 1993).

160. Ibid., p. 400.

161. Niccolò Machiavelli, "The Exhortation to Penance" in *The Prince*, trans. Robert M. Adams (New York: W. W. Norton & Co., 1977), p. 126. Cf. Lefort, *Le travail de l'oeuvre Machiavel*, pp. 767–68.

162. Arendt, *On Revolution*, p. 159.

163. Ibid., pp. 38–39. *The Life of the Mind*, however, credits "the lonely figure, Machiavelli" with providing the Age of Enlightenment with the model of a "revival of antiquity [which] ceased to be a matter of erudition and responded to highly political purposes" (p. 211).

164. Unlike other modern revolutionaries, Arendt claims, the American revolutionaries understood that "foundation, augmentation, and conservation are intimately interrelated," that uninterrupted continuity of this augmentation and its inherent authority could come about only through tradition" (ibid., p. 201). Still she admits "it was not tradition that bound them back to the beginnings of Western history but, on the contrary, their own experiences, for which they

needed models and precedents" (ibid., p. 197). Hence the problem of our own "forgetfulness" regarding the revolutionary tradition. None of this distinguishes Lefort and Arendt, whose differences I will further analyze elsewhere. Pocock's thesis again affirms their agreement, tracing the development of the humanist tradition from Florentine political thought to the Atlantic Republican tradition. Again see *The Machiavellian Moment*.

165. Montesquieu, *The Spirit of the Laws*, XI. 4.

166. G. W. F. Hegel, "Prefatory Lectures on the Philosophy of Law," *Clio* 8, no. 1 (1978), p. 52 [1822–23].

167. See PR: Introduction. The exclusion of matters pertaining to application is even stronger in the "Prefatory Lectures." See pp. 65–66.

168. Jean-Luc Nancy, "The Jurisdiction of the Hegelian Monarch," *Social Research* 49, no. 2 (1982).

169. Ibid., p. 496. See Arendt, *On Revolution*, p. 39.

170. J. N. Findlay, *Hegel: A Re-examination* (London: George Allen & Unwin, 1958), p. 302.

171. This event is unwieldy—indeed the opening of a "night-like pit," to use Hegel's term. It was, as Findlay immediately states in a retraction, the problem of "dialectical method," itself a method Findlay previously denied existed in Hegel (*Hegel: A Re-examination*, pp. 353–54). This interface between creative imagination ("symbolic, allegoric, or poetic imagination" [PS: 209, §456]) and productive memory in one sense is lacking in method, in the same way that discovery always lacks a logic. Yet it remains the remnant of *epagoge* itself, as has been seen, divided between invention and discovery, its "night-like pit" equally divided between conscious and unconscious. This is not, pace positivist reductions, or deconstructive suspicions, simply to poison the well, dissolving the paradoxical warrant that accompanies its evidence. Rather it is to articulate the "divided" character of evidencing itself.

172. Otto Pöggeler, "Hegel et Machiavel. Renaissance italienne et idéalisme allemand," *Archives* 41, no. 3 (1978): 435–68. It is clear from Hegel's concerns that he agrees in this regard with Stephen Toulmin's recent account of the rise of the modernity: "Whatever was gained by Galileo, Descartes, and Newton's excursions into natural philosophy, something was lost through the abandonment of Erasmus and Rabelais, Shakespeare and Montaigne." See *Cosmopolis: The Hidden Agenda of Modernity* (Chicago: University of Chicago Press, 1990), p. 43.

173. See Leo Strauss, *The Political Philosophy of Hobbes*, p. 88f.

174. Sir Francis Bacon, *The Works of Francis Bacon*, vol. viii, p. 438. Cited in Strauss, ibid. p. 88. Again, while Strauss would connect Bacon's account of history to Hobbes, Gadamer would insist on its continuity with Aristotle (TM:23). Both are true, I am suggesting, which is why Gadamer's Aristoteleanism likewise turns to the problem of recognition—and nascently thereby to Hobbes, as will be seen.

175. Theodor Adorno, *Aesthetic Theory,* trans. C. Lerhardt (London: Routledge & Kegan Paul, 1984), p. 361.

176. As will become evident the problem of recognition accompanies ethical theory, especially in continental theory, in Hegel's wake, originating in Hegel's post-Kantian predecessors and extending to contemporary thinkers such as Sartre and Levinas. On Hegel's ambiguous relation to Hobbes as well as his "speculative correction," see Jacques Taminiaux, "Hegel and Hobbes" in *Dialectic and Difference,* trans. Robert Crease and James T. Decker (Atlantic Highlands, NJ: Humanities Press, 1985). Likewise see Axel Honneth, *The Struggle for Recognition,* trans. Joel Anderson (Cambridge, MA: Polity Press, 1995). What distinguishes these treatments is Taminiaux's excellent articulation of the link between Hobbes's (and Hegel's) struggle for domination and the elevation of *mathesis.*

177. See Hegel, *Aesthetics,* trans. T. M. Knox (Oxford: Clarendon Press, 1975), vol. II, pp. 972f ("Poetic and Prosaic Treatment") where all these issues become intertwined.

178. Sigmund Freud, *The Psychopathology of Everyday Life,* trans. Alan Tyson, ed. James Strachey (New York: Norton, 1966).

179. John Locke, *Questions Concerning the Law of Nature* (Ithaca: Cornell University Press, 1990), pp. 127, 129.

180. Leo Strauss, "The Three Waves of Modernity" in *An Introduction to Political Philosophy,* ed. Hilail Gilden (Detroit: Wayne State University Press, 1989), p. 86.

181. Maurice Merleau-Ponty, *The Prose of the World,* pp. 85, 113. As noted previously Sartre had written on the problem of the everyday (*tous les jours*) in his *What Is Literature?* Nonetheless the notion remained (as it had for Husserl before him, who conceived of it in terms of the natural attitude) intelligible only within the series of antinomies that continuously undercut his insight: being and nothingness, subject and object, plenitude and negation, prose and poetry. Merleau-Ponty doubtless here as elsewhere attempts to undercut these dichotomies.

182. Cf. Lefort, *Le travail de l'oeuvre Machiavel,* p. 407.

183. Edmund Husserl, *Formal and Transcendental Logic,* trans. Dorion Cairns (The Hague: Martinus Nijhoff, 1978), p. 199.

184. Ibid., p. 223.

185. See Charles Taylor, *Sources of the Self* (Cambridge: Harvard University Press, 1989), p. 257; Jean-François Lyotard, "The Sublime and the Avant-Garde" in *The Lyotard Reader,* ed. Andrew Benjamin (Oxford: Blackwell, 1989).

186. See Stanley Cavell, *In Quest of the Ordinary* (Chicago: University of Chicago Press, 1988), p. 177. See Kierkegaard, *Fear and Trembling,* trans. Howard V. Hong and Edna H. Hong (Princeton: Princeton University Press, 1983), pp. 41, 79.

187. Søren Kierkegaard, *Attack Upon "Christendom,"* trans. Walter Lowrie (Princeton: Princton University Press, 1944, 1968), p. 159.

188. Since the beginning—or at least since Hobbes's reduction of the copula to mathematical equation and Vico's claim that we are certain of history because we make it—modernists had tended to equate truth with certainty, invention with creation and 'history' as the 'dramatization' of such coincidence. The result lost sight of the fertility and rationality of both invention and interpretation. Heidegger had seen the failure of both: the former in the early works, the latter in the later work.

189. See Michel de Certeu, *The Practice of Everyday Life,* trans. Steven F. Rendell (Berkeley and Los Angeles: University of California Press, 1984), pp. 2–3.

190. Cf. TM:26; Mikhail Bakhtin, *The Dialogic Imagination,* trans. Caryl Emerson and Michael Holquist (Austin: University of Texas Press, 1992), pp. 167ff. As Bakhtin put it, transforming the traditional hierarchies resulted in "the disunification of what had been traditionally linked, and the bringing together of that which had been traditionally kept distant and disunified" (ibid., p. 170).

191. Harold Rosenberg, *The Tradition of the New* (New York: Horizon Press, 1959), p. 12.

192. Bakhtin, *The Dialogic Imagination,* p. 25.

193. Hans-Georg Gadamer, *The Relevance of the Beautiful,* ed. R. Bernasconi, trans. Nicholas Walker (Cambridge: Cambridge University Press, 1986), p. 49.

194. Martin Heidegger, "The Origin of the Work of Art" in *Poetry, Language, Thought,* trans. Albert Hofstadter (New York: Harper & Row, 1971), p. 54.

195. Ibid.

196. Edmund Husserl, "Phenomonology," *Encyclopedia Britannica,* vol. 17 (1937), p. 700.

197. Husserl, *Formal and Transcendental Logic,* p. 276. The term "urtradition-alität" is found in later unpublished manuscripts.

198. See Jean-Paul Sartre, *The Transcendence of the Ego,* trans. Forrest Williams and Robert Kirkpatrick (New York: Farrar, Strauss, and Giroux, 1957).

199. Bakhtin, *The Dialogic Imagination,* p. 171.

200. See Ralph Waldo Emerson, "Poetry and Imagination" in *Letters and Social Aims* (Boston: Houghton Mifflin, 1883), p. 20. It is also not insignificant to note that not only the authority of tradition, but the authority of the "elderly" became questioned at the same time. Compare Thoreau's claim early in *Walden* that "age is no better, hardly so well, qualified for an instructor as youth, for it has not profited so much as it has lost." *Walden* (New York: Literary Classics of the United States, 1985), p. 329.

201. Henry James, "The Art of Fiction," in *The Art of Fiction and Other Essays* (New York: Oxford University Press, 1948), p. 238.

202. See Theodor Adorno, *Aesthetic Theory,* p. 68.

203. Karl Marx, *The Eighteenth Brumaire of Louis Bonaparte* (New York: International Publishers, 1963), p. 15.

204. Baudelaire, *"Salon of 1846."* ("On the Heroism of Modern Life"), trans. Jonathan Mayne (New York: Doubleday & Company Inc., 1956), pp. 126–27.

205. Ibid., p. 128. On Baudelaire's own reception of Piranesi see Luzius Keller, *Piranèse et les romantiques français* (Paris: Librairie Jose Corti, 1966).

206. Burke, *Reflections on the Revolution in France*, p. 44.

207. See Danielle Sallenave, Julia Kristeva, "L'expérience littéraire est-elle encore possible," *L'Infini*, No. 53 (Printemps 1996): p. 39. This tradition of revolt and its experience is one that even escapes, she claims, Foucault's archaeology of knowledge. In this passage, its major figures include Cartesian doubt, the Heideggerean 'parole', and the unconscious of Freud, all of which are brought to bear on the analysis of Proust in her recent work.

208. See the analysis of George McCarthy, *Marx and the Ancients* (Savage, MD: Rowman & Littlefield, 1990).

209. Walter Benjamin, *Charles Baudelaire: A Lyric Poet in the Era of High Capitalism*, trans. Harry Zohn (London: NLB, 1973), p. 81.

210. Ibid., p. 82.

211. An attempt to explore such a history can be found, for example, in *Counter-tradition*, ed. Sheila Delaney (New York: Basic Books, 1971).

212. See Theodor W. Adorno, *Aesthetic Theory*, pp. 31–32.

213. Ibid., p. 30.

214. Theodor W. Adorno, "On Tradition," collaborative translations, *Telos*, N. 94 (Winter 1992–93): p. 82.

215. Jean-Paul Sartre, *Being and Nothingness*, trans. Hazel Barnes (New York: Washington Square Press, 1966), p. 73.

216. Jean-Paul Sartre, *Saint Genet*, trans. Bernard Frechtman (New York: Pantheon, 1963), p. 25.

217. Walter Benjamin, *Schriften I* (Frankfurt am Main: Surkamp Verlag, 1995), p. 255.

218. Lefort, *The Political Forms of Modern Society*, p. 305.

219. Hans Georg Gadamer, *Reason in the Age of Science*, trans. Frederick G. Lawrence (Cambridge, MA: MIT Press, 1989), pp. 76–77.

220. See Lefort, *Le travail de l'oeuvre machiavel*, part six, "L'oeuvre, l'idéologie, et l'interprétation," which centers on the problem of interpretation and indeterminacy.

221. Claude Lefort, "Novelty and the Appeal of Repetition," in *The Political Forms of Modern Society*, p. 124.

222. Ibid., p. 136.

223. Lefort, *Democracy and Political Theory*, p. 255.

224. See Alasdair MacIntyre, *Herbert Marcuse: An Exposition and A Polemic* (New York: Viking, 1970), p. 103. Likewise see Jacques Lacan, "Kant avec Sade," *Ecrits* (Paris: Editions du Seuil, 1966), pp. 765–93.

225. Emmanuel Levinas, "Meaning and Sense" in *Collected Papers,* trans. Alphonso Lingis (The Hague: Martinus Nijhoff, 1987), p. 117.

226. Ibid.

227. Emmanuel Levinas, *Totality and Infinity,* p. 276.

228. Emmanuel Levinas, *Otherwise than Being or Beyond Essence,* trans. Alphonso Lingis (The Hague: Martinus Nijhoff, 1981), p. 10.

229. Arendt, *On Revolution,* p. 152. Emmanuel Levinas, *Philosophical Papers,* trans. Alphonso Lingus (The Hague: Martinus Nijhoff, 1986), p. 89.

230. Hannah Arendt, *On Revolution,* p. 42.

231. See Werner Marx, *Heidegger and the Tradition,* trans. Theodore Kisiel and Murray Greene (Evanston: Northwestern University Press, 1971), p. 8. Nonetheless he saw it too: the poetics that results remains, he concludes, divorced from the everyday: "Heidegger's later writings do not deal with everyday men but with creative men. Accordingly, Heidegger's remarks on 'ethics' are presumably only for them," p. 250.

232. Martin Heidegger, "Die Kategorien und Bedeutungslehre des Duns Scotus," in *Frühe Schriften* (Frankfurt-am-Main: Klostermann, 1972), pp. 348, 155.

233. Ibid., p. 204.

234. Ibid., p. 197. Although Heidegger's *Seinsfrage* would intend to radically transform both the problems of *transcendens* and analogy that traditionally formed the economy of the conceptual operators within ontology, these never simply disappeared from Heidegger's development. As the 1943 *Parmenides* lecture discloses in its attempts, *inter alia* to confront the problem of the *polis* and its interpretation, once again committed to the greatness of Greek origins — and (it could be argued) the strictness of the distinction between poetics and prosaics:

> Sight into the unconcealed transpires first, and only, in the disclosive word. Sight looks, and is the appearing self-showing that it is, only in the disclosive domain of the word and of telling perception. Only if we recognize the original relation between the word and the essence of Being will we be capable of grasping why, for the Greeks and only for them, to the divine (τὸ θεῖον) must correspond the legendary (ὁ μῦθος). This correspondence is indeed the primordial essence of analogy (homology), the word "ana-logy" taken essentially and literally. (Heidegger, *Parmenides:* 114)

235. Indeed when in the *Letter on Humanism* Heidegger claimed that thinking was an *aventure* not only as a search and inquiry into the unthought "but also a relation as to what arrives (*l'avenant*)," we can gauge both its *Erwiderung,* its lingering relation to *fortuna,* and in both the complications of *legitimacy:* moreover such are the complications of interpretation and the claims of such hermeneutics itself. See LH:240.

2. Kant, the Architectonics of Reason, and the Ruins of the Ancient Systems

1. The case for this interpretation was originally made by Paul Wittichen, "Kant und Burke," *Historische Zeitschrift* 93 (1904), 252–55. For further discussion of the issue see Frederick Beiser, *Enlightenment, Revolution, and Romanticism* (Cambridge: Harvard University Press, 1992), pp. 39ff.

Gadamer has equally asserted its importance for his own discussion of hermeneutics and tradition, stating that along with the theological account of Christian religion as a true prejudice, Burke prepares the way for German romanticism (TM:273).

2. Gottfried von Herder, *Outlines of a Philosophy of the History of Man*, trans. T. Churchill (New York: Bergman), pp. 227–28.

3. Immanuel Kant, "Review of Herder's Ideas for a Philosophy of the History of Mankind," OH:48.

4. Herder, *Outlines*, p. 352.

5. Kant, "Review of Herder," OH:49.

6. OH:38. Moreover Kant shows misgivings at one point about the explanatory force of the concept itself: "It is true that songbirds teach their young certain songs and transmit them by tradition. . . . But where did the first song come from?" (Anth:184).

7. OH:148 (cf. CJ: para 83, p. 320).

8. Kant, "What Is Enlightenment?" OH:4.

9. Ibid.

10. Moreover, Kant's "principled improvement of the ancient Greek philosophy" was likewise held to be already operative in natural understanding, a move itself not without further internal transformations, as will become evident.

11. See Hannah Arendt, *The Life of the Mind/Willing* (New York: Harcourt Brace Jovanovich, Inc., 1978), p. 16. It is indeed striking, granted Arendt's commitment to Kant's account of judgment, that she omits Kant from her treatment of the will. Elsewhere I have further elaborated on the Kantian origins of this abyss. See "Abysses," in my *Extensions: Essays on Interpretation, Rationality, and the Closure of Modernism* (Albany: SUNY Press, 1992), chap. I.

12. I take this formulation, again, from Jürgen Habermas, *Justification and Application*, trans. Ciaran P. Cronin (Cambridge: MIT Press, 1993), p. 119.

13. See Immanuel Kant, *Philosophical Correspondence 1759–99*, ed. and trans. A. Zweig (Chicago: Chicago University Press, 1967), p. 190–94.

14. I take this formulation from Cassirer's 1929 Davos exchange with Heidegger, who had indeed tied the ethical to time and the transcendental schematism—at the risk, Cassirer claimed, of losing not only the link between the ethical and eternity but also the intrinsic autonomy and objectivity at stake in both. See Martin Heidegger and Ernst Cassirer in the "Davos Lectures," appendix to Martin Heidegger, *Kant and the Problem of Metaphysics*, trans. Richard

Taft (Bloomington: Indiana University Press, 1990), p. 173. Without simply deciding either for or against either antagonist, in what follows I will in effect detail such a hermeneutics of the ethical within Kant's own text. The issue between Cassirer and Heidegger is still contested in contemporary thought in Heidegger's wake, as can be seen for example in Alain Renault's concluding chapter to *L'ère de l'individu* (Paris: Gallimard, 1989). Tacitly however, it might be claimed that this issue overshadows many of the debates that surround the status of ethics in Heidegger's thought.

15. Again, this formulation of Heidegger dates from the Davos exchange. See ibid., p. 175.

16. Wilfred Sellars in his own study on Kant had argued for the significance of analogy, claiming that while both "obscure and difficult" analogy is "nevertheless as essential to the philosophy of science as it has been to theology." See Wilfred Sellars, *Science and Metaphysics* (New York: Humanities Press, 1982), p. 18. We will trace, however, its hermeneutics internal to Kant's own work and its impact on hermeneutics in general beyond Kant.

17. Jacob Klein, *Greek Mathematical Thought and the Origin of Algebra*, pp. 118–19. We should be careful, nonetheless, not to confuse such "geneologies" with semantic primitivism, which is their denial. And this distinction is perhaps especially important here. Indeed it is just because the *arché* of the ancients became suspect that the problem of principled virtue emerges. Moreover, once it has emerged, any attempt to simply return to a substantive basis for virtue, denying the problem of interpretation and underdetermination that the emergence of principled enquiry entails (this 'emergence' is not historical but logical in force) in short, to deny that other bases for virtue are possible—is always 'illusory' in the Kantian sense.

18. By invoking the Freudian term "cathexis," we are reminded of the proximity of Freud and Kant. As Paul Ricoeur has similarly claimed, "the network of the functions of consciousness constitutes, in Freud's works, the sketch of a true transcendental aesthetic, perfectly comparable to Kant's, inasmuch as it groups together all the conditions of exteriority." See Paul Ricoeur, *Freud and Philosophy,* trans. Denis Savage (New Haven: Yale University Press, 1970), p. 182. In fact, however, as is evident from Kant's own account of the connection between the *facultas signatrix* and the faculty of desire, such a cathexis is already outlined within the complex set of issues (epistemic and ontological) at stake in the Typic, where the relation to 'exteriority' surely complicates the limits of transcendental analytics. Moreover these complications are doubtless indicative of a complexity at the heart of transcendental analytics, the prominence of transcendental imagination, and Kant's transformation of the ancient problem of the categories.

In a gloss that would not be missed by thinkers as diverse as Husserl and

Frege in his wake, Kant had compared the discovery of the categories to collecting "the elements for a grammar (in fact both researches are very nearly related)." See Kant, *Prolegomena to Any Future Metaphysics,* trans. Lewis White Beck (Indianapolis: Bobbs-Merrill, 1950), p. 70. As will become increasingly evident in articulating the extensions of the Kantian account, however, such analysis of the "logical syntax" of transcendental understanding could not exhaust the problem of meaning or the account of the rational that accompanied it. Indeed this is the force of Kant's acknowledgment that, strictly taken, the determinations of *Sinn und Bedeutung* did not exhaust meaning—precisely to the extent that "we have an understanding which *problematically* extends further" (A255/B310). As the continual return of the problem of analogy in the critical system indicates, the problematic character of human rationality evidences both its demonstrative shortfall, as Hume had seen, but equally its inevitably dialectical and analogical status, and thereby the recurrence of the ancients' question of the *pros hen.* We have noted previously the incursion of the problem of significance that accompanied the *ars analytica.* In addition to such pure analyses, the question of interpretation continually intrudes; beyond such analyses of the 'logical syntax', the problem of meaning would be augmented not only by Kant's complicated account of semantics but equally a hermeneutics, the latter doubtless inseparably bound to the problem of the noumenon, to what extends beyond what strictly taken can be known. While transcendental analytics could be distinguished from questions of ontology, the latter, as becomes especially glaring in the problem of practical reason's intelligibility (or symbolic *cathexis*), could not. Obviously, this problem is not simply confined to practical reason, however: indeed such is the problem of Kantian extension in general. Without denying the strictness of Kantian principles, then, to reduce the Kantian project in this regard to transcendental semantics will always miss its complexity, the complexity of its "mixed message"—and thereby the complicated relations that adjoin sign and symbol, principle and transcendence, regulative and constitutive judgment.

19. Klein, *Greek Mathematical Thought and the Origin of Algebra,* p. 118.

20. Cf. Adolf Trendelenburg, "A Contribution to the History of the Word Person," ed. Rudolf Eucken, *The Monist* XX, no. 5, (July 1910). This work was written in 1870 and only posthumously published in *Kantstudien* in 1908.

21. Compare, for example, *De Officiis* III. V. 23: "No man shall be allowed for the sake of his own advantage to injure his neighbor. For it is to this that the laws have regard; this is their intent, that the bonds of union between citizens should not be impaired." Trans. Walter Miller (Cambridge: Harvard University Press, 1990). Granted Kant's account of the requisite of pure practical reasoning, such a precept must *denaturalize* such bond of its "empirical" con-

tent, i.e., "the principle of humanity . . . is not borrowed from experience, first because of its universality, since it applies to all rational beings generally" (Found:49).

22. Kant's complex relation to phenomenology has been the subject of a number of studies. See Iso Kern, *Kant und Husserl* (The Hague: Nijhoff, 1964) as well as the classical study of Paul Ricoeur, "Kant and Husserl" in *Husserl: An Analysis of his Phenomenology,* trans. Edward G. Ballard and Lester E. Embree (Evanston: Northwestern University Press, 1967). Kant's *epoché* with respect to the phenomenon of moral consciousness of the good will, which "dwells already in the natural sound understanding and which does not so much need to be taught as brought to light," sets the stage for such a phenomenology. At the same time it trumps both Husserl's and Kant's own texts. As is well known, Kant's first *Critique* was originally conceived in relation to a phenomenology—a term he takes over from Lambert, whose *Neues Organon* contained a concluding section entitled *Phänomenologie oder von dem schein,* distinguishing therein a hermeneutic or doctrine of signs from a phenomenology or doctrine of appearance. Kant explains (as early as the *Inaugural Dissertation* of 1770) that the critical project could not be identified with such a positive account of appearance, or phenomenology in his sense, since it is rather an account of the limits of appearance which, for reasons now evident, can only emerge in dialectic. Lacking extrinsic criteria sufficient for deduction, truth claims grounded only phenomenologically would amount to a logic of illusion (*Schein*), to use the predicates of the Transcendental Dialectic. Still, Kant was likewise clear that the ideas generated from such a logic would not be mere "figments of the brain" but would instead be both inevitable and ultimately undecidable from the theoretical standpoint.

The opening of the *Faktum* of practical reason explicates precisely the 'appearing' of moral obligation and the event of such an appearing. It does so nonetheless only in explicating again a pure theoretics of phenomenology. In other words, the very abandonment of phenomenology within the critical system only underlines the disequilibrium of all phenomenology: lacking extrinsic criteria, phenomenology will always be insufficient to meet the requisites of knowledge, understood from the Kantian standpoint. Secondly, as this clause itself demonstrates, all phenomenology will be theory-laden, and its 'theoretics' will be equivalent to the narratives of explication itself. All phenomenology is hermeneutic. Here Husserl (and those after him who engaged in moral 'phenomenologies') lost the critical difference that the problem of the noumenon had indicated, returning to a naive realism. As Ricoeur rightly recognized, "Like the Neo-Kantians, Husserl lost the ontological dimension of the phenomenon and simultaneously lost the possibility of a meditation on the limits and foundations of phenomenality" ("Kant and Husserl," p. 190).

At the same time, however, we should see another problem indicated in the

Kantian text concerning this phenomenological exchange: namely the phenomenological horizons that the critical text constantly narrates, as already evidenced in Kant's phenomenology of the domain of the natural, and which we have also seen in the assertions of the *Nun sage ich* with respect to humanity as an end in itself or the beautiful as a symbol of the good. In this sense all such "symbolizations," as we termed them, must be viewed precisely as phenomenological *explicata*. Elsewhere I will further explore the complex relation between semantics and hermeneutics that has already begun to unfold here. For now it will become even further evident that Kant himself felt obliged to explicate more fully the phenomena of the 'natural' consciousness: first with respect to the phenomenological horizons of moral consciousness, and then finally with respect to the appearance of the everyday lifeworld and its failures in civil society. And as underdetermined in this respect as all such phenomenological claims must be, they open themselves further to the counterphenomenologies and (to use Ricoeur's term) the hermeneutics of suspicion that loomed at the limits of Enlightenment, as seen in positions such as Lacan's (which we will discuss later).

23. See my "On the Agon of the Phenomenological: Intentional Idioms and the Foundations of Justification" in *Extensions*.

24. See Edmund Husserl, *Formal and Transcendental Logic*, p. 316.

25. See, for example, Jacques Lacan, "Kant with Sade."

26. For an account of the Stoic *kataleptike*, an impression that itself compels assent by its intrinsic character, see F. Sandbach, "Phantasia Kataleptike, in *Problems in Stoicism*, ed. A. A. Long (London: Althone Press, 1971), pp. 9–21. That its effect may have wide impact upon matters of nineteenth- and twentieth-century moral theory is wagered by Martha Nussbaum in her reading of Proust. See *Love's Knowledge* (New York: Oxford University Press, 1990), chap. 11. I am suggesting this retrieval is more widespread, not only in the Romantic account of the sublime but even in Kant's phenomenology of the passions. At the same time it will be necessary to deny simplistic readings of Kant (or Proust for that matter) as simply affirming a kind of masochism. As is evident in Kant's 'refiguration' of the passions, any emphasis placed on 'humiliation' in the Kantian text must be understood in the wake of the failure of the classical hierarchies, precisely as overcoming the nihilism of the modern (egoistic) accounts. In this respect it belongs in the tradition of *Kataleptike* itself, understood, to use Pierre Hadot's term, as a "dialectical exercise in which we dialogue with events which pose the question." See Pierre Hadot, *La citadelle intérieure* (Paris: Fayard, 1992), p. 101.

27. If, to use Lacan's terms, beneath all such considerations—even its recovering of the sovereign good of the ancients, not as a certain "counterweight (*contrepoids*) but so to speak, as an antiweight (*antipoids*)" ["Kant with Sade," p. 56]—there lurks the Stoic split (and desire) before the Other, this 'Other'

and reason's plunge into the transcendent remain principled. Moreover if it is true that the law here is always "something else" (*autre chose*; ibid, p. 68) it is not simply the law of desire. Indeed, pace those following Hobbes, there is no law of desire, no calculable law, or algebra of pleasure: indeed it is just because of this that any such theoretization of the Good is always symbolic. Finally when Lacan identifies this 'something else' with the 'law' of tragedy ("But the Law is something else, as has been known since Antigone") he is mistaken. If the Law is not readily identifiable with the institutions of law (and the police, as Lacan feared)—if that is, ontic law and Justice itself must be distinguished— Justice still cannot be identified through the mechanations of *caesura* alone. And it is surely Kant who recognized this. Again, whatever 'law' will be, it will be principled. This is not, pace some of Kant's critics, to accede to the claim or even the commitment that required adherence to the eternity of law: it is instead to think the inevitable jointure between concept and intuition, symbol and *symbiosis*, law and desire. Again, the analysis of this event will require both principle and interpretative.

28. See *Opus postumum*, trans. Eckart Förster and Michael Rosen (Cambridge: Cambridge University Press, 1993), pp. 200ff. Here Kant claims, for example, that "the Holy Ghost judges, punishes, and absolves through the categorical imperative of duty" (217).

29. Kant's letter to J. G. Fichte, February 2, 1792, *Philosophical Correspondence*, trans. Arnulf Zweig (Chicago: University of Chicago Press, 1967), pp. 186–87.

30. Hence the importance of narrative and myth in those after Kant. Fittingly, only the third *Kritik* will fully expound this symbolics, without however abandoning any of the earlier accomplishments. If it is decisive that we see the gesture underlying Kant's account of symbolization and its narratological retrievals, however, it must equally be paired with his refusal of fanaticism: what is at stake, as the first *Critique*'s canon concludes, cannot be mistaken for "a demonstrated dogma" (A818/B846). And as the *Religion* equally declares in this regard, admonishing hopes for inner illumination (Rel:78), such symbolization remains always "perilous" and underdetermined, undertaken, as he puts it, "in fear and trembling" (Rel:62). Kant was adamant in the *Tugendlehre* that he had distinguished the metaphysics of pure practical reason from both history and revelation, claiming in turn that *Religion with the Limits of Reason Alone* "contains only the agreement of pure practical reason with history and revelation (that they do not conflict with reason)" (Tugend:158). We have traced (without calling into question) both how complex that "agreement" is as well as the effect of that history's incursion within the analytics of pure reason—that is, the constant dialogue with the past that Kant's critical elaboration inevitably undertook.

31. For further discussion of this issue, see my "Hermeneutics and the Retrieval of the Sacred," *Extensions,* chap. 3.

32. See Cicero, *De Officiis,* I. IV.

33. See Pierre Hadot, *La citadelle intérieure,* p. 329. Indeed to speak fairly, on Hadot's account Kant would be repeating the strategy of Stoic ethics with regard to the status of the moral law itself—in affirming a reason independent of nature. Hadot here appeals to Marcus Aurelius's claim that whether or not there is providence or chaos is irrelevant: it suffices that *we* be moral to affirm the presence of univeral reason. See Hadot, pp. 169, 328. But Kant of course, perhaps more from awareness of the complexity (and the ideology) of such "proofs," cannot affirm such a view, realizing the lingering illusion to such claims. The proof of the reality of human reason, that is, freedom, is theoretically precluded: it is not the actual existence of freedom but its possibility alone that has been defended. The "act as if" of the categorical imperative must mean something different for Kant and for Marcus Aurelius, and this difference involves the intersection of philosophy as a form of life and philosophy as a form of critique, linked intrinsically to the (modern) problem of demonstration and certainty.

34. Cicero, *De Amicitia* VIII, I. iv. ff.

35. Ibid., xvi. Against the view which "limits friendship to an exact exchange of duties and kindness," Cicero replied that this "demands a far too nice and narrow calculation of friendship, to make sure that there is a precise balance between income and outgo. In my opinion true friendship is too rich, yes, too affluent for this sort of thing."

36. Hannah Arendt, "On Humanity in Dark Times: Thoughts About Lessing," trans. Clara and Richard Winston, in *Men in Dark Times* (New York: Harcourt Brace Javanovich, 1983), p. 24.

37. Ibid., p. 24.

38. Ibid., p. 25.

39. Ibid., p. 27.

40. Ibid., p. 15.

41. Hence, it might be charged, the problematic character of Arendt's nostalgia for the Greeks at this point. Arendt on the one hand had sought strongly to distinguish the dialogue that had characterized ancient friendship under the gloss of Aristotle's account of the friendship of the citizen. On the other hand, she held that the modern account of friendship, exemplified by Jasper's or Buber's account, doubtless based more upon intimacy, could not aspire to the "We" of Greek *praxis.* See Arendt, *The Life of the Mind,* p. 200. Doubtless this is true. But her account leaves out the problematic status of the "We" in modern civil society, as Kant's text attests. Here the Stoic natural love of humanity—one to which Arendt also appeals over against egoistic reductions of theoretical

modernity—has been rendered both historically and theoretically problematic (morally ideal). Hence the epistemic dialogue between the self and itself (or the friend as 'another' self, conjoined by Arendt to that of I-thou) is inextricably bound up with the problem of the "We" without being reducible to this problem (à la Fichte). Friendship, as Aristotle realized, will take various forms, including both the intimate and the political, ultimately united only by the Good itself. What he did not know perhaps were the critical problems that would befall the bond of *praxis*. Hence emerges Kant's transformation of the natural bonds of beneficence into respect. Finally, it might be wondered whether Arendt's criticism of Kantian respect, devoid of the "We," is more appropriately aimed at Heidegger's gloss on it as "Dasein's respect for itself" (BP:135).

42. See Francis Bacon, "Of Friendship," *The Works of Francis Bacon*, vol. VI, p. 441.

43. Interestingly, all that Arendt calls the mainstay of classical friendship, such as gladness taken for the other person's sake, the connection between moral love and friendship (and later tenderness), now becomes restricted to the nucleus of private life. For example, notwithstanding Kant's strict distinction between aesthetic and moral friendship, the close affinity between ethical friendship and the culmination of aesthetic friendship now appears in marriage. It is striking that, after all Kant had endowed both war and self-interest as positive forces in the development of humanity, both love of life and sexual love are moved by "a power higher than human reason" that keeps it moving forward (Anth:142–43). Despite all that characterizes Kant's Augustinian condemnation of lust, the failures of his gender analyses and his view of the passions as "cancerous sores" as the *Anthropology* puts it (Anth:133), a certain higher Augustinianism likewise returns in the contract of marriage, unifying the highest physical and the highest moral goods. This explains, for example, the 1797 *Tugendlehre*'s invocation of the third *Critique*'s lexicon for its analysis of sexual love as "truly the greatest sensuous pleasure that can be taken in an object." And yet "it is not merely sensible pleasure taken in objects that please in the mere act of contemplating them (the susceptibility to this being called taste), but pleasure from the enjoyment of another person" (Tugend:87). Moreover, while strict in distinguishing sexual from moral love, he declares the sexual to be a love *sui generis*, irreducible to other forms, and yet one which enters into "close connection" with moral love (Tugend:88). But this close connection makes such pre-Romantic views indeed the culmination of "humanity," the "way of thinking that unites well being with virtue" (Anth:143). *The Lectures on Ethics* similarly declared that "sexuality leads to a union of human beings, and in that union alone is its exercise possible" (Ethics:167). And this is not simply, it should be insisted, because it made possible the moral exercise of the *facultas sexuales*, but equally because it facilitated the union of two persons, body and soul, a reciprocal "unity of will," as Kant put it. If moral friendship "is the complete confidence of two persons in the mutual openness

of their private judgements and sensations" (Tugend:138) there is, then, indeed a sense in which Kant had surely excluded it from the public realm.

44. See OH:14.

45. See for example, Wilhelm von Humboldt, *The Limits of State Action* [1791–92], ed. J. W. Burrow (London: Cambridge University Press, 1969); or Friederich Schlegel, "Der universelle Republikanismus" [1796] in *Schriften und Fragmente* (Stuttgart: Alfred Kroner, 1956), pp. 292–301. Also see Friedrich Schleiermacher, *On Freedom* [1790–93], in *Schleiermacher: Studies and Translations*, vol. 9, trans. Albert L. Blackwell (Lampeter: The Edwin Mellen Press, 1992). We will see that Fichte too should surely be included here, though as will become evident in the analysis of the following chapter, I include him here likewise anticipating the internal conflicts that his position generates.

46. Montaigne, "Of the Education of Children," *The Complete Essays of Montaigne*, trans. Donald M. Frame (Stanford: Stanford University Press, 1965), p. 115.

47. Commentators have noted this Aristotelian backdrop to Kant's discussion. Not only does Kant directly cite Aristotle's text, "Oh my friend there is no friend," in many respects he both depends upon and (critically) rewrites it. Much can be said about this significant retrieval of Aristotle and I will return to it. In fact the *Lectures on Ethics* distinguishes, as did Aristotle, three types of friendship (based on need, taste, and moral attitude [*Gessinung*] (203). Throughout, friendship is seen to complete love by adding reciprocity (and nascently recognition) to it and thus to overcome the distinction between moral friendship and (modern) egoism or self-love (cf. *Lectures*, p. 202). Similarly, Kant, like Aristotle, links the issue of friendship to self-knowledge—although Aristotle surely would not follow him in claiming that truth itself *requires* such iterable communicability. The latter doubtless, again, attests to the incursion of modern theoretical practices and the elevation of *mathesis* on classical accounts of friendship and community, both of which are at stake in the modern conception of "objectivity."

Aristotle remained committed to the reliability of the community in this regard, whereas the moderns were led to be more suspicious. Hence friendship, which, as Kant states, "is not of heaven but of the earth," will encounter its difficulties. Friends should always be treated as if they might be potential enemies for Kant: "We must so conduct ourselves towards a friend that there is no harm done if he should turn into an enemy" (p. 208). In the case of Fichte and the problem of the *Atheismas-streit,* Kant thought of course he had encountered just such a problem. Hence the 1799 open letter on the *Wissenschaftslehre* cited another "old Italian proverb": "May God protect us from our friends, and we shall watch out for our enemies" (*Philosophical Correspondence*, p. 254). More to the point, Kant claimed a certain distance is then required for intersubjectivity, both prudentially and morally: respect itself requires this distance in order to make secure the instability of emotion. A similar distance and complication has been noted with respect to Aristotle. Neither, however, saw reason to doubt the possibility of friendship, even if Kant himself clearly delegated perfect friendship to the status of an idea. Still Kant, as has been seen, doubts the possibility of moral friendship less than he does the possibility of morality itself, as the 'black swan' claim attests. Finally, both Kant and Aristotle see friendship's fundamental importance to the notion of community. While both acknowledge that friendship itself is always between friends, and one cannot be a friend to everyone (or just anyone), both attest to a kind of friendship (the friendship of the citizen) which transcends such limitations and moreover is essential to sustaining justice (cf. *Politics* 1280bf).

48. OH:11.

49. OH:12.

3. On the Rights of Nature

1. Johann Gottfried Herder, *God: Some Conversations,* trans. F. Burkhardt (New York: Veritas Press, 1946), p. 195.

2. F. Schlegel, *Kritische Friederich Schlegel-Ausgabe,* ed. Ernst Behler (Munich: Paderborn, Vienna: Verlag Ferdinand Schoningh, 1958), xviii:396.

3. Fichte, SK:240.

4. Friedrich Schiller, *On the Aesthetic Education of Man,* trans. Reginald Snell (New York: Frederick Unger, 1971), p. 65.

5. F. W. J. Schelling, *Of Human Freedom,* trans. James Gutmann (Chicago: Open Court, 1985), pp. 97, 98.

6. Such an 'abandonment'—in effect the abandonment of the question of the meaning of Being for the meaning of meaning—has been a recent focus in a number of contexts in contemporary thought, as has been noted by Manfred Frank. Since it will be the focus of later analyses, I will not further detail the implication for semantics here, one with broad implication. See *What Is Neo-structuralism,* lecture 14. That it has implications for political philosophy arising in the wake of post-Kantian thought is likewise variously affirmed. See for example, Alain Renault, *Le system du droit: philosophie et droit dans la pensée de Fichte* (Paris: Presses Universitaires de France, 1986), p. 171.

7. Cited in Paul Friedländer, *Plato: An Introduction,* trans. Hans Meyerhoff (Princeton: Princeton University Press, 1970), p. 144.

8. Giambattista Vico, *The New Science,* trans. Thomas Goddard Bergin and Max Harold Fisch (Ithaca: Cornell University Press, 1988), §338, p. 394. Against the medievals' (or patristic) transformation of the ancient account of natural "law," which connected it with a *habitus* or *syndereis* comprised of practical principles (but grounded in the unchangeable character of divinity), the early modern's secularization of natural law refigured it mathematically. Grotius claimed in fact that even if there were no God, the dictates of right reason would obtain: "Just as God cannot cause that two and two should not make four, so he cannot cause that which is intrinsically evil be not evil." Pufendorf claimed

that natural law itself was a necessary and immutable set of laws deduced from the nature of things. As Strauss has noted, and as we have witnessed in Kant, the modern conception of natural law is closest in this regard to Cicero's account of the universal bonds of nature and community—though again decisively refigured. All of this would complicate again Aristotelian retrievals: Aristotle after all had clearly argued for a context-specific manifestation of *politeia*, even though the latter is everywhere one and the same. See NR:chap. 4; TM:318–19. As will become evident, however, even Vico's own attempts to escape the limitations of the model of mathematics in this regard were not successful.

9. Caspar David Friederich's link to "Jena mysticism which is at present insinuating itself everywhere, in art as in science, in philosophy as in religion" had been the subject of denunciation by Friederich Bailius von Ramdohr— whose neoclassical theory of landscape had in turn been criticized earlier by the Schlegels. A summary of these events can be found in Hugh Honour, *Romanticism* (New York: Harper & Row, 1979), pp. 28–29.

10. Herder, cited in Christa Karoli, *Ideal und Krise, enthusiastichen Kunstlertums in der deutschen Romantik* (Bonn: H. Bouvier, 1968), p. 7. On the relationship between Herder and Winckelmann on this matter, see ibid., pp. 48–49.

11. Johann Joachim Winckelmann, *Reflections on the Imitation of Greek Works in Painting and Sculpture* [1755], trans. Elfriede Heyer and Roger C. Norton (LaSalle, IL: Open Court, 1987), p. 5.

12. Friedrich Schlegel, "Atheneaum Fragment," *Philosophical Fragments*, trans. Peter Firchow (Minneapolis, University of Minnesota Press, 1991), §149, p. 37.

13. Friedrich Schlegel, "Dialogue on Poetry," trans. Ernst Behler and Roman Structure in *German Romantic Criticism*, ed. Leslie Wilson (New York: Continuum, 1982), p. 94.

14. For further discussion of Kant's metaphorics in this text, see for example John Sallis, *Spacings—Of Reason and Imagination* (Chicago: University of Chicago Press, 1987), chap. 1.

15. See F. W. J. Schelling, *Of Human Freedom*, p. 98.

16. This account of the significance of the image of the lived body has emerged in recent French Fichte scholarship. Here the claim is that the description of the lived body provides the schema for the application of freedom in the natural world, an image that defies the criteria of external constraints. See, for example, Renault, *Le système du droit: philosophie et droit dans la pensée de Fichte* (Paris: Presses Universitaires de France, 1986) p. 215.

17. Karl Marx, "Difference Between the Democritean and Epicurean Philosophy of Nature" in K. Marx, F. Engels, *Collected Works,* vol. I (New York: International Publishers, 1975), p. 64.

18. See Walter Benjamin, "The Work of Art in the Age of Mechanical Reproduction," in *Illuminations,* trans. Harry Zohn (New York: Schocken Books, 1969), §XIII.

19. Marquis de Sade, *The Complete Justine, Philosophy in the Bedroom, and Other Writings* [1795], trans. Richard Seaver and Austryn Wainhouse (New York: Grove Press, 1965), III:226.

20. Arne Naess, *Ecology, Community, and Lifestyle,* trans. David Rothenburg (Cambridge: Cambridge University Press, 1990), p. 51.

21. Albert Einstein, "Physics and Reality" in *Ideas and Opinions* (New York: Crown Publishers, 1954), pp. 302ff.

22. Immanuel Kant, letter to Marcus Herz, 1772, *Philosophical Correspondence,* p. 59.

23. See Ludwig Wittgenstein, *Philosophical Investigations,* p. 216; §289, p. 99.

24. See Philippe Lacoue-Labarthe, "The Caesura of the Speculative," in *Typography: Mimesis, Philosophy, Politics,* ed. Chistopher Fynsk (Cambridge: Harvard University Press, 1989), p. 214.

25. Stanley Cavell, *In Quest of the Ordinary, Lines of Skepticism and Romanticism* (Chicago: University of Chicago Press, 1988), preface.

26. Ibid., pp. 14–15.

27. See Martin Heidegger, *Schelling's Treatise on the Essence of Human Freedom,* trans. Joan Stambaugh (Athens: Ohio University Press, 1985), p. 26.

28. F. H. Jacobi, *Über die Lehre des Spinoza in Briefen an den Herrn Moses Mendelssohn, Werke* (Darmstadt: Wissenschaftsliche Buchgesellschaft, 1968); and Sigmund Freud, *Gesammelte Werke,* vol. 4, 8:211.

29. F. W. J. Schelling, "Philosophical Letters on Dogmatism and Criticism" in *The Unconditional in Human Knowledge: Four Early Essays,* trans. Fritz Marti (Lewisburg: Bucknell University Press, 1980), p. 177.

30. Schelegel, Athenaeum Fragment, *Philosophical Fragments,* §427.

31. Henri Bergson, *The Creative Mind* (New York: Philosophical Library, 1946), p. 139.

32. Edmund Husserl, *Erst Philosophie* (The Hague: Martinus Nijhoff, 1956).

33. J. G. Fichte, "The Spirit and the Letter Within Philosophy," *Early Philosophical Writings,* trans. Daniel Breazeale (Ithaca: Cornell University Press, 1988), p. 204.

34. J. G. Fichte, "Review of Aenesidemus," trans. George de Giovanni, in *Between Kant and Hegel,* trans. Giovanni and H. S. Harris (Albany: SUNY Press, 1985), pp. 149, 152.

35. See, for example, Ludwig Siep, *Anerkennung als Prinzip der praktischen Philosophie* (Freiburg: Karl Alber, 1979); Marc Richir, *Phénoménologie et institution symbolique* (Grenoble: Jerome Millon, 1988); Robert R. Williams, *Recognition: Fichte and Hegel on the Other* (Albany: SUNY Press, 1992).

36. Fichte, "Review of Aenesidemus," p. 152.

37. Novalis, *Materialen zur Encyclopaedie,* 1798–99, *Novalis Schriften Zweite Hältfe,* ed. Heilborn (Stuttgart: W. Kuhlhammer Verlag), p. 431.

38. See Luc Ferry, *Political Philosophy,* vol. 2, trans. Franklin Philip (Chicago: University of Chicago Pres, 1992), pp. 122–23.

39. Fichte's defense of the French Revolution can be found in *Beiträge zur Berichtigung der Urteile des Publicans über die Französische Revolution*, which can be found in *Fichteswerk* VI (Berlin: Walter de Gruyter & Co., 1971), pp. 39–288.

40. Ibid., p. 177.

41. Ibid., p. 184.

42. See Xavier Léon, *Fichte et son temps I* (Paris: Librairie Armand Colin, 1954), pp. 510ff.

43. Cf. CprR:128.

44. For further discussion of Fichte's account of nature and its difference vis à vis Schelling, cf. Reinhard Lauth, *Dies transzendentale Naturlehre Fichtes nach den Prinzipien der Wissenschaftslehre* (Marburg: Felix Meiner, 1984).

45. Spinoza, *Ethics*, bk III, prop. IV.

46. See Manfred Frank, *Die Unhintergehbarkeit von Individualität* (Frankfurt am Main: Suhrkamp, 1986), p. 66.

47. Fichte, "On the Spirit and the Letter in Philosophy," trans. Elizabeth Rubenstein in *German Aesthetic and Literary Criticism: Kant, Fichte, Schelling, Schopenhauer, Hegel*, ed. David Simpson (Cambridge: Cambridge University Press, 1984), p. 89.

48. Fichtes, *Nachgelassene Werke*, ed. I. H. Fichte (Bonn: A. Marcus, 1834–35), Bd. II, p. 477.

49. Schlegel, *Lucinde and the Fragments*, trans. Peter Firchow (Minneapolis: Minnesota University Press, 1971), p. 249.

50. See Gerard Ginette, *Mimologiques* (Paris: Seuil, 1976), pp. 227ff. Likewise see Philippe Lacoue-Labarthe and Jean-Luc Nancy, *The Literary Absolute*, trans. Philip Barnard and Cheryl Lester (Albany: SUNY Press, 1988), pp. 93–94.

51. See J. G. Fichte, "On the Linguistic Capacity and the Origin of Language," trans. Jere Paul Serber, in *Language and German Idealism: Fichte's Linguistic Philosophy* (New Jersey: Humanities Press, 1996). Despite the richness of Fichte's text—*inter alia* its rich discussion (again) of "the drive to realize a language" when "rational beings enter into reciprocity with one another" (124), or his discussion of *Seyn* and pure representation (131f.), Fichte's account of language doubtless remains more representationalist than expressivist. The economics of such a position are driven by the axiom that "the concept must have been present before a signification" (131)—a thesis that both the expressivist and the formalist must ultimately deny. Here the classical work of von Humboldt remains closer to the Romantics, to Schlegel and Schleiermacher than to Fichte. All of the former were in accord, after all, that *Seyn* is not simply the correlate of pure representation. We will return to this issue in the sequel to this work.

52. Fichte's complicated relation to the humanists is not only evident in the problem of education and the *humaniora*, but equally in his later writings on Machiavelli. In this regard see the presentation of Luc Ferry and Alain Renault in their translation, J. G. Fichte, *Machiavel et autres écrits philosophiques et politiques de 1806–7* (Paris: Payot, 1981), pp. 10–35.

53. F. W. J. Schelling, *On University Studies,* trans. E. S. Morgan (Athens: Ohio University Press, 1966), pp. 12–13.

54. Cf. Alain Renault, "Les deux logiques de l'idée de nation," *Cahiers de philosophie politique et juridique* 14 (1988): 7–21.

55. See Luc Ferry, *Political Philosophy,* volume II, p. 163ff.

56. Mikhail Bakhtin, *The Dialogic Imagination,* trans. Steven F. Rendell (Berkeley and Los Angeles, 1984), pp. 170–71.

57. See Ernst Kantorowicz, *The King's Two Bodies: A Study in Medieval Political Theology.*

58. Claude Lefort, "The Image of the Body and Totalitarianism" in *The Political Forms of Modern Society,* p. 302.

59. Bakhtin, *The Dialogic Imagination,* p. 169.

60. Marcus Aurelius, *Meditations* VII, 67–68.

61. Here again one would need to further examine Fichte's own political writings on the German nation, including his nationalist reading of Machiavelli.

62. See Maurice Merleau-Ponty, "An Unpublished Text by Maurice Merleau-Ponty: A Prospective of His Work," trans. Arleen B. Dallery, in *The Primacy of Perception,* ed. James B. Edie (Evanston: Northwestern University Press, 1964). For further discussion of this text see my "Merleau-Ponty, the Ethics of Ambiguity, and the Dialectics of Virtue," in *Merleau-Ponty in Contemporary Perspective,* ed. Patrick Burke and Jan Van Der Veken (Dordrecth: Kluwer, 1993).

63. Fichte, *Early Philosophical Writings,* p. 159.

64. Fichte, "The Spirit and the Letter within Philosophy," *Early Philosophical Writings,* p. 196.

65. Leo Strauss, *Spinoza's Critique of Religion* (New York: Schocken Books, 1965), p. 15.

66. See Benedict de Spinoza, *A Theological-Political Treatise,* trans. R. H. M. Elwes (New York: Dover, 1951), chap. IV.

67. Adolf Trendelenburg, *Naturrecht: Auf den Grunde der Ethik* (Leipzig: S. Hirzel, 1860), pp. 39ff.

68. Spinoza, *Ethics* II, XLIV.

69. Fichte to Schelling, 31 May 1801. F. W. J. Schelling, *Briefe und Dokumente* Bd. II, Herausgegeben von Horst Fuhrmans (Bonn: Grundmann, 1973), pp. 339–40.

70. Schelling to Fichte, 3 Oct. 1801, ibid., pp. 348–49.

71. Schelling-Hegel (authorship disputed), "On the Relationship of the Philosophy of Nature to Philosophy in General" [1802 "System Fragment"], *Between Kant and Hegel,* ed. George DiGiovani and H. S. Harris (Albany: SUNY Press, 1985), p. 372.

72. See Bradley, *Ethical Studies* (New York: Liberal Arts Press, 1951).

73. J. G. Fichte, *Addresses to the German Nation,* ed. G. A. Kelly, trans. R. F. Jones and G. H. Turnbull (New York: Harper & Brothers, 1968), second address.

74. See G. W. F. Hegel, *Philosophy of Nature,* part II of the *Encyclopaedia of*

Philosophical Sciences, trans. A. V. Miller (Oxford: Clarendon Oxford University Press), §247, 259.

75. See G. W. F. Hegel, "The Tübingen Essay of 1793: Religion ist ein...," trans. H. S. Harris, *Hegel's Development: Toward the Sunlight* (London: Oxford University Press, 1972), p. 506.

76. Hegel, *Philosophy of Nature*, §285.

77. Lucretius, *De rerum naturae*, bk. II.

78. Johann Joachim Winckelmann, "Gedanken über die Nachhamung der Griechischen Werke in der Mahlerey und Bildhauer-Kunst," *Kleinere Schriften* (Berlin: Walter Rehm, 1968), p. 29—cited, in the context of his analysis of modern nostalgia for the Greeks, in Jacques Taminiaux, "The Nostalgia for Greece at the Dawn of Classical Germany," in *Poetics, Speculation, and Judgment*, trans. Michael Gendre (Albany: SUNY Press, 1993), p. 75.

79. Hegel, *Philosophy of Nature*, §281zu.

80. Ibid., §286.

81. Strauss, *Spinoza's Critique of Religion*, p. 198: "The issue here is not between a rational and an irrational philosophy but between the unbelieving and the believing manner of experiencing the world."

82. F. W. J. Schelling, *The Philosophy of Art*, trans. Douglas W. Stott (Minneapolis: University of Minnesota Press, 1989), p. 225.

83. F. W. J. Schelling, "New Deduction of Natural Right," *The Unconditional in Human Knowledge: Four Early Essays*, p. 232.

84. This commentary is translated as *Philosophy of Poetry: The Genius of Lucretius*, trans. Wade Baskin (New York: Philosophical Library, 1959).

85. See "Becoming in Dissolution" in *Friederich Hölderlin: Essays and Letters of Theory*, trans. Thomas Pfau (Albany: SUNY Press, 1988).

86. "Concerning the Relation of the Plastic Arts to Nature" [1807], trans. Michael Bullock, in Herbert Read, *The True Voice of Feeling* (New York: Pantheon, 1953): 341–42.

87. Ibid., p. 342.

88. Ibid., p. 361n.

89. Ibid., p. 344.

90. Emerson, "Quotation and Originality" in *Letters and Social Aims* (Boston: Houghton, Mifflin, 1890), pp. 181–82.

91. Emerson, "Manners," *Emerson's Essays*, first and second series (New York: Harper & Brothers, 1926), p. 368.

92. Ibid., "Experience," pp. 309, 292.

93. Ibid., p. 320.

94. Ibid., "Nature," p. 395.

95. Ibid., "Experience," p. 315.

96. Ibid., pp. 306, 53.

97. Ibid., p. 313.

98. Ibid., "Self-Reliance," p. 50.

99. C. S. Peirce, "The Law of the Mind," *Collected Papers,* vol. 6 (Cambridge: Belknap Press/Harvard University Press, 1967), pp. 86–87.

100. Ibid.

101. Deleuze, "Lucretius and the Simulacrum," *The Logic of Sense,* trans. Mark Lester with Charles Stivale (New York: Columbia University Press, 1990), p. 279.

102. See Gilles Deleuze, *Expressionism in Philosophy: Spinoza,* trans. Martin Joughin (New York: Zone Books, 1990), chap. 16.

103. Ibid., p. 270.

104. See Leo Strauss, "What Is Political Philosophy?" in *What Is Political Philosophy and Other Studies* (Chicago: University of Chicago Press, 1959), p. 50.

105. Ibid.

106. Ibid., p. 55.

107. The same omission occurs in the work of Alasdair MacIntyre, who reduces the "tradition which Kant, Fichte, and Hegel tried but failed to universalize" to merely a "Prussian tradition in which public law and Luthern theology were blended"—see *Whose Justice? Which Rationality?* (Notre Dame, IN: University of Notre Dame Press, 1988), p. 11.

108. Deleuze, *Expressionism in Philosophy: Spinoza,* p. 259. Deleuze's citation of Strauss occurs in a footnote, p. 259n.

109. Ibid., p. 268.

110. I have further elaborated the relation between Strauss's work and the hermeneutic models that descend from German Idealism in my "Quarreling Between the Ancients and the Moderns," in *Extensions: Essays on Interpretation, Rationality, and the Closure of Modernism.*

111. In "The Vocation of Man," Fichte worries openly whether the intuition to which he appealed "is dream [and] thought—the source of all the being and all the reality I picture, the source of my own being, my own powers, and my own purposes—is the dream of that dream." See J. G. Fichte, *The Vocation of Man,* trans. Roderick M. Chisholm (Indianapolis: Bobbs-Merrill, 1956), p. 80.

112. F. W. J. Schelling, *System of Transcendental Idealism* [1800], trans. Peter Heath (Charlottesville: University Press of Virginia, 1978), p. 204.

113. See in this regard Henri Maldiney, "Pulsion et presence," *Psychanalyse à l'Université* 12, no. 5 (Dec. 1976).

114. "One may say that Kant's *Critique of Judgment* . . . has been influential up to now only on the basis of misunderstandings, a happenstance of no little significance for the history of philosophy. Schiller alone grasped some essentials in relation to Kant's doctrine of the Beautiful"—Martin Heidegger, *Nietzsche,* vol. 1, pp. 107–108.

115. Friedrich Schiller, *On the Aesthetic Education of Man,* p. 31n.

116. Ibid., p. 65.

117. Ibid., p. 64.

118. Ibid., p. 66.

119. Ibid., p. 74.

120. Ibid., p. 84. Hence, *inter alia,* the ultimate split between Fichte and Schiller. See Fichte's letter to Schiller June 27, 1795, concerning Schiller's refusal to publish the former's "On the Spirit and the Letter in Philosophy"—eventually published in his own *Philosophisches Journal* in 1800. This letter appears in translation in *Early Philosophical Writings,* p. 392. The essay "On the Spirit and the Letter . . ." is translated in *German Aesthetic and Literary Criticism: Kant, Fichte, Schelling, Schopenhauer, Hegel,* ed. David Simpson (Cambridge: Cambridge University Press, 1984). What is striking, however, is the extent to which this transformation of consciousness and desire (*Trieb*), is closely paired with the aesthetic, especially in the essay's claim that the objects of consciousness provide "an expression of its own action outside itself . . . as if in a mirror." Fichte's account of practical versus aesthetic reason provides a certain *Elementlehre* for Schelling's elevation of Leibniz and later the aesthetic itself and the resolution of transcendental antinomy.

121. See Jacques Taminiaux, "The Nostalgia for Greece at the Dawn of Classical Germany" in Taminiaux, *Poetics, Speculation, and Judgment,* trans. Michael Gendre (Albany: SUNY Press, 1993), p. 79.

122. For a fuller treatment of Schiller's work and its context, see Taminiaux's earlier book-length study, *La nostalgie de la Grèce à l'aube de l'idéalisme allemand* (The Hague: Martinus Nijhoff, 1967).

123. See again Hölderlin, "Remarks on Oedipus," *Essays and Letters on Theory,* p. 102, and Lacoue-Labarthe's essay with this title in *Typography: Mimesis, Philosophy, Politics,* ch. 3. It is important again to recall—perhaps critical at this point—Lacoue-Labarthe's devaluation of *Naturphilosophie.* As Lacoue-Labarthe also realized, the *caesura* also played a speculative role in Hölderlin. And both Schelling and Hegel would not miss it in their expositions of the Absolute. Doubtless, however, Hölderlin (and perhaps Lacoue-Labarthe after him) also depends on the speculative, even in calling the link between 'speculation' and the 'Absolute' into question: this too after all is the effect of the *caesura* of the speculative—that its 'genitive' becomes unrestrictedly an economy without reserve, belying both 'subjective' and 'objective' reduction.

124. G. W. F. Hegel, *Faith and Knowledge,* trans. Walter Cerf and H. S. Harris (Albany: SUNY Press, 1977), p. 174.

125. G. W. F. Hegel, *Philosophy of Nature,* §276.

126. See Hölderlin, Thalia Fragment, *Sämtliche Werke,* ed. F. Beisner (Stuttgart: Kohlhammer, 1985), vol. III.

127. Heidegger, *Nietzsche,* vol. 1, p. 144; Vol. 2, p. 28.

128. Walter Benjamin, *Charles Baudelaire: A Lyric Poet in the Era of High Capitalism,* trans. Harry Zohn (New York: Verso, 1973), p. 43.

129. See *English Works of Thomas Hobbes,* vol. I: *The Elements; Logic,* ch. 1.

130. Stanley Cavell, *In Quest of the Ordinary,* pp. 175–76. Here again, it might be thought, we encounter a certain Kierkegaardian defiance concerning irony

in its refusal of the concrete: that is, that irony must instead be *resolved* in the concrete. See Kierkegaard, *The Concept of Irony*, pp. 296–97. As has been noted previously, Kierkegaard's religious solution to irony misses its (hermeneutic) venture. Simple affirmations of the ordinary, again, miss its (positive) ambiguity—the moment in which it remains problematic, i.e., *Ausserordentlich*.

131. Edmund Husserl, *Formal and Transcendental Logic*, p. 240.

132. Edmund Husserl, "Foundational Investigations of the Phenomenological Origin of the Spatiality of Nature," trans. Fred Kesten in *Husserl: Shorter Work*, ed. Peter McCormick and Frederick Elliston (Notre Dame, IN: University of Notre Dame Press, 1981), p. 225, 229.

133. Martin Heidegger, "The Nature of Language," *On the Way to Language*, trans. Peter Hertz (San Francisco: Harper & Row, 1971), p. 84.

134. Martin Heidegger, "On the Being and Conception of *Physis* in Aristotle's *Physics* B, 1," trans. Thomas J. Sheehan, *Man and World* 9 (1976): p. 221.

135. Ibid., p. 222.

136. Ibid., p. 245.

137. Ibid., pp. 252–53.

138. Ibid., p. 253.

139. Max Scheler, *Formalism in Ethics and Non-Formal Ethics of Values*, trans. Manfred S. Frings and Roger L. Funk (Evanston: Northwestern University Press, 1975), p. 422.

140. Scheler, *Formalism in Ethics and Non-Formal Ethics of Values*, p. 423.

141. Jean-Paul Sartre, "Merleau-Ponty," *Situations*, trans. Benita Eisler (New York: Fawcett, 1965), p. 214.

142. Maurice Merleau-Ponty, *The Visible and the Invisible*, trans. Alphonso Lingus (Evanston: Northwestern University Press, 1968) p. 135.

143. See Merleau-Ponty, *Themes from the Lectures at the College de France*, trans. John O'Neil (Evanston: Northwestern University Press, 1970), p. 98. In addition see the notes on Merleau-Ponty's 1957–58 course, "Husserl's Concept of Nature," trans. Drew Leder in Merleau-Ponty, *Text and Dialogues*, ed. Hugh J. Silverman and James Barry, Jr. (Atlantic Highlands, NJ: Humanities Press, 1992).

144. Merleau-Ponty, *The Visible and the Invisible*, p. 81.

145. Ibid., p. 82.

146. Merleau-Ponty, *Signs*, trans. Richard C. McCleary (Evanston: Northwestern University Press, 1964), p. 178.

147. Heidegger, *Schelling's Treatise on the Essence of Human Freedom*, pp. 14ff.

148. Schelling, *System of Transcendental Idealism*, p. 211.

149. On the continuity of Schelling's thought concerning the *Abfall* and its equally perduring criticism of Fichte, see Xavier Tilliette, *Schelling: une philosophie en devenir*, vol. I (Paris: Urin, 1970), p. 487.

150. Maurice Merleau-Ponty, *The Phenomenology of Perception*, trans. and rev. by Forrest Williams and David Guerriere (London: Routledge & Kegan Paul, 1962), p. 427.

151. Ibid.

152. Heidegger, *Schelling's Treatise on the Essence of Human Freedom,* p. 158.

153. Fichte, Letter to Schelling, 3 October 1801, F. W. J. Schelling, *Briefe und Dokumente* Bd. II, pp. 346–47.

154. Vico, *The New Science,* section 349. While Vico's argument may seem to be "anti-Hobbesian," insofar as it elevates history over mathematics, the reduction of Being to historical enactment, modeled upon geometrical construction is one that Hobbes also affirms:

> The science of every subject is derived from a pre-cognition of the causes, generation, and construction of the same; and consequently where the causes are known, there is place of demonstration, but not where the causes are to seek for. Geometry therefore is demonstrable, for the lines and figures from which we reason are drawn and described by ourselves; and civil philosophy is demonstrable, because we make the commonwealth ourselves. (See *The English Works of Thomas Hobbes,* vol. 7, p. 184)

For an account of this legacy of Hobbes's work in German Idealism, see Jacques Taminiaux, "Hegel and Hobbes," trans. James Decker and Shaun Gallagher in *Dialectic and Difference,* ed. James Decker and Robert Crease. I have further discussed Fichte's mathematical analogue in my "On the De-lineation of the Visible," *Extensions,* chap. 7.

155. Heidegger, Appendix to *Schelling's Treatise on the Essence of Human Freedom,* p. 168.

156. Merleau-Ponty, *The Visible and the Invisible,* p. 33

157. Martin Heidegger, "Excerpt from the Manuscripts in Preparation for the Seminar on Schelling, Summer Semester, 1941," Appendix to *Schelling's Treatise on the Essence of Human Freedom,* p. 188.

158. Heidegger, "On the Being and Conception of *Physics* in Aristotle's *Physics B, 1,*" p. 224. On the importance of the *Ethics* in the early Heidegger see for example his "Phenomenological Interpretations with Respect to Aristotle: Indication of the Hermeneutical Situation," trans. Michael Bauer, *Man and World* 25 (1992): pp. 355–93.

159. Ibid., p. 235.

160. Ibid., p. 240; cf. *Physics* 193a

161. Hegel, *Philosophy of Nature,* §246.

162. Heidegger, *Schelling's Treatise on the Essence of Human Freedom,* pp. 186–87.

163. Spinoza, *Theologico-Political Treatise,* I. 61.

164. Giambattisto Vico, *The New Science,* p. 116.

165. Heidegger, "On the Being and Conception of *Physics* in Aristotle's *Physics B, 1,*" pp. 228–29.

166. See, for example, Heidegger's discussion of decision and its highest forms, "enthusiasm, heroism, and faith," in *Schelling's Treatise on the Essence of Human Freedom,* p. 157.

167. Martin Heidegger, *Parmenides,* trans. André Schuwer and Richard Rojcewicz (Bloomington: Indiana University Press, 1992), p. 95.

168. Heidegger, LH:238–39; *Parmenides,* p. 137.

169. See, for example, Savigny, *Vom Beruf unserer Zeit für Gesetzgebung und Rechtswissenschaft* (Heidelberg, 1814), pp. 11–13. This work receives considerate analyses in Robert Legros, "La Metaphysique Romantique," *Phénoménologie et politique: Mélanges offerts à Jacques Taminiaux,* ed. B. Stevens (Bruxelles: Ousia, 1989), p. 433.

170. As Lefort has rightly realized the proclamation of human rights both exceeds and abandons appeals to human essence, beyond both naturalism and historicism, divided between individual and universal 'natures'. It is both 'speculative' and empirical at once. The survival of the public space requires precisely the preservation of this ambiguity. See "Human Rights and the Welfare State" in *Democracy and Political Theory,* pp. 37–38.

171. See Max Scheler, *Gessammelte Werke,* vol. 9, "Späte Schriften [Aus Kleineren Manuskripten zu *Sein und Zeit*]," herausgegeben von Manfred S. Frings (München: Franke, 1976), p. 297.

172. Hence unlike recent French scholarship attempting to align Merleau-Ponty and Fichte (e.g., Ferry), we regard him as in this respect closer to Schelling, as commentators such as Xavier Tilliette realized. See Tilliette's *Merleau-Ponty: ou, la mesure de l'homme* (Paris: Seghers, 1970), and *Schelling: une philosophie en devenir* (Paris: Vrin, 1970). In the latter, the later work of Merleau-Ponty is seen as continuing the legacy of Schelling's "hermeneutiqué [qui] se forment au contact" (vol. II, p. 422).

173. Maurice Merleau-Ponty, *Sense and Non-Sense,* trans. Hubert L. Dreyfus and Patricia Allen Dreyfus (Evanston: Northwestern University Press, 1964), p. 103.

174. J. G. Fichte, *Beitrage zur Berichtigung der Urtheile des Publicums über dies französische Revolution* (Frankfurt: Ulstein, 1973), p. 107.

175. Compare Søren Kierkegaard, *Fear and Trembling,* p. 57.

176. Schelling, *Of Human Freedom,* p. 97.

177. Heidegger, *Schelling's Treatise on the Essence of Human Freedom,* p. 179.

178. See in this regard, Marc Richir's introduction to the French translation of Schelling's *Philosophie de la mythologie,* trans. Alain Pernet (Grenoble: Jerome Millon, 1994).

179. Heidegger, *Schelling's Treatise on the Essence of Human Freedom,* p. 146.

180. Granted the disequilibrium of Heidegger's account of origins, beyond the plurality of narrative, it is perhaps not surprising then to see the failure of Fichte's nationalist discourse return in the instrumentalism of Heidegger's own *Rektorataddress.*

181. Cf. A646/B674. On the role of the transition from phlogiston theory to the chemistry of Lavosier in Kant's work, see Michael Friedman, *Kant and the Exact Sciences* (Cambridge: Harvard University Press, 1992), pp. 264–65. That

reflective judgment and this transition itself concerning the interrogation (*befragen*) of nature could not be reduced to this event was evident from the outset, however; the latter conflates regulative and constitutive accounts and loses the *Wechsel* between ideal and nature, as we have seen.

182. Compare in this regard Arne Naess's "Pluralistic Theorizing in Physics and Philosophy," *Danish Yearbook of Philosophy*, vol. 1 (1964), a work whose theoretical questions emerge in dialogue with Popper and Feyerabend. The same is doubtless true of Michel Serres's recent attempts to "romanticize" the "contract" with nature. See *Le contrat natural* (Paris: Editions François Bouin, 1990).

183. An example of such reliance is to be found in the *locus classicus* of such considerations, Rachel Carson's *Silent Spring* (Cambridge, MA: Houghton-Mifflin, 1962). While the concluding chapter itself concludes in decrying the arrogance of the figure of "the control of nature," it does so precisely having delineated the development of the science of biological control and the alternatives it opens up.

184. For an analysis of the history of such attempts, see Roderick Frazier Nash, *The Rights of Nature: A History of Environmental Ethics* (Madison: The University of Wisconsin Press, 1989), chap. 6, "Liberating Nature."

185. Arne Naess, "Spinoza and Ecology," *Speculum Spinozanum* (Boston: Routledge & Paul, 1977), p. 418.

186. J. G. Fichte, "The Spirit and the Letter within Philosophy," *Early Philosophical Writings*, p. 207.

187. See for example Michele Le Doeff, "L'homme et la nature dans les jardins de la science," *Revue Internationale de Philosophie*, no. 159 (1986).

188. Hence it becomes apparent how recent attempts to contrast "the radical antimodernism" of the ecology movement and the "humanism" of the modern republican tradition are overly abstract, missing the 'tradition' that united both from the start of the modern. See, for example, Luc Ferry, *Le nouvel ordre écologique* (Paris: Grasset, 1992).

189. I allude once more to Heidegger's own allusion to Seneca on care, not only to underline the lingering presence of Stoicism in Fichte's account but also the presence of the Stoics themselves in this itinerary. See M. Aurelius III. 13, and the discussion of Victor Goldschmidt, *Le système stoicien et l'idée de temps* (Paris: Vrin, 1969), "Harmonie et implication rèciproque," p. 27.

190. See Luc Ferry, *Political Philosophy*, vol. II, pp. 67–68.

191. Maurice Merleau-Ponty, *Phenomenology of Perception*, p. 432.

192. Kant, *The Metaphysical Elements of Justice*, trans. John Ladd (Indianapolis: Bobbs-Merrill, 1965), p. 112.

193. Merleau-Ponty, *Sense and Non-Sense*, p. 102.

194. A whole tradition, beginning with immediately post-Kantian thinkers, would then claim the importance of Spinoza over Kant in this regard. This tradition continued after Trendelenburg, to Cohen, all the way to Alexis

Philolenko. See for example, the latter's discussion in *L'oeuvre de Kant II* (Paris: Vrin, 1972), p. 234. But on this reading Kant's shortcomings at the same time occur only by a certain "advance" that demonstrates the dialectic and the withdrawal of the sacred—or of transcendence—that subtends pure ethics. If, as has been seen, Spinoza had seen both the problem of interpretation and the 'analogical' status of law, he likewise identified the necessity underlying both with the divine—insofar as both "express" the latter. See *A Theological-Political Treatise*, ch. 4. Hence, again, the complication of Spinoza's own naturalism.

195. See Martin Heidegger, "On Time and Being" in *On Time and Being*, trans. Joan Stambaugh (New York: Harper & Row, 1972), p. 23.

4. Hegel, the "Plasticity" of Character, and the Prose of the World

1. F. W. J. Schelling, *The Philosophy of Art*, trans. Douglas W. Stott (Minneapolis: University of Minnesota Press, 1989), p. 271.

2. Ibid.

3. In addition to Schelling's own 1796 "New Deduction of Natural Right" see, for example, Hegel's essay on *Natural Law* (1802). The works of Kant, Humboldt, Maimon, and Fichte on this topic equally belong to this archive.

4. Schelling, *The Philosophy of Art*, p. 270.

5. Emerson, *Representative Men*, (Boston: Houghton-Mifflin & Co., 1891), p. 195.

6. Ibid., p. 241.

7. Johann Gottfried Herder, "Shakespeare," translated in *The Origins of Modern Critical Thought: German Aesthetic and Literary Criticism from Lessing to Hegel*, trans. Joyce P. Crick, ed. David Simpson (Cambridge University Press, 1988), pp. 80–81.

8. Cf. Aristotle, *Poetics*, 1448.

9. See Friedrich Hölderlin's letter No. 172 (to his brother, Jan. 1, 1799) in *Friedrich Hölderlin: Essays and Letters on Theory*, p. 137.

10. David Hume, *A Treatise of Human Nature* (Oxford: Oxford University Press, 1968), p. 575.

11. See Johann Heinrich Lambert, *Semiotik*, BdI, *Philosophische Schriften*, (Hildeshein: Georg Olms, 1965). The link between characterization and semiotics—i.e. characteristic—however, is by no means without precedent. That character is a spiritual power and "the nature of a sign" can be found, for example, in Aquinas' *Summa Theologicae* III 63. 3, who takes it over from Albert the Great and Bonaventure. What is specific to modern 'characteristics'—and Kant's use of the term reflects this—is its link with mathematics and the *ars analytica*, where Leibniz's account of characteristic lies in the background. See Friederich Kaulbach, "Der Begriff des Charakters in der Philosophie von Leibniz," *Kant-Studien*, 57 (1966), pp. 126–41.

12. Cicero, *De Officiis,* I. XXXI. There may well be Heraclitean origins to the figure of the world stage. See Heraclitus fragments D-K 118, 89.

13. Diogenes Laertius, *Lives of Eminent Philosophers,* vol. II, trans. R. D. Hicks (Cambridge: Harvard University Press, 1965) VII, 160 (citing Ariston).

14. See the discussion of Philippe Lacoue-Labarthe, "La cesure du speculatif" in *L'Imitation des modernes* (Paris: Galilee, 1986).

15. Cicero, *De Officiis,* I. XXVII.

16. The 'theatricality' of expression as characteristic occurs in a manner Shakespeare himself affirms in a passage from *Twelfth Night,* one cited by the O. E. D. as exemplifying a now-obsolete usage of "character" in terms of "the face of features as betokening moral qualities": "I will believe thou had a mind that suits with this thy fair and outward character" (I:ii:51).

17. See Jean-Paul Sartre, *Being and Nothingness,* pp. 142–43. For further discussion of this archive, see my "Reason and the Face of the Other," *Journal of the American Academy of Religion* LIV, no. 1.

18. Hume, *Treatise,* p. 608.

19. See Hegel's *The Science of Logic,* vol. I, book II, section II (WdL:479), which includes Hegel's attempt to overcome the Kantian distinction between the phenomenal and the noumenal and its accompanying epistemic commitments.

20. See Friedrich Schlegel, "Athenaeum Fragments" §418, *Philosophical Fragments,* pp. 83–84.

21. Friedrich Schlegel, "Lessing (Vom kombinatorischen Geist)," in *Schriften und Fragmente,* ed. E. Behler (Stuttgart: Kroner, 1956).

22. See von Humboldt, "Das achtzehnte Jahrhundert," *Gesammelte Schriften,* Bd. II hrsg. von der Königlichen Preussischen Akademie der Wissenschaften (Berlin, 1903). A monograph detailing this project's emergence from von Humboldt's classical studies is Youngkun Tschong, *Charakter & Bildung* (Würzburg: Königshausen und Neumann, 1991).

23. Jean Paul's own discussion of character occurs in his *Horn of Oberon: Jean Paul's School for Aesthetics,* trans. Margaret R. Hale (Detroit: Wayne State University Press, 1973), pp. 158–59. It is obvious however that Jean Paul had already lost the fertility in Schlegel's (and von Humboldt's) task, since for him the matter is fully an aesthetic one, i.e., a matter of "technical presentation." The claim that the stress on individuality misses the role of judgment, the background of concept formation and hence succumbs to psychologism in beginning simply from the standpoint of the spectator can be found in a number of contemporary treatments. Perhaps most persuasively it can be found in Alasdair MacIntyre's discussion of Shaftesbury and the English moralists, who, as has become apparent, played a significant role in the Romantic's discussion of genius. I am proposing instead that both arguments must still be seen against the complexity of their Hobbesean backdrop. See Alasdair MacIntyre: *A Short History of Ethics* (New York: Collier Books, 1966), p. 163. Schlegel's discussion must be under-

stood as emerging from (and transforming) Kant's (and perhaps Hume's) own criticism of Hutchinson and Shaftesbury: the point is, beyond all (dogmatic) metaphysics of a 'moral' or common sense, to articulate how ethics is possible.

24. See Frederich Schlegel, "Critical Fragments," §9, 37, 42; *Philosophical Fragments,* pp. 2–5.

25. Schlegel, "On Philosophy," cited in Philippe Lacoue-Labarthe and Jean-Luc Nancy, *The Literary Absolute,* p. 116, whose account I follow at this point.

26. Schlegel, "Athenaeum Fragments," §310, *Philosophical Fragments,* pp. 61–62.

27. See Hans Eichner, "Friederich Schlegel's Theory of Literary Criticism" in *Romanticism Today,* ed. Reinhold Grimm (Bonn: Inter Nationes, 1973), pp. 17–26.

28. Schlegel, "Critical Fragments," §83 and §78, *Philosophical Fragments,* p. 10.

29. See my "On the Rationality of the Fragment" in *Extensions: Essays on Interpretation, Rationality, and the Closure of Modernity* (Albany: SUNY Press, 1992).

30. Friedrich Schlegel, "Lessing" (*Vom Wesen der Kritik*), p. 54.

31. Schlegel, *Philosophical Fragments,* Ideas, §36, p. 97.

32. Schlegel, *Philosophical Fragments,* "Ideas," §60, p. 99.

33. Schlegel, Ibid., "Ideas," §49, p. 98.

34. See, for example, H. S. Harris, *Hegel's Development* (Oxford University Press, 1972), pp. 272–73.

35. It could be argued however that this was precisely the fecundity of Aristotle's doctrine of the mean, an indeterminacy which demanded the exploration of the singular—or in Hegel's term, an indeterminacy which was precisely the "rational impulse towards what is good" (HP:II.204).

36. Ludwig Wittgenstein, *Culture and Value,* trans. Peter Winch (Chicago: University of Chicago Press, 1980), p. 84.

37. On the elevation of family as ethical substance, see PR:§158ff and for further discussion of the mother as the genius of the child, PS:§405. Finally, compare Schlegel's claim that "the family is pure poetry." See "Ideas," §152, *Philosophical Fragments,* p. 37.

38. Boethius, "De duabus naturis et una persona Christi," III, *Patrologiae Latina,* ed. Migne, vol. LXIV, 13430.

39. See F. Hölderlin's discussion of the rhythm of tragic representation, "Remarks on 'Oedipus'" in *Essay and Letters on Theory,* trans. Thomas Pfau (Albany: SUNY Press, 1988), and Hegel's discussion of the rhythm of the speculative proposition (Phen:38). Hölderlin's account of tragedy as a metaphor of intellectual intuition should be kept strictly in mind. Its antecedents in Aristotle's *perpeteia* can be found in chapter 11 of the *Poetics.*

40. See Theodor Litt, "Hegel's Begriff des 'Geistes' und das Problem der Tradition," *Studium Generale* (June 1951): pp. 311–21.

41. Aristotle, *Politics*, 1235.

42. See Aristotle, *Rhetoric*, I:15.

43. Hooker, *Ecclesiastical Polity*, I:10.

44. For Hegel's gloss on the problem of conceptualization and its difficulties concerning determination, categorization, plurality, and alterity, "pure difference," see for example Phen:§235ff and WdL:409ff.

45. Novalis, *"Logological Fragments,"* trans. Alexander Gelley, in *German Romantic Criticism*, ed. Leslie Wilson (New York: Continuum, 1982), p. 71.

46. See *Poetics* 1448b, *Rhetoric* 1371a-b.

47. I borrow these terms, not without altering them, from Paul Ricoeur. See *Time and Narrative*, vol. I, trans. Kathleen McLaughlin and David Pellauer (Chicago: University of Chicago Press, 1984), chap. 2. Ricoeur's concurrence with Hegel should likewise be noted: "Whereas Aristotle had subordinated characters to plot, taken as the encompassing concept in relation to the incidents, characters, and thoughts, in the modern novel we see the notion of character overtake that of plot, becoming equal with it, then finally surpass it entirely" (vol. II, p. 9). Ricoeur's account of this 'surpassing' nonetheless in the end falls short, *grounded* still in the category of action, and ultimately intention.

48. Hence emerges the argument concerning 'unhappy consciousness' against Novalis (Aesth:159) and perhaps even more importantly, against Solger, crucially as the latter enters into the development of the argument of the *Philosophy of Right*'s transgression of the claims of conscience (PR:101).

49. Compare Schlegel's account, in which Shakespeare not only stands at the center of Romantic art, and is more correct and systematic than any other modern poet, but is so "often by a parody of the letter and an irony on the spirit of romantic drama." The result, however, he concurs, is "the most sublime and complete individuality." See "Athenaeum Fragments," §247, §253, *Philosophical Fragments*, pp. 52–54.

50. See Walter Benjamin, "The Destructive Character," in *Reflections* (New York: Schocken Books, 1986), p. 302, Hölderlin, "Becoming in Dissolution," in *Essays and Letters on Theory*, p. 97.

51. Bakhtin, *The Dialogic Imagination*, trans. Caryl Emerson and Michael Holquist (Austin: University of Texas Press, 1981), p. 38.

52. Ibid., p. 291.

53. Ibid., p. 39.

54. Ibid., p. 31.

55. Ibid., p. 10.

56. In his 1823 address elevating the task of translation in the exposition of the rational, Schleiermacher similarly appealed to "the living power of the individual that creates new forms by means of the plastic material of language." See Friederich Schleiermacher, "On the Different Methods of Translator," trans. André Lefevre in *German Romantic Criticism*, ed. Leslie Wilson (New York: Continuum, 1982), p. 6. For Schleiermacher, this appeal to the foreign (*das Fremde*) at stake

in translation—like the individuality it involved—remained insurpassable. Here the dialectics (and the ironies) of the *Athenaeum* remain intact.

57. Søren Kierkegaard, *Fear and Trembling*, p. 59.

58. Edmund Burke, *Considerations*, p. 149.

59. Burke, *Considerations*, p. 75.

60. First Introduction to the *Critique of Judgment*, trans. James Haden (Indianapolis: Bobbs-Merrill, 1965), p. 18.

61. The account of dialectic as "the science of all sciences" represents dialectic's elevated role in the *Trivium*. These (representative) citations are from Rhabanus Maurus, *Education of the Clergy*, trans. F. V. N. Painter in *Readings in the History of Education*, ed. Ellwood P. Cubberly (Boston: Houghton Mifflin, 1920), p. 107.

62. Friedrich Nietzsche, *The Birth of Tragedy*, trans. Walter Kaufmann (Vintage/Random House, 1967), §13.

63. Ibid., §14.

64. We should deny the claim that tragedy (and irony) had simply been effaced from philosophy. As is often noted, Aristotle's concern in the *Ethics* with *arete* is from beginning to end a concern that measures itself against the problem of tragic fate or bad luck. Moreover the undeterminacy of tragic action finds itself mirrored in the multiplicity that metaphysics confronts in inventing the interpretive response of the *pros hen*, that Being can be said in many different ways: both are ventures, after all, irreducible to 'certainty' or logical schematism as much as they are irreducible to the opposite, simple agonistic as such. The itinerary of the fragment that we have followed through Schlegel doubtless acknowledged both—as did the recognition of hermeneutics as a general problem of understanding. While Hegel saw Socratic irony to be an exploration of the possible, "the development of the universal from the concrete case—and Socrates himself to be a thinker of the 'prosaic' world who proceeds" by going to the workplaces of tailors and shoemakers and entering in to discourses with them as also with youths and old men, Sophists, statesmen, and citizens of all kinds—irony itself, Hegel claimed, fell short of *method*. See HP:397-98.

65. Kant, "Idea for a Universal History" [1784] in *On History*, pp. 11–12.

66. Ibid., p. 16.

67. F. W. J. Schelling, "Philosophical Letters on Dogmatism and Criticism" in *The Unconditional in Human Knowledge*, trans. Fritz Marti (Lewisburg: Bucknell University Press, 1980), p. 193.

68. Hölderlin, *Essays & Letters on Theory*, Letter no. 172.

69. See Luce Irigaray, "The Eternal Irony of the Community," in *Speculum of the Other Woman*, trans. Gillian C. Gill (Ithaca: Cornell University Press, 1985), p. 217.

70. Ibid.

71. Ralph Waldo Emerson, *The Conduct of Life* (Boston: Houghton Mifflin, 1890), p. 183.

72. Ibid., p. 182.

73. Ibid., p. 184. Elsewhere Emerson would similarly declare of this event that it too was Shakespearean: "Now, literature, philosophy and thought, are Shakespearized," and the nineteenth century's "speculative genius is a sort of living Hamlet." *Representative Men,* p. 195.

74. Ibid.

75. Bakhtin, *The Dialogic Imagination,* p. 39.

76. Emerson, "Lecture on the Times" (Dec. 1841), in *Nature, Addresses, and Lectures* (Boston: Houghton, Mifflin, 1890), p. 249.

77. Hans Robert Jauss, *Aesthetic Experience and Literary Hermeneutics,* trans. Michael Shaw, (Minneapolis: University of Minnesota Press, 1982), p. 141.

78. Aristotle, *Nicomachean Ethics,* 1155b.

79. See especially "The Spirit of Christianity and its Fate" in Hegel, *Early Theological Writings,* trans. T. M. Knox (Philadelphia: University of Pennsylvania, 1981).

80. See Friedrich Nietzsche, *Will to Power,* trans. Walter Kaufman and R. J. Hollingdale (New York: Vintage Books, 1968), §849:

> It is an amazing comedy at which we have only now learned to laugh, which we only now see: that the contemporaries of Herder, Winckelmann, Goethe, and Hegel claimed to have *rediscovered the classical* ideal—and at the same time Shakespeare!

81. See Philippe Lacoue-Labarthe, *Heidegger, Art and Politics,* pp. 84–85. Such an immanent connection between *physis, nomos,* and *ergein,* he rightly argues, became an object of criticism for Heidegger in his later discussions of the *Gestell.*

82. Cf. Hegel's own discussion of Creuzer's symbolics (Aesth:310f).

83. The term 'pantragicism' is taken from Hyppolite: see Jean Hyppolite, *Introduction à la Philosophie de l'Histoire de Hegel* (Paris: M. Rivière, 1948), p. 78. For an analysis of the complex interface between Christian theology and Hegel's account of the tragic, centered on the Natural Law, see Jacques Taminiaux, *Naissance de la philosophie hégélienne de l'État* (Paris: Payot, 1984). The impact of such syntheses even in the physiognomies of Nietzsche's *grand style* should not be missed:

> To "give style" to one's character—a great and rare art! It is practiced by those who survey all the strengths and weaknesses of their nature and then fit them into an artistic plan until every one of them appears as art and reason and even weaknesses delight the eye. Here a large mass of second nature has been added, there a piece of original nature has been removed—both times through long practice and daily work at it. . . . It will be the strong and domineering natures that enjoy their finest gaiety and perfection under a law of their own. (Friedrich Nietzsche, *The Gay Science,* bk. IV, §290)

Kierkegaard's account of personal virtue, on the other hand, had decried the metaphysics of such self-creation—again, in arguing against the Romantic's conception of ironic character:

> By living poetically irony understood something other, something more, than what this signifies to every rational person with some regard for human being, some sense for what is original in man. It did not understand by this the artistic seriousness which lends assistance to the divine in man, which listens hushed and silently to the voice of what is unique in individuality, disclosing to it its movements so as to predominate in the individual, and so cause the whole of individuality to develop harmoniously into a plastic shape [*plastisk*] culminating in itself. It did not understand by this what the pious Christian understands when he becomes conscious of the fact that life is an upbringing, an education, which, to be sure, is not going to make him other than he is. . . . It is one thing poetically to produce oneself, quite another to allow oneself to be poetically produced. [(Kierkegaard, *The Concept of Irony*, p. 297) Here I cite the more literal translation of Lee M. Capel (Bloomington: Indiana University Press, 1968).]

Against these (strict) antinomies, we have suggested, the 'hermeneutics' of character that emerges from Schlegel, von Humboldt, and Schleiermacher is the exploration of their possibility without simply denying either—and without as Kierkegaard believes, requiring that either interpretation or irony would deny or "overcome historical actuality" (ibid., p. 296).

84. *History of Ancient Art,* bk. IV, ch. I. "The conception of high or ideal beauty is . . . not equally clear to all, and one might suppose, from remarks made on the Ideal, that it can be formed only in the mind. By the Ideal is to be understood merely the highest possible beauty of the whole figure which can hardly exist in nature in the same high degree in which it appears in some statues" (49).

85. Again, see Cicero, *De Officiis:* I. XXVIIff.

86. I take these terms from Philippe Lacoue-Labarthe, see *Heidegger, Art and Politics,* p. 81. Still, one must not equate the two: the figural, that is could not be transformed into pure malleability (*techne*)—which is doubtless why Lacoue-Labarthe immediately argues that "the subject of imitation" must be thought ek-statically, "This is precisely what Heideggerean *Da-sein* 'is'" (82).

87. Schlegel, "Athenaeum Fragments," §58, *Philosophical Fragments,* p. 25.

88. Leo Strauss, "Restatement on Xenophon's *Hiero*" in Leo Strauss, *On Tyranny: Including the Strauss-Kojève Correspondence,* ed. Victor Gourevitch and Michael S. Roth (New York: The Free Press, 1991), p. 194.

89. Alexander Kojève, "Tyranny and Wisdom," in Strauss, *On Tyranny,* p. 154. See Kojève, *Equisse d'une phenomenologie du droit* (Paris: Gallimard, 1981), part 1.

90. Aristotle, *Nicomachean Ethics,* 1155b; 1171a.

91. Kojève, "Tyranny and Wisdom," p. 152.

92. Kojève, Letter to Strauss, October 29, 1953, in *On Tyranny,* p. 261.

93. See, for example, Ludwig Siep, "Der Kampf um Anerkennung: zu Hegels Auseinandersetzung mit Hobbes in den Jenaer Schriften," *Hegel-Studien* 9 (1974): pp. 155ff.

94. Kojève, "Tyranny and Wisdom," p. 167.

95. Ibid., p. 154.

96. Strauss, "Restatement on Xenophon's *Hiero,*" ibid., p. 196.

97. See Kojève letter to Strauss, July 1, 1957, ibid, pp. 280–81. The problem here, and it is doubtless anything but accidental that it arises in relation to the problem of friendship, is the question of community (*Koinonia*) and the status of epistemic certainty with respect to it.

98. Leo Strauss, *The Political Philosophy of Hobbes,* p. 54.

99. Ibid., p. 55.

100. Ibid., pp. 57–58. It is worth noting that this analysis ends with a footnote in which Strauss states that "Mr. Alexandre Kojevitkoff and the writer intend to undertake a detailed investigation of the connexion between Hegel and Hobbes."

101. See Karl-Heinz Ilting, "Hegels Auseinandersetzung mit der aristotelischen Politik," *Philosophisches Jahrbuch,* vol. 71 (1963–64), pp. 38–58.

102. Strauss, *The Philosophy of Hobbes,* p. 88, citing *The English Works of Francis Bacon,* ed. Spedding and Ellis, vol. VI, p. 438.

103. Ibid., p. 88.

104. See Hannah Arendt, *Lectures on Kant's Political Philosophy,* ed. Ronald Beiner (Chicago: University of Chicago Press, 1982), p. 37.

105. See George Herbert Mead, *Mind, Self, and Society from the Standpoint of a Behaviorist* (Chicago: University of Chicago Press, 1934), pp. 260ff. This interface between Hegel and Mead has been the subject of a number of recent analyses by members of the Frankfurt school (e.g., Habermas, Honneth), where, however, Mead's linguistic community becomes construed through Wittgenstein. I am arguing that such assimilation loses both the complication and the fertility of its interpretation, especially prominent in the status of individuality that results.

106. Compare on the other hand Adorno's denial of this risk:

> If you focus sociological attention on Shakespeare, at least one thing becomes clear, and that is that he differed from Francis Bacon. Shakespeare was a dialectical dramatist who, unlike Bacon, looked at the *theatrum mundi* from the perspective of the victims of progress. (See T. W. Adorno, *Aesthetic Theory,* p. 361)

As has become evident, Adorno perhaps missed in the end the dialectic at stake: both the extension of Shakespeare's 'modernism' but equally the risk—and the fragmentation—which underwrites Bacon's attempt. That is, we have insisted on viewing the experience that accompanies Bacon's experimentalism—and the problem of application to which its turn to history gives rise—as arising out of the experience of detraditionalization itself, i.e., the tragedy of the past. On the other hand, as Schlegel notes, an account that no longer restricted tragedy to the past would require both a "liberal mentality" and the republican idea. See "Athenaeum Fragment," §138, *Philosophical Fragments,* pp. 35–36. We are reminded again of Castoriadis's recognition, too often missing in post-Enlightenment encounters with 'Greece', that the Athenians, not without irony, created *both* tragedy *and* democracy. See Cornelius Castoriadis, "The Greek *Polis* and the Creation of Democracy," in *Philosophy, Politics, Autonomy,* ed. David Ames Curtis (New York: Oxford University Press, 1991), chap. 5.

107. These ideological investments are doubtless complex. Compare for example Alasdair MacIntyre's characterization of the accounts of Kant, Fichte, and Hegel as (failed) attempts to universalize "the whole Prussian tradition in which public law and Luthern theology were blended," in *Whose Justice? Which Rationality?* (Notre Dame, IN: University of Notre Dame Press, 1988), p. 11. At the same time, their attempts remained invested in the ideology of universality and objectivity itself. As Mary Hesse has put it, we have yet to unravel all that was at stake in this new notion of objectivity. In both regards the ventures at stake remained hermeneutic, interpretive, rational, and doubtless ideological. The problem again is grasping the relation between principle and narrative.

108. For further discussion of this issue see my "Heidegger, Rationality, and the Critique of Judgment," *Review of Metaphysics* XLI no. 3, (1988).

109. See Aristotle, *Nicomachean Ethics* 1102b, *Rhetoric* 1374a.

110. See Pierre Hadot, *Philosophy as a Way of Life,* trans. Michael Chase (Chicago: University of Chicago Press, 1995).

111. See Kierkegaard, *Fear and Trembling,* preface.

112. See Martin Heidegger, *Hegel's Concept of Experience,* trans. Kenley Royce Dove (New York: Harper & Row, 1970), pp. 95, 144–45.

113. Gadamer provides a history of the concept *Erlebnis* in TM:64ff.

114. See Martin Heidegger, "Phenomenological Interpretations with Respect to Aristotle: Indication of the Hermeneutical Situation," trans. Michael Baur, *Man and World* 25 (1992). "The confusing ambiguity of the word 'life' and its application must not become grounds for simply getting rid of the word," p. 361. Instead the ambiguities themselves, traced to "Greek-Christian interpretations of human Dasein" in this important 1922 document, became explicated through the basic notion of caring (*Sorge*), a matter to which I will return in further analysis.

115. Compare Hadot's analysis of Plotinus's position in his *Plotinus or The Simplicity of Vision,* trans. Michael Chase (Chicago: University of Chicago Press, 1993), chap. 1. The text in question again, is the *Enneads* I, 6 {9} in which Plotinus compares "inner vision" to work of the sculptor:

> How can one see the beauty of a good soul? Withdraw into yourself and look.
> If you do not as yet see beauty within you, do as does the sculptor of a statue

that is to be beautified. . . . Never stop working at the statue until the sacred radiance of virtue shines through it.

The remnants of this Plotinian 'vision' of the Idea are doubtless at stake in German neoclassicism following Winckelmann.

116. Aristotle, *Nicomachean Ethics* 1140b.

117. See Michel Foucault, *The Care of the Self,* vol. 3 of *The History of Sexuality,* trans. Robert Hurley (New York: Vintage Books, 1988) and Pierre Hadot, "Reflections on the Idea of the Cultivation of the Self," *Philosophy as a Way of Life,* chap. 7. Hadot rightly argues against the identification of the ancients' account of joy with (modern) reductivist views of pleasure (and worries, in Foucault's case, about the reduction of ethics to aesthetics, or even worse, to a new form of 'dandyism'). We have witnessed Kant's retrieval of the Stoics in this regard and Hadot again confirms it:

> If the Stoics insist on the word *gaudium*/"joy," it is precisely because they refuse to introduce the principle of pleasure into moral life. For them, happiness does not consist in pleasure, but in virtue itself, which is it own reward. Long before Kant, the Stoics strove jealously to preserve the purity of intention of the moral consciousness. (p. 207)

It is also true that unlike the transcendence revealed in the ancients' account of *gaudium* and *Eudaimonia,* we have traced the problematic status of their metaphysics, politics, and ethics within modern theoretics.

118. Heidegger, "Phenomenological Interpretations with Respect to Aristotle," p. 361; see Aristotle, *Metaphysics* 1003a.

119. Kierkegaard, *Fear and Trembling,* p. 62. We have previously noted (without simply affirming) the link between irony, the "plasticity" of character and individuality in Kierkegaard, one he developed in his own dialectic with Romanticism.

120. Leo Strauss, *Liberalism Ancient and Modern* (Chicago: University of Chicago Press, 1995), p. 266.

STEPHEN H. WATSON is Professor and Chair of the Department of Philosophy at the University of Notre Dame. He is the author of *Extensions: Essays on Interpretation, Rationality, and the Closure of Modernism* (Albany: SUNY Press, 1992) and *On the Dispensations of the Good*—a forthcoming sequel to this volume. In addition to being the author of many articles, he has co-edited three collections on contemporary continental thought: *Transitions in Continental Philosophy* (Albany: SUNY Press, 1994), *Phenomenology, Interpretation and Community* (Albany: SUNY Press, 1996), and *Reinterpreting the Political: Continental Philosophy and Political Theory* (Albany: SUNY Press, 1998).